THE SOLE SPOKESMAN

*Jinnah, the Muslim League
and the demand for Pakistan*

AYESHA JALAL
Columbia University

CAMBRIDGE
UNIVERSITY PRESS

CAMBRIDGE UNIVERSITY PRESS

Cambridge, New York, Melbourne, Madrid, Cape Town, Singapore,
São Paulo, Delhi, Dubai, Tokyo, Mexico City

Cambridge University Press
The Edinburgh Building, Cambridge CB2 8RU, UK

Published in the United States of America by
Cambridge University Press, New York

www.cambridge.org
Information on this title: www.cambridge.org/9780521458504

First published 1985
This paperback edition published 1994

A catalogue record for this publication is available from the British Library

Library of Congress catalogue card number: 84-17439

ISBN 978-0-521-24462-6 Hardback
ISBN 978-0-521-45850-4 Paperback

THE SOLE SPOKESMAN

In memory of my father,
Hamid Jalal

CONTENTS

MAPS

The maps are based on Joseph E. Schwartzberg (ed.), *A Historical Atlas of South Asia* (Chicago and London, 1978), pp. 94 (a, b), 76 (b), 72 (a, l), 77.

PREFACE

This book took its initial shape as a fellowship dissertation submitted to Trinity College in 1980. It derives its present form from a doctoral dissertation submitted to the University of Cambridge in 1982. During the five years of its incubation I have incurred many debts of gratitude. My greatest debt is to Dr Anil Seal, my research supervisor, whose critical scrutiny of my various drafts and exacting standards of scholarship have helped me to avoid many errors in argument and style. We had hoped to place my findings on Jinnah, the Muslim League and the demand for Pakistan in the wider context of Indian politics and British policy. But his other preoccupations persuaded us that this work was itself a significant advance towards understanding the transfer of power in India and should be brought before the public eye.

I would also like to thank the Master and Fellows of Trinity College for supporting me with an overseas bursary in the first year of my research, an external studentship during 1979–80 and a research fellowship since October 1980. I am grateful to Trinity College and the Managers of the Smuts Memorial Fund for their generous contributions towards travel and expenses of research in Britain, Pakistan and India. I am much obliged to the Librarians and staff of the India Office Library (London), to the Director and staff of the National Archives in Islamabad and to Khalid Shamsul Hassan for their time and trouble in finding material for me, and to all those persons who talked to me about their role in the events which led to the partition of India.

This work is a personal tribute to my father who first aroused my interest in the subject but who unfortunately did not live to see it in its final form. My mother's support and understanding has been an invaluable source of strength for me. I am grateful to many of my friends and colleagues in Pakistan and Britain for helping me survive the trials and tribulations of scholarship. It is impossible to list everyone by name. But I thank Dr Christopher Bayly, Dr Gordon Johnson and Professor Ronald Robinson for reading and commenting on my work. I would like to thank Sugata Bose with whom I have had many useful discussions on various aspects of the work and who has given me enormous assistance in getting the manuscript ready for publication.

I am of course entirely responsible for the contents of this book. Any errors of fact or style are unintended, but mine alone.

Ayesha Jalal

Trinity College
Cambridge, December 1983

PREFACE TO THE PAPERBACK EDITION

When it first appeared in 1985, *The Sole Spokesman* was seen as questioning ruling orthodoxies about historical processes that led to the partition of India. The publication of a new paperback edition eight years later might suggest that the book in the meantime has come to be recognized in scholarly circles as something of a new 'orthodoxy' surrounding the central event in the history of twentieth-century South Asia. For someone uncomfortable with orthodoxies of all kinds, this perception is at best a mixed compliment. While it is gratifying to find the main arguments of the book informing scholarly and intellectual debates on South Asia, *The Sole Spokesman* continues to represent a challenge to the fossilized political thinking sustaining centralized state structures and monolithic ideologies of sovereignty in the subcontinent.

One of the principal aims of the book was to tease out the inwardness of the real political aims of Muhammad Ali Jinnah and the All-India Muslim League in the final decade of the British raj in India. Whatever the merits or demerits of the Muslim claim to nationhood orchestrated after 1940, the lasting relevance of Jinnah's view of the imperative to renegotiate the union of India cannot be denied. Jinnah had held that at the moment of the British withdrawal the unitary centre of the colonial state would stand dissolved. Any new all-India arrangements had to be based on an agreement among the constituent units. In the historical context of the 1940s the main constituent units were to have been the existing Muslim- and Hindu-majority provinces of British India as well as the princely states. While in the post-colonial era linguistic states and provinces arguably are the primary, though not exclusive, constituent units, the need for a renegotiation of central powers in India and Pakistan has become more urgent than ever.

Jinnah had claimed to be the sole spokesman of all Indian Muslims, not only in the north-west and the north-east where they were in a majority but also for the geographically dispersed Muslim minorities in the rest of India. The fact of Muslim majorities in certain regions of India was sought to be deployed to protect Muslim interests throughout the subcontinent by winning for them an equitable share of power at the all-India centre. Jinnah and the Muslim League were unable at the end of the day to square the contradictory interests of Muslims in majority and minority provinces which had been accentuated by the British policy of alternatively attempting to communalize and provincialize Indian politics. The lack of congruence between the regional and specifically communal interests of Muslims left Jinnah's strategy particularly vulnerable during the end game of the raj. His uncertain hold over the politics of the Muslim-majority provinces, Congress's readiness to partition Punjab and Bengal as the price for acquiring centralized state power, and the British eagerness to quit with the least possible damage to imperial interests compelled Jinnah to acquiesce in the creation of the very 'maimed, mutilated and moth-eaten' Pakistan which he had rejected out of hand in 1944 and then again in 1946. As it came about in 1947 the partition of India effectively foreclosed the possibility of the Muslim-majority areas raising a shield in defence of Muslim-minority interests outside the pale of a sovereign Muslim state. The territorial demand for a state or states accompanying the Muslim claim to nationhood was much more nuanced than has been generally appreciated in late colonial and post-colonial discourse and historiography.

This study's revisionist flavour arose from a determination to rectify the cardinal historiographical error of treating the end result of the 1947 partition as the ultimate goal not only of Muslim politics but also of larger historical trends subsumed under the theme of communalism. The uncertainties, ambiguities and indeterminacies of politics in the late colonial era condemn this sort of an approach to the status of an unacceptable and flawed teleology. Illusions of an inexorable drift to the telos of partition are to be found in abundance even in the otherwise refreshing new trends in South Asian historiography. It requires a methodological leap of faith to connect all too easily the 'communal consciousness' in the 'subaltern mind' as well as the periodic outbreaks of inter-communal violence in the 'public arenas' of localities with the partition of the subcontinent ostensibly along religious lines at the moment of formal decolonization. An historical analysis of the level of high politics and the arena of the state is of critical importance in understanding the dynamics of the post-colonial transition. The critique of over-centralized state monoliths has to rest on more than a simple celebration of its fragmentary parts. Communal consciousness too has been subject to far greater recent and dramatic historical change than is commonly acknowledged. What is needed are explorations of the relationship between the social and cultural formation of communities as they respond and react to political processes and structures of colonial and post-colonial states at the local, regional and central levels. This is not to deny the agency of subordinated social groups in the making of history, but to underline that even active agents can be tragic though not passive victims of political manoeuvrings and decisions taken by the claimants, makers and managers of states.

Jinnah and the Muslim League achieved Pakistan, if not the 'Pakistan' which fully encapsulated their political demands on behalf of India's Muslims. The consummate Muslim lawyer had a constitutional point, but lost command of the case in the realm of hard politics when he argued that only Hindustan and Pakistan together could constitute a true union of India. This book had emphasised in 1985 that the partition of 1947 was no more than a partial solution to the Muslim minority problem in the subcontinent. The point has been made more poignant by the resurgence of communal tensions in India and the repercussions in Pakistan and Bangladesh. Apart from targeting their own non-Muslim minorities, citizens of Pakistan and Bangladesh can merely look helplessly across the borders at the plight of India's Muslim minority under siege.

When I argued in *The Sole Spokesman* that Islam should not be seen as the only driving force behind the creation of Pakistan, the intention was to draw the links between the twin dialectics in modern South Asian history – all-India nationalism and religiously based communalism as well as centralism and regionalism. The spectre of a communal divide has a way of obscuring the centre–region contradiction in the unfolding of political processes. It did so in 1947 and has the potential of repeating that role in the 1990s and beyond. Using a subcontinental communal divide as its lever, the Congress in 1947 was able not only to cut the Muslim League's demands to size but to use its inheritance of the colonial state apparatus to impose central authority over the regions. In recent decades Hindu-majoritarian communalism in India and a state-sponsored Islam in Pakistan have been called in to buttress the centre's waning political authority in the face of regional and sub-regional threats. One way to contest the power of rigid post-colonial state monoliths is to defend the fragments; the other is to rethink and reconstitute the structural and ideational bases of states through the pooling of sovereignties of its fragmentary parts. Until that happens this book will remain a goad to new thinking and a challenge to all ruling orthodoxies.

Ayesha Jalal

ABBREVIATIONS

A.I.C.C.	All-India Congress Committee
A.I.M.L.	All-India Muslim League
AIML	All-India Muslim League Records
Cmd.	Command Papers
C.P.	Central Provinces
H.M.G.	His Majesty's Government
I.O.L.	India Office Library
LAD	Legislative Assembly Debates
M.L.A.	Member of the Legislative Assembly
N.W.F.P.	North West Frontier Province
QAP	Quaid-i-Azam Papers
SHC	Syed Shamsul Hassan Collection
T.P.	*Transfer of Power* series
U.P.	United Provinces

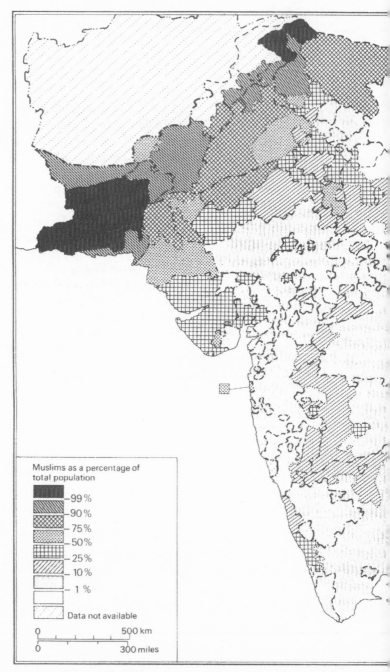

Map 1(a). Muslims 1931. Data by minor administrative subdivisions.

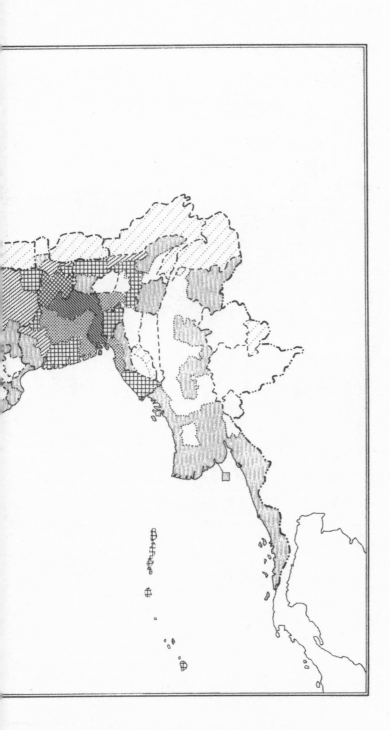

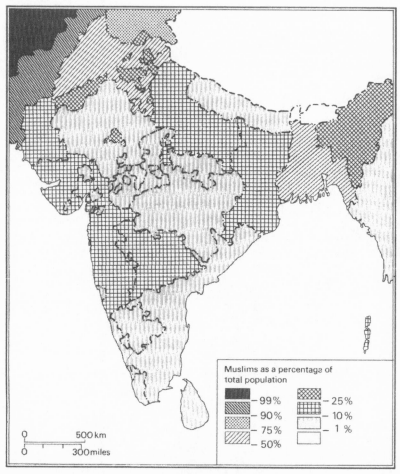

Map 1(b). Muslims 1931. Data by major administrative divisions. Indian total: 77,677,545 (22.2%); Ceylon total (est.): 356,000 (6.7%).

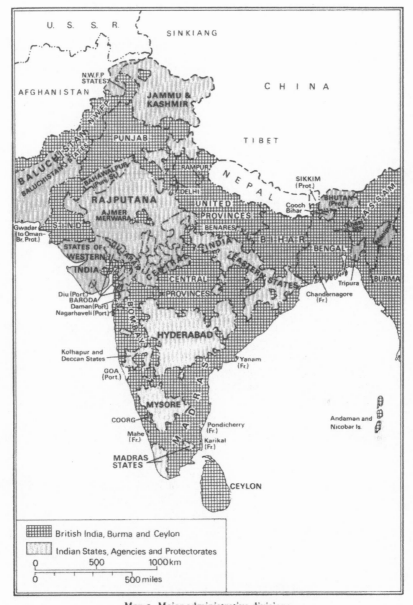

Map 2. Major administrative divisions.

Introduction

In August 1947, the British transferred power in India to two separate Dominions. When they established dominion over India, the political map of the subcontinent did not reflect the religious affiliations of its peoples. But by the time of the British withdrawal, rivalries between Hindus and Muslims had come to dominate Indian politics. When the British Raj was dismantled, the frontiers of the new states were drawn mainly along the lines of religion. In the making of Pakistan[1] religion appears to have been the determinant of nationality. The Raj came to its end amidst convulsions in which not only Hindus and Muslims, but also Sikhs and Muslims slaughtered one another, a holocaust unprecedented even in the blood-stained annals of India's past. Within less than a year refugees in their millions had moved both ways between the two wings of Pakistan and India, the largest transfer of populations in recorded history.[2]

There have been various theories to explain these cataclysmic events. The most common argument is that the Indian Muslims were always a separate and identifiable community. India, this theory argues, always contained the seeds of two nations; the Muslims were never wholly assimilated into their Indian environment and had their own distinctive traditions.[3] Another theory has emphasised the role of imperialism in dividing two communities which history and tradition had joined. The concept of Pakistan, according to this view, arose from the efforts of the British to divide and rule their Indian empire (and eventually to divide and quit).[4] Unfortunately these theories raise more questions than they answer.

---

[1] Pakistan at that time consisted of western Punjab, Sind, the North West Frontier Province, Baluchistan and eastern Bengal.

[2] The total movements of peoples after partition has been estimated to be around seventeen million, but just how many died in the riots that accompanied partition will never be exactly known. (See O. H. K. Spate, *India and Pakistan: A General and Regional Geography* (London, 1954), p. 119.)

[3] A well-known exposition of this view is in I. H. Qureshi, *The Muslim Community of the Indo-Pakistan Subcontinent (610–1947): A Brief Historical Analysis* (The Hague, 1962).

[4] There have been other theories as well which stress the economic gulf between Hindus and Muslims, the 'backwardness' of most Muslims, their failure to adapt to British rule,

At the time of partition some ninety-five million Muslims lived in the subcontinent, about one person in four. Of these, about eighty million were in British India, the remainder in the Princely States. In British India, most Muslims lived in the two provinces of Bengal and the Punjab. In these provinces, they had a bare majority over other communities.[5] In the marcher regions of the north-west, Sind, the North West Frontier Province and Baluchistan, there were much smaller Muslim populations, but they had larger, and sometimes overwhelming majorities over other communities.[6] Elsewhere in British India, Muslims were relatively small minorities, the most numerous and important being in the United Provinces.[7] Of this Muslim population, some sixty million in 1947 became citizens of Pakistan, the largest Muslim state in the world at that time, but a state cut in two by a thousand miles of Indian territory. Another thirty-five million were left inside India, remarkably, the largest number of Muslims in a non-Muslim state.

Yet the most striking fact about Pakistan is how it failed to satisfy the interests of the very Muslims who are supposed to have demanded its creation. The main centres of Muslim population, the Punjab and Bengal, ended up by being sliced in two. In both these provinces, which enjoyed an increasing measure of autonomy in the twentieth century, Muslims had come more and more to dominate the ministries. The partition of the Punjab and Bengal deprived Muslims of the benefits of undivided provinces. Muslim Punjab lost its fertile eastern districts in Ambala, Ludhiana and Jullundur; it also lost the advantages that its Muslim majority had gained from the working relations between Punjab's three main communities, the hallmark of the Unionist government which had run the Punjab since the nineteen-twenties. Muslim Bengal lost Calcutta, its capital city and economic 'heart', as well as the hinterlands of west Bengal, breaking the identity of a province proud of

and point to the religious barriers which prevent Muslims everywhere from adapting successfully to secular Western rule. Most Muslims may have been 'backward' in Bengal where economic cleavages certainly embittered disputes between the two religions; but some Muslims were 'advanced' in much of north India. Some Muslims may have failed to adapt to secular rule; others triumphantly succeeded in doing so.

5 About thirty-three million Muslims lived in Bengal (where they were 55 per cent of the population), and sixteen million lived in the Punjab (where they were 57 per cent of the population). (*Census of India*, 1941, Command Paper No. 6479, Table VI, II.)

6 In Sind, there were over three million Muslims, about three-quarters of the population; in the N.W.F.P. less than three-quarters of a million, or about 92 per cent of the population; and in Baluchistan, less than half a million Muslims were about 88 per cent of the population. (Ibid.)

7 In the U.P., there were more than eight million Muslims (14.5 per cent of the population). (Ibid.)

its common culture, language and distinctive traditions. Stripped of Calcutta and western Bengal, eastern Bengal was reduced to the status of an over-populated rural slum, capable neither of being defended from external attack nor of being developed as an equal partner inside a Muslim state.[8] As for Muslim minorities in other provinces of British India, they were left high and dry inside a country over which their more numerous co-religionists to the east and west had no influence. In the U.P., Muslim notables had successfully deployed the arguments and facts of large Muslim populations elsewhere in India to their local advantage.[9] At a stroke, partition stripped them of their convenient cohorts and dropped the shield that the Muslim-majority provinces might have raised in their defence inside undivided India. Thus it would seem that the main beneficiaries of the creation of Pakistan were the Muslim regions of the north-west, with their small but predominantly Muslim populations. But the Muslims of Sind, the N.W.F.P. and Baluchistan had one thing in common: a fierce attachment to their particularist traditions, and a deep antipathy to any central control. The creation of Pakistan bundled them willy-nilly into a state dominated by their more numerous co-religionists from western Punjab and placed them under the tight central control which Pakistan had to impose if it was to survive. The enthusiasm of these patriots of 'Pakhtunistan', Sind and Baluchistan for this union can be gauged by their efforts since independence to throw off the yoke of the Punjab.[10] This raises the

[8] Bengali resentment of West Pakistani domination was dramatically highlighted in the civil war of 1971 which led to the creation of Bangladesh.

[9] Since the later nineteenth century, members of the Urdu-speaking elite of north India, the traditional centre of Muslim power, were the most energetic claimants for the role of spokesman of all Indian Muslims. Anxious to preserve their standing in their own province, they were keen to shake off the taint of disloyalty which after 1857 had embarrassed their relations with the Raj. This was the strategy of Sir Syed Ahmad Khan and his Aligarh school; it inspired the 'Muslim breakaway' from the Indian National Congress which he orchestrated in 1886; and it was his political heirs who led the deputation of Muslims in 1906 which demanded a share of representation for Muslims not in accordance with their numbers but in line with their 'political importance'. (See Peter Hardy, *The Muslims of British India*, Cambridge, 1972, pp. 154–7.) The founding of the All-India Muslim League followed soon after. On 30 December 1906 at Dacca, the Mohammedan Educational Conference converted itself into the All-India Muslim League. (See S. S. Pirzada (ed.), *Foundations of Pakistan: All-India Muslim League Documents: 1906–1947*, vol. I (Karachi, 1969), pp. 1–15.)

[10] At the time of partition, the N.W.F.P. had a Congress ministry, led by the brother of the renowned Frontier Gandhi, Abdul Ghaffar Khan; the Pathans had scant reason to fear Hindu domination in a region where hardly a Hindu could be seen above the ground. In Sind, there were communities other than Muslims, but they were mainly urban-based and not a real threat to the sway of Muslim notables who ran Sind as their domain. As for Baluchistan, the tribal *sardars* had no reason to fear the British, let alone the Hindus.

question: how did a Pakistan come about which fitted the interests of most Muslims so poorly?

This is the central problem to which the book will address itself. It will do so by concentrating upon the politics of Mohammad Ali Jinnah, the All-India Muslim League which he led, and the demand for 'Pakistan' with which he is associated, during the last decade of British rule. It was not until 1934 that the A.I.M.L., moribund for much of the nineteen-twenties, was revived under Jinnah's leadership. Until 1937, the League continued to ground itself on the old charter of Muslim rights – separate representation, first granted to Muslims in 1909 and confirmed in the Government of India Act of 1935 – but, in contrast with the Muslim politicians of the Punjab and Bengal, it had been ready to make common cause with the Indian National Congress in attacking the constitutional arrangements of 1935 which gave Indians something in the provinces but little at the centre. Only after the elections of 1937, when its overtures to the Congress had been rebuffed did the League adopt a new line. In 1940, a mere seven and a half years before partition, it formally demanded independent Muslim states, repudiating the minority status which separate representation necessarily entailed, and instead asserted that Muslims were a nation. This was Jinnah and the League's bid to register their claim to speak for all Indian Muslims, not only Muslims in the minority provinces where they had achieved their only success in the 1937 elections, but also Muslims in the majority provinces where they had been unequivocally rejected. This work will trace how this claim came to be accepted by the British, was conceded to a greater or lesser degree by many Muslims in minority and majority provinces alike, and was not effectively contradicted by the Congress, even though it continued to deny it until the very end. The claim was built upon the demand for 'Pakistan'. But from first to last, Jinnah avoided giving the demand a precise definition, leaving the League's followers to make of it what they wished. A host of conflicting shapes and forms, most of them vague, were given to what remained little more than a catch-all, an undefined slogan. So it is important to identify the aims of Jinnah's political strategy, the reasons why he was so reluctant to bring them into the open, and the extent to which he succeeded, or failed, in realising them.

Jinnah sought to be recognised as the sole spokesman of Indian Muslims on the all-India stage. Throughout his long political career, he saw his role to be at the all-India level. From the late nineteen-thirties his main concern was the arrangements by which power at the centre was to be shared once the British quit India. But if Jinnah and the League were to play their part at the centre, they needed a mandate from Muslims in the provinces. Given the imprecision of the demand for 'Pakistan' it is necessary to establish how and to what extent Jinnah was able to win that mandate, and the measure of discipline the League's High Command was able to impose on provincial Muslim interests. This will require an assessment of the balance of power between the High Command and the provincial arms, and an investigation into the nature of the League's organisation (or lack of it), both at the centre and in the Muslim provinces. Although this is not a study of provincial politics, it will look at the particularist concerns of the Muslim provinces and the disjunction between the interests of Muslims in provinces where they were in a majority and provinces where they were in a minority. This is principally a work on politics at the all-India level, but it does not ignore the uses made by Jinnah and the League of religion or the importance of communal consciousness at the social base. Jinnah's appeal to religion was always ambiguous; certainly it was not characteristic of his political style before 1937, and evidence suggests that his use of the communal factor was a political tactic, not an ideological commitment. A detailed analysis of the complex social and economic ingredients of 'communal' passions which erupted so violently in the last days of the Raj is beyond the scope of this work. It will, however, consider whether Jinnah was able to deploy the communal card to his advantage and how far it constrained or helped him in achieving his political aims.

A work on Jinnah, the League and the demand for Pakistan must take account of the other two sides in the Indian political triangle, the Indian National Congress and the British. At every stage of the story, particularly in its final outcome, the Congress had a critically important role to play. The Congress, whether its manoeuvrings at the centre or its politics in the provinces, will be seen primarily from Jinnah's angle of vision, and implicitly as a gauge against which the League's political organisation can be compared. British policies and initiatives were a vital factor in Indian political calculations and responses, and will also be viewed from the perspective of Jinnah and the League. This is an appropriate moment for a study of this sort. Most of the critical sources have become available – the monumental *Transfer of Power* documents from the British end, and the Muslim League papers and the private correspondence of Jinnah himself.

1

Jinnah between the wars

Section 1

Mohammad Ali Jinnah began his political career firmly inside the tradition of moderate nationalist politics. A Muslim lawyer based in Bombay where the Indian National Congress had been founded in 1885, Jinnah was one of the foremost proponents of a share of power for Indians at the all-India centre. Anxious to forge a common nationalist front against the British, Jinnah joined the Congress and regularly attended its annual gatherings. Interestingly enough, Jinnah never showed much enthusiasm for the principle of separate electorates which were granted to Muslims by Morley and Minto in 1909.[1] It was not until 1913, some seven years after its foundation, that Jinnah formally enrolled as a member of the A.I.M.L.[2] In 1916 it was Jinnah who persuaded the League and the Congress to agree upon a common scheme of reforms. At the League's Lucknow session (over which he presided), Jinnah confessed that he had always been 'a staunch Congressman' and had 'no love for sectarian cries'. He considered the 'reproach of "separatism" sometimes levelled at Mussalmans' as 'singularly inept and wide of the mark'. In Jinnah's opinion, the League, 'this great communal organisation [was] rapidly growing into a powerful factor for the birth of United India'.[3]

Between 1917 and 1920 many of the developments in Indian politics went against Jinnah's grain – the provincial bias of the Montagu–

---

[1] At the annual Congress session in 1910 Jinnah moved the resolution deploring the extension of that principle to local boards, even though he himself had been the beneficiary, albeit indirectly, of separate representation. He had been elected to the central legislative council as the Muslim member from Bombay. (Matlubul Hasan Saiyid, *Mohammad Ali Jinnah: A Political Study*, 3rd edn. (Lahore, 1962).

[2] He made his two sponsors, Mohammad Ali and Wazir Hasan, solemnly assure him that 'loyalty to the Muslim League and Muslim interest would in no way and at no time imply even a shadow of disloyalty to the National cause to which his life was dedicated'. (Ibid., p. 54.)

[3] Jinnah's address to the A.I.M.L., Lucknow, December 1916, in M. Rafique Afzal (ed.), *Speeches and Statements of the Quaid-i-Azam Mohammad Ali Jinnah, 1911–34 and 1947–48* (Lahore, 1966), pp. 56–62.

Chelmsford reforms and the Government of India Act of 1919, and Gandhi's capture of the Congress in 1920 with the help of pro-Khilafat Muslims. By declaring his support for the Khilafat, Gandhi secured the allegiance of an impressive array of Muslim *ulema* and political activists for his policy of non-violent non-cooperation.[4] This fusion of religion and politics had left Jinnah cold in the wings. He denounced Gandhi for causing schism and split 'not only amongst Hindus and Muslims but between Hindus and Hindus and Muslims and Muslims and even between fathers and sons . . . [indeed] in almost every institution' that the Mahatma had anything to do with. Gandhi's programme would lead to 'complete disorganisation and chaos'.[5] At the Congress's Nagpur session in December 1920 when Gandhi's non-cooperation programme was ratified, Jinnah alone had the courage of his convictions and spoke openly against non-cooperation. Speaking for the 'intellectual and reasonable section' of public opinion, Jinnah derided the false and dangerous religious frenzy which had confused Indian politics, and the zealots, both Hindu and Muslim, who were harming the national cause.[6] Jinnah now resigned as a member of the Congress. This was a parting of the ways between Jinnah and the Congress under Gandhi, a parting which he always hoped would be temporary not permanent. But as revealing as his contempt and worries about Gandhi's methods was his total antipathy to the religious militancy of those Muslims who had joined Gandhi in pushing the moderate nationalists out.

All this indicates a great deal about Jinnah's political priorities, which were to remain constant throughout his career. A nationalist who preferred constitutional methods, Jinnah's moderation in politics was tactical, not strategic; he recognised the need to keep inarticulate, but potentially disruptive communal passions at bay. There was nothing mendicant about his approach. Proud, with an assurance painfully constructed in difficult circumstances, he was never prepared to compromise over principles and had little liking for India's white masters with whom he never felt wholly at ease. A pragmatic politician, he realistically gauged how much the British were ready to concede at this juncture and reluctantly accepted separate electorates as a fact of political life for the time being, but not necessarily for all time. He did not approve of the

---

[4] See Richard Gordon, 'Non-cooperation and council entry, 1919 to 1920', in John Gallagher, Gordon Johnson and Anil Seal (eds.), *Locality, Province and Nation, Essays on Indian Politics 1870–1940* (Cambridge, 1973), pp. 128–41; and Francis Robinson, *Separatism Among Indian Muslims: The Politics of the United Provinces' Muslims (1860–1923)* (Cambridge, 1974), chapter 8.

[5] See Saiyid, *Mohammad Ali Jinnah: A Political Study*, p. 130.

[6] Ibid., pp. 134–6.

principle; he was against its extension, but he recognised that Muslim politicians were not yet ready to give it up. Jinnah, the 'ambassador of Hindu–Muslim unity', had worked hard to get the Congress and the League to co-operate and deplored the opportunistic alliance between the Mahatma and the Khilafat Muslims. In Jinnah's eyes, that coalition, remarkable even in a country used to the oddest combinations, threatened the stability of the existing political structures and orderly progress along moderate and nationalist lines. The alarming rise in communal tensions in the remaining three years of the Khilafat agitation is a commentary on the soundness of Jinnah's assessment. After 1919, the Khilafat movement overwhelmed the League,[7] and despite the fanfare of Hindu–Muslim unity eventually broke the fragile constitutional understanding between Congress and League which Jinnah had so painstakingly helped to construct. In his later years, Jinnah time and again tried unsuccessfully to snatch back the unity which for a brief moment after 1916 had seemed to promise so much for the nationalist cause.

During most of the nineteen-twenties Jinnah spent his life in relative political isolation. The 1919 reforms were not intended to be a first step towards the grant of responsible government at the centre. They merely tacked on some political concessions to divert Indian attention to the provincial arenas. The principle of diarchy aimed to limit the Indian say in provincial self-government to the less important subjects, and the new franchise was tilted to favour the Raj's friends, not its critics. By design, the way to diarchic heights in the province under the new rules lay less through separate Muslim constituencies and specifically Muslim parties, than through alliances which cut across community. Separate representation by itself was not enough if Muslim politicians were to do well, whether in the U.P. where they were in a minority, or in the Punjab and Bengal where they had majorities.[8] The reforms had provincialised Indian politics and had driven a wedge between the interests of provin-

[7] For an account see Gail Minault, *The Khilafat Movement, Religious Symbolism and Political Mobilization in India* (New York, 1982).

[8] The reforms ensured that no single community would dominate the ministries; the balance of power was kept firmly in the government's hands. Throughout the nineteen-twenties, cross-communal alliances of landed interests formed the ministries in the U.P. and the Punjab. In Bengal, the situation was different; by the late nineteen-twenties Muslims depending on government support and the European members dominated the ministries. For the actual working of the 1919 reforms in these provinces see Ayesha Jalal and Anil Seal, 'Alternative to partition: Muslim politics between the wars', *Modern Asian Studies*, 15, 3 (1981) 417–29; David Page, *Prelude to Partition: The Indian Muslims and the Imperial System of Control 1920–1932* (Oxford, 1982) and J. H. Broomfield, *Elite Conflict in a Plural Society: Twentieth Century Bengal* (Berkeley, 1968), pp. 278–81 and 284–8.

cial politicians, who could see advantages in working the new system, and the interests of all-India politicians who wanted to push for advance at the centre. Indeed there was no all-India party which could speak for Muslims at the all-India level. The British strategy of depriving the all-India stage of political relevance had largely succeeded. The Muslim League was moribund, spurned by all the provincial bases of Muslim power, and the Congress itself was split down the middle with its Khilafat allies in disarray.

In November 1927, the appointment of the Simon Commission opened the prospect of new constitutional reforms. Provincial politicians had to look to the all-India stage if they were to influence the shape of these reforms. Jinnah was ready to use the opening to try again to forge a common front between the League and the Congress. He faced two main difficulties: persuading the divided factions of the Congress to join him and bringing in the Muslim provinces behind his strategy. The Congress was committed to a strong unitary centre, while the Muslim provinces wanted a weak federal structure in which the provinces and not the centre would be the real bearers of power. Jinnah's own view of the future shape of the centre was closer to that of the Congress. But he had to find a way of reconciling the conflicting demands of the Muslim provinces and the Congress. There remained the old problem of separate electorates. Jinnah was ready to give up separate representation in return for other concessions – the creation of a Muslim province in Sind, a higher status for the N.W.F.P. and Baluchistan, representation for the Punjabi and Bengali Muslims in line with their populations and a guaranteed third of the seats in the central legislature for Muslims. But by May 1928 Jinnah had failed to convince both the Congress and the Muslim provinces. The Nehru report of August 1928, which made no concessions at all, was rejected by all shades of Muslim opinion.[9]

By the late nineteen-twenties the demands of the Muslim provinces, the Punjab in particular, had swamped Jinnah's centralist strategy. Jinnah, the nationalist concerned with securing a share of power for Muslims at a strong centre, had to recognise the forces of provincialism and appear to come out in favour of a weak federal structure. But this was a tactical concession, not a modification of his ultimate objective. A confirmed centralist, Jinnah was merely seeking a way of uniting the Muslims behind a common line and then negotiating a joint front with the Congress against the British. His famous 'fourteen points' were simply a reiteration of the demands raised at the Punjabi-dominated All-

[9] See Mushirul Hasan, *Nationalism and Communal Politics in India, 1916–1928* (New Delhi, 1979), chapter 8.

India Muslim Conference in December 1928.[10] Yet Jinnah's real intentions are revealed by his willingness to bargain on the question of separate electorates provided the other Muslim demands were accepted by the Congress. Unfortunately for Jinnah, the Congress dismissed his formula for a Hindu–Muslim settlement. Motilal Nehru considered the 'fourteen points' to be 'preposterous' and thought Congress could safely 'ignore Mr Jinnah'.[11] This may have been a short-sighted conclusion, but for the time being it did toss Jinnah into the wilderness. For the next few years Jinnah was in self-imposed exile in London.

The constitutional negotiations of the early nineteen-thirties called for some Muslim voice. This Fazl-i-Husain, the leader of the Punjab Unionist 'party', a cross-communal alliance of Muslim, Hindu and Sikh agriculturist interests, stepped forward to provide. He backed his claim to speak for Indian Muslims by organising the All-India Muslim Conference. Fazl-i-Husain's conditions for Muslim co-operation at the Round Table Conferences in London were unequivocal. He wanted separate electorates to be retained, clear majorities for Punjabi and Bengali Muslims, the separation of Sind from Bombay, provincial status for the N.W.F.P. and full autonomy for all the provinces. Until these were conceded, Fazl-i-Husain was against any advance towards a responsible centre.[12]

Jinnah was a potential, if ineffectual, threat to the Muslim Conference position at the First Round Table Conference. He became a member of the sub-committee appointed to discuss the component elements of an all-India federation and the future relationship between the centre and the provinces. Jinnah opposed the notion of a weak federation, but only indirectly. He was against bringing the Indian Princely States into the all-India federation on a basis different from that of the British Indian provinces. He wanted the federation 'to be a real one', not 'watered down or weakened' so that in fact there was 'no Federation at all'.[13] This is why he wanted to postpone all discussion on the relationship between the centre and the provinces. Instead he preferred the old nationalist line of advance at the centre before the settlement of the communal question.

By the time the First Round Table Conference collapsed, it was Fazl-i-Husain's views which had largely prevailed. The Muslim delegates had

[10] See K. K. Aziz, *The All-India Muslim Conference, 1928–35, a Documentary Record* (Karachi, 1972), pp. 44–7 and Afzal (ed.), *Speeches and Statements of the Quaid-i-Azam*, pp. 302–5.

[11] Cited in Page, *Prelude to Partition*, p. 200, fn. 6.

[12] See Jalal and Seal, *Modern Asian Studies*, 15, 3 (1981), 434–5.

[13] See Jinnah's address to the federal structure sub-committee, 1 December 1930, in Afzal (ed.), *Speeches and Statements of the Quaid-i-Azam*, p. 320.

refused to sanction any advance towards a responsible centre unless their communal safeguards were maintained. Even amongst the British participants there was talk of a federation rather than a strong unitary centre. Fazl-i-Husain's Punjab thesis had come to dominate the constitutional negotiations. But it was only one among a range of strategies being aired in Muslim circles. The most important was the strategy of Sir Muhammad Iqbal. In his December 1930 presidential address to the A.I.M.L., Iqbal called for the creation of a Muslim India, a state in the north-west consisting of the Muslim-majority regions of the Punjab, Sind, the N.W.F.P. and Baluchistan. This was not the first call for Pakistan, or for the division of India. Iqbal's proposal was set firmly within an all-India context.[14] Fazl-i-Husain now pressed the All-India Muslim Conference to spell out its strategy in more concrete terms. In April 1931, the Conference demanded a loose federation in which the constituent units would have the fullest autonomy; all residuary powers had to be vested in the provinces which would be on an equal footing with the Princely States.[15] This was to be the Punjabi Muslim construct of India's future: playing states' rights against a weak federal centre. But the question of Muslim representation still had to be settled first.

After the Second Round Table Conference failed to make any headway on the question of communal proportions, London decided to make an award. Macdonald's Communal Award of 16 August 1932 left the Muslims of the Punjab and Bengal in a strong position. In these two

---

[14] Muhammad Iqbal, the famous poet–philosopher argued that the 'life of Islam as a cultural force in this country very largely depends on its centralisation in a specified territory', and once this was recognised it would 'deepen the patriotic feeling' of Muslims. Iqbal assured the British and the non-Muslims that when the Muslims were allowed to develop 'within the body-politic of India, the North-West Indian Muslims will prove the best defenders [of] India against foreign invasion, be that invasion one of ideas or bayonets'. (See Iqbal's speech at the twenty-first session of the A.I.M.L., 29 December 1930, in Jamil-ud-Din Ahmad (ed,), *Historic Documents of the Muslim Freedom Movement* (Lahore, 1970), pp. 126–7.

Muslim politicians ignored Iqbal's speech. But it did inspire yet another Punjabi Muslim, Chaudhuri Rahmat Ali, a student at Cambridge, to coin the word 'Pakistan'. Rahmat Ali drew up a scheme for an independent Muslim state in north-western India for the Muslim delegates attending the Round Table Conferences in London. The ingenuity of the scheme was more contrived than remarkable – 'P' stood for the Punjab; 'A' for Afghanistan or the North West Frontier Province; 'K' for Kashmir; 'S' for Sind and 'tan' for Baluchistan. The literal translation of 'Pakistan' was 'the land of the pure or the holy'. Since the scheme (unlike Iqbal's) envisaged massive transfers of Muslim populations from other parts of India, it was understandably dismissed by the Muslim delegates as a 'student scheme' which was 'chimerical' and 'impractical'.

[15] No subject would be given to the centre without the prior agreement of the federating units. As a further safeguard, the provinces would have the right of secession from the Indian union.

provinces they retained not only their separate electorates but they were also given more seats than any other community in the provincial assemblies.[16] Provincial autonomy was now a pleasing prospect for Muslims in the Punjab and Bengal, and also for Muslims in the newly-created province of Sind as well as the N.W.F.P., which was to be elevated to the status of a Governor's province. But what suited Muslims in the majority provinces did not suit Muslims in those parts of India where they were small minorities.[17] Given the unevenness of Muslim gains under the Award and the new reforms, there was plenty of opportunity for those opposed to the Muslim Conference to exploit provincial Muslim grievances, especially in the minority provinces.

This gave Jinnah another opportunity. He was invited to revive the Muslim League by Muslims in the minority provinces, the U.P. in particular. His opposition to the federal scheme had kept him out of the Third Round Table Conference.[18] He could now rally Muslim opinion against the forthcoming reforms. After March 1934 he was back in the saddle of a resuscitated A.I.M.L. Once again he hoped to play the role of mediator at the centre. In October 1934, Jinnah was re-elected to the central assembly. There he attempted to win support among Congress members to strengthen his claim to be a national leader in his own right, and a spokesman of Muslim interests with a standing greater than that of the Muslim Conference. By broadening the basis of the League and following his old tactic of coming to terms with the Congress at the all-India level, Jinnah hoped not only to get Congress agreement to the fact of Muslim majorities in the Punjab and Bengal, but to do so without losing his position as the voice of minority Muslim interests.

Congress's terms for a deal with Jinnah were Muslim acceptance of joint electorates, and this seemed on offer from the Muslims of eastern Bengal provided they were given a secure majority in the province. This gave Jinnah an alternative to the Punjab line. He now offered his strong support to the Congress in attacking the British proposals for a loose federal structure. His talks with the Congress president, Rajendra Prasad, in January and February 1935 showed, as Prasad's own words confirm, the 'great possibilities for the future' which a joint operation by

---

[16] For details of the Communal Award and reactions to it, see Jalal and Seal, *Modern Asian Studies*, 15, 3 (1981), 443–6.
[17] Full autonomy for the provinces would eliminate the official bloc, the one safeguard for minority Muslim interests.
[18] As Jinnah explained, he was 'the keenest Round Tabler' but 'not . . . an enthusiastic Federalist'. He had not been invited to the Third Round Table Conference because he was 'the strongest opponent of the [federal] scheme'. (See *Legislative Assembly Debates*, 7 February 1935, I, V/9/124, I.O.L.)

Congress and the League might have.[19] Jinnah, the centralist, saw that the real security for Muslims, especially the Muslims in the minority provinces, lay not in the outworn device of separate electorates, which he had never favoured, but in an agreement with the Congress at the centre. Just as the Punjab was Jinnah's Achilles' heel, time and again, so now Bengali Hindu opposition to the Communal Award proved to be Congress's stumbling-block. The Bengal Hindu Mahasabha's unwavering opposition ensured that the Jinnah–Prasad talks came to naught.[20]

Although the talks failed, there remained the possibility of the Congress party in the central assembly coming to some understanding with Jinnah. Jinnah had taken care to present his case simultaneously in the central assembly. He urged its members to accept the Communal Award since agreement between the communities on any other basis seemed unlikely. Without an agreement there could be no constitutional framework. Speaking for himself, Jinnah admitted that he was 'not satisfied with the Communal Award . . . my self-respect will never be satisfied until we produce our own scheme'. The Communal Award did not validate the notion that religious differences were the most important factor in Indian politics. As far as Jinnah was concerned, 'religion should not enter politics'. The Award was not simply a question of religion:

this is a question of minorities and it is a political issue . . . . Now, what are the minorities? Minorities mean a combination of things. It may be that a minority has a different religion from the other citizens of a country. Their language may be different, their race may be different, their culture may be different, and the combination of all these elements – religion, culture, race, language, art, music and so forth makes the minority a separate entity in the State, and that separate entity wants safeguards. Surely, therefore, we must face this question as a political problem, we must solve it and not evade it.[21]

This confirms that Jinnah did not consider communal differences to be an obstacle to agreement at the all-India level, and that his solutions to the communal problem were cast in political, not religious, terms. He could see that without an acceptance of the Communal Award the entire reform scheme would have to be abandoned. He did not like the new constitution and thought it was 'humiliating' and 'intolerable'. But he realised that the Muslim provinces were anxious to work provincial autonomy and he could not reject the new reforms out of hand.

---

[19] Cited in John Gallagher, 'Congress in decline: Bengal, 1930–1939', in Gallagher, Johnson and Seal (eds.), *Locality, Province and Nation*, p. 310.

[20] Ibid., pp. 309–13.

[21] Jinnah's speech in the central assembly, 7 February 1935 (LAD) 1935, I, V/9/124, I.O.L.

As ever Jinnah had to strike a delicate balance between his own priorities and those of his potential constituents. He was clearly opposed to the federal scheme; it postponed responsible government and left the centre weak and ineffectual. If he openly called for Congress's unitary centre, he would almost certainly be repudiated by the Muslim provinces. So he tried to reassure everyone, especially the Muslim provinces, that he was not opposed to the idea of *any* all-India federation. But he disliked the one proposed under the reforms since it allowed the princes to come in on their own terms. Jinnah was willing to accept the provincial aspect of the reforms although he shared Congress's objection to the special powers conferred upon the Governors. It was the central aspects of the reforms and the Viceroy's overriding powers in fiscal matters that Jinnah wanted modified. Jinnah's proposed amendments to the federal scheme set out in the Joint Select Committee's report were passed by a majority in the central assembly. Yet he could hardly claim this to be an agreement between the Congress and the League. Without such an agreement at the centre, Jinnah was still a long way from becoming an effective spokesman for Muslims on the all-India stage.

Section 2

In 1935 the Government of India Act and the Communal Award which had preceded it were finally passed by the British Parliament. The Act widened the franchise to nearly thirty-five millions[22] and gave the provinces of British India a large measure of self-government. Diarchy was abolished and Indians were now to be associated with decision-making in virtually every department of provincial government. But complete responsibility at the centre was still something for the future; the executive was not responsible to the legislature and many of the central subjects were 'reserved'. By granting provincial autonomy and beating a retreat to the centre, the British planned to give autonomy to their friends and collaborators, and to retain control at the top. Encouraging provincial ambitions and keeping the centre firmly in British hands was not a strategy for getting out of India, but a way of staying on. There was no mention of Dominion Status in the Act, an omission which aroused grave suspicions in the minds of Indian nationalists. Yet the most disturbing feature of the Act, from the point of view of those familiar with constitutional law, was the clear disjunction between provincial autonomy and the creation of an all-India federation. The provinces were to become autonomous as soon as elections had been held

---

[22] *Report of the Indian Franchise Committee*, 1932, Cmd. 4086, V6485.

under the extended franchise. But the first step towards a federation was to be taken only after one-half of the Indian States, on the basis of population, had voluntarily agreed to accede. While each Indian State was to negotiate its way into the federation, the British Indian provinces would automatically come into the federation. The future relationship between the federating units and the federation was bound to be complicated. The Indian States would demand extravagant terms for their accession. There was always the possibility that the provinces, certainly the Muslim provinces, would want more autonomy from the centre. During the Round Table Conferences Indian opinion had been sharply divided on the question of residuary powers. Those committed to retaining a strong central government wanted residuary powers to remain with the federal centre, while spokesmen of the Muslim provinces, the Punjab in particular, wanted residuary powers to be given to the provinces. To tide over the difficulty, the Act provided for three legislative lists – the federal,[23] the provincial[24] and the concurrent. Both the federal and the provincial legislatures could deal with the subjects covered under the concurrent list. By parcelling out most of the legislative field, the authors of the Act hoped to obviate the importance of giving residuary powers either to the federal centre or to the federating units. Whatever remained of the residuary powers was vested in the Governor-General who could permit either the federal or a provincial legislature to enact laws not specified in any of the three lists. So although the Act avoided addressing itself to the issue of residuary powers, this was another potential stumbling-block in the way of an all-India federation.

But these were difficulties of the future. The debate on the relationship between the federal centre and the federating units could assume real

---

[23] The federal list included defence, external affairs, ecclesiastical affairs, currency, posts and telegraphs, census, banking, insurance, shipping, aircraft and air navigation, import and export, customs duties, income tax, capital levies, corporation tax, railways, salt tax and naturalisation. (See *The Government of India Act, 1935*, Schedule VII, Delhi 1936.)

[24] The provincial list included public order, the administration of justice, courts of law (except the Federal Court), police, prisons, provincial public services, local government, public health, education, communications (except railways), water supply and irrigation, agriculture, land and land tenures, production (i.e. supply and distribution of goods), trade and commerce within the province, fisheries, etc. The provinces were also given the following heads of taxation: land revenue, taxes on agricultural income, taxes on mineral rights, taxes on professions, on luxury and entertainments, stamps on specific documents, and tolls. The concurrent list allowed the provinces to legislate on criminal law, criminal and civil procedure, marriage and divorce, wills and succession, transfer of property, trusts, contracts, medical and other professions, factories, newspapers, labour, trade unions and electricity. (Ibid.)

significance only when the British were ready to transfer power. For the time being, this was not likely to happen. The Act had been designed to safeguard British rule in India, not to weaken it. At the centre, the British proposed to hold on to many of the vital attributes of sovereignty by limiting the powers of the federal legislature, and by bringing in Princely India to redress the balance in British India. Much of the centre's budget was kept immune from the federal legislatures' vote; Indians had no say over defence; ninety-four sections of the Act gave the Viceroy discretionary powers, and defence and external affairs were kept firmly in his hands. Although the provinces had been given a great deal of autonomy in legislative, administrative and financial matters, the centre was equipped with all the powers to stamp its authority and to keep centrifugal tendencies in check. Section 102 of the Act which gave the Viceroy the power to direct the federal legislature to make laws for the provinces during an 'emergency', caused either by a war or an internal disturbance, effectively limited provincial autonomy. The Governors had special powers and could take over the administration of a province under Section 93 of the Act. With special powers for the Viceroy and the Governors in both the executive and the legislative spheres, the 1935 Act had provided the 'steel frame' which could preserve British rule in India.

The distribution of seats in the federal legislature reveals how the British proposed to keep nationalist opposition at bay. The federal legislature was to consist of a council of state and an assembly, as it were an upper and lower house on a model half-way between Westminster and Washington. States and minorities were conceived as safeguards against a nationalist domination at the centre. In the council of state there were 156 representatives of British India and 104 of the Indian States. The federal assembly had 250 representatives from British India and not more than 125 representatives from the Indian States. Of the 156 representatives of British India in the council of state there were seventy-five general seats, six seats for the Scheduled Castes, four seats for the Sikhs, six for women and forty-nine for the Muslims.[25] Indian Muslims had eighty-two of the 250 seats in the federal assembly. The Muslim provinces in particular were given favoured treatment. More than half the total number of seats for Muslims in the council of state were for the Muslim-majority provinces. Bengal had ten, Punjab eight, the N.W.F.P. four, Sind three and Baluchistan one; the U.P. only had seven seats. In the federal assembly the Muslim provinces had thirty-nine of the eighty-two seats reserved for Muslims. Bengal had seventeen, Punjab fourteen, Sind three, the N.W.F.P. four and Baluchistan one.[26]

---

[25] *The Government of India Act, 1935*, Schedule I.   [26] Ibid.

On the face of it Muslims in the federal legislature had received more than their fair share and could hope to safeguard their interests. But all the calculations about Muslim security, particularly at the centre (the only real security for Muslims in the minority provinces), depended critically on the premise, the spoken and unspoken assumption of the British and Muslims alike, that the Muslims were a community possessing a solidarity of political opinion and capable of acting unitedly in defence of their separate and distinctive interests. The first elections under the 1935 Act with an extended franchise would make it possible to test British assumptions and the claims of the Muslim leadership about communal unity against the irrefutable evidence of the polls – irrefutable because Muslims had their separate electorates and did not have to face any competition from the non-Muslims. Since there were other special and minority interests with reserved seats, not to mention Princely India, the Muslim position in the federal legislature was not much worse than that of the Caste Hindus. If only the Muslims voted solidly as a group at the centre they could convert their perpetual minority status into an effective and powerful bargaining factor *vis-à-vis* the Congress. This is why Jinnah and the A.I.M.L. had now to stress that Muslims, whatever their complexion, had to accept the whip of a single leader. But the only reason for divided Muslims to have an united body at the all-India level was if the British planned to give away real power at the centre on the basis of elections held in the provinces. Until the British showed their readiness to give away something at the centre, and this did not seem an immediate possibility, the need for an all-India Muslim organisation speaking for its provincial bases was less urgent.

Between 1934 and 1937, Jinnah kept his eye firmly fixed upon the centre. Just as much as the Congress, he did not like the federal provisions of the 1935 Act. They would weaken the old unitary form of government, introduce the Indian States to muddy the waters of British India and make it impossible for nationalists to get a working majority at the centre even if Congress and the Muslims came to terms. But above all, Jinnah disliked the Act because it kept a firm hold over power at the centre which he had fought to wrest from British hands. Congress, now stressing its all-India role, pressed for a revision of these federal arrangements. However, its capacity to influence the centre depended upon how well it did in the provincial elections of 1937. Thus Congress and Jinnah had a common interest in breaking the old provincial structure of politics upon which the British depended. If the old structure survived the elections, the British might still be able to hold a balance between Congress (and of course the League) and their old friends in the provinces. This added up to a basis, however shaky, for an alliance between Jinnah and the Congress bosses in a joint attack on the old provincial hands and a pincer movement from two sides against the British at the centre. Until the results of the 1937 elections were known, no one could be sure how well the Congress would do, whether smashing its rivals or absorbing them into its organisation. If in its turn the League succeeded in rallying Muslims in the minority provinces solidly behind its banner, Jinnah's League might have had something to offer the Congress. By an electoral success, the League might conceivably have held the balance in minority provinces and its support might have proved to be essential for the Congress to achieve office. Equally, if the League could make a dent on the Muslim-majority provinces, this would give Jinnah a standing in all-India politics as the spokesman of Muslims, ostensibly more united than they had ever been. All this would have given Jinnah something real to offer the Congress in return for an alliance against the proposed federal provisions of the 1935 Act.

But Jinnah's strategy depended on several assumptions. First, he assumed that the old guard of provincial politics would not be demolished in the elections, and Congress would therefore need help from the League if it was to rivet its own control over the Hindu provinces. Secondly he believed that the imperatives of all-India politics would bear upon the thinking of those who ran the Muslim provinces. But Jinnah did not understand provincial politics before 1937 – indeed, it is doubtful if he ever understood them. Paradoxically, separate representation proved to be the big obstacle in his way. Ever since separate representation had been granted in 1909, Muslim politicians had little incentive to organise real parties, or indeed even to join parties, as a way of consolidating their hold over local constituencies. In contrast, local politicians who were not Muslim increasingly came to see the advantages of affiliating themselves with more organised bodies such as the Congress, mainly to strengthen their grip over their own factions. But politicians, safe inside the protective walls of Muslim constituencies, had less reason to change their old tactics. Local influence was enough to get themselves elected; and factional alliances seemed to give them enough freedom to play their hands both locally and provincially without the constraints of links with parties above or real organisations at the base. Sticking to a party line, and organising its machine, was not essential to their political interests. This was the case even in minority provinces, but it was particularly the case in the Muslim provinces. So even though the League and Congress had similar purposes before the 1937 elections, the League had little to offer Muslim politicians in the provinces; recently revived, the League even in its better days had been little more than a debating forum for a few articulate Muslims in the minority provinces and had made no impact upon the majority provinces.[27]

In April 1936, Jinnah asked Fazl-i-Husain to preside over the A.I.M.L. at Bombay. But it was a belated gesture, and the Punjabi leader was not about to bite upon such uninviting bait.[28] So Jinnah was left to dominate a rump at the League's session; it accepted the Communal Award and provincial autonomy 'for what it is worth'; but it came out against the federal provisions of the 1935 Act as 'fundamentally bad'. They were described as: 'most reactionary, retrograde, injurious and fatal to the vital interest of British India *vis-à-vis* the Indian States, and . . . calculated to thwart and delay indefinitely the realisation of India's most cherished goal of complete responsible government and is totally unacceptable'.[29] This was hardly the best way of winning round Fazl-i-Husain who had influenced the making of these reforms so powerfully. Jinnah's Central Parliamentary Board set up to nominate Muslim candidates throughout India was another challenge to the Muslim leaders in the majority provinces. Declaring that all Muslim candidates must run on communal tickets alone was throwing the gauntlet down to the old parties, particularly the Unionists in the Punjab, and also such cross-communal groups as the Prajas in Bengal and the Agriculturist 'party' in the League's home base.

[27] Its Council of 310 members 'reflected neither the subscription-paying membership nor the aspirations of the leaders from these Muslim majority provinces' (Z. H. Zaidi (ed.), *M. A. Jinnah–Ispahani Correspondence, 1936–1948* (Karachi, 1976), p. 11 (henceforth *Correspondence*). The Punjab with its thirteen million Muslims had the same number of seats on the Council as the U.P. where there were seven million Muslims; Sind and the N.W.F.P. had only half as many seats as Bombay. Until 1938, well after the elections, the League's constitution remained unchanged, and its Council did not reflect where power was coming to lie in Muslim India – in majority provinces more powerful if less vocal than the Muslims of the Gangetic plains. The seats on the Council were distributed as follows:

Delhi	10	United Provinces	50
Punjab	50	Bombay	20
Bihar and Orissa	30	Sind	10
Madras	18	N.W.F.P.	10
Baluchistan	4	Bengal	60
Burma	10	Assam	12
C.P. and Berar	10	Central India & Ajmer	6

Ten seats were for the Indian States and others. ('The Constitution and Rules of the All-India Muslim League', AIML/File No. 111 and Zaidi (ed.), *Correspondence*, pp. 11–12).

[28] Jinnah wrote to Fazl-i-Husain that it was the 'unanimous desire' of the League's Council and 'I along with many others feel that at this moment no one can give a better lead to the Mussalmans of India than yourself' (Jinnah to Fazl-i-Husain, 5 January 1936, Mss.Eur.E.352/17/I.O.L.). For Fazl-i-Husain's reactions, see Jalal and Seal, *Modern Asian Studies*, 15, 3, (1981), p. 448.

[29] See A.I.M.L.'s twenty-fourth session, Bombay, April 1936, in Pirzada (ed,), *Foundations of Pakistan*, vol. 11, pp. 260–1.

Not surprisingly, Jinnah faced formidable opposition to these moves in the Punjab where the politicians had most to gain from provincial autonomy and most to lose by permitting outsiders to rock their Unionist boat. Fazl-i-Husain warned this actor on a stage which had yet to be set to keep out of his territory. Punjab was the biggest prize for the Muslim League. It was also to prove the most elusive. Dominated by the Unionist alliance, Fazl-i-Husain had enough support from Hindus and Sikhs to win a clear majority in the assembly and to form yet another Unionist ministry after the 1934 elections. No doubt there were factional rivalries among the Muslim ranks in the Punjab, and Jinnah sanguinely hoped to take advantage of them by offering to give shelter to Muslim candidates under the banner of the League. He was even ready to allow them to co-operate with non-Muslim groups in the assembly, once they were elected on a League ticket. But even this device attracted no defections from the Unionists. In fact Jinnah's only supporters in the Punjab proved to be a handful of urban-based men, most of them non-Unionists.[30] Fazl-i-Husain and Sikander Hayat Khan warned Jinnah to 'keep his finger out of the Punjab pie'; his meddling would simply encourage 'vociferous [sic]' tendencies among some Muslims; 'we cannot possibly allow "provincial autonomy" to be tampered in any sphere and by anybody be he a nominee of the powers who have given us this autonomy or a president of the Muslim League'.[31] Their prediction that Jinnah would achieve nothing if he came to the Punjab proved to be correct.[32] In Fazl-i-Husain's opinion, Jinnah's tactics were an 'utter failure'. A mere handful of 'miscellaneous urbanites like Iqbal, Shuja, Barkat Ali, have naturally been trying to make something out of this'; Jinnah simply could 'talk and talk and talk'; he had done nothing to revive the provincial League in the

---

30 They included Sir Muhammad Iqbal, the poet and philosopher of Pakistan. Jinnah did manage to set up a Punjab Muslim League Parliamentary Board, but it had little organisation and less support. It was reduced to blaming the Unionists for dividing urban and rural Punjab and making an appeal to religion which the Unionists did not like but as yet had no reason to fear. (See 'An important appeal to the Punjab Muslims' (Urdu), in M. Rafique Afzal (ed.), *Malik Barkat Ali: His Life and Writings* (Lahore, 1969), p. 36.)

31 Sikander Hayat Khan to Fazl-i-Husain, 1 May 1936, in Waheed Ahmad (ed.), *Letters of Mian Fazl-i-Husain* (Lahore, 1976), p. 528.

32 The Unionists refused to join him; so had the faction of the Ittihad-i-Millat (literally the 'unity of the community'), also known as the Blue Shirt Volunteers. It was formed by Maulana Zafar Ali Khan in 1935 to work for the return of the Shahidganj Mosque to Muslims from the Sikhs. But even this little pressure group was divided; Iqbal had another small faction of his own and its membership was hardly two hundred strong. Another Muslim group, the Ahrars, also refused to join Jinnah's Parliamentary Board (Ashiq Husain Batalvi, *Iqbal Ke Akhari Do Saal*, 3rd edn. (Lahore, 1978), pp. 319–47).

Punjab, or taken even the most elementary steps that any 'ordinary practical man' would have done if he wanted a base in the districts. Shrewdly Fazl-i-Husain judged that Jinnah's tactic was simply to persuade the powers that be to agree to don the League cap, take a seat on a nominal Central Parliamentary Board, and then run the elections in the province just as they would have before. In other words, the League scheme was 'purely a paper one',[33] but that was all Jinnah wanted it to be, provided he got his mandate at the centre.

Jinnah did not get his mandate.[34] He left the Punjab swearing: 'I shall never come to the Punjab again; it is such a hopeless place.'[35] The 1937 elections were fought in the Punjab on the old lines with personal, tribal and factional rivalries, not party creeds, dominating the choice of the voters.[36] The Muslim candidates who won these factional struggles in their constituencies agreed once again to come under the umbrella of the Unionists. In 1936 the Grand Old Man of Unionism, Fazl-i-Husain, had died, but Sikander Hayat Khan was unanimously elected as his successor even by his rivals in the Noon–Tiwana faction. This suggests that the provincial strategy of Fazl-i-Husain was capable of surviving in the Punjab. On 22 February 1937, the Governor happily noted 'that on the surface at least the party is in a strong position'.[37] At the final count, the Unionists claimed seventy-one of the seventy-five Muslim rural seats; and, all in all, they won the allegiance of ninety-nine of the 175 members of the assembly. Only in the urban seats did the Unionists do badly,

---

33 Fazl-i-Husain to Sikander Hayat Khan, 6 May 1936, Ahmad (ed.), *Letters of Mian Fazl-i-Husain*, p. 534.

34 Even the eleven members from the Punjab on Jinnah's fifty-four-member Central Parliamentary Board, had shunned the League ticket – only two of them actually contested the election on such a ticket and one of them was later to join the Unionist party.

35 Cited in Azim Husain, *Mian Fazl-i-Husain: A Political Biography* (London, 1966), p. 311.

36 As the Governor noted: 'In the forthcoming elections the Unionist Party will often not be represented by a single candidate in a particular constituency. In fact the usual position will be two or more Muslim candidates fighting the same constituency, all of whom are prepared to support the Unionist Party if elected. The elections will be fought on personal or tribal lines, and the fact that the candidates subscribe to the same political creed will not mitigate local animosity which will long survive the result.' (Emerson to Linlithgow, 19 October 1936, R/3/1/1, I.O.L.).

     None of this was new. There had been a longstanding rivalry, for example, between the families of Noon-Tiwana of Shahpur and the Wah faction of Sikander Hayat. Despite all the factional shifts, the Governor predicted that 'future prospects are probably less unstable than existing circumstances would suggest'; and despite all the manoeuvring and bargaining between the groups after the elections, a Unionist ministry was clearly on the cards.

37 Emerson to Linlithgow, 22 February 1937, R/3/1/1, I.O.L.

winning two of the nine reserved seats. But these few urban seats were expendable. The League ended up with one seat.[38] In March 1937, the first Punjab ministry under the 1935 Act was formed, with Sikander Hayat Khan as chief minister. It included three Muslims, all drawn from the ranks of the rural Unionists; two Hindus (Chhotu Ram in the rural interest, and Manohar Lal for the towns); and there was one Sikh in it as well. In the Punjab at least the aims of the 1935 Act had been achieved – a ministry drawn from all the communities that mattered, ready to work provincial autonomy, and in the hands of the proven friends of the Raj.

Despite the failure of his initiative in early 1935, the prospects for Jinnah, it seemed, were better in Bengal than they were in the Punjab.

[38] *The 1937 election in the Punjab**

Party	Muslim U	R	O	General U	R	O	Sikh U	R	O	Other	Total
Unionist	2	71	1	—	13	—	—	—	—	8	95
Hindu Electoral Board	—	—	—	1	8	1	—	—	—	1	11
Khalsa National	—	—	—	—	—	—	2	11	1	—	14
Government	2	71	1	1	21	1	2	11	1	9	120
Indian National Congress	—	2	—	7	3	1	—	4●	1●	—	18
Shiromani Akali Dal	—	—	—	—	—	—	—	10	—	—	10
Majlis-i-Ahrar	2	—	—	—	—	—	—	—	—	—	2
Ittihid-i-Millat	2	—	—	—	—	—	—	—	—	—	2
Muslim League	1	—	—	—	—	—	—	—	—	—	1
Congress Nationalist	—	—	—	—	1	—	—	—	—	—	1
Socialist	—	—	—	—	—	—	1	—	—	—	1
Labour	—	—	—	—	—	—	—	—	—	1	1
Independent	2	2	3	—	9	—	—	3	—	—	19
Opposition	7	4	3	7	13	1	—	18	1	1	55
TOTAL	9	75	4	8	34	2	2	29	2	10	175

* Although all eleven members of the Hindu Electoral Board are listed as pro-government, the party was divided into two factions: the Narendra Nath faction of perhaps eight members which supported the government and the Gokal Chand Narang faction of perhaps three members which opposed it.
● Congress Socialists.
Symbols: U = urban, R = rural, O = other (women, landowners). The 'other' seats includes those of small communal groups, Europeans, Anglo-Indians and Indian Christians; and those of functional groups such as commerce, labour and university graduates. The functional seats might be held by members of any community and their constituency included members of all communities.
Source: United Kingdom: House of Commons, *Parliamentary Papers 1937–38, XXI (Accounts and Papers VI)*, Cmd. 5589, 'Returns Showing the Results of elections in India, 1937', pp. 80–93. (From Stephen Oren, 'The Sikhs, Congress and the Unionists in British Punjab, 1937–1945', *Modern Asian Studies*, 8, 3 (1974), 398.)

The clash of interests between Muslims in the eastern and western districts had been made sharper by the Communal Award.[39] In the east Muslims could see that they had little to fear from joint electorates; but in the west where they were generally in small minorities, separate electorates were essential if they were to have adequate representation.[40] For the Hindus it was the other way round. Consequently, any demand for joint electorates would neatly divide the interests of Hindus and Muslims at the two points of the compass. In 1935, Fazlul Huq, sensing this trend, decided to put it to political use by making a bid for control of the Nikhil Banga Praja Samity supported by Muslims from eastern Bengal.[41] In April 1936 the old guard reacted by forming an United Muslim party which unconvincingly claimed to be united and concerned about the lot of peasants and workers. The two parties – the United Muslim and Huq's Krishak Praja – soon fell out, and most of the leaders from Calcutta and the west (including some who had been in the old Nikhil Banga Praja Samity, such as Akram Khan, Abdur Rahim and Shaheed Suhrawardy) joined the United Muslim party. But the key to Muslim success in Bengal under the reformed constitution was the support of the eastern districts. An united front between the United Muslim party and the Krishak Praja party was mooted, but the talks broke down over the usual problem about who was to lead and who was to follow. At this point, two Calcutta businessmen, Ispahani and Abdur Rahman Siddiqui, decided to attend the Lahore meeting of the A.I.M.L.'s Parliamentary Board. There Jinnah gave them the job of organising the Bengal League. After yet another attempt to get the United Muslim party and Krishak Praja to agree failed, Ispahani thought he saw a chance of doing down both, if only Jinnah came to Calcutta immediately and took a hand.[42] The Krishak Praja party was sticking to its guns about abolishing zamindari without compensation; it also wanted to keep its identity, and to be

---

[39] By the nineteen-thirties, Muslim politicians in the east were beginning to gain control of districts which had long been dominated by Hindus. Members of local boards in Bengal were chosen by joint electorates; this enabled Hindus and Muslims alike to gauge what would happen in the council and assembly if separate electorates, in force since 1909, were given up.

[40] See Jinnah–Prasad negotiations, pp. 13–14, above.

[41] Huq was elected president against the candidate backed by Muslims from the west, Khan Bahadur Abdul Momin of Burdwan. This presented a serious challenge to the old guard of Muslim politicians who had their base in Calcutta and the western districts. The newly enfranchised voters included many who would respond to radical demands for land reform, and Huq saw the political advantage of linking himself with the Praja Samities in the east. In February 1936, he succeeded in making a deal with the Krishak Praja leaders of Tippera.

[42] See Ispahani to Jinnah, 9 August 1936, Zaidi (ed.), *Correspondence*, p. 76.

allowed to contest general seats. The zamindar interest in the United Muslim party, with their access to ministerial patronage, were not having any of this. Once Jinnah's initiative on joint electorates had failed, the United Muslims wanted all their candidates to run on purely communal tickets. This was in line with the League's policy but Huq wanted his men on the League's Parliamentary Board to sign the Praja party's creed. This Jinnah could not accept, so he willy-nilly had to end up by settling for the United Muslim party, although he came to Calcutta hoping to bring both these groups under the League's wing. The United Muslim party had no organisation or support in the eastern districts where the Krishak Prajas held sway, so it saw some advantage in getting the League's High Command to ratify its claims to represent all Bengal Muslims.[43] Nawabs, zamindars and Muslim businessmen all could see that the best defence against the Krishak's undoubted electoral advantages in eastern Bengal, lay in the claim that the Praja party, with its radical social demands, was 'not a purely Muslim organisation'.[44] So the United Muslim party went into voluntary liquidation and joined the League on a limited liability basis. All this really meant was that the United Muslim party took over the mantle of a moribund Muslim League in Bengal. But Jinnah now was entitled to nominate representatives on to the Bengal Parliamentary Board. Jinnah's nominees to the Bengal Muslim League's Parliamentary Board inevitably were drawn from the old United Muslim party, mainly big landlords or non-Bengali businessmen from Calcutta. So Jinnah had to settle for support mainly from the western districts and Calcutta. In turn Huq formed his own rival parliamentary board. It was plain that 'in effect the Muslim League in Bengal was "the United Muslim Party" writ large'.[45]

Forming a League Parliamentary Board in Bengal did not impose order on Muslim politics in Bengal. The rivalry between the League and Huq's group intensified. The League may have had more money and ministerial patronage, but it had no formal organisation and depended on the support of existing factions. It had no clear programme. Of course the Krishak Praja was hardly united and solid in its purpose.[46] So the

---

[43] Of course when it came to forming a ministry, this would depend upon its patronage and ability to win over enough members of the assembly, not on the League's support from the centre.

[44] This was Nazimuddin's line. By stressing the need for communal solidarity the United Muslim party hoped to undermine the supra-communal policies of its rival. (Shila Sen, *Muslim Politics in Bengal: 1937–1947* (New Delhi, 1976), p. 75.)

[45] Zaidi (ed.), *Correspondence*, p. 23.

[46] Huq, described by the Governor as the 'most uncertain quantity in Muslim politics', 'devoid of principle and trusted by nobody', made much of his agrarian programme, but

Bengali Muslims remained at sixes and sevens at the eve of the 1937 provincial elections. By contrast the Hindus had gone some way towards closing their ranks. Their unanimous dismay at the Communal Award had welded them into an unprecedented (if impermanent) unity. Despite its long history of factional squabbles, the Congress, according to the Governor, entered the elections as the 'only organised party in Bengal'.[47] The Congress and the Krishak Praja had an unwritten agreement not to poach on each other's territory, and this worked to the electoral advantage of both. The League was left complaining that the Krishak Praja party was merely the running dog of the Congress.

The 1937 election results showed just how divided the Bengal Muslims were. Of all the Muslim candidates, about two-thirds fought the elections as independents and won forty-three seats. The Muslim League (or the old United Muslim party) won thirty-nine seats out of the eighty-two that it contested, which included all six of the urban seats and four in special constituencies. The Krishak Praja party did almost as well, winning thirty-six seats out of the seventy-five it contested, and the Tippera Krishak Samity won five. The Muslim League had three more seats than the Krishaks but it polled fewer votes.[48] The Krishak Praja naturally did best in the eastern districts. The League for its part did best in the west, and in a few constituencies in north and central Bengal, and of course, Dacca was still its preserve by courtesy of the Nawab. But when Nazimuddin and Huq tested their strength in Patuakhali, Huq won hands down.[49]

The results of the 1937 elections in Bengal meant that Huq was bound to have a say in putting together any ministry. Congress, with its fifty-

---

he and many of the members of his alliance were mainly concerned to oust the Dacca faction. Despite all his radical pretensions, Huq, the Governor predicted, was ready to 'make a bid for office by scraping up support from among Muslims whose chances of advancement from the United or other Parties was small and selling himself and them to the highest bidder'. The Governor also drew attention to Huq's 'chronic indebtedness [which] places him at the mercy of anyone who, for the time being, can buy up the interest of a substantial creditor'. Although he was useful to the Congress, and perhaps even in their pay, since it was 'their inveterate policy of splitting the Muslims' in order to get control themselves, Huq was 'liable to double-cross and they know it'. (See Anderson to Linlithgow, 3 December 1936, R/3/2/2, I.O.L.)

[47] Ibid.

[48] The League polled 61.4% of the urban votes, only 26.5% of the rural votes and 27.10% of the total Muslim vote. The Krishak Praja party won 31.78% of the rural votes, only 15.39% of the urban votes and 31.51% of the total Muslim votes. (Government of India, Home Political File 129/37: Returns showing the Results of Elections in India, 1937, Cmd. 5589, cited in Sen, *Muslim Politics in Bengal*, pp. 88–97.)

[49] Humaira Momen, *Muslim Politics in Bengal: A Study of Krishak Praja Party and the Elections of 1937* (Dacca, 1972), p. 64.

four seats, was the largest single bloc.[50] Fortunately for the League in Bengal, the All-India Congress Committee was slow to accept office, and this gave them their chance to put together a ministry at Calcutta. Once Huq's negotiations with the Bengal Congress broke down, he quickly came to terms with the League. It involved paying a heavy price. His Praja party was to have only two of the six Muslim posts in the new ministry, the Muslim League was to have four, three went to caste Hindus who did not belong to the Congress, and another two to representatives of the Scheduled Castes, also outside the Congress camp. In a ministry dominated by zamindars, Huq had to dilute his programme. For example, he was allowed to press for the repeal of repressive laws and the release of political prisoners only so far as this was 'consistent with public safety'; free primary education was to be free only to a few; and Huq had to settle for a commission of enquiry to look into the Permanent Settlement rather than an outright commitment to abolish the zamindari system.[51] Huq's own followers were bitter about this compromise; twenty-eight of the Krishak Praja men now deserted Huq. These defections forced Huq to depend increasingly upon the Muslim League. In Bengal, then, the Muslim League (the old United Muslim party in all but name) had managed to cobble together an unstable ministry, the only ministry the League could claim to have formed in any province after the elections. But this was a success built upon the shifting sands of Bengali factionalism.

In the other two Muslim-majority provinces, Sind and the N.W.F.P. Jinnah had no success at all. In Sind, the politics of Muslims were ridden by faction, but this was true of all politics in Sind, whether Hindu or Muslim. As late as October 1936, Sir Lancelot Graham reported that no 'definite party had been constituted in Sind for the purpose of contesting the provincial elections'. The 'leading man' was Sir Ghulam Hussain,

---

[50] *Strength of the various parties in the Bengal legislature after the 1937 election*

Congress	54
Hindu Nationalists (caste Hindus)	3
Hindu Sabha (Scheduled Caste)	2
Independent Hindus	37
Muslim League	39
Praja Party	40
Independent Muslims	42
Europeans	25
Anglo-Indians	4
Indian Christians	2
TOTAL	248*

* Two by-elections pending.
(See Anderson to Linlithgow, 8 February 1937, R/3/2/2, I.O.L.)

[51] See Sen, *Muslim Politics in Bengal*, pp. 90–1.

loyalist, former minister and member of the Viceroy's Executive Council, and by far the 'ablest politician in Sind'. Sir Shah Nawaz Bhutto from Larkana was another important man in Sind but the Governor had failed to get Ghulam Hussain and Bhutto to work together. With many parties, Sind prepared for the elections in a festive mood. A Muslim businessman from Karachi, Seth Haji Abdullah Haroon, formed the United 'party', a favourite name when unity was difficult to find. It had a non-communal programme, and managed to win Bhutto over. Ghulam Hussain formed his own Sind Muslim 'party'; and Abdul Majid Sindhi's faction took on the title of the Sind Azad 'party'.[52] In 1936, Jinnah tried but failed to create a League Parliamentary Board in Sind. Sind went to the polls in 1937 without any League presence, and this was a province where nearly seventy-two per cent of the population was Muslim. Although the United party won more seats, its leader and deputy leader lost their elections, and so the Governor had to invite Ghulam Hussain to form a ministry.[53]

In the N.W.F.P., Jinnah was asked by a handful of Muslims in Peshawar to set up a League Parliamentary Board, but he learnt that the pro-Congress Khudai Khidmatgars (literally, the servants of God) were bound to win and their Muslim rivals were a broken reed since they were too busy fighting each other to listen to Jinnah. So he abandoned even the pretence of trying to set up a Parliamentary Board. The Governor encouraged the loyalist Khans to close their ranks against these pro-Congress Khudai Khidmatgars. But the Khudai Khidmatgars surprisingly had something resembling an organisation, with an over-all parliamentary board as well as local boards in some districts.[54] Factionalism was the order of the day among the Frontier Muslims, and 101 candidates fought over thirty-six Muslim seats.[55] The Congress High

[52] Graham to Linlithgow, 16 October 1936, R/3/1/1, I.O.L.
[53] The United party won sixteen rural and one urban Muslim seat. Ghulam Hussain's Sind Muslim party won two urban and thirteen rural Muslim seats as well as the special landlord constituency. The Sind Azad party was able to win only one seat. Since Shah Nawaz Bhutto, the leader, and Abdullah Haroon, the deputy leader of the United party lost their elections, Ghulam Hussain was called in to form the ministry. (See Graham to Linlithgow, 18 February 1937 and 22 March 1937, ibid.)
[54] According to the Governor 'Their loyalty to their organisation and its principles, and their firm suppression of individual interests, compel admiration, and may possibly result in the undoing of the loyalists, who are so rent by faction and jealousy that up to now they have found it quite impossible to combine, or to achieve any sort of effective organisation'. (Griffiths to Linlithgow, 9 November 1936, ibid.)
[55] The Khudai Khidmatgars/Congress party under Dr Khan Sahib contested twenty-nine Muslim seats, the Ittihad–i–Millat one, the Independent party five, and various Khans contested thirty-five seats with sixty-six candidates. (Griffiths to Linlithgow, 12 January 1937, ibid.)

Command's indecision whether or not to accept office gave the 'no party Muslims' under Sir Abdul Qaiyum Khan an opportunity to enjoy the fruits of office with some Hindu and Sikh support in the assembly. But once the High Command gave the signal, the local Congress assembly party under Dr Khan Sahib quickly defeated Qaiyum's ministry.[56]

This dismal record in the Muslim-majority provinces made it essential for Jinnah to rescue something in the Muslim-minority provinces, where the League's appeal was likely to be greater. The U.P. were the key. Here the ungenerous provisions of the Communal Award, endorsed in the 1935 Act, had put at risk the comfortable position that the landlord politicians had enjoyed under diarchy. The Montagu–Chelmsford reforms had been worked here by cross-communal alliances of land-owners, organised in an Agriculturist 'party' at the behest of British governors. The coming of a new constitution with a wider franchise made it more imperative than ever for the British to try and keep this group together. It was an obvious favourite. It was conservative, loyal and inter-communal – the best guarantee that provincial autonomy would not be used against British purposes. But the 'party of stability' upon which the British hoped to rely had always been loosely organised. In the early nineteen-thirties it had done nothing except bide time. Only when the Congress began to organise for the central legislative assembly elections in 1934, having declared that the policy, at least of its socialist wing, was to abolish zamindari without compensation, did the landlords give serious thought to pulling themselves together. By August 1934 they had set up a National Agriculturist party in both Agra and Oudh. But it existed mainly on paper.[57] Until 1936 it continued to depend on the personal influence of its members. The Governor thought its prospects might still be reasonable, 'if they [the landlords] could only prevent their supporters fighting each other on personal grounds'.[58]

---

[56] The party position in the assembly was:

Congress	19
Hindu–Sikh nationalists	7
Independent Hindus	1
Independent Muslims	2
'No party Muslims'	21
TOTAL	50

(Griffiths to Linlithgow, 22 February 1937, ibid.)

[57] As the Governor noted, 'Many of the landlords frankly disbelieved in the necessity of organisation. Their view was that they could by their personal influence control the votes of their tenants and that the ordinary methods of propaganda were superfluous, while their political horizon was limited to their own personal success at the election.' (Haig to Linlithgow, 29 October 1936, ibid.)

[58] Ibid.

So in the U.P. at least Jinnah could expect to recruit disenchanted landowners and ex-Congress Muslims. The impact of the civil disobedience movement and the increasing politicisation of the peasantry had shown some landlords that the old policy of relying upon government to protect Muslim property was no longer enough, 'so even those Muslims who have so far been with government will go against it or lose all influence with the public'.[59] Increasingly many of the prominent landlords in the Agriculturist camp began to forge links with communal organisations, whether with the Hindu Mahasabha or, in the case of Muslim landlords, with the League or the Conference. Two of the most prominent Muslim landlords in Agra, the Nawab of Chhatari and Nawab Sir Muhammad Yusuf, decided to keep their options open by flirting with Jinnah's newly revived League. In the Governor's opinion, this was a tactical blunder since 'it was obvious that the All-India Muslim League was to be merely the means whereby Mr Jinnah was to utilise the Muslim vote for the purpose of his own advanced Nationalist policy'. Both Chhatari and Muhammad Yusuf wanted to avoid difficult electoral fights against nationalist Muslims in Agra who would have the League's support. But by hedging their bets they undermined their own position inside the Agra branch of the National Agriculturists. In Oudh, the Agriculturists were no better placed. The Hindu *taluqdars* had reorganised the Oudh Liberal League in 1935 and they now claimed to speak for the Hindu landlord interest, while in the early nineteen-thirties the Muslim *taluqdars* took up their place in the Muslim Conference and Unity Boards and helped to revive the Muslim League in the U.P.[60] The Raja of Mahmudabad, an old friend of Jinnah, and the Raja of Salempur in fact joined the League's Parliamentary Board, and the Raja of Jehangirabad, who had been the vice-president of the Oudh Agriculturist party, announced that he would fight the elections as an independent, fearing the outcry from nationalist and League Muslims alike if he stood again on an Agriculturist ticket. By October 1936 many Muslim members of the Agriculturist party were leaving the sinking ship, because they had been tipped the wink that if they stood as independents they would 'not be opposed so vigorously'.[61] Some nationalist Muslims, until now in the Congress camp, crossed over to the League since a Congress ticket was hardly the passport to success in a Muslim constituency. Reluctantly they accepted that they would do better by wearing the League cap. Among them was Choudhry Khaliquzzaman, later the secretary of the U.P. League, who continued to keep his links with the

[59] Mushir Husain Kidwai to Fazl-i-Husain, 3 April 1931, in Ahmad (ed.), *Letters of Mian Fazl-i-Husain*, p. 129.
[60] Haig to Linlithgow, 29 October 1936, R 3 1 1, I.O.L.   [61] Ibid.

Congress. Not surprisingly, the Muslim League in the U.P., drawing its support from such diverse sources, was hardly a solid organisation. Some of the more socially conservative notables who had joined it (for example, Raja Ali Ahmed Khan of Salempur, who was chairman of the League), fell out with the secretary, Khaliquzzaman; and even the Raja of Mahmudabad soon began 'to regret his association with the Muslim League and . . . [was] not likely to take any very active part in the elections on its behalf'.[62] As the elections drew closer, the U.P. League, a ramshackle coalition, never more than a 'patchwork . . . never likely to stand much strain'[63] began to split at its seams. There were sixty-four Muslim constituencies in the U.P., and the contestants had the enviable choice either of fighting them under the League's banner, remaining with the Agriculturists or standing out as independents. All except seven seats were contested, and the measure of the politicians' uncertainty is the fact that sixty-six independents contested forty Muslim rural seats. The League put up only twenty-seven candidates in the countryside, and its remaining twelve were in urban constituencies. The real casualties were the Agriculturists who contested only ten Muslim seats in Agra and nine in Oudh. The Congress did not fight any urban Muslim seat, evidence perhaps that it had an unwritten pact with the League since there were still many Congress Muslims in the U.P.[64]

In the 1937 elections, the Agriculturists did much worse than their friends had expected and the Congress and the League did at least as well as their most optimistic supporters had hoped. The Congress won 134 of the 140 general seats. The League won nine urban Muslim seats and, most remarkably, twenty in the rural constituencies, and one special seat to boot. The Agriculturist party was virtually wiped out. The Oudh section did a little better than its counterpart in Agra but the Agriculturists came back with only three of the forty rural seats they had fought, and were ignominiously driven out of the four urban general seats where they had dared to stand.[65] This was a real turn-about; the Agriculturists had the advantage of holding office and disbursing patronage; they were beloved in Government House, and they knew their countryside. Here again, it was more a consequence of Congress's rural activism with the *kisan* agitation and its potential threat to landlords, which persuaded the notables either to make terms with their potential enemies or to organise against them under a new banner. Even in the League's home-base – the

---

62 Haig to Linlithgow, 2 December 1936, ibid.
63 Haig to Linlithgow, 6 January 1937, R/3/I/I, I.O.L.
64 See P. D. Reeves, 'Changing patterns of political alignment in the General Elections to the United Provinces Legislative Assembly, 1937 and 1946', *Modern Asian Studies*, 5, 2 (1971), 127.   65 Ibid., 114–15.

U.P. – a success, relative, rather than absolute, had been bought more by a change of allegiance at the top than by a surge of populist support at the base.

In the U.P. the Congress emerged as the largest party in the assembly and did not need an alliance with any other group to form a ministry.[66] Since the Congress itself, especially in the U.P., was divided between right and left wings, which had opposing ideologies and different strategies for the land, a coalition between Congress and the League with its landed notables, whatever its attractions in terms of a common front at the all-India centre, was likely to strengthen the right-wing inside the U.P. ministry. But if there was to be no coalition between the Congress and the League in the U.P., where the League had its only real success in the elections of 1937, this put paid to Jinnah's hopes of forming coalition ministries with the Congress in other Muslim-minority provinces,[67] and

[66] The composition of the Muslim members of the new U.P. legislative assembly was:

Muslim League	29 + 1 special seat
Independents	24
Congress	1
NAPA*	7
NAPO●	3
TOTAL	64

The composition of the non-Muslim members of the legislature, i.e. the 140 general seats and 24 special seats, along party lines was as follows:

Congress	134 (8 special seats)
NAPA*	6 (3 special seats)
NAPO●	9 (3 special seats)
Liberals	1 (special seat)
Independents	14 (8 special seats)
TOTAL	164

* National Agriculturist party of Agra; ●National Agriculturist party of Oudh. (Ibid.).

[67] The following shows the complete election returns for the Muslim League.

Province	Total Muslim seats	Seats won by the League*	Percentage
Madras	28	11	39
Bombay	39	20	51
Bengal	119	37	31
U.P.	64	27	43
Punjab	86	1	1.1
Assam	34	9	26.4
N.W.F.P.	36	—	—
Orissa	4	—	—
Sind	36	—	—
Bihar	39	—	—
C.P.	14	—	—

* Only those seats which were actually won by the League candidates are included.

Of the total Muslim votes cast (7,319,445), the League was able to poll only 321,772, or 4.4 per cent. *Returns showing the Results of Election in India, 1937* (Cmd. 5589.)

to his strategy of using these provincial alliances as the basis for an agreement with the Congress at the centre.

The election of 1937 destroyed the foundations upon which Jinnah had built his strategy ever since his return to India in 1934. By its success at the polls (surprising only to those who fail to understand the inwardness of civil disobedience and the dividends it was to pay at the ballot box) Congress had shown that it could do without the League which had not been able to match Congress's attractions to the floating vote. Congress formed ministries in six provinces, and had troubles enough with its own factions without wanting to add to its difficulties by bringing in Leaguers who owed allegiance to a rival High Command. In the Muslim provinces, Sikander Hayat brought the Unionists back to office, with a single Leaguer keeping Jinnah's flag aloft in the Punjab assembly. In Sind and the N.W.F.P., the League did not win a single seat. In Bengal, Fazlul Huq's ministry was a coalition, and this was in a Muslim province where the League could claim (uncertainly) to have done best. Anyone except Jinnah would have been tempted to throw in the towel; indeed Congress generously invited him to do just that, and said it would welcome back into its house his would-be nationalists. But Jinnah was a fighter and he was the master of a long slow game, an expert at seeing chances in the worst reverses. Although he was outraged by this further example of perfidy from Congressmen whose purposes he shared but whose priorities and personalities he frequently despised, he could spot a silver lining in these clouds. Congress's triumph in the 1937 elections, orchestrated by its High Command, heralded the coming victory of centre over province. It also signalled the collapse of many of the old provincial structures upon which the British strategy of retreat to the centre depended. This meant that the way was clearer for the Congress High Command to make a bid for power at the centre, and it also meant that Congress just as much as the League had reason to want to break the residues of provincial autonomy, especially in the Muslim provinces, in pursuit of this aim. Muslim provinces would now feel the brunt of Congress pressure. In its turn this might give the League at the centre a chance both to mediate on behalf of these Muslim provinces and perhaps in due course to help in disciplining them itself. In the meantime, the Muslim provinces would be forced to recognise their need to have a spokesman at the centre; and their own embattled provincialism had left Jinnah and his League as the only plausible candidate for this role. Taken with the cold draughts of exclusion which minority Muslims now could feel inside their provinces, these new imperatives gave Jinnah some hope for an otherwise gloomy future. He was able to reject the condescending offer of a Congress High Command which should have known that what it had achieved yesterday, Jinnah might achieve tomorrow – disciplining provincial factions from above and persuading them to accept a spokesman at the centre. Paradoxically, the Congress High Command, anxious to storm the centre, and the British, anxious to ward them off, also needed someone to speak for Muslims at the all-India level. The fact that Muslims had proved yet again to be divided at the polls did not remove them as a formidable political category in discussions about the future of India. All this enabled Jinnah to live to fight another day.

2

Jinnah and the League's search for survival

Section 1

Before the 1937 elections Jinnah's plan had been to claim for the League
the undisputed spokesmanship of Muslims at the all-India level. This
plan required the Muslim-majority provinces to come under the
League's banner and Muslims in provinces where they were in a minority
to vote solidly for the League. If he had won this mandate from Muslim
voters, Jinnah might have been able to offer Congress something worth
having: at the centre, support from Muslim provinces for a combined
assault upon the federal provisions of the 1935 Act and, in the minority
provinces, solid League backing which might have tipped the balance
against the old guard upon whom the British depended and have brought
into office coalition Congress–League ministries.

But for Jinnah the results of the 1937 elections proved another setback
in a career marked more by snakes than by ladders. In the Punjab, the
Unionists swept the board; in Bengal, Jinnah and the League had to
accept a coalition led by Huq who did not acknowledge their writ; in Sind
they faced an independent ministry; and in the N.W.F.P., where almost
the entire population was Muslim, the worst humiliation of all, a
Congress ministry. In each of the majority provinces, Jinnah's strategy
had been repudiated by the voters' choice. In the Muslim-minority
provinces, where the League did best, the Congress did much better than
anyone had expected, and did not need the League's help to form stable
ministries. Despite a measure of agreement with Jinnah about the future
shape of the centre, the Congress High Command could now plausibly
do without the League; understandings with the League were, in the
aftermath of the 1937 elections, the expenditure of the expendable.
Rejected by the Muslim provinces, the League had nothing to offer the
Congress at the centre; so in the provinces where it had won comfortable
majorities the Congress saw no reason to dilute its control by giving the
League a share of office. The way in which the Muslim vote had split in
the elections of 1937 lent some credence to the old Congress line that it
was a secular party, ready and able to speak for Muslims, many of whom
had entered its camp. Indeed, the Congress now saw the possibility of

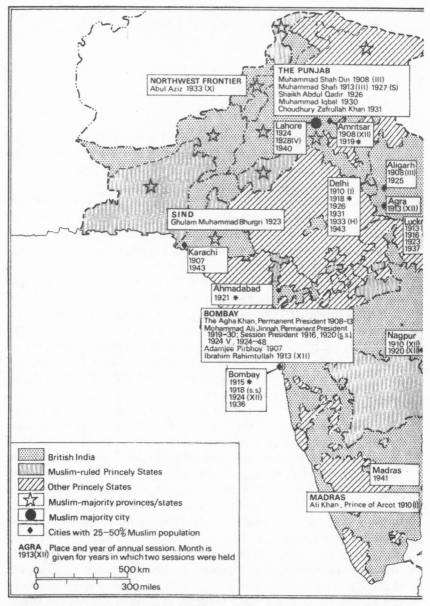

Map 3. All-India Muslim League: presidents and sessions, 1906–1943. Presidents are grouped by regions. Dates for both permanent presidents and sessional presidents are given. From 1908 to 1930 the League designated a permanent president (see the Aga Khan, the Raja of Mahmudabad and M. A. Jinnah) as well as a sessional president. (N.B. All boundaries are as at July 1947, all population data as at 1941.)

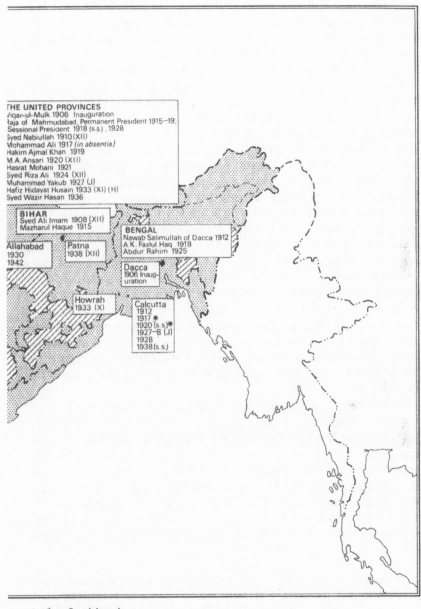

THE UNITED PROVINCES
Viqar-ul-Mulk 1906 Inauguration
Raja of Mahmudabad, Permanent President 1915–19;
Sessional President 1918 (s.s.), 1928
Syed Nabiullah 1910 (XII)
Mohammad Ali 1917 *(in absentia)*
Hakim Ajmal Khan 1919
M.A. Ansari 1920 (XII)
Hasrat Mohani 1921
Syed Riza Ali 1924 (XII)
Muhammad Yakub 1927 (J)
Hafiz Hidayat Husain 1933 (XI) (H)
Syed Wazir Hasan 1936

BIHAR
Syed Ali Imam 1908 (XII)
Mazharul Haque 1915

BENGAL
Nawab Salimullah of Dacca 1912
A.K. Fazlul Haq 1918
Abdur Rahim 1925

Allahabad
1930
1942

Patna
1938 (XII)

Dacca
1906 Inaug-
uration

Howrah
1933 (X)

Calcutta
1912
1917 *
1920 (s.s.) *
1927–8 (J)
1928
1938 (s.s.)

(s.s.) = Special session
* = Simultaneous session with Congress
(H) = Hidayat group
(J) = Jinnah group   } (temporary factions
(S) = Shafi group   within League)

breaking the grip of rival political groups in the provincial assemblies. Muslim members outside its whip in provincial assemblies might be persuaded to cross the floor; a mass contact programme directed specifically at Muslims might give substance to the claim that Congress spoke for many of them. Above all, the High Command calculated that Congress's eventual dominance at a federal centre was unlikely to be threatened by an united Muslim bloc. On the basis of the 1937 elections, the League could at best expect to control less than half of the Muslim seats in the federal legislature, or just over fifteen per cent of the seats for British Indian representatives. The triennial election system meant that it would be long before the League, even on the assumption that it could win the Muslim-majority province vote, could get its one-third say among the British Indian representatives. Moreover, if the federal provisions of the 1935 Act could be changed so that representatives from the Princely States were elected, not nominated, then the Congress would have little to fear at the centre from even a powerful Muslim combination, let alone the rump led by Jinnah.[1] Once Congress succeeded in getting a constituent assembly along the lines it wanted, that assembly, even if it were to be elected on the existing franchise and even if Muslims continued to have separate representation, would contain a mere handful of League members. So there seemed little point in paying much heed to the League – an assessment which seemed reasonable enough in the first flush of victory in 1937, but one which was to prove to be one of the gravest miscalculations by the Congress leadership in its long history.

Faced with the threat of being snuffed out politically, the League urgently needed a new strategy for survival. Some appearance of support, however nominal, from the Muslim-majority provinces was the first requirement if the League was to secure any role for itself at the centre. Admittedly the Muslim-majority provinces needed a spokesman in Delhi since it was there that the Congress's ambitions were coming increasingly to be directed. At the centre, one voice was more likely to be heard than a babel of conflicting tongues. But Jinnah, an obvious candidate for the role of spokesman, was not well placed to exact terms

---

[1] The Indian States were of course divided. But the Muslim States were grossly outnumbered by the Hindu States. Kashmir with its Hindu Maharaja had only three seats and Hyderabad, which had a predominantly Hindu population and a Muslim ruler, had only five seats. So the Hindus would have a certain majority of the representatives from the Indian States. If they were to be elected, then they might join the Congress, since Congress had a powerful States' movement while the League had nothing of the sort even in the Muslim States.

from the majority provinces for acting as their *vakil*; a briefless advocate, he had to accept any terms they cared to offer. Predictably their terms were not generous. In October 1937, Sikander and Huq rescued Jinnah from political oblivion by allowing him to speak for Punjab and Bengal at the centre; but they both made the League pay a heavy price for the privilege. By agreeing to bring their followers nominally into the Punjab League, the Unionists were in fact ensuring the obliteration of an independent League in their province. Moreover, Sikander insisted that in return for this limited mandate to represent their interests at the centre, the A.I.M.L. was to have no say in Punjabi affairs. There was more to it than that: Jinnah was forced in the Punjab to call to heel the few loyal Leaguers, urban out-groups who actually acknowledged his authority. That the Jinnah–Sikander agreement at Lucknow was a victory for the Unionists is proved by the reaction of Iqbal and the League's urban supporters in Punjab. Iqbal saw the move as 'handing over the League to Sir Sikander and his friends', which had 'already damaged the prestige of the League in this province' and 'may damage it still further', and warned that Muslim Unionists had no intention of signing the League's creed.[2] In December 1938 some 'honest and genuine [L]eaguers', predicted that the Punjab League, now simply an Unionist creature, a bogus organisation, existing only on paper, would soon be 'absolutely dead';[3] but Jinnah had no alternative but to sacrifice what little organisation the League possessed in the Punjab in exchange for the limited right to speak for it at the centre. With characteristic political realism, he told his Punjabi supporters what his line towards the provinces was now going to have to be. Any Muslim ready to accept the League's 'creed, Policy and Programme' (or simply that the League spoke for him at the centre), whatever his political persuasion, 'is no longer any thing else but a leaguer and those who have been already in the League are no better than the [new] leaguers'. With so few in his camp, Jinnah had no option except to fling the gates wide open to all comers. Any Muslim who now gave the League his nominal allegiance became a Leaguer on an equal footing with those who had actually worked for the party in the past. As Jinnah explained with unusual candour, 'there is no such thing as this group or that group, or that party or this party, because then it really means various cliques'.[4]

---

[2] Iqbal was proved to be right. Until the summer of 1944, the League possessed not even the pretence of an organisation in the Punjab. (See Iqbal to Jinnah, 10 November 1937, Ahmad (ed.), *Historic Documents*, p. 213.)

[3] Shaikh Zafar Ali to Jinnah, 21 December 1938, QAP/11/File No. 1094, pp. 479–80.

[4] Jinnah to Barkat Ali, no date, in S. Qaim Hussain Jafri (ed.), *Quaid-i-Azam's Correspondence with Punjab Muslim Leaders* (Lahore, 1977), p. 48.

Bengal's backing at the centre was purchased by Jinnah at an even higher price. Here M.L.A.s in the League camp had a fighting chance of pulling down Huq and having a ministry of their own. In September 1937, another section of the Krishak Praja party had broken with Huq, leaving him as the leader of a minority group in the coalition ministry. This strengthened the claims of Nazimuddin, the leader of the League's assembly party, to become prime minister, particularly since he had Government House's favour, backing from the European bloc in the assembly and support from the non-Bengali Muslim businessmen of Calcutta. This is why Huq now identified himself with the League and led Bengal's delegates to the League's Lucknow session. To get the immediate support from the ministry in Bengal, Jinnah had to permit Huq and his Krishak Praja followers, who straddled the communities, to appropriate the League's colours. In return, all Huq promised to do was to advise his few remaining Muslim followers in the Krishak Praja party to 'follow' the League's policy at the centre, while in every other respect he and his men remained free to go their own way. In the short-term, this prevented the Nazimuddin faction, which after all was much closer to Jinnah and the A.I.M.L., from throwing Huq out of office, and perhaps bringing in a League ministry in its stead.

Of course Jinnah would have liked to impose structure and control from the centre over the provincial Leagues, as the A.I.M.L.'s new constitution, drafted along Congress lines, proves. But the gap between Jinnah's centralist pretensions and the realities in the provinces was shown by the concessions he had to make even in the paper constitution. The A.I.M.L.s new constitution which came into effect in February 1938 gave the Muslim-majority provinces a much larger say than before on the All-India Council. But it still did not reflect the real balance of power in Muslim politics. The total membership of the Council was raised from 310 to 465, the Punjab and Bengal each receiving an additional forty representatives, Sind fifteen and the N.W.F.P. ten. But the U.P. was also given an additional twenty seats.[5] The two largest

---

[5] Seats on the A.I.M.L. Council were distributed as follows (the old numbers are in parenthesis):

Delhi	15 (10)	Baluchistan	5 (4)
U.P.	70 (50)	Bengal	100 (60)
Punjab	90 (50)	Bihar ⎱	30 (30)
Bombay	30 (20)	Orissa ⎰	10
Sind	25 (10)	Assam	25 (12)
Madras	20 (18)	Ajmer	5 (6)
N.W.F.P.	20 (10)	TOTAL:	445

(See 'The Constitution and Rules of the All-India Muslim League', AIML/File No. 111.)

Muslim provinces had just over forty per cent of the votes on the League's Council, and even with Sind, the N.W.F.P. and Baluchistan thrown in, the Muslim-majority provinces had only just over half the votes. The method of election to the League Council was closely in line with the principles adopted by the Congress. The representatives of the League Council were to be elected by the provincial branches. Provinces were to be split into divisions which were further sub-divided into wards, and branches in a ward or a district were named primary Leagues. The membership fee was reduced to only two annas (two annas less than that of the Congress). For every one hundred primary League members there was to be one representative on the district League. The district Leagues would annually elect members to the provincial Leagues – the precise number from each district was to be fixed in the newly revised provincial League constitutions. The provincial Leagues in turn would elect representatives to the A.I.M.L.'s Council. In the event that the process of election was not completed by a province, the All-India Council had the authority to select members from each province. The League Council also had the power to disaffiliate Leagues in a majority of the districts. Rules for the enrolment of members, conduct of meetings, election of office bearers, maintenance of accounts, etc., were also framed. The most significant change was the increased powers of the Working Committee – the executive of the All-India League's High Command. It was to consist of twenty-one members, to be nominated from the Council by the president; it would consider and pass all resolutions before they were put before the Council and was empowered to prepare the annual budget of the League and to sanction all payments exceeding fifty rupees not included in the budget. The Working Committee also had the authority to appoint all sub-committees.[6] This was almost a carbon copy of the Congress constitution; and it followed its model by concentrating power at the top, in the hands of the Working Committee. With the right to select all the members of the Working Committee, Jinnah at least in theory had equipped himself with all the necessary powers to impose centralised authority over the League's provincial arms. But the continued dominance of minority-province Muslims in the Working Committee, the U.P. in particular, suggests that the League was still far from becoming the voice of the Muslim provinces.

After the elections, Iqbal had advised Jinnah to 'ignore Muslim minority provinces' and to look to the Muslims of north-west India and Bengal, an irony not lost on the leader of a party whose only electoral success had been in the minority provinces which he was now being

---

[6] Ibid.

invited to spurn. Seven years after his famous speech in Allahabad on 29 December 1930, Iqbal crystallised his thoughts:

Why should not the Muslims of North West India and Bengal be considered as nations entitled to self-determination just as other nations in India are? Personally I think that the Muslims of North West India and Bengal ought at present [to] ignore Muslim minority provinces. This is the best course to adopt in the interests of both Muslim majority and minority provinces.[7]

But as even Iqbal could see the lip-service paid by the two main Muslim-majority provinces in October 1937 could be turned into political advantage only if the League could now find a line which would appeal to all Muslims, whether in the majority or in the minority provinces. Once the Congress had launched its Muslim mass contact movement in March 1937, Iqbal was convinced that the League would now have to decide 'whether it will remain a body representing the upper classes of Indian Muslims or [the] Muslim masses who have so far, with good reason, taken no interest in it'. The real issue as Iqbal saw it, was: 'how . . . to solve the problem of Muslim poverty? And the whole future of the League depends on the League's activity to solve the question.' The 'only way to solve the problem of bread for Muslims' was to enforce the 'Law of Islam'.[8] A bold social and economic programme based on the 'Law of Islam' for the Muslim masses would, according to Iqbal, do the trick; but what such a 'Law' involved or how it could be implemented was not very clear, and in any case Jinnah was too shrewd and too secular to chase this particular hare. If the 'Law of Islam' was to be interpreted by the ulema, the traditional guardians of the law, then Jinnah would certainly have nothing to do with it. Any recourse to the 'Law of Islam' would have sparked off an ideological debate between the ulema and the more progressive Muslims. This was clearly the last thing Jinnah needed at this stage. As his old friend the Raja of Mahmudabad has reminisced, Jinnah 'thoroughly disapproved' of such traditional remedies; he asked Mahmudabad not to express them from the League's platform since this might mislead people into thinking that Jinnah had given them his endorsement.[9] Moreover, Jinnah could see that any appeal to religion, or to a radical economic programme, might only too easily boomerang upon its proponents. The League could not even begin to set out a plausible facsimile of a social programme to eradicate Muslim poverty since such support as it possessed came from vested landed and business interests at

[7] See Iqbal to Jinnah, 21 June 1937, SHC/Press and Publications, vol. I.
[8] Iqbal to Jinnah, 28 May 1937, ibid.
[9] See the Raja of Mahmudabad, 'Some Memories', in C. H. Philips and M. Wainwright (eds.), *The Partition of India: Policies and Perspectives, 1935–1947* (London, 1970), p. 388.

the apex of society. In any event, such appeals were irrelevant to Jinnah's predicament.

But the Congress's siren calls to the Muslims, both to the elected representatives in the assemblies and to the people below, its efforts to seek accommodations with provincial Muslim factions and to launch a mass contact movement,[10] had somehow urgently to be countered. All Jinnah could do was to make much of the Congress threat to Muslim interests, portraying it as a perfidious party no Muslim after the U.P. experience could ever trust again; its mass contact movement a knife at the throat of every Muslim politician; its ministries blatantly favouring their own; a High Command whose iron control over its own provinces clearly hinted at what lay ahead for the Muslim-majority provinces once it came to dominate the centre. Much of the League's propaganda at this stage was directed against the Congress ministries and their alleged attacks on Muslim culture; the heightened activity of the Hindu Mahasabha, the hoisting of the Congress tricolour, the singing of *bandemataram*, the Vidya Mandir scheme in the Central Provinces and the Wardha scheme of education – all were interpreted as proof of 'Congress atrocities'. So Congress was clearly incapable of representing Muslim interests, yet it was trying to 'annihilate every other party'. Jinnah wanted the League's claim to 'complete equality with the Congress' to be recognised. While he was prepared to come to an understanding on this basis: 'we cannot surrender, submerge or submit to the dictates or the ukase of the High Command of the Congress, which is developing into a totalitarian and authoritative causes [sic – ?caucus], functioning under the name of the Working Committee, and aspiring to the position of a shadow cabinet in a future republic'.[11] He warned that Congress was taking the offensive deep into the Muslim provinces, and hoping by dividing to rule. In Sind, his line was that Congress had contrived a split among the Muslims;[12] certainly it had helped to keep a League ministry out of office.[13] In the C.P., the very provinces where,

---

10 See A.I.C.C. Papers, Files 24/1936 ad 41/1937.
11 See Jinnah's presidential address to the A.I.M.L.'s special session at Calcutta on 17–18 April 1938, in Pirzada (ed.), *Foundations of Pakistan*, vol. II, pp. 293–5.
12 But of course the Sindhi Muslims were already hopelessly split, and seemed destined to remain so. In the assembly there were at least four different Muslim groups.
13 In March 1938, Ghulam Hussain's ministry in Sind had been forced to resign. A new ministry under Allah Baksh was formed, supported in the assembly by members of the Congress and the Hindu Independent party. When Allah Baksh increased the assessment rates, some Muslim landed interests who were pro-League brought a no-confidence motion against him. Sir Abdullah Haroon, the president of the Sind Muslim League, thought there was now a chance of forming a League ministry. (See Abdullah Haroon to Jinnah, 2 August 1938, QAP/10/File No. 1090, p. 57.)

according to League propaganda, Congress had ridden roughshod over Muslims, it was accused of dangling carrots before Muslim League M.L.A.s.[14] These were some of the arguments, according to Jinnah, why Muslims needed to unite under his leadership.

Much of this propaganda was simply a response to Congress's attempts to further consolidate its electoral success by winning Muslim support both inside and outside the legislatures. But by now some elements in the Congress High Command were coming to realise that they had perhaps underestimated the League's capacity for survival, or the fears among Muslims upon which it would play. So they called off the Muslim contact movement and made tentative approaches to Jinnah through Subhas Chandra Bose, an appropriate choice since Bose, as a Bengali, could see the advantages for his own province in some understanding between the Congress and the Muslims. But at this point Jinnah was not ready to parley with the Congress unless it accepted the League as the 'authoritative and representative organisation of the Indian Muslims', just as he was ready somewhat provocatively to admit that the Congress was the 'authoritative and representative organisation of the solid body of *Hindu* opinion'.[15]

Congress saw no reason to make a concession which cut against the

In October 1938, Jinnah came to Karachi hoping to stamp some unity upon the divided Muslim ranks of Sind, and then to impose the League's imprimatur on whatever alliance they were prepared to form. Just when it seemed that Baksh might come to terms with Jinnah, the Congress High Command ordered its party in the provincial assembly to support Baksh against the no-confidence motion. So Baksh saw no reason to forge an alliance with the League. Jinnah left Sind plaintively complaining that the Congress High Command was 'obsessed with one and only one idea of destroying any effort which will bring solidarity among the Musalmans'. (See Jinnah's statement to the Associated Press of India in Karachi, 13 October 1938, QAP/4/File No. 160.)

[14] Of course the C.P. and Berar Muslim League was riven with factionalism and many League M.L.A.s were prepared to cross the floor and join the Congress. In mid-January 1939, a group of C.P. Leaguers agreed to call a meeting of the Muslim members of the legislature to present their common demands to the Congress ministry. Of the fourteen Muslim M.L.A.s, ten were Leaguers and four were Congressmen, and it proved impossible for them to agree. The Congress Muslim M.L.A.s had no reason to join in attacking the Vidya Mandir scheme and were not impressed by the alleged anti-Muslim activities of the ministry. As the vice-president of the Jubbulpur League lamented: 'to go to the enemy with different aims and aspirations is to court disaster from the beginning' and 'to exhibit community's demoralised position before the bar of . . . world opinion in a manner not befitting to its aims and objectives'. (See Taj-ud-din to Jinnah, no date, SHC/File No. 4.) Jinnah was warned that if he did not intervene personally and put an end to the 'scandalous' activities of some of the C.P. Leaguers, he would find 'Provincial PACTS [sic] being arranged ignoring the All-India organisation which is the new game of the Congress'. (Taj-ud-din to Jinnah, 1938 (undated), ibid.)

[15] Quoted in Subhas Chandra Bose's note to Jinnah, 14 May 1938, AIML/File No. 122 (my italics).

very basis of its creed, and so Jinnah turned to the British, a last resort for so dedicated a nationalist who had devoted his political life to battling against the alien rulers. In August 1938, he asked to meet Lord Brabourne, the acting Viceroy, and hinted at a deal by which the League might support the British at the centre if in return the British accepted the League as the sole spokesman of the Muslims. According to Lord Brabourne, Jinnah had ended up with the suggestion that 'we [the British] should keep the centre as it is now' and that 'we should make friends with Muslims' by protecting them in the Congress provinces, and if this was done, 'Muslims would protect us at the centre'.[16] Jinnah himself confessed that, if the League's interests so demanded, he was ready to be 'the ally of even the devil'. 'It is not because we are in love with Imperialism', Jinnah explained to the annual League session in December 1938, 'but in Politics one has to play one's game as on a chessboard.'[17] But still trying to implement the federal provisions of the 1935 Act, Viceregal Lodge saw little attraction in a deal with a man who besides being bitterly opposed to the federal scheme seemed as trivial an enemy as he was lightweight as a friend.[18]

However, when war seemed imminent and certainly once it had broken out, Delhi's relative assessment of Jinnah and the Congress changed sharply. To fight a war from an Indian base, the British now needed both to hold firm at the centre and to reassert control over the provinces. With the war on its way, Delhi judged that Congress would demand a high price for its collaboration and might threaten to pull out its provincial ministries. But far from being a frightening prospect, this threat was good news for Delhi, since even collaborating Congress provinces were likely to be more of a nuisance in running India during the war than provinces deprived of their Congress ministries. By April 1939 Delhi had persuaded Parliament to give it powers to take over and run the provinces if the need arose.[19] So the Viceroy and his advisers were

[16] Lord Brabourne to Zetland, August 1938, in John L. Dundas (ed.), *Essayez, the Memoirs of Lawrence, Second Marquess of Zetland* (London, 1956), p. 190.

[17] See Jinnah's address at the twenty-sixth session of the A.I.M.L. at Patna, 26 December 1938, in Pirzada (ed,), *Foundations of Pakistan*, vol. II, p. 309.

[18] But already the year before, London was taking a somewhat different line: Lord Zetland, the Secretary of State for India, could 'not resist a steadily growing conviction that the dominant factor in determining the future form of government would prove to be the All-India Muslim League'. (See Dundas (ed.), *Essayez*, p. 247.) But Linlithgow in Delhi did not expect any 'serious trouble' from the Muslims and thought they would ultimately come into the federation if it was imposed upon them. (See Gowher Rizvi, *Linlithgow and India: A Study of British Policy and the Political Impasse in India, 1936–1943* (London, 1978), p. 84.)

[19] Six months before the war broke out, a new section (Section 126A) in the 1935 Act was

ready, indeed eager, to ditch the eight Congress ministries. Here the British made a reasoned assessment of the Congress's weaknesses. Even in the two brief years of provincial autonomy, they could see that the Congress High Command was increasingly facing the dangers of splits between Congress movements outside the legislatures and the ministerial groups in office. Congress in office was bound to disappoint many of the aspirations of its followers. There were splits between the Congress right wing and the radicals, between rival factions bidding for government patronage, and of course between 'ins' and 'outs'. The war was bound to make the problems worse, since the provincial governments would have less of a free hand and, with little prospect of large concessions at the centre during the war, provincial bosses would have less reason to accept the dictates of the High Command. This added up to a strong argument for the High Command to pull the Congress out of the provinces. The High Command still had the power to tell its provincial ministries to resign, however reluctant they themselves might be to do so. But if Congress promised to be an uncertain ally during the war, a way had to be found which combined the requirement that no concessions of substance be made to it, and yet succeeded in putting the blame for the breakdown of negotiations upon Indian politicians and their inability to agree among themselves.

This is where Jinnah proved to have his uses. This ambassador of Hindu – Muslim unity now seemed the best guarantee the British could find in India against an united political demand. With his limited mandate from the Muslim-majority provinces, Jinnah now had a semblance of a right to speak for Muslims at the centre. This is where the British needed him and where they were ready to acknowledge his standing. But they wanted to keep him out of the affairs of the Muslim-majority provinces. The fact that Jinnah was hardly a free agent, a mere *vakil* of the Muslim provinces, made him a particularly convenient instrument from the British point of view. It still seemed unlikely that Jinnah could produce a demand which would seriously embarrass the British, and he had no power to create problems for the war effort in the Muslim-majority provinces, especially in the Punjab, the main recruiting ground for the Indian army, and in Bengal, the Raj's eastern front against Japan.

introduced by Westminster; this enabled the Government of India, during an emergency such as war or the threat of war, to instruct provincial governments on the exercise of executive authority; permitted the central legislature to make laws for the provinces and gave the centre full executive powers if it needed them. At a stroke, this negated most of the provincial autonomy which the 1935 Act had granted. (See Rizvi, *Linlithgow and India*, pp. 131–2.)

Just how confident Delhi was of its ability to exploit the weaknesses both of the Congress High Command and its much weaker counterpart, the League, was shown on 3 September 1939, when Linlithgow, without consulting any Indian politician, simply announced that by declaring war on Germany Britain had automatically turned India into a belligerent in the allied cause. This was correct by the letter of the law; but it was hardly the action of rulers concerned about the reactions of their subjects. The next day the Viceroy invited Jinnah, on an equal footing with Gandhi, for talks, and informed them that the efforts to implement the federal provisions of the 1935 Act would be suspended until after the war.

This blunt announcement placed the Congress in a more acute dilemma than it did Jinnah. Ever since Congress ministries had taken office in the provinces in 1937, tension had been growing between them and the High Command. Rivalries between Congressmen in office and Congressmen out of office were becoming increasingly tiresome for the all-India leadership. These struggles for power and position at a provincial level played back upon the centre where the High Command itself was not as solid as it liked to pretend. As usual Gandhi remained in the wings, the ultimate arbiter whose commitment to non-violence complicated the Congress response to the blood and iron of war. Subhas Bose and his Forward Bloc, outmanoeuvred by the old guard earlier in 1939, now argued that Britain's difficulties were India's opportunity, and the divisions inside the Congress over its response to the war gave the Tiger of Bengal another chance to spring back into the ring from which he had been ousted. Nehru, who was permitted the role of Congress expert on foreign affairs, had enthusiastic but idiosyncratic views in which his commitment against fascism was qualified by notions of a world movement against imperialism. More to the point, there were discontents at central and provincial levels, sufficient and ready to embarrass the leadership and to force it to react in a more uncompromising way than the High Command itself deemed politic. Some of its members, particularly those with business interests, could see advantage in a pragmatic response to secure an accommodation with the British which would permit the Congress to co-operate during the war to its advantage. But the High Command was already finding it difficult to keep its movement together. If it was to preserve its fragile unity, it had somehow to make its bid for power at the centre compatible with ostensibly mobilising the base, and appearing to steer 'leftwards'. Not surprisingly it took the Congress a week of agonising before it could cobble together a compromise out of these conflicting elements and make its public response to Linlithgow's curt announcement. That response was the Congress's impractical demand on 14 September 1939 for immediate independence and for a constituent assembly to make the arrangements. This was the price Congress had to pay in order to maintain a semblance of solidarity over its own divided camp.[20]

Once Congress had stated its demands, Linlithgow urgently needed a means by which he could challenge its claim to be speaking for all-India. Four days later, the League's more measured resolution calling for the abandonment of the 'Federal objective' and a guarantee that no scheme of constitutional reform would be enforced without its approval gave the Viceroy the opening he needed.[21] On 18 October 1939, Linlithgow assured Muslims that 'full weight would be given to their views and interests'. 'It is unthinkable', Linlithgow added, 'that we should now proceed to plan afresh, or to modify in any respect any important part of India's future constitution without again taking counsel with those who have in the recent past been so closely associated on a like task with His Majesty's Government and with Parliament'.[22] The League's Working Committee interpreted this statement as an emphatic repudiation of the Congress claim to represent the whole of India, and an indication that H.M.G. 'recognise the fact that the All-India Muslim League alone truly represent the Mussalmans of India and can speak on their behalf',[23] even though this was not quite how Linlithgow had intended his response to be understood.[24] By making prior agreement between the Congress and the Muslims the condition for any advance at the centre, Linlithgow in effect handed a veto to whoever could claim to speak for Muslims. At the same time he shifted the blame for failure to achieve constitutional advance squarely upon Indian politicians. As Delhi had hoped, the Congress High Command now had no option but to ask its eight provincial ministries to resign; they did so on 10 November 1939 and the Governors took charge of their administration under Section 93.[25]

---

[20] See B. R. Tomlinson, *The Indian National Congress and the Raj, 1929–1942, The Penultimate Phase* (London, 1976) and Rizvi, *Linlithgow and India*.

[21] A.I.M.L. Working Committee's resolution, 18 September 1939, in Ahmad (ed.), *Historic Documents*, p. 349.

[22] Ibid., p. 352.

[23] A.I.M.L. Working Committee's resolution, 22 October 1939, AIML/File No. 128, p. 116.

[24] Linlithgow had spoken of Muslims, not of the Muslim League. But it was convenient for the League's Working Committee to claim Linlithgow's assurance as a further step in the direction of gaining recognition as the sole authoritative spokesman of the Indian Muslims.

[25] The Government of India's *Quarterly Survey* noted that the Governors of the Section 93 provinces were much relieved at being rid of the Congress ministries and were pleased with the results. (Cited in Rizvi, *Linlithgow and India*, p. 145.)

With the constitutional question now effectively in cold storage, Linlithgow turned increasingly towards Jinnah and the League. He frankly admitted that Jinnah had given him 'valuable help by standing against Congress claims and I was duly grateful'. Had Jinnah supported the Congress and 'confronted me with a joint demand, the strain upon me and His Majesty's Government would have been very great indeed . . . therefore, I could claim to have a vested interest in his position'.[26] On his side, Jinnah, mindful of the risks of making an open declaration of collaboration in the war effort, preferred to sit on the fence. In private, however, he thanked Linlithgow 'with much graciousness' for what the Viceroy had done to 'assist him in keeping his party together'.[27] Here and now, the Viceroy's favour was worth more than any agreement with the Congress. After all, an anti-Congress stance was the main, perhaps the only, common factor in the divided ranks that Jinnah was trying to lead. Linlithgow himself thought he had more to gain from a deal with the League than with the Congress. When London pressed him to try and reach an accord with Indian leaders, Linlithgow argued that so long as Congress failed to meet Muslim demands, it was a mistake to try 'swapping horses or doing anything which might lose us Muslim support'.[28]

So for the time being neither Jinnah nor the British were ready to negotiate with the Congress. But they were ready to come to an accommodation with each other which offered prospects of setting Jinnah and the League on the road to recovery. But from the British point of view such an accommodation required the League to spell out its policy in public. During the course of his talks with Jinnah, the Viceroy had: 'again put forward the familiar argument for formulating and publishing a constructive policy and in the light of our discussion he [Jinnah] said that he was disposed to think it would be wise for his friends and himself to make public at any rate the outlines of their position in good time'.[29] Since Jinnah and the League were to be used to alleviate a problem of propaganda, Linlithgow pressed Jinnah to state the League's 'constructive policy' as a counterweight to the Congress's demand for independence and a constituent assembly. There was public opinion in

---

26 Linlithgow to Zetland, note of interview with Jinnah on 4 November 1939, L/P&J/8/506, I.O.L. and Rizvi, *Linlithgow and India*, pp. 113–14.
27 Note of interview between Linlithgow and Jinnah, 5 October 1939, L/P&J/8/505, cited in Rizvi, *Linlithgow and India*, p. 110, fn. 4.
28 Linlithgow to Zetland, 25 October 1939, Mss.Eur.F.125/18/409, cited in ibid., p. 148, fn. 3.
29 See Linlithgow to Zetland, 16 January 1940, Mss. Eur.F.125/19/6, I.O.L., cited in Rizvi, *Linlithgow and India*, p. 116, fn. 2.

Britain; there was the need to get America to join the allies and to counter the threat in Asia of the Japanese, portraying themselves as the champions of Asian nationalism; and above all there was the need to maintain the existing systems of collaboration in the provinces. So it was mainly a matter of finding reasonable grounds for carrying on under British management while avoiding a serious backlash, whether in India, Britain or abroad. The complexities of the Indian communal problem seemed to offer the best pretext for doing nothing. Since Jinnah also needed time in which to build the League's case, he was ready to recognise this conformity of interest between the League and Viceregal Lodge, and to proceed on that basis for the time being.

Section 2

Linlithgow's call to Muslims to produce a 'constructive policy' was an opportunity for Jinnah, the potential spokesman for Muslims at the centre, but it was also something of an embarrassment. Such a policy would have to walk a tight-rope between the conflicting requirements of the divided constituents on whose behalf he was purporting to speak. In particular Jinnah had to find a way of squaring the dominant interests in Muslim-majority provinces over which he had no control. At this juncture his most urgent priority was to persuade everyone – the British, the Congress High Command and his own uncertain followers – to accept his claim to be the sole spokesman for Muslims without being too precise about the demand – precision and unanimity were incompatible. Yet Linlithgow's invitation, and the chance of official recognition which it offered, required Jinnah to spell out a policy at a point in time when his true hand, if revealed, was bound to be repudiated by the most influential of his principals, the leaders of the majority provinces. Congress's demand for independence and a constituent assembly was itself the product of its own disunities and dilemmas. Since the disunities among the Muslims were far greater, and the League's High Command was neither high nor commanding, it is not surprising that Jinnah's problem in papering over the cracks in his movement was more difficult. A demand which was the highest common factor of Muslim differences would, almost by definition, have to be imprecise and vague.

There were a number of important constraints upon Jinnah in formulating a policy. The new policy had to make a break with the past. It had to reject the federal provisions of the 1935 Act since there was no security there for Muslims, whether at the centre for the majority provinces, or in the provinces where they were minorities. It had to turn back upon the old principle of separate representation for much the same reasons. Even

if Muslims voted solidly for one party – an unlikely prospect at this time –
they would be outnumbered, and outvoted in the making of the
constitution. So a single constituent assembly offered no security for
Muslim interests, however construed. What Muslims needed was a quite
different basis to overcome the fatal defect of being a minority in British
India, and a divided minority to boot. As far as the Muslim-majority
provinces were concerned, they might have been content simply to see
the British remain for ever in charge at the centre. But if some transfer of
power was inevitable, then they preferred strong autonomous provinces
and a weak federal centre. Yet the preferences of the Muslim-majority
provinces had awkward implications for Jinnah: if these provinces
openly called on the British to stay on, this would leave the Congress
unchallenged as the spokesman of nationalist demands; if, however, the
centre was to be weak and the provinces strong, any Muslim party at the
centre would be the servant, not the master, of powerful provincial
satraps. This, in turn, would give little security to Muslims in minority
provinces. Their approach was bound to be very different. The only way
minority Muslims could achieve security and a real share of power and
patronage was by calling in the centre to redress the provincial balance.
This required a strong centre, and at that centre a Congress High
Command with an incentive, and the authority, to order its provincial
arms to cut against the grain of their narrow interests, and cut in the
Muslims. Such incentive could be found only in terms of all-India, not
provincial, imperatives. The context in which the Congress High Command might have an incentive to instruct its provinces to treat Muslim
minorities well would be if it needed Muslim co-operation at the centre.
It would need such co-operation on two assumptions: first, that India had
an unitary government (including Muslim-majority provinces) with a
relatively strong centre, and second that at this centre there was a strong
Muslim party, speaking for majority and minority provinces alike,
whose co-operation was vital for effective government. If there was no
strong Muslim party at the centre, or if the Congress could make terms
separately with majority Muslims, province by province, then Muslims
in minority provinces would not be able to get the centre to alleviate their
provincial disadvantages. So Muslims in the minority provinces above all
needed a strong party at the centre speaking for all Muslims. This was
closer to Jinnah's own vision of the role he envisaged for the League. But
the circumstances of the time had placed him at the mercy of the majority
provinces: they were paying the piper; they could call the tune.

The new development of which Jinnah could take advantage was that
the majority provinces, however reluctantly, now were coming to
recognise that they too needed a piper at the centre playing a strong new

tune. No juggling of the political arithmetic could prevent safe provincial Muslim majorities from being turned into an ineffectual minority at the centre. Asserting that Muslims were a nation avoided the logic of numbers. As a community, they were consigned to being a perpetual minority in an united India. As a nation they were entitled to equal status, irrespective of their numbers, since the family of nations contains the big and the small. This was a large step and a bold assertion. But it had a pedigree of sorts. There had been talk along similar lines for at least half a century.[30] In the nineteen-twenties and early nineteen-thirties, when the British tactic had been to retreat to the centre, the idea of Indian Muslims constituting a nation had very little to commend it politically since it was relevant only if the distribution of power at the centre was at stake. The constitutional negotiations which led to the 1935 Act gave the notion a slight stimulus, but it remained an idea more cultural than political, for example in Iqbal's famous presidential address to the A.I.M.L. in December 1930, or a fantasy more utopian than practical, as in the student scheme for a 'Pakistan' (see above, p. 12, fn. 14). The strongest Muslim influence on the making of the 1935 Act had been the Punjab's provincial thesis which argued states' rights against the centre, and envisaged an United States of Southern Asia in the long-term.[31] Yet for the time being the Punjab statesmen had been happy to leave the centre firmly in British hands – which suited the rulers perfectly.

However, the Congress triumph at the polls in 1937 had implications for centre and province alike and it brought the Muslim dilemma into the open, and a flurry of schemes looking for some way out were doing the

[30] Syed Ahmad Khan spoke of 'two nations' in the eighteen-eighties when he urged Muslims to disassociate themselves from the Indian National Congress, and asked the British to give them recognition in terms of their political importance, not their numbers. Of course this early hint of Muslim 'separatism' needs to be set into the context of north India in the late-nineteenth century: the particular interests of its Muslim elite, their response to the categories the Raj employed, and the opportunities of exploiting its patronage and favour. Later developments robbed this notion of its political utility. (See above, pp. 9–10.)

[31] As early as 1935, the Aga Khan could see that Indian Muslims needed an entirely new basis on which to make their demands. The best course, he thought, was to take advantage of the 'impregnable position' of Muslims in the north-western regions and in Bengal; at the centre, Muslims should be 'out and out Federalists' and 'make India what she is, i.e. a United States of Southern Asia', where the Muslims would use the majority provinces against the centre. But 'our Indian patriotism, of course, should never leave any doubt and our Hindu countrymen must realise that the welfare of India as a whole . . . is as dear to us as it is to them . . .'. (Aga Khan to Fazl-i-Husain, Fazl-i-Husain Papers (Aga Khan File); see also Jalal and Seal, *Modern Asian Studies*, 15, 3 (1981), 448–9.)

rounds. In March 1939, the A.I.M.L. appointed a special committee to look into schemes which had little in common with each other except the assertion, explicit or implicit, that Indian Muslims, whatever their differences and however defined, were a nation. These were not merely the tattered remnants of kites flown long ago; they included at least five new variants of varying degrees of practicality. The weightiest, because it had the stamp of Sikander Hayat Khan, who had taken on the mantle of Fazl-i-Husain, was a version of the time-honoured Punjab strategy, up-dated to prepare against the probability that the Congress would have a solid majority at the centre. The Punjab would afforce its autonomy by exerting its sway over other Muslim-majority provinces in its north-western neighbourhood, and by weakening the centre further still.[32] The Punjab, the most viable base for Muslim consolidation, was not surprisingly the most fertile source for schemes of a federal nature. Another version, rather more extreme than Sikander's, robbed the centre of any real substance.[33] And of course there was the notorious 'Pakistan' scheme of the irrepressible Chaudhuri Rahmat Ali, an even more fantastical variant of his earlier dreams.[34] None of this had much to offer Muslims in the minority provinces. As small scattered islands in a non-Muslim ocean, their dilemma was underlined by the impossible knots into which they tied themselves when they tried to deploy the idea of Muslims as a nation in their own interest. Some professors at Aligarh, a seminary noted for its political inventiveness,[35] conceived the plan of slicing India into three separate states. Two of them were to be dominated by Muslims, and Hindustan, the one non-Muslim state, was to be subjected to a further surgery which would carve two autonomous

---

[32] Sikander's scheme published in the summer of 1939 advocated the loosest of federations with a weak centre and 'blocs' of provinces which would have regional or zonal legislatures dealing with common subjects. The Punjab in this way would dominate the north-western 'bloc' (which would include Sind, the N.W.F.P. and Baluchistan) and enjoy many of the attributes of sovereignty that belonged to the centre.

[33] This was the 'Industan scheme' outlined in a *Confederacy of India* by 'A Punjabi'; it proposed to split India into five different federations to be reassembled into a confederacy with common links, so vague and unspecific as to make the federal provisions of the 1935 Act appear in comparison an iron frame. (See 'A Punjabi', *Confederacy of India* (Lahore, 1939.)

[34] Rahmat Ali now called for the establishment of no less than eight Muslim states and their consolidation into a 'Pakistan Commonwealth of Nations', which in turn would be re-integrated with that heterogeneous Muslim belt all the way from Central Asia to the Bosporus, the 'original Pakistan'. (Chaudhuri Rahmat Ali, *Pakistan: The Fatherland of the Pak Nation*, rev. edn., (Lahore, 1978), pp. 228–9.)

[35] Aligarh was rewarded in Jinnah's will, made in 1939. It left substantial sums to Aligarh and to Bombay universities – a will which, significantly, Jinnah never changed, even though he had ample time to do so.

provinces out of its heart and its southern extremities: Delhi, the old
centre of Muslim power in north India, and a somewhat improbable
Muslim Malabar, built around the Moplahs.[36] In their different way, all
these schemes were trying to rescue Muslims from having a perpetual
minority status at the centre, and they all, with the exception of Rahmat
Ali's, envisaged linkages of some sort between the Muslim blocs and
their non-Muslim counterparts. No one accepted an unqualified
balkanisation of India.[37]

Out of these unpromising and contradictory opinions, the League had
to find a way forward. Its sub-committee had been in existence since
March 1939. When Linlithgow pressed Jinnah, the League's Working
Committee decided that it had to give its sub-committee a brief. That
took it four days of constant meetings between 3 and 6 February 1940. In
constructing a brief, the Working Committee had to bear in mind that
the only point of general agreement was the decision to declare that
Muslims were a nation, not a minority, and to reject constitution-making
based on the counting of heads.[38] Of course the real problem was to steer
a path between majority and minority Muslims and somehow give Jinnah
a hand to play at the centre.[39] The new balance of power in Muslim

[36] The Aligarh professors justified the creation of two autonomous provinces inside
Hindustan on the grounds that Muslims in the minority provinces needed the 'full and
effective support by the Muslim majority provinces'. Muslims inside Hindustan were to
be regarded as a 'nation in minority and part of a larger nation inhabiting Pakistan and
Bengal'. There would be defence alliances between the two Muslim states and
Hindustan, and adequate safeguards would be incorporated in 'the constitution', which
obviously would have to be agreed upon by all three states. Moreover, the A.I.M.L.
would be the 'sole official representative body of the Muslims in Hindustan'. (Mohammad Afzal Husain Qadri, 'The problem of Indian Muslims and its solution', 2 February
1939, QAP/File No. 135.)
   Another variant of the Aligarh scheme came from Dr Latif from Hyderabad Deccan,
which, interestingly enough, thought in terms of a minimal federation of homogeneous
cultural zones, to be created after massive transfers of population. (See R. Coupland,
Indian Politics: 1936–1942 (London, 1944), pp. 201–2.)

[37] It is significant that the premiers of the two most important Muslim-majority provinces,
namely the Punjab and Bengal, were mainly concerned with protecting, and if possible,
furthering provincial autonomy. Sikander's scheme has already been discussed in
footnote 32, p. 53 above. Less than a month before the League's Working Committee
was scheduled to meet, Fazlul Huq sent a resolution to it, passed by the Bengal
Provincial League's Working Committee. This called for a Royal Commission to look
into the working of provincial autonomy 'with a view to decide how far and in what
direction any further advance in constitutional progress may be made'. (Fazlul Huq to
Liaquat Ali Khan, 18 January 1940, QAP/File No. 129.)

[38] See minutes of the A.I.M.L. Working Committee meetings between 3 and 6 February
1940, New Delhi, QAP/File No. 137.

[39] It was not an easy task. Jinnah saw Dr Latif's scheme as well as the Aligarh scheme. (See
secretary of the Sind Muslim League to Jinnah, March 1939, QAP/File No. 136 and

politics was reflected in the Working Committee's brief to its sub-committee: it contained an uncompromising version of the Punjab thesis – both in the west and east the Muslim-majority provinces were to constitute two 'Independent dominions in direct relationship with Great Britain'. Moreover, the 'various units in each zone shall form component parts of the Federation in that zone as autonomous units'. This was the assurance which had to be made to the Muslim politicians of Sind and the N.W.F.P.[40] Minority Muslims had to be content with unspecified assurances of 'adequate' safeguards.

This, then, was the brief that the Working Committee gave its constitutional sub-committee. There are no records of the sub-committee's deliberations. So the particular mix which produced the Lahore resolution cannot be analysed and documented precisely. But there are clear hints of what parts made up the whole. Sikander was later to deny that the resolution was based on his draft; the resolution, he claimed, was the League's view, not that of the Punjab.[41] But the Punjab thesis was a powerful – perhaps the most powerful – influence on the making of the resolution. Zafrullah Khan's paper (which he gave to Linlithgow) shows the lines of Punjab's thinking. Zafrullah, a distinguished lawyer from the Punjab, and a member of the Viceroy's Executive Council wrote it in the later half of February 1940, that is, after the Working Committee's brief, but some time before the Lahore resolution was passed on 23 March 1940. In it, Zafrullah was looking for a constitutional scheme acceptable to Muslim opinion generally. He considered three schemes. The first was the 'Pakistan scheme' along Rahmat Ali's lines which he swiftly dismissed as 'utterly impracticable'.[42] The second, closest to the League Working Committee's brief, envisaged two Muslim federations, in the north-west and the north-east, in 'direct relation with the Crown', but with treaty agreements with the non-Muslim federation (or federations) to cover matters of common interest.[43] The short shrift he gave this

Mohammad Afzal Husain Qadri to Jinnah, QAP/File No. 135.) But the supporters of Rahmat Ali's scheme, who had formed a 'Pakistan Majlis' in Lahore, condemned these schemes; they wanted to ensure the political integrity of Pakistan (which the cultural zones scheme did not do) and demanded that the League should 'allow the Pakistan Movement [to go] its own way'. (See Ahmad Bashir to Jinnah, 22 March 1939, QAP/File No. 136.) Fortunately for Jinnah, the 'Pakistan Majlis' had little weight and could be ignored, but its separatist inclinations reveal the problems facing whoever purported to speak for Muslims in the all-India arena.

[40] See minutes of the A.I.M.L. Working Committee meetings between 3 and 6 February 1940, New Delhi, QAP/File No. 137.

[41] See Sikander's speech to the Punjab legislative assembly on 11 March 1941 below, p. 67.

[42] Sir Muhammad Zafrullah Khan's note, no date, Mss.Eur.F.125/135, Sl. no. 20, vol. v, pp. 119–50, I.O.L.   [43] Ibid.

'separation scheme', his hardly disguised scepticism about its practicality, shows that while everyone had to take account of the new direction which seemed to have emerged from the Working Committee's deliberations, Zafrullah himself was not sure that it could be sustained. Significantly the 'separation scheme', as Zafrullah understood it, demarcated the 'Muslim Federations' not on communal lines, but along the boundaries of existing provinces – this was the only way of safeguarding Muslim minorities in the non-Muslim federation (or federations).[44]

When he argued, with tongue in cheek, that 'devotion to the principle of all-India unity may in the end prove too strong to permit wisdom and foresight to govern the situation', and the 'separation scheme' might have to be abandoned, he hinted at the more pragmatic approach of an all-India federation which he preferred.[45] Zafrullah knew the British; he knew the Congress; he knew the real interests of the Punjab; but, above all, he had the measure of Jinnah. Of course, the all-India federation scheme, which Zafrullah went on to outline, was familiar to the Punjab school and its British masters; but now the scheme envisaged a 'radically modified' version of the 1935 provisions. Instead of an apportionment of power between centre and provinces, the provinces had first to be replaced as sovereign units under the Crown, and then would 'delegate such minimum authority to the centre as may be necessary for the setting up and working of the All-India Federation'. In other words, the centre 'must not be invested with any greater authority than the minimum necessary to secure the working of the Federation, nor must the scope of the Federation be any wider than is absolutely essential'.[46]

Zafrullah's note was seen by Jinnah. Indeed, Linlithgow thought it had been written specifically 'for adoption by the Muslim League with a view to its being given the fullest publicity'.[47] It is reasonable to assume that the League's constitutional sub-committee also considered it, and the Lahore resolution bears some marks of this note. But the resolution as cast shows Jinnah's dilemma, the delicate balance between what he wanted, and what the majority provinces, especially the Punjab, were after, but which he could not afford to accept. If the League accepted Zafrullah's all-India federal scheme, it would have had to accept forever its role as a cipher at an impotent centre, the mere agent of provincial forces which it did not control. The federal scheme denied the need for a strong party at the centre capable of negotiating for all Muslims, in particular those in minority provinces. Worst of all it specified a construct of the centre which the majority provinces liked and which

[44] Ibid.   [45] Ibid.   [46] Ibid.
[47] Linlithgow to Zetland, 12 March 1940, Mss.Eur.F.125/9, Sl. no. 13, vol. v, pp. 169–76, I.O.L.

Jinnah was unprepared to accept. This may have reflected the balance of power in Muslim politics in March 1940; but Jinnah's entire strategy depended on somehow changing that balance by the end of the day. In some respects the 'separation scheme' was even less attractive. It envisaged two Muslim federations constituted out of the Muslim-majority provinces. It abolished the centre as it had existed in British India, and it left minority Muslims high and dry. It envisaged the relationship between the federations being made by treaties. At best this gave the A.I.M.L. an equivocal role. It beggars belief that such a scheme could have recommended itself to Jinnah whose entire career and thinking had concentrated upon the centre, and getting Muslims a share of power in it. Only two months before the Lahore resolution was passed, Jinnah had spoken of a constitution which recognised that there were 'in India two nations who both must share the governance of their common motherland'.[48]

Jinnah now decided to make a virtue out of his weakness. He took the logic of the provincial demand to its extreme, decided to espouse some features of the 'separation scheme' and made no mention at all of the centre, its future shape, and how it was to be arrived at. Just as Zafrullah had realised, Jinnah knew only too well that the Muslims were not the sole arbiters of their political destiny. The Congress High Command and the British alike had powerful reasons for wanting a strong unitary centre – the Congress High Command – to hold its movement together, and to discipline its own followers (not to mention cracking a whip over the Indian princes) and the British for their imperial interests, both strategic and economic. By apparently repudiating the need for any centre, and keeping quiet about its shape, Jinnah calculated that when eventually the time came to discuss an all-India federation, British and Congress alike would be forced to negotiate with organised Muslim opinion, and would be ready to make substantial concessions to create or retain that centre. The Lahore resolution should therefore be seen as a bargaining counter, which had the merit of being acceptable (on the face of it) to the majority-province Muslims, and of being totally unacceptable to the Congress and in the last resort to the British also. This in turn provided the best insurance that the League would not be given what it now apparently was asking for, but which Jinnah in fact did not really want.

[48] Article published in *Time and Tide*, London, 19 January 1940, cited in Rizvi, *Linlithgow and India*, p. 116. In an unpublished draft of the A.I.M.L. Working Committee's resolution of 22 October 1939 immediate independence for India was demanded on the basis of a 'constitution of a confederation of free states', in which the 'rights and interests of all communities and interests shall be adequately safeguarded'. (See A.I.M.L. Working Committee's resolution, 22 October 1939, AIML/File No. 128, p. 116.)

Some parts of the Lahore resolution were by now predictable. All Muslims agreed that separate representation was not enough; that the 1935 federal provisions would have to be scrapped; that Congress's notion of a constituent assembly, where 'brother Gandhi has three votes and I [Jinnah] have only one',[49] was unacceptable; and that all further arrangements now had to be 'reconsidered *de novo*', on the basis that Muslims were a 'nation' repudiating once and for all their minority status.[50] This cleared the way for that 'constructive scheme' for which Linlithgow had been pressing. Here Jinnah had to tread carefully, balancing, trimming, obfuscating, giving with one hand, and sur-reptitiously taking away with the other. The resolution made no mention of 'partition', certainly none of 'Pakistan'. In the League's 'considered view', the Muslim-majority provinces were to be 'grouped to constitute Independent States in which the constituent units shall be autonomous and sovereign'.[51] But the sovereignty of these 'Independent States' was something for the future. Admittedly, the League's Working Committee was authorised to frame a scheme along the lines of the resolution 'providing for the assumption finally, by the respective regions, of all the powers, such as defence, external affairs, communications, customs and such other matters as may be necessary'.[52] The critical word was 'finally'; this implied a transitional period, and plenty of opportunity to negotiate along the way.

In the resolution, Jinnah had been forced to make large concessions to get the backing of the majority provinces.[53] Yet he had prevented their more specific proposals for the centre from being adopted. A critically important resolution which said nothing about the centre might seem the greatest setback for a politician whose whole career had been committed to promoting a nationalist demand at an all-India centre; but the

[49] See Jinnah's presidential address to the A.I.M.L., 22 March 1940, Pirzada (ed.), *Foundations of Pakistan*, vol. II, p. 332.

[50] The A.I.M.L.'s resolution, 23 March 1940, ibid., p. 340.

[51] Paragraph three of the League's resolution reads: 'Resolved that it is the considered view of this Session of the All-India Muslim League that no constitutional plan would be workable in this country or acceptable to the Muslims unless it is designed on the following basic principles, viz. that geographically contiguous units are demarcated into regions which should be so constituted, with such territorial readjustments as may be necessary, that the areas in which the Muslims are numerically in a majority, as in the North-Western and Eastern zones of India, should be grouped to constitute Independent States in which the constituent units shall be autonomous and sovereign'. (Ibid., p. 341.)   [52] Ibid.

[53] The provision, that even inside the 'Independent States' the units would be 'auton-omous and sovereign', was clearly intended to appease the politicians of Sind and the N.W.F.P. Significantly, Jinnah asked Huq to move the resolution. He did so; Sikander voted for it and the resolution was adopted unanimously.

inwardness of the resolution was that Jinnah, with his characteristic political skill, took account of all the factors in the game, not only the present demands of strong Muslim-majority provinces, but also the future constraints which he believed the British and the Congress and indeed he himself would be able to put upon them. In this way he managed to make some real gains, while living to fight another day.

The contradictions inside the resolution, and evidence of Jinnah's line of thinking, can be seen in its fourth paragraph which deals with the minorities. Just as Zafrullah Khan himself had envisaged, the resolution assumed that the boundaries of the 'Independent States' would in the main be the existing boundaries of the provinces.[54] That would leave the Muslims in minority provinces outside Muslim 'autonomous and sovereign' areas.[55] By trading safeguards for non-Muslims in the Muslim-dominated 'units', the fourth paragraph asked for the protection of Muslim minorities in those units outside the Muslim sphere. But it is significant that this paragraph talks of 'the constitution' (and not of treaty arrangements) to govern arrangements for both sets of minorities, Muslim and non-Muslim. In other words, Jinnah was keeping his options open for a constitutional arrangement which would cover the whole of India.

No one can argue that the Lahore resolution was a complete or coherent statement of Muslim demands. At no point between 1940 and the Cabinet Mission's arrival in 1946 did the League expand, revise, or make more specific this incomplete and contradictory statement, even when its position was ostensibly stronger, and the need for clarification most urgent. This suggests that Jinnah was never in a position to confront his constituents in the majority provinces with the inwardness of his strategy. There were contradictions between Muslim interests in

---

[54] According to the third paragraph of the resolution, there were to be some 'territorial readjustments'. This was put in not because anyone was ready to give up any part of the majority provinces, but as a bid to get more territories, and better lines of communication between them. In October 1942, that is after the Cripps offer, Choudhry Khaliquzzaman wrote to Jinnah about the potential disadvantages of such 'territorial readjustments'; he stressed the importance of retaining links between the Pakistan areas and the minority provinces; 'Long and hostile distances will intervene against the cultural influences of the minority Provinces on the Pakistan Zone.' Moreover, 'one of the basic principles lying behind the Pakistan idea is that of keeping hostages in Muslim Provinces as against the Muslims in the Hindu Provinces. If we allow millions of Hindus to go out of our orbit of influence, the security of the Muslims in the minority Provinces will greatly be minimised.' (See Khaliquzzaman to Jinnah, 7 October 1942, SHC/U.P. vol. IV and Choudhry Khaliquzzaman, *Pathway to Pakistan* (Lahore, 1961), pp. 424–7.) Significantly, in April 1946, the phrase about 'territorial readjustments' was dropped from the League's revised version of the Lahore resolution.

[55] And by inference inside 'autonomous and sovereign' non-Muslim states.

majority and minority provinces, and between an apparently separatist demand for autonomous Muslim states and the need for a centre capable of ensuring the interests of Muslims in the rest of India. At no point was Jinnah able to reconcile these contradictions. He came away from Lahore not with a coherent demand which squared the circle of these difficulties, but simply with the right to negotiate for Muslims on a completely new basis. He also had the advantage of being able to do so without being hindered by too specific a programme. Jinnah's priorities are revealed by his continued insistence after 1940 that he, as the president of the A.I.M.L., should be recognised as the sole spokesman of all Indian Muslims.

No amount of detective work on what led to the resolution or how it came to be interpreted afterwards can hope to tease out its inwardness. It can only be discovered by looking at Jinnah's shifting tactics in attempting to control followers more powerful than himself, and to negotiate with rivals who were not only more formidable but better organised than his own party. Contemporaries and historians have often described Jinnah as a player who kept his cards close to his chest; and a good player with a poor hand has to pretend to have different cards than those he is actually holding. So there is nothing surprising about Jinnah's inscrutability, or that the final result was so different from the one which he had so skilfully planned and fought so hard to achieve.

Section 3

The timing of the Lahore resolution had been dictated by British needs, which in their turn had been made more urgent by Congress's demands. Its context had been deeply influenced by the weaknesses in Jinnah's standing in relation to the British and the Congress, but particularly in relation to his potential constituents in the majority provinces. From the British point of view – and the angles of vision from London, New Delhi and the provincial headquarters were very different – the Lahore resolution was useful, but far from ideal. Its demand for 'autonomous and sovereign units', hedged though it was with ambiguities and qualifications, seemed to threaten the unity of India, so dear to the British.[56] But for the time being Delhi saw a clear balance of advantage in accepting

[56] This unity was important to British interests even in an independent India. As Zetland wrote, it was something 'which we aim to perpetuate after British rule ceases'; the League's resolution was a 'counsel of despair' and added up to a 'Silly . . . scheme for partition'. (See Zetland to Linlithgow, telegram, 4 April 1940, Mss.Eur.F.125/19/94, I.O.L. and Linlithgow to Zetland, 5 April 1940, Mss.Eur.D.609/19, I.O.L.)

the resolution at face value, and not exposing 'the absurdity of the idea'.[57] For the moment it was satisfied that the resolution made it most unlikely that Congress and League would come to terms. This would justify the British in making 'no further moves towards Congress', 'taking no action and . . . lying back'.[58] The Lahore resolution cleared some obstacles in the way of the Viceroy's tactic of concentrating upon the war and putting the question of constitutional change to one side. He urged London to leave the 'post-war period to post-war man'.[59] Since the Viceroy could see that Jinnah and the League had little influence in the Muslim provinces that mattered for the war effort, he was encouraged by the Punjab Governor's reaction that 'responsible Muslim opinion' did not think much of the resolution, seeing it mainly as a bargaining counter. As one Lahore newspaper boss told Craik, 'everybody knew it was a perfectly impracticable scheme, but it had the merit of having exposed the Congress pretensions to represent the whole of India'.[60] As yet there were no strong Punjab reasons for Delhi to take a stand on the resolution. But the League's stature in the government's eyes as spokesman for Muslim opinion had been enhanced, albeit by default of an alternative.

This cleared the way for the next step in Jinnah's strategy, which was to get the government to accept him as the sole spokesman of Muslim India and to make no arrangements, now or in the future, without giving the League a standing equal to that of the Congress. Congress, on the other hand, now faced a situation which was less than promising; for one thing, it was difficult for its leaders to continue to claim that there were only 'two parties', the British and the Congress, in settling the Indian question.[61] Now that the merits of co-operation were coming to be realised, Congress's revised terms, less uncompromising than its earlier demand for immediate independence, had less chance of being accepted. As it brought down its terms, Jinnah (to the Viceroy's relief) raised the

---

57 Which the new Secretary of State in London, L. S. Amery, wanted. (See Amery to Linlithgow, 25 January 1941, Mss.Eur.F.125/10/3, I.O.L.)
58 Linlithgow to Zetland, telegram, 8 March 1940, Mss.Eur.D.609/26, I.O.L. cited in Rizvi, *Linlithgow and India*, p. 148, fn. 2.
59 Amery to Linlithgow, 11 December 1941, Mss.Eur.F.125/10/38, Linlithgow's comment is in the margin, I.O.L. cited in Rizvi, *Linlithgow and India*, p. 119.
60 Craik to Linlithgow, 30 April 1940, L/P&J/5/243/ff. 198, I.O.L.
61 On 15 June 1940, Gandhi repeated his old line that: 'There is only one democratic elected political organisation, i.e. the Congress. All the others are self-appointed or elected on a sectional basis. The Muslim League is an organisation which, like the Congress, is popularly elected. But it is frankly communal and wants to divide India into two parts . . . Thus for the present purposes there are only two parties – the Congress and those who side with the Congress, and the parties who do not . . .' (See *Harijan*, Ahmedabad, 15 June 1940.)

League's demands. When Congress, setting Gandhi's principle of non-violence to one side, announced it would be satisfied with a 'National Government' *now*, and a promise of independence *after* the war, the 'composite cabinet not limited to any single party'[62] it had in mind was conveniently torpedoed by Jinnah's insistence that such a cabinet would only be acceptable if the British 'associate the Muslim leadership as equal partners in the Government both at the Centre and in all the provinces'. By 'Muslim leadership', Jinnah of course meant the Muslim League; Leaguers 'must be fully trusted as equals and have equal share in the authority and control of the Governments, Central and Provincial'.[63] Congress could not swallow such a demand; and Linlithgow was able to keep things as they were, giving Jinnah a vague assurance that he recognised the 'importance' of 'securing adequate representation of Muslim interests' in any constitutional change that might be made.[64]

The way was now clear for the Viceroy to issue a declaration of British policy in response to the Congress's and the League's statements of demands. It emerged as Linlithgow's August offer of 1940. Despite its bland statements of goodwill and concern about the future, the Viceroy's aim was simple: to block the Congress's proposals for a National Government during the war, stand pat at the centre, and run the provinces wherever necessary through Section 93. If Congress did not bend, it would be broken. The Government of India was prepared 'to crush the organisation as a whole' if Congress resorted to its ultimate agitational weapon, civil disobedience.[65] The August offer,[66] as it emerged from London's revision, simply stated that H.M.G. would set up a representative body after the war to work out India's future; Dominion Status was the goal; but no system of government denied 'by

---

[62] Maulana Azad quoted in Rizvi, *Linlithgow and India*, p. 155.

[63] Jinnah's tentative proposals for intensifying the war effort, 1 July 1940, in L. A. Sherwani (ed.), *Pakistan Resolution to Pakistan, 1940–1947: A Selection of Documents Presenting the Case for Pakistan* (Karachi, 1969), pp. 44–5.

[64] Linlithgow pointed out that an expanded Executive Council would work together as a single Government of India, and there was no case for striking a balance between the different interests or of preserving proportions between important parties. As for Muslim representation in all British Indian provinces, it was entirely up to the Governors of Section 93 provinces to appoint advisers. If provincial ministries were formed in the Section 93 provinces, the 'importance of the community from which Advisers are drawn in a particular province has a direct bearing'. In other words, the Viceroy assured Jinnah that even if equal representation could not be guaranteed, it might be granted *ex gratia*. (Linlithgow to Jinnah, 6 July 1940, ibid., pp. 45–6.)

[65] Linlithgow to all Governors, 8 August 1940, L/P&J/8/507, I.O.L. The August offer was made on the same day.

[66] London chopped and changed the Viceroy's proposals. (See Rizvi, *Linlithgow and India*, pp. 156–8.)

large and powerful elements in India's national life' would be forced upon Indians.[67] In other words, Indians would have to agree. For the time being, Indians would be invited to join the Executive Council and the proposed war advisory committee. This effectively put paid to the Congress's initiative. It was not as specific in recognising Jinnah's claims to speak for Muslims as he would have liked it to be, but at least it set up the target at which he was aiming. Not surprisingly, both the Congress and the League rejected the August offer; it had been cast in terms to achieve just that result.

After the offer had been made and rejected, Jinnah could afford to wait upon events. The real casualty of the abortive offer was Congress, not the League. Its offer of co-operation rejected, the Congress reluctantly was forced to try to save face by non-cooperation. Yet many powerful elements inside the Congress, whether on calculations of interest or ideology were against shaking foundations and removing the roof during a hurricane. Gandhi's characteristic compromise of launching a campaign of individual satyagraha was intended to save face; it certainly did not frighten the British or bring the war effort to a stand-still.[68] Its real aim was to encourage the British to offer the Congress something new and to allow it to return to the negotiating table. But no one in London or Delhi was ready to do so for the time being.

With Congress ministries out of office and much of its leadership under arrest, Jinnah could turn to his other main preoccupation – achieving a better balance between the League at the centre and its provincial satraps. The key province was of course the Punjab; everyone agreed 'that Jinnah's writ does not run in the Punjab' and a 'final split between him and Sikander cannot be long delayed'.[69] The 'so-called Muslim League' in the province consisted mainly of 'Unionists who owe allegiance from first to last to Sir Sikander'.[70] If Jinnah pressed him, Sikander was not likely to budge, but would simply break with the League.[71] When the League tentatively tried to call the shots by dictating

---

[67] Linlithgow's speech of 8 August 1940, *Speeches by the Marquess of Linlithgow*, vol. II, (Simla, 1944), pp. 238–42.

[68] By June 1941 over twenty thousand Congressmen had been arrested, but the campaign had lost such impetus as it had. In October 1941, there were only 5,600 satyagrahis in jail and many in the Congress wanted to call off the campaign. The movement had failed to obstruct the war effort; the British were not ready to make any new offers, and symbolic acts of defiance had proven to be a dismal failure particularly in the Muslim-majority provinces. (See Tomlinson, *The Indian National Congress and the Raj*, pp. 151–2.)

[69] Craik to Linlithgow, 20 June 1940, L/P&J/5/243, p. 172, I.O.L.

[70] Barkat Ali to Jinnah, 4 December 1940, QAP/File No. 215.

[71] Barkat Ali complained that the Punjab League, dominated by the Unionists, had no intention or incentive to improve its organisation in the province. As a result: 'the cause

that Leaguers should stand aloof from district war committees, in the Punjab no one paid the slightest heed.[72] Nor did they do so in Bengal, certainly not as far as Huq and his followers were concerned. Here again if Huq were forced to choose between his provincial priorities and his distant commitment to the League, it was clear which way he would go,[73] and it was not in Jinnah's direction. So neither Sikander nor Huq, as Ispahani reported gloomily, 'care two brass buttons whether they go over anyone's head or throw the Muslims in the minority provinces to the wolves'.[74] Of course Huq's coalition in Bengal was much less secure than Sikander's in the Punjab, and Jinnah could hope for better things in the future from the play of Bengali factionalism although he hardly controlled the game. In the outlying Muslim provinces of the north-west, the disjunction between Jinnah's claims at the centre and the provincial realities was even more marked. In Sind, where no one could discover 'any enthusiasm for Pakistan',[75] whether among those in office or those

of the League has suffered a most irretrievable setback, and unless you seriously take in hand the question of the reorganisation of the League in this Province the organisation will die before long, however much [sic] politically minded Mussalmans agree with the League'. (Barkat Ali to Jinnah, ibid.) All Jinnah could tell Barkat Ali was that he had 'no power to take action', and matters concerning the League's organisation had to be referred to the Working Committee of which Sikander was still a member. (Jinnah to Barkat Ali, 11 January 1941, ibid., p. 66.)

[72] On 16 June 1940, the League's Working Committee had passed a resolution asking Leaguers not to serve on the war committees but to await further instructions from Jinnah. In this way Jinnah hoped to gain some leverage during his negotiations with Linlithgow. But in the Punjab, many Leaguers including Sikander joined the war committees.

[73] Huq had defined his attitude towards the war effort in December 1939. As a member of the provincial government, he saw his duty to support the war effort. Indeed, if it came to deciding between his membership of the League and his responsibilities as chief minister, the latter must prevail. (See Zaidi (ed.), *Correspondence*, pp. 137–8.)

[74] Ispahani complained that both Huq and Sikander were openly flaunting the High Command's authority, and the League had become the 'laughing stock of our political opponents'. As for the so-called League members of the Bengal ministry, they were the same 'reactionary forces' which had made the 'old League so undemocratic and moribund'. For the time being the 'progressives will wait patiently until such time as existing conditions change or until you [Jinnah] feel that the salvation of the Muslim nation does not lie in the hands of such indisciplined and undependable colleagues'. (Ispahani to Jinnah, 21 June 1940, ibid., pp. 142–3.)

[75] In February 1940, Allah Baksh had been forced to resign. Mir Bandeh Ali Khan, the leader of the Baluch group in the assembly, formed a new ministry which included three League ministers: K. B. Khuhro, Sheikh Abdul Majid and G. M. Syed. Jinnah would have liked to have some say over the ministry, and indeed the Sind Provincial Parliamentary Committee did try to force the League ministers to take orders from it. But the League trio contended that the ministry was neither a League cabinet nor a coalition League cabinet. (See Graham to Linlithgow, 25 July 1940, L/P&J/5/256,

hoping to get in, and where loyalties were qualified by self-interest, politics continued to see-saw in an intensive series of in-fights.[76] In the N.W.F.P. Jinnah's sanguine hopes of getting a League ministry, however nominal, came to naught,[77] breaking on the factionalism of the Khans and the self-seeking interests of the local Leaguers.[78] Here the Governor was less likely than his opposite number in Sind to help the factions resolve their differences inside a League ministry since he was content to run the province under Section 93, particularly after the Congress civil disobedience proved a failure.[79] The 'refreshingly local

I.O.L.) Not surprisingly, the so-called League ministers ignored the resolution prohibiting Leaguers from participating in the war committees, and the Governor did 'not encounter any enthusiasm for Pakistan either among my ministers or in the local press or in my visitors'. (Graham to Linlithgow, 9 October 1940, ibid.)

76 With the formation of Bandeh Ali Khan's ministry, communal relations in Sind deteriorated. So the Governor wanted Allah Baksh back, since 'the Muslim League is not so powerful as it pretends to be and . . . Allah Baksh still has a very considerable following not only in the Assembly but in the country'. (Graham to Linlithgow, 25 September 1940, ibid.) In November 1940, two of the League ministers resigned in favour of Allah Baksh and Ghulam Hussain without the permission of the League Provincial Parliamentary Committee. In March 1941, Bandeh Ali Khan, by now a member of the League, 'collapsed through fear' and resigned. Allah Baksh formed a new ministry; every one of the new Muslim ministers had been in Graham's cabinets before, and he quipped: *'Plus ça change, plus c'est la même chose.'* (Graham to Linlithgow, 12 March 1941, L/P&J/5/257, I.O.L.)

77 Ever since Dr Khan Sahib's Congress ministry resigned in November 1939, Jinnah had been desperate to form a League ministry in this predominantly Muslim province. Just note the tone of his telegrams: 'Form Ministry at any cost, even interim Ministry, waverers and others will come afterwards'; and when he was informed that it was impossible to form even a League coalition ministry, he wrote: 'Your telegram. Great mistake, missing opportunity, form coalition Ministry, make every sacrifice, let others be ministers'. (Cunningham to Linlithgow, 12 November 1939, L/P&J/5/215, I.O.L.)

78 Since 1939, the Governor had been urging the local Khans to form a 'party strong enough to win the next elections'. (Cunningham to Linlithgow, 9 May 1939, L/P&J/5/214, pp. 34–5.) The League was the obvious alternative for the Khans, and it now became an essentially Khanate party with little popular support. The local League was known to consist of 'self-seekers'; 'they were not the men to excite either fervour or loyalty' among the Pathans; not surprisingly it became the hotbed for 'selfish, ambitious and private feuds' among the Khans. There was a leadership struggle between Khan Bahadur Sadullah Khan and Aurengzeb Khan, not to mention other feuds amongst the many contenders for leadership in the province. (Cunningham to Linlithgow, 9 January 1940, L/P&J/5/216, p. 105, I.O.L.)

79 Understandably, most of the local Congress leaders in the Frontier were less interested in political questions involving the rest of India than in their local manoeuvrings. Dr Khan Sahib, although he did resign when ordered to do so by the Congress High Command, was strongly opposed to civil disobedience. Even Gandhi had to admit that the Frontier possessed no one fit to carry out civil disobedience in a non-violent manner. The Governor's view was that Pathans were 'simply not interested in Congress'. (Cunningham to Linlithgow, 9 April 1941, L/P&J/5/218, p. 107, I.O.L.)

outlook',[80] the 'local jealousies',[81] and a hardly remarkable lack of interest among the Pathans in the affairs of all-India meant that the Frontier ignored Jinnah, and even the local League became less active except in their 'quarrelling among themselves about the election of office-bearers'.[82]

The experience of the first year after the resolution was passed dashed Jinnah's hopes of redressing the balance in the League between the centre and its provinces. Not one of the Muslim-majority provinces had fallen into line. In the Punjab, Jinnah's precarious compromise faced a new threat when some of the implications of the Lahore resolution began to sink in. As Jinnah himself told the Punjabis on more than one occasion, they held a 'key position in the scheme for the realisation in practice of the Lahore resolution'.[83] But the Lahore resolution had been cast in terms which were unacceptable to Punjab's other two main communities, the Hindus and especially the Sikhs. In early 1941, the Khalsa Nationalists (a small section of pro-British Sikhs who had forged an alliance with the Unionists in 1937) entered into an agreement with some members of the Akali Dal (who had a larger base of popular support in eastern Punjab, had links with Bose's Forward Bloc and were anti-British) to form the Khalsa Defence of India League; they called on Sikhs to participate in the war effort and warned the Unionists that unless they denounced 'Pakistan' openly, the Khalsa Nationalists would join the opposite benches.[84] Anxious not to lose Sikh support, particularly from the Khalsa Nationalist party, the Unionist bosses realised that their own provincial imperatives called for distancing themselves from the Lahore resolution. So Muslim ministers and prominent Muslim

---

[80] The Governor found it remarkable that the Pathans were completely unconcerned with what was happening in the rest of India. Admittedly they liked war and wanted more opportunities of enlisting in the army. Satyagraha was hardly their style and 'even the war, now that it is going well, is of less importance to them than the weather and crops'. (Cunningham to Linlithgow, 9 February 1941, ibid., pp. 132–3.)

[81] Linlithgow also wanted a different ministry in the Frontier. But he had to admit that 'local jealousies' were a 'very serious obstacle to any real progress'. (Linlithgow to Cunningham, 16 March 1940, Mss.Eur.F.125/75, pp. 7–8, I.O.L.)

[82] While the 'Congress stock continues to fall', there was a marked lull in the League's activities; its leaders were now concentrating wholly upon waging family feuds under the League's banner. (Cunningham to Linlithgow, 23 November 1941, L/P&J/5/218, p. 15, I.O.L.)

[83] Interestingly enough, Jinnah did not himself refer to the League's resolution as the 'Pakistan Resolution'. (See Jinnah's address to the Pakistan Conference, *Civil and Military Gazette*, Lahore, 2 March 1941.)

[84] See Stephen Oren, 'The Sikhs, Congress and the Unionists in British Punjab, 1937–1945', *Modern Asian Studies*, 8, 3 (1974), 409.

Unionists stayed away from the Pakistan Conference of March 1941.[85] Sikander went further; in the Punjab legislative assembly, he denounced the Lahore resolution saying that it was not his doing, and in fact was an amended version which he liked less the more he understood it. He repeated the old axioms of the Punjab – complete autonomy for the provinces; Muslim opposition to an 'all powerful Centre' because it threatened provincial autonomy; a weak centre, not a 'domineering hostile Centre looking for opportunities to interfere with the work of provincial Governments'. Significantly, Sikander admitted that the Muslim-majority provinces wanted complete autonomy only 'because they are afraid that a communal oligarchy in power might undermine or altogether nullify the autonomy and freedom of the provinces. That is the suspicion that haunts them. It may not be well founded but there it is; and we must face facts'.[86] But above all, Sikander wanted to show 'the rest of India, that we in the Punjab stand united and will not brook any interference . . . then only we will be able to tell meddling busybodies from outside 'hands off the Punjab'.[87] This was virtually a unilateral declaration of independence at a time when Jinnah could not afford to pick a quarrel with the Punjab leaders. Fortunately for Jinnah, matters did not come to a head because of a conveniently-timed distraction at the all-India level.

By the middle of 1941, the Congress civil disobedience movement had started petering out. The Viceroy thought it was an appropriate moment to expand his Executive Council and to create a National Defence Council. The Executive Council was to have eight Indian and four British members, so for the first time there was to be a non-official Indian majority even though most of the important portfolios were held by the British members. On 21 July, Linlithgow announced the names of the National Defence Council; the list included Fazlul Huq, Sikander Hayat and Muhammad Sadullah (the premier of Assam); all three were nominal members of the League and had been invited to the Council without reference to Jinnah. The Viceroy had 'concluded that it would be preferable not to embarrass . . . [Jinnah] by inviting . . . [him] to make suggestions'.[88] For Jinnah the inclusion of Leaguers in the Defence Council was indeed an embarrassment since it was hardly 'fair or proper

85 The Pakistan Conference had been organised by the Punjab Muslim Students Federation, with the object of a 'revival of enthusiasm for the Pakistan movement'. (Punjab
   Chief Secretary's Report, first half of March 1941, L/P&J/5/244, I.O.L.)
86 Sikander's speech in the Punjab legislative assembly, 11 March 1941, *The Punjab
   Legislative Assembly Debates*, vol. XVI, (Lahore, 1942), pp. 350–6; cited in Sherwani
   (ed.), *Pakistan Resolution to Pakistan*, pp. 30–2.
87 Ibid., cited in Khaliquzzaman, *Pathway to Pakistan*, p. 254.
88 See Ahmad (ed.), *Historic Documents*, p. 415.

that they should be approached by His Excellency over the head of the President and the executive of the All-India Muslim League'.[89] The Viceroy's invitation to Muslim leaders to join the Defence Council had raised an issue critically important to Jinnah; it tested his claim at the centre to be consulted, and his authority to instruct provincial Leaguers on the line they should take at the centre. He had no choice but to direct the League's Working Committee to pass a resolution demanding the resignation of the three Leaguers on threat of disciplinary action. Jinnah argued that the three League premiers had been invited in their capacity as representatives of Muslims, and not in their official capacity. Sikander went to Bombay for consultations with Jinnah; he could see the danger of being branded as a traitor to the Muslim cause if he refused to toe the League's line. This would give his opponents in the Punjab an excuse to launch a campaign against him which would inevitably disrupt the fragile communal balance of the Punjab. By accepting Jinnah's line, Sikander not only kept the High Command at bay, but also ensured that the war effort would not be disrupted. Sikander agreed to accept no proposal from the Government without first discussing it with Jinnah. 'The situation is such', Jinnah wrote to Sikander, 'that the slightest mistake on our part now well [sic] undo all the work done by us hitherto.'[90] Later Jinnah admitted that the Viceroy had 'double-crossed' Sikander by giving the impression that the Muslim premiers had been invited in their official capacity, and thanked the Punjab premier for his 'willing assistance'.[91]

Sikander's resignation from the Viceroy's Defence Council saved Jinnah's face. But the Bengal premier was less generous. Huq refused to bend to the dictates of the High Command and broke with the A.I.M.L., protesting 'against the manner in which the interests of the Muslims of Bengal and the Punjab are being imperilled by Muslim leaders of the Provinces where the Muslims are in a minority'. Huq attacked Jinnah for the 'arbitrary use of powers'; recent events had 'forcibly brought home to me that the principles of democracy and autonomy are being subordinated to the arbitrary wishes of a single individual who seeks to rule as an omnipotent authority over the destiny of 33 millions of Muslims in the province of Bengal who occupy the key position in Indian Muslim Politics'.[92] Huq's revolt gave his rivals in the Bengal League their chance to bid for power. Suhrawardy called out students and workers to

[89] Ibid., pp. 415–16.
[90] Jinnah to Sikander, 29 August 1941, QAP/File No. 353, p. 38.
[91] Jinnah to Sikander, 13 September 1941, ibid.
[92] Huq to Liaquat Ali Khan, 8 September 1941, in Ahmad (ed.), *Historic Documents*, pp. 418–19.

demonstrate against Huq, who retaliated by getting his friends to table no-confidence motions against these rebels inside his camp, Suhrawardy and Nazimuddin. On 1 December all the League ministers resigned, certain that the Governor would call on them to form a new ministry. Since the Leaguers had more votes, Huq had to offer his cabinet's resignation. But the Governor was having none of it; he decided to call on Huq again to form the new ministry. This ministry brought in, as finance minister, the leader of the Hindu Mahasabha, Shyma Prasad Mookerji – the symbol of Hindu fanaticism. The move startled Muslim India; it was a red rag to Jinnah and the League. The Bengal League was now an opposition party, and Huq was able to survive as premier in Bengal by restructuring his ministry with the support of the Progressive Coalition party.[93]

By the time Cripps was sent to India, Jinnah had neither made nor broken a single ministry in the Muslim provinces; for the time being he had been deprived of the support of even the Bengal ministry; the Punjab was going its own way; Sind had a pro-Congress faction under Allah Baksh in power, and Section 93 ruled the N.W.F.P. Leaguers in the provinces had shown that they were ready to get into office by hook or by crook.[94] In this anarchy of self-interest effective linkages between centre and provinces, created or controlled by the League, hardly existed.

So Linlithgow had no reason to bother to get 'an appreciation of local Muslim reactions to Pakistan', whether public or private and Jinnah conveniently 'had been at great pains not to define exactly what he means by that blessed word, and all we should get would be something pretty woolly and general'.[95] After a tour (admittedly mainly in the Hindu-

---

[93] A grand name covering a multitude of political factions, some of Bose's Forward Bloc, various Krishak Praja men, Hindu Mahasabhites, a few Indian Christians, Anglo-Indians and Scheduled Caste members.

[94] For instance the Mamdot–Daultana faction in the Punjab; Suhrawardy and Nazimuddin in Bengal; Aurangzeb Khan in the N.W.F.P.; and Khuhro amongst many others in Sind. Aurangzeb Khan had gone so far as openly to denounce Jinnah's policy on the National Defence Council issue and 'would jump at the offer of a seat on the Defence Council had it been made to him'; and he would do so without reference to Jinnah. Not only had Aurangzeb promised the Governor all aid including help in the war effort, but had rubbed in the fact that Jinnah's 'real trouble is his jealousy for [sic] Sir Sikander Hayat, and not any anti-British bias'. (See Cunningham to Linlithgow, 8 and 24 August 1941, L/P&J/5/218, p. 69 and p. 63, I.O.L.) The situation in Sind was even more dismal. Here the Governor found 'no regard at all for Jinnah and the League's extra-Sind affiliations' amongst the 'Sindhi Leaguers'; they were quite willing to support Allah Baksh if he broke with the Congress. (See Dow to Linlithgow, 12 December 1941, L P&J/5/257, and 29 January 1942, L/P&J/5/258, I.O.L.)

[95] Linlithgow to Amery, 8 January 1942, in N. Mansergh and E. W. R. Lumby (eds.), *The Transfer of Power 1942–7*, vol. I (London, 1970), p. 17 (henceforth *T.P.* I, and so on; all references are to page numbers).

majority provinces, but also covering Bengal and Assam) H. V. Hodson, the Reforms Commissioner, made a characteristically acute assessment of Muslim opinion. Most Muslims with whom he had spoken, including 'orthodox supporters of Pakistan . . . from Jinnah downwards', were thinking in terms of the British staying on, with defence in British hands for an undefined 'transitional period'. The real point was that 'every Muslim Leaguer . . . interpreted Pakistan as consistent with a confederation of India for common purposes like defence, provided the Hindu and Muslim element therein stood on equal terms'.[96] This hardly surprised Hodson since no one with any political foresight in the Muslim-minority provinces believed in his heart of hearts that Pakistan could solve their problems. Pakistan, as this intelligent observer realised, was in essence a 'revolt' against the notion of minority status with safeguards. At best, such a status relegated Muslims to being 'a Cinderella with trade--union rights and a radio in the kitchen but still below-stairs'. The 'two-nation' theory was a better way of describing Muslim aims than 'Pakistan', since it turned from safeguards and minority rights to the solid gains of national status. There would be 'no retreat' from this new outlook, Hodson prophesied. What was now needed was a 'new terminology' which 'recognises that the problem is one of sharing power rather [than of] qualifying the terms on which power is exercised by a majority'.[97] So even though there was no 'genuine enthusiasm for Pakistan', no Muslim was ready actually to repudiate it, since it was an expression, however vague and contradictory, of 'Muslim solidarity which they feel to be vitally necessary at the present time'.[98]

The Reforms Commissioner was looking at the Pakistan demand from the outside. But the insiders' view confirms his analysis. I. I. Chundrigar[99] from Bombay, a Leaguer of pelf and persuasion, told the men down the line that the object of the Lahore resolution was not to create 'Ulsters', but to achieve 'two nations . . . welded into united India on the basis of equality'.[100] 'Bold departure' though it seemed to be, the resolution was hunting for an alternative to majority rule, not seeking to

---

[96] Note on the tour of the Reforms Commissioner from 8 November to 7 December 1941, to Madras, Orissa, Assam, Bengal and Bihar. (Annexe to document No. 30, ibid., 63). The only exception was Fazlul Huq, who ironically had moved the Lahore resolution. Among those who saw the Union Jack continuing to flutter over Government House were Khwaja Nazimuddin, Suhrawardy, Muhammad Sadullah, Sobhan Khan, Abdul Hamid Khan, Abdul Matin Choudhry, and Khan Bahadur Saiyid Muhammad Ismail. (Ibid., 66.)   [97] Ibid., 67.   [98] Ibid., 66.

[99] I. I. Chundrigar, a member of Independent Pakistan's first cabinet, later had the distinction of serving as prime minister for two long months. But then life in Karachi, which was not Bombay, required some compensations.

[100] Note by Chundrigar, April 1940, 'Must Face Facts', QAP/File No. 103.

destroy the unity of India.[101] That Chundrigar's interpretation was on the right tracks is suggested by the fact that Jinnah himself, Chundrigar's neighbour in Bombay, often stated that 'Pakistan', with its connotations of partition, was not the League's idea but a caricature thrust upon it by the Hindu press: 'They fathered this word upon us',[102] he complained at Delhi in 1943. As he told Nawab Ismail in November 1941, he could not openly and forcibly come out with these truths 'because it is likely to be misunderstood especially at present'. In a line which reveals more than a thousand pages of research and propaganda, Jinnah admitted: 'I think Mr. Hodson finally understands as to what our demand is.'[103] But sadly for the course of the subcontinent's history, the Reforms Commissioner's note was not digested by those who drafted the declaration which Cripps brought to India.

Section 4

By the end of 1941, events abroad were coming to bear more powerfully upon the situation in India than what was happening in India itself. The Congress satyagraha movement had turned out to be something of a contrived fiasco; and Congress leaders, who had given up power in the provinces in their bid for a share of power at the centre, found themselves increasingly at a loss about how to get out of the cul-de-sac into which they had driven. What they needed was a British initiative which they could meet half-way, but Linlithgow was not prepared to give anything away. So Congress leaders were reduced to sending surreptitious messages to Westminster through the usual intermediary, that respectable channel of 'moderate-liberal opinion', Tej Bahadur Sapru, who for long had been reduced to being a mere postman between correspondents who mattered. Yet their urgent plea to London calling for an act of statesmanship to break the deadlock[104] would have been ignored by the Cabinet, which had more pressing problems at hand, if it had not been subjected to pressures from outside India.

These came in part from Britain's allies, deeply concerned about the fighting in the east and in part from the Labour members of Churchill's National Government. The Japanese assault on Pearl Harbour had brought America into the war. America's entry was Churchill's best security for ultimate victory against the Axis Powers. But it also had its inconveniences. One of these was the President's rather jejune, but well-

[101] Ibid.
[102] See Jinnah's address to the A.I.M.L., Delhi, April 1943, Pirzada (ed.), *Foundations of Pakistan*, vol. II, p. 425.
[103] Jinnah to Nawab S. M. Ismail, 25 November 1941, QAP/10/File No. 1092, p. 143.
[104] R. J. Moore, *Churchill, Cripps, and India, 1939–1945* (Oxford, 1979), p. 45.

meaning, interest in India. Roosevelt's view, typical of the State Department's naivety about the nature of the world which America was beginning to join, was that Indian co-operation was the answer to Japan's unchallenged advance through colonial Asia. The fall of Singapore in February 1942 seemed to confirm Washington's reasoning that the best way of securing the gates of India against the Japanese was to promise Indians their freedom from colonial tyranny. This view, orchestrated by Roosevelt and fiercely resisted by Churchill, was echoed by Chiang Kai-shek who had paid a flying visit to India in February 1942.

But American pressure, though embarrassing, would not have been sufficient if it had not coincided with a reciprocal trend inside the Cabinet, not merely among Labour but also some Conservative members (as well as pressure groups outside Parliament) who were unconvinced by the diehard attitudes of the Prime Minister and his Viceroy. In the Cabinet, Attlee, who was second in command, Cripps who had recently returned from Russia with his reputation for statesmanship in fine order, and even Bevin, who had more urgent matters to deal with, felt that the time had come to give thought to the future of India, particularly since such an initiative might bring immediate benefits: public opinion at home and abroad would be reassured that British promises to India were genuine; the Americans would be placated, and those political groups in India which Labour had been conditioned to believe mattered most would be brought into active co-operation instead of being left grumbling outside. Attlee and Cripps argued that by grasping the nettle and by being specific about Britain's post-war intentions in India, large gains could be achieved at little immediate cost. There was no question of loosening control over the executive in India, over defence or indeed over anything serious that related to the war effort. Little harm and some good might come by associating Indians in that effort, particularly at the centre. By February, pressure inside the Cabinet had built up and Churchill was forced to try and side-step the issue by his fantasy of creating a nominated Defence Council of Indians, later to be India's constituent assembly. But this was soon exposed for what it really was: an impudent rejection of the democratic process. Attlee and Cripps returned to the attack, and demanded a declaration of British intentions. If such a declaration forced the Viceroy to resign that would be all to the good since they considered Linlithgow to be unfit for the job;[105] and they believed that Congress was likely to be more co-operative under a new Viceroy.[106]

---

[105] As Wavell later learnt to his cost, Attlee did not hesitate to give Britain's proconsuls short shrift from the metropolis.

[106] Attlee's memorandum on the Indian question rejected the policy of doing nothing. He called for an 'act of statesmanship'; and was convinced that the Viceroy was 'not the man

But of course the resources of the old team, the Prime Minister, the Secretary of State, and Linlithgow, though strained, were not exhausted. A draft declaration owing something to many sources – Cripps's schemes of 1939,[107] Amery's view that 'strengthening Provincial sentiment is the best corrective to the present over-centralised party dictatorships' (of both Congress and the League) and, what was rapidly becoming the ark of the covenant, the interests of Muslims, particularly the martial races in the north-west – was prepared.[108] The draft declaration, amended this way and that by successive hands, did however, suggest some new directions in British policy: the most important was the explicit statement that Dominion Status after the war would not depend upon a prior agreement between India's conflicting parties; in other words, freedom would come even if unity could not be assured. What made this possible was the decision to allow provinces to opt out of an Indian union; they could, if they wished, stay under the British or achieve independent Dominion Status in their own right.[109]

The draft declaration, if declared, would have precipitated a general crisis, in the metropolis and in India. Churchill would have fiercely resisted it; the Cabinet would have split and the Viceroy would have resigned immediately. That crisis was averted by Cripps's timely offer to go to India to test reactions to the draft before it was given the formal status of declared policy.[110] Churchill, and his embattled Viceroy, confidently expected Cripps to arrive in India with high hopes but to return from it with empty hands and a tarnished reputation. So from

to do this'. So he concluded: 'Lord Durham saved Canada to the British Empire. We need a man to do in India what Durham did in Canada . . . A representative with power to negotiate within wide limits should be sent to India now, either as a special envoy or in replacement of the present Viceroy . . . ' (Memorandum by Attlee, 2 February 1942, L/PO/6/106a, War Cabinet Paper (42).)

107 Towards the end of 1939, Cripps prepared a scheme for a constituent assembly composed on the basis of the 1936–7 elections. There were to be a total of 2,000 representatives, 700 from Congress, about 450 from the League, 400 from other parties and 500 from the States. If he could obtain a general consensus in India, Cripps intended to propose that H.M.G. set up an assembly to frame a constitution for India by a two-thirds or three-fifths majority. The minority problem, and the question of the Indian States and defence, was to be settled through a treaty between Britain and India. (See Rizvi, *Linlithgow and India*, pp. 146–7.)

108 In his proposal for the expansion of the Defence Council, Amery argued that the best course 'from the point of view of defence liaison with the provincial war effort and from that of future constitution-making' was to get the provincial legislatures to elect the representatives. (Note by Amery, 7 February 1942, *T.P.*, I, 125.)

109 See draft declaration as published in *T.P.*, I, 565–6.

110 Churchill was sure that the offer would be torpedoed. And so it turned out; there were more than enough torpedoes for the task.

their point of view some good at least would come from the charade. The critics of perfidious Albion would be given token of her good intentions; Indian politicians would be shown in their true colours; and business would continue as usual. And so it proved to be – but only up to a point.

The real interest of the abortive Cripps mission lies not in the fact that it failed, or even in the reasons why it failed, but in the novel commodity which now was being touted around the great Indian political bazaar: the option for provinces to stay out of an independent Indian union. On the face of it, this was a break with the most sacred principle of British policy – the unity of India. So it is important to be clear how this had come about. Despite the apparently casual manner in which this new direction was taken, it cannot be ascribed to such varied factors as the war going badly, or its architects failing to realise the implications of local option.[111] More to the point, it was emphatically not a case of a sudden conversion, whether by Whitehall or by Cripps, to the idea of 'Pakistan'. Rather, the option that provinces could keep out of a future Indian union was an effort to bring into the open the contradictions in the League's demand for Pakistan, to force the followers of the League to realise the implications of the Lahore resolution, and to drive a wedge between Jinnah and the League at the centre and their constituents in the Muslim-majority provinces. There was method in the draft declaration and policy in Cripps's offer. During his 1939 visit to India Cripps had sensed the nascent fear of the Punjab and Bengal of a centre which Congress was bound to dominate; and had also seen clearly that Congress's aim was to get power at the centre. By taking advantage of these provincial fears and by encouraging Jinnah to act as the spokesman of Muslim-majority provinces, Linlithgow had found a way of allowing the arguments for provincial autonomy and for a weak centre to merge into and, in a sense to be overlaid by, the rather different and broader question of the rights of Muslim minorities and relations between the communities throughout India. One main advantage that had flowed from this deliberate obfuscation was that the whole question of constitutional advance could be put into cold storage. Cripps's aim was to reopen the question of India's constitutional future by removing the obstacle which Jinnah's demand

---

[111] On 6 March, the provincial Governors sent a flurry of telegrams protesting against the local option clause. Some ministers and the India Office did not like it. R. A. Butler, for example, wrote to Hoare: 'it would appear that the powers-that-be are reconciled to the idea of a Moslem Confederation in the North. This means two Indias, and I am pressing for some form of central government'; and the declaration, according to Butler, gave the impression that 'the unity of India – the goal of British policy hitherto – must be set aside'. (Butler to Hoare, 6 March 1942, Templewood Papers, cited in Moore, *Churchill, Cripps, and India*, p. 73.)

for Pakistan had placed in its way. His plan was to achieve this by driving a clear distinction between on the one hand real attachment to provincial autonomy and the fears among provincial leaders of a strong centre once the British left, and on the other the vaguer sentiments of communal solidarity. Cripps could see that the politicians of the Punjab and Bengal had an outlook which was more provincial than communal. Their first concern was to retain Punjab for the Punjabis, Bengal for the Bengalis, and to shut out 'busybodies' from outside.[112] The politics of these two provinces, with their very large non-Muslim populations, forced the provincial leaders, even when they were Muslims, such as Sikander or Huq, to realise that they needed to come to terms with other communities. Muslim leaders were concerned with their own provincial constituencies, not with Muslim minorities and their worries in other parts of India. They had been prepared to go along with Jinnah mainly because he had a limited utility for them at the centre. It suited Jinnah to metamorphose the provincial thesis into something rather different, and it suited the Viceroy to allow Jinnah his head (even though the more perceptive of the Governors were beginning to see the dangers of this course). But the provincial leaders had no urgent reason before Cripps came to India to challenge and deny Jinnah's purposes. Cripps hoped to give them reason to do so.

Unlike the Viceroy's short-term priorities, Cripps's offer took a longer view of political futures. British India, with the Congress out of the picture, may have been a convenient scenario while the war lasted. But once India began to move towards self-government after the war, it was inconceivable to think of it without the Congress. Congress and a strong centre were the best insurance the British could take out to prevent chaos and balkanisation in the India they proposed to leave. But giving Congress the strong centre it wanted was difficult to square with the provincial thesis of the Punjab and Bengal. This was the dilemma that Cripps was trying to resolve. His proposed solution was to give provinces, but not communities, the right to decide whether to come into the Indian union or not; it had the additional merit of showing what the logical consequences of Jinnah's unspecific demand for Pakistan were likely to be, and how feeble the League's grip was over its most important constituents, namely the Muslim-majority provinces. By offering a provincial not a communal option, Cripps hoped to provide a powerful incentive for those very constituents on whom Jinnah's strategy depended to unhitch their wagons from the League's train.

112 As for Sind and the N.W.F.P., although they were predominantly Muslim, they were more particularist and even more divided than the two majority provinces that really mattered.

This is why the Viceroy did not like Cripps's initiative, and this is why Cripps's offer, far from being a step in the direction of giving Jinnah what he was after, represented the gravest threat to his entire strategy. At a stroke the draft declaration threatened to pull the rug, which had so painstakingly been woven together, from under the Viceroy's feet – destroying 'the whole policy of throwing the primary responsibility on Indians to settle their own internal problem'.[113] By forcing Congress to take account of provincial demands, Cripps's offer, if accepted, would have removed the communal sting from the political debate. The inwardness of Cripps's offer can be most clearly seen in the way it embarrassed Jinnah. The local option clause in fact gave the Punjab (and other Muslim-majority provinces) precisely what Jinnah had been compelled reluctantly to demand on their behalf. Until now, he had managed to keep the Lahore resolution silent about the relationship of Muslim provinces to any centre, and in this way had managed to avoid an explicit endorsement of the Punjab's preferences for a weak federal centre. Jinnah's strategy had depended on the assumption that the British would never entertain such an extreme version of the provincial thesis – the right of provinces to secede. Yet here was Cripps doing the unthinkable and taking the provincial demand, implicit in the Lahore resolution, at its face value. It was a way of flushing Jinnah out into the open and forcing him to show where he stood on the question of the centre. Jinnah's tactic, which had the Viceroy's tacit approval, had been to keep quiet about the awkward choice between his more immediate need to back the Muslim-majority provinces, and hence their demand for provincial autonomy and a very weak centre (if there was to be a centre at all) and the unswerving commitment to a strong centre which his overall strategy, as representative of all Muslims rather than of particular provinces, demanded.

The Punjab of course was the key province, and until now Linlithgow, just as many politicians in the Punjab, had avoided facing the imperatives which the delicate balance between the communities imposed upon its politics. By offering the Punjab what it wanted Cripps was forcing its politicians and Government House to recognise these imperatives and to see how rampant communalism would undermine, not secure, provincial prospects. So now the Viceroy warned London: 'if we go too far towards meeting Jinnah we are bound to get into trouble either with Sikhs (and consequently in Punjab with Muslims) or Hindus or both'. Therefore, he preferred a formula which 'avoids laying down precisely

---

[113] See Linlithgow to Amery, 9 March 1942, *T.P.*, I, 381. What of course the Viceroy meant was that the declaration would destroy the policy of depending upon Indians to *fail* to settle their own problems.

the post-war plan . . . does not exclude Pakistan but does not advertise local option'.[114] In other words, things should return to the *status quo ante* Cripps. The Viceroy did not wish to face all the contradictions inherent in the situation: the potential clash between the communal and the provincial approach, the fact that the 'Pakistan agitation' with its communal overtones was bound to endanger the intra-communal alliances upon which the stability of the Punjab and Bengal depended, and the divisions inside the League about the future of the centre.[115] Linlithgow simply wanted Jinnah's imprecision to be mirrored by a continuing imprecision on the British side, since British interests at the centre would at this stage benefit from imprecision. Both Linlithgow and Jinnah realised that Cripps's offer would concentrate attention upon the facts of political life in the Muslim-majority provinces, and make it clear where power lay in the balance between these provinces and their all-India spokesman. Once local option was on the table, it became an urgent matter for communal feeling in the Punjab to be damped down. Unless this was done, Punjab would not be able to take advantage of that option. As the ex-Governor of the Punjab warned: 'moderate Muslims in the Punjab do not really like . . . Pakistan'; local option if exercised under the umbrella of an all-India communal party, would break the fragile intra-communal balance – Pakistan for the Punjab would be interpreted by other communities, the Sikhs in particular, as an invitation to demand the right for minorities to opt out: 'Sikhs will certainly resist by force inclusion in Pakistan.'[116]

Punjab was also critically important for Jinnah's strategy. Yet his most loyal supporters were not in the Punjab, or in Bengal, but in the minority

---

[114] Linlithgow to Amery, 9 March 1942, ibid., 384.

[115] Linlithgow pointed out that: 'the fatal defect in the present draft is the precision given by the local option pledge to the still shadowy prospect of a decisive struggle for power after British authority departs among Hindus, Muslims and Sikhs in areas where none of them holds an obviously commanding position and above all in the Punjab . . . any fresh undertakings . . . must be confined to generalities on procedure . . . once we go beyond a broad offer we shall be obliged to define prematurely our attitude towards communal proportions'. (Linlithgow to Amery, 8 March 1942, ibid., 366–7.)

[116] Craik's comments are enclosed in Linlithgow's letter to Amery, 9 March 1942, ibid., 384. Glancy endorsed Craik's view, and felt that Punjabi Muslims were bound to exercise local option to remain separate; the Sikhs would probably want to go their own way, and so the spectre of civil war in the Punjab would rear its head. (See Glancy to Linlithgow, 4 March 1942, ibid., p. 321.) Linlithgow told Amery that the Hindus would interpret the draft declaration as 'a virtual promise not merely of Pakistan but of Sikhistan also, and as containing greater possibilities of disintegrating India than even Jinnah claims' and would almost certainly be regarded by them as an invitation to minorities in the Muslim-majority provinces to 'force separation on exorbitant terms by mere refusal to agree'. (Linlithgow to Amery, 9 March 1942, ibid., 384–5.)

provinces. Local option gave them nothing. There was 'no comfort' here 'to Muslims in the U.P. and Bihar',[117] for example. The emphasis of Cripps's offer (in much the same way, it must be said, as the Lahore resolution itself), was provincial not communal. Local option showed just how hopeless the League's plan of covering Muslim bets in minority as well as majority provinces was likely to prove if there was no all-India centre which included them both. So Jinnah himself might be forced to come out against local option, and hence lose even the appearance of support from the Muslim-majority provinces, thus removing a main obstacle to a political settlement between the British, the Congress and the Muslim provinces severally.

When Churchill failed to prevent this roving envoy from going to India, he took comfort in the prospect that Cripps's efforts would prove a 'thankless and hazardous' task, and would show 'the problem . . . to be for the time being insoluble'. But it would also show the Americans 'our honesty of purpose' and would buy time, the most precious commodity of all.[118] Amery as usual took comfort by getting hold of not quite the right end of the stick. Just as he had been persuaded by the merits of local option because it might breach the powerful dictatorships of all-India parties, so now he took pleasure at Congress's fury that the draft declaration had apparently laid 'Pakistan cuckoo's egg' in the Indian nest. He had a better insight into a rather different consequence of this initiative: Cripps's offer would force Congress and Muslims alike to face the need for 'compromise'; an 'entirely new constitutional solution' was now the only alternative to 'a divided India'; but if Congress had now to come to terms with Muslim provinces, Muslims themselves would be forced to 'realise what Pakistan may involve in respect of Muslim minorities elsewhere, of the Sikh difficulty, of holding down the richer and more numerous Bengal Hindu minority, and last but not least of economic dislocation',[119] realisations which neither Jinnah nor the Viceroy felt the Muslims were ready to swallow and digest.

At the first meeting of the Executive Council at which the Cripps offer was discussed, Firoz Khan Noon brought out other important implications of local option for the Punjab and Bengal. In both these provinces, Muslim members of the assembly were in a bare majority; in both the population was predominantly Muslim, but not by a large margin. On a straight vote on local option, Muslims would have to vote solidly, with

---

117 Linlithgow to Amery, 6 March 1942, ibid., 328; and Linlithgow to Amery, 6 March 1942, ibid., 330.
118 Churchill to Linlithgow, 10 March 1942, ibid., 394-5.
119 Amery to Linlithgow, 10 March 1942, pp. 396-7 and Amery to Linlithgow, 10 March 1942, ibid., 402.

hardly a defection, if they were to prevent accession or assure secession. Such unanimity would be without precedent; and it was not at all likely. When pressed, Cripps was ready to lower the requirement: if less than sixty per cent voted for accession, then a plebiscite of the entire electorate would decide the issue.[120] But this was a typically double-edged concession. If the elected Muslim representatives were an uncertain factor, it was likely that the voters at large might be equally unpredictable in the way they voted in a plebiscite. But the plebiscite that Cripps envisaged gave a vote to the entire electorate of the province, not simply the voters of the majority community – this too was consistent with having a settlement on provincial rather than communal lines. The long and the short of it was that those in favour of exercising the local option to keep out of the union would have to win a majority of voters drawn from all communities and, to be certain of winning that vote, required cross-communal understandings in the Punjab and Bengal. These two provinces could remain autonomous and undivided only if Muslims kept their alliances with other communities in good repair, not by steering a communal line. Local option obviously held many attractions for the Muslim politicians in power in the majority provinces. That Jinnah at least could see the pitfalls of the Cripps offer is shown by the way he concentrated on the problems of how local option was to be worked in the Punjab and Bengal, while the Congress leaders, anxious to have an immediate say at the centre, failed to seize the opportunity of using local option to undermine Jinnah.[121] If Congress had accepted it, Jinnah would have been in danger of being dumped unceremoniously but permanently into a wilderness from which this time there would be no return. So he tried to blunt the point of Cripps's thrust by stressing the communal line, and demanding a plebiscite of Muslims alone to decide the question of secession in their majority provinces – self-determination for Muslims alone.[122] The irony of Jinnah's contention that he was 'rather surprised' at the 'distance . . . [local option] went to meet the Pakistan case' may not have been lost on Cripps.[123] One sharp lawyer had met another. Since Cripps's proposal for a plebiscite did not form any

[120] See note by Cripps on his interview with Jinnah, 25 March 1942, ibid., 480.

[121] Of course Congress had to take account of the fact that its acceptance of the local option clause might encourage its provinces to go their own way. For the moment it seemed easier to reject local option and keep 'Pakistan' with its communal connotations on board. Once again Congress's imperatives kept Jinnah's strategy in play.

[122] Initially Jinnah thought that Cripps's suggestion of a plebiscite was better than a vote in the provincial assemblies, but he did not like the 40% requirement to get a plebiscite. Later, Jinnah denounced plebiscites where everyone voted, claiming that Muslims alone should decide the issue.

[123] See note by Cripps on his interview with Jinnah, 25 March 1942, *T.P.*, 1, 480.

part of the draft declaration, it was safe for Jinnah to raise the issue of self-determination for Muslims only without risking an outright rejection from London. As for the draft declaration itself, it ensured that the constituent assembly would be a sovereign body 'with a preference for an all-India Union', since it would be elected proportionally from *all* the provincial assemblies meeting together as one electoral college. Hence it would be predominantly Hindu and could not 'come to any other conclusion except the Union'. Not only were the Muslims to be deprived of the old security of separate representation, but the decisions of the proposed constituent assembly would be on the basis of a bare majority. Gandhi would enter the assembly 'with a dead certainty' of getting a Congress-dominated all-India union. [124]

Once again it was the Congress which unsuspectingly came to Jinnah's rescue. Since the nineteen-twenties, Bengal and the Punjab had been its blind spots, mainly because it had failed to control the politics of these provinces. Now instead of making the most of the local option clause to allay the fears of these two provinces, the Congress concentrated all its attention upon the centre, and upon the steps that Cripps might take to give it a share of power there right away. But the High Command was asking for concessions in just those matters where Cripps's hands had been most firmly tied before he left London: the executive authority of the Viceroy was not to be touched during the war. It was out of the question to have an Indian defence minister with effective powers on the Viceroy's Executive Council, which was what the Congress wanted. The Executive Council would not be given joint responsibility; and a Congress majority would not be allowed to dominate its proceedings. Understandably, the War Cabinet in London was adamant on these points. So Congress, frustrated at the centre, turned down the offer, and Cripps had to admit failure. Naturally, he felt let down and thought that the Congress had lost an opportunity both to cut Jinnah down to size and to clear the way for advance at the centre. But it is a telling comment on how far the question of the Muslims and minorities had come to dominate everyone's thinking that Cripps blamed the failure of his mission upon the communal problem, by now the universal scapegoat in abortive constitution-making. Jinnah's own standing had survived a grave threat. He was now ready to turn Congress's rejection of the offer to his advantage; he could point with renewed emphasis to the dangers ahead of overweening Congress ambition which was unwilling to countenance the concessions made by Cripps to the Muslim-majority provinces. Provincial option, he argued, was clearly an insufficient security.

[124] Jinnah's address to the A.I.M.L. session at Allahabad, 4 April 1942, in Pirzada (ed.), *Foundations of Pakistan*, vol. II, 386–7.

An explicit acceptance of the principle of Pakistan offered the only safeguard for Muslim interests throughout India and had to be the precondition for any advance at the centre. So he exhorted all Indian Muslims to unite under his leadership to force the British and the Congress to concede 'Pakistan'. If the real reasons for Jinnah's rejection of the offer were rather different, it was not Jinnah but his rivals who had failed to make the point publicly.[125] A commentary perhaps on the fact that neither the Congress leadership nor the politicians of the Muslim-majority provinces had as yet recognised the need to take Jinnah and the League seriously.

[125] The failure of his mission left Cripps with the choice of either blaming the Viceroy and some of his colleagues in the War Cabinet, or the Congress. Not surprisingly, he chose to blame Congress and its demand for an immediate National Government at the centre. He interpreted Congress's stand as implying a demand for a system of government 'responsible to no legislature or electorate . . . and the majority of whom would be in a position to dominate large minorities'. (Broadcast by Cripps, 11 April 1942, cited in Rizvi, *Linlithgow and India*, p. 203, fn. 2.)

3

Jinnah and the Muslim-majority provinces

Although the Cripps mission had failed, it had underlined the basic contradiction in the League's demand for Pakistan. Offering provinces and not communities the right to opt out posed a potential threat to Jinnah's efforts to bring the Muslim-majority provinces under a specifically communal banner at the centre. A few of the more perceptive politicians could see that the provincial option was incompatible with following the lead of a communal party at the all-India level. It raised the awkward issue of what might happen to non-Muslim minorities in the Muslim-majority provinces if Muslim politicians in these provinces rallied behind Jinnah and the League. Here was an opportunity for the Congress to exploit the inherent weakness in Jinnah's strategy. Certainly it now became crucial for Jinnah to somehow secure the allegiance of Muslim politicians, particularly in the legislatures of the Muslim-majority provinces.[1]

At least one Congressman was aware of Jinnah's difficulties, and ready to make the most of them. Rajagopalachari urged his High Command to give the Muslim provinces the option to go their own way. This would enable the Indian union to have a strong government at the centre. In his opinion, 'partition' was by far the lesser evil than forcing Muslim provinces to stay in. By accepting local option, Congress at the end of the day would safeguard its power at the centre and in all probability the League would be tossed into oblivion. A wedge might successfully be driven between Muslim politicians who wanted to keep their provinces intact and the Leaguers at the centre whose undefined demand, inevitably communal rather than provincial, threatened the cross-communal understandings upon which the provincial integrity of the Punjab and Bengal depended. But the Congress High Command shirked from taking

---

[1] In a constituent assembly set up along the lines suggested in Cripps's proposals, the League could hope to have a say only if a majority of the Muslim representatives in the provincial legislatures of both the majority and the minority provinces were in its camp. But since the majority provinces were more likely to use local option, it was particularly important for the League to have a majority in the Punjab, Bengal, Sind and the N.W.F.P. legislatures. This alone could guarantee Jinnah a place in the constitutional negotiations which were to follow at the end of the war.

this step: on 2 May 1942 an overwhelming majority of 120 against fifteen voted down Rajagopalachari's cynical but far-sighted resolution.[2]

But even if the Congress High Command failed to make the point publicly, Sikander Hayat had taken it on board in the Punjab. He recognised that a demand for Pakistan, cut loose from the strict disciplines of the Punjab thesis, threatened the unity of his province. In May 1942 he resigned from the League's Working Committee and in July subtly demonstrated that the demand for Muslim self-determination might bring about the partition of the Punjab. Once Punjabi Muslims realised this, they would, Sikander hoped, think twice before blindly following Jinnah.[3] Significantly, the Viceroy and the Governor of the Punjab understood the real purpose of Sikander's July proposal, but they did not give it the publicity it deserved.[4]

Yet again a combination of factors, the unwillingness of the Congress to recognise its own limitations and the expediency of the British – saved Jinnah from having the fatal weaknesses of his position publicly exposed. With the Congress leadership conveniently in jail in the aftermath of the 'Quit India' resolution,[5] Jinnah returned to his safe but negative line of attack, condemning Congress dictatorship, past and future, and standing pat on a demand which remained conveniently unspecific.[6] Asked if

[2] In April 1942, Rajagopalachari persuaded the Congress assembly party in Madras to pass a resolution which urged the High Command to let the Muslim provinces go their own way; this would give Congress a chance of forming a strong 'National Government' instead of making a futile attempt to maintain 'the unity of India'. (*Civil and Military Gazette*, 25 April 1942.)

[3] Sikander proposed that if the Punjab assembly failed to settle clearly for accession to or separation from the Indian union, then Muslims should decide the issue by a referendum; but in those parts of the Punjab where Muslims were not in a majority (the eastern districts in the main), there should also be another referendum giving those parts the option to sever themselves from the province. At first glance, Sikander might appear to be advocating the partition of the Punjab, something that was anathema to him. But, as Glancy realised, Sikander's subtle hope was to show that Jinnah's 'Pakistan' would smash the unity of his province and in this way to kill unthinking enthusiasm for it. (Glancy to Linlithgow, 10 July 1942, *T.P.*, II, 359–60.)

[4] Glancy and Linlithgow persuaded themselves that Sikander's proposal would not in fact expose the fundamental weakness of Pakistan, and that discretion was the better part of the new Punjab tradition. (Linlithgow to Glancy, 17 July 1942, ibid., p. 402.)

[5] On 8 August 1942, the A.I.C.C. called for an immediate British withdrawal and sanctioned a mass movement under Gandhi's leadership. The next day, Government arrested Gandhi and the members of the Working Committee, and outlawed the Congress organisation. With its experience of handling the second civil disobedience movement behind it, and with its powers massively afforced by wartime authority, the Raj was ready to tackle a movement which was designed to move the British towards the table while most of its own activists sat still, or at worst rested, in jail.

[6] The 'Quit India' slogan, Jinnah contended, was 'a mere camouflage and what is really aimed at is supreme control of the Government of the country by the Congress'.

the League might now trim its demands, Jinnah retorted: 'If you start by asking for sixteen annas, there is room for bargaining . . . Hindu India has got three-fourths of India in its pocket and it is Hindu India which is bargaining to see if it can get the remaining one-fourth for itself and diddle us out of it.'[7] This, as even the Viceroy had guessed, was a 'highly ingenious move in Jinnah's game of poker'.[8] Wanting and needing a centre, Jinnah's bid for the whole rupee was intended not to buy a ticket away from Delhi but a seat at the centre. Jinnah, the Viceroy speculated:

anxious as he may be to turn this question [Pakistan] to advantage in his political battle, must in his own mind, for his intelligence is considerable, realise that problems of finance, tariff control, of assistance from the Centre, and the like which any separation must involve, are all of first class importance and significance, and must realise too both that they have to be faced, and how hard a battle would be fought over them by the Hindu side in any negotiations or discussions designed to lead to any agreement on the basis of partition.[9]

But these were matters which Jinnah could not even begin to consider until he had brought the Muslim-majority provinces behind the League. This chapter considers how much Jinnah had to concede to the Muslim provinces to win what was little more than a semblance of a mandate from them at the centre, and how little able he was to challenge the authority of the provincial bosses in their own domains.

Section 1

(a) The Punjab

The key to the League's future lay in the Punjab. Government House at Lahore and the Punjab politicians were at one: they wanted the *status quo*, fences between the communities to be mended, and a League ministry to be kept out. In May 1942 Sikander had shown his hand and he began to probe the possibility of a deal with the Congress. But his death later the same year removed one of the main obstacles to Jinnah's plan of cajoling Muslim politicians of the Unionist persuasion to cross the floor into a League ministry. Sikander was succeeded by Khizar Hayat Tiwana, a man belonging to the same tradition as Fazl-i-Husain and Sikander, but not of their calibre. However the scramble among the leaders to grab Sikander's mantle meant that for the one who got in, there

Gandhi's pious hopes that the Hindu–Muslim problem would resolve itself as soon as the British departed was a 'fantastic theory'. The Quaid-i-Azam preferred his own theories. (See Sherwani (ed.), *Pakistan Resolution to Pakistan*, pp. 72–3.)

[7] Jinnah's press conference, 13 September 1942, *T.P.*, II, 958.
[8] Linlithgow to Amery, 24 August 1942, ibid., 810.
[9] Linlithgow to Amery, 14 September 1942, ibid., 964.

were the many who were left out. In the Unionist chain, Hayats and Daultanas were now the weakest link.[10] But exploiting Unionist splits was quite a different matter from backing the rump of genuine Leaguers, protesting noisily but unimpressively from the urban margins of the Punjab. Barkat Ali, used by now to rough treatment from his leader, was slapped down when he suggested that Jinnah should give a lead to his embattled loyalists.[11] Jinnah denounced the Muslim League Workers' Board, designed specifically to challenge the Unionist stranglehold over the Provincial League.[12] With Khizar's allegiance hanging very much in the balance, Jinnah was not prepared to risk losing his passport to the centre issued by a Punjab ministry in the vain hope of building up a disciplined League party in the provincial assembly, or having a real organisation in the localities and districts of the Punjab.[13]

[10] Selecting Sikander's heir was a problem because no rules and precedents existed for settling the succession. Chhotu Ram, who spoke for the Hindu Jats from Hariana was the senior member of the Unionist coalition, but he wisely recognised that the Punjab had to have a Muslim premier. Three main Muslim families had their eyes on this prize: the Noon-Tiwanas of Sargodha, the Hayats of Wah (Sikander's family) and the Daultanas of Multan. The Hayats of Wah had links with the Daultanas who fought it out with the Noon-Tiwanas locally in Sargodha constituency. When Khizar was appointed, the Hayats and Daultanas were understandably put out. On the surface, Khizar's election on 23 January 1943 as Unionist boss was unanimous, but union among the Unionists had been badly damaged underneath. To appease the Hayats of Wah, Khizar gave Sikander's eldest son, Shaukat Hayat, a consolation prize in his ministry. Nawab Shah of Mamdot, the president of the Unionist-dominated Provincial League, had also died in 1942; his son, Nawab Iftikhar Husain Khan of Mamdot, succeeded him. He also belonged to Sikander's camp.

[11] Sikander's death encouraged the improbably buoyant Barkat Ali to ask Jinnah to organise a separate League party in the assembly, but of course Jinnah could not risk endorsing such a move. He ordered Barkat Ali to stand back; he was 'watching the situation and let us wait and see how things develop'. (Jinnah to Barkat Ali, 3 January 1943, in Afzal (ed.), *Malik Barkat Ali: His Life and Writings*, pp. 309–10.)

[12] In January 1943, a Muslim League Workers' Conference was held in Lahore with Nawabzada Rashid Ali Khan, the Lahore City League's president, in the chair. The Conference elected seven permanent members on the Workers' Board: Maulana Zafar Ali Khan (president); Barkat Ali and Mian Nurullah (senior vice-presidents); Nawabzada Rashid Ali Khan (general secretary); Syed Mustafa Shah Gilani (secretary); Haji Abul Karim (financial secretary); and Khan Rab Nawaz Khan (propaganda secretary). See Punjab Provincial Muslim League 1943–1944, AIML/File 162.

[13] Jinnah immediately denounced this as mutiny and called the Board to order. (Jinnah to Nawabzada Rashid Ali Khan, 13 February 1943, Jafri (ed.), *Correspondence with Punjab Muslim Leaders*, p. 318.) The Board wanted all Muslim members of the assembly to resign from the Unionists and join the League assembly party, and on 7 March 1943 Maulana Abdul Hamid Badauni actually moved a resolution to that effect in the Provincial League Council. Khizar retorted that a League assembly party already existed under the terms of the 1937 Sikander–Jinnah pact. So Jinnah had no choice but

Jinnah, the pragmatist, had one concern: his strategy at the centre. His tactics paid some dividends: at the A.I.M.L.'s annual session in April 1943 he was able at least to claim that the Punjab ministry was behind the League. His only, and seemingly innocuous, message to the League ministries in the majority provinces was that they should beware of becoming tools in gubernatorial hands.[14] Even this mild intervention presented a potential threat to the Unionists. By paying lip-service to the League, Khizar hoped to continue to keep Punjab out of Jinnah's ken, but there was always the danger that some Muslim politicians might 'sell the Unionist fort for their own personal advantage'.[15] Uninformed enthusiasm for 'Pakistan' in Muslim circles was a political resource which Punjab's many factions, even more numerous opportunists and rather fewer ideologues could use to undermine the Unionist coalition. So it would have suited Khizar if the British had stated, loud and clear, what grave implications Pakistan had for the Punjab. But the priorities and prejudices of the Viceroy at the centre saved Jinnah from having to define the indefinable.

By May 1943, Khizar's fears began to come true. Sikander's son, Shaukat Hayat, who had been brought into ministry as a gesture to the Hayats of Wah, having fallen out with Khizar, fell in with Jinnah.[16] But for Khizar it was worse than that. Shaukat was urged on by the chiefs of two other big families, Mamdot and Daultana.[17] The fragile unity of the grandees of Shahpur and Wah was visibly cracking. The Sikander–Jinnah pact, which gave the Unionists hard local bases in the Punjab and Jinnah his will-o'-the-wisp at the centre, was now coming to be questioned by the very politicians in whose provincial interest it had been made. Here was an opportunity to push Khizar out, and put more League stuffing into the ministerial carcass.[18] Everything was now grist

to insist that this awkward resolution should be withdrawn – hardly the action of a man in command of Punjabi affairs.

[14] See Jinnah's address to the A.I.M.L. session at Delhi, 24 April 1943, in Pirzada (ed.), *Foundations of Pakistan*, vol. II, 405–6 and *T.P.*, II, 919–20.

[15] Glancy to Linlithgow, 17 April 1943, *T.P.*, III, 899.

[16] Shaukat Hayat, who had been bought out of the army to be brought into the cabinet, wanted his father's place on the *gadi* (throne). But he calculated that the League might serve his purpose better than the Unionists since it had fewer plausible leaders to do down. Jinnah had no time for this impertinent youth and advised him to go back to posturing in the army and to leave politics alone. Later Jinnah had to curb his disdain for Shaukat and saw the wisdom of making terms with the son of Punjab's ex-premier who, unlike the trader's son who had made his own world, had been born with the silver spoon in his mouth.

[17] This factional alignment augured well for the League's prospects in the Punjab, as the elections of 1945–6 were to show.

[18] In May 1943, Mamdot claimed that the Sikander–Jinnah pact had come to an end; he

to the anti-Khizar mill: the grievances of professional groups hit by rising prices,[19] and the ambitions of families, whether rising or falling, who saw a chance of tipping the balance in their own favour.[20]

By the middle of 1943, Khizar's opponents were ready to make a bid for power. Their tactic was to challenge Khizar either to reaffirm his allegiance to the League or to declare his independence from it. The survival of Khizar and his Unionist coalition depended on their taking a stand on the Sikander–Jinnah pact.[21] On his side, Jinnah had to decide

wrote spirited letters to Jinnah about the League's changing fortunes: 'We have now reached a stage where nobody has the guts to say anything against the League. I have purposely tried to involve the Muslim Ministers knowing that none of them will have the courage to say 'no'. We must assert ourselves because we know that the masses are with us.' (Mamdot to Jinnah, 19 May 1943, Jafri (ed.), *Correspondence with Punjab Muslim Leaders*, p. 222.) Jinnah's satisfaction at this turn of events is apparent from his comments to Barkat Ali; he admitted that: 'the position of the Muslim League in the Punjab is very sad indeed . . . All I can say is – patience. The League is bound now to go ahead. I have full confidence that our opponents and enemies will fail.' (Jinnah to Barkat Ali, 23 June 1943, ibid., p. 72.)

19 The anti-Khizar groups were able to turn Punjab's economic troubles against the Unionist ministry. In January 1943, firms buying supplies of wheat for the army had been exempted from price control. This encouraged zamindars and urban dealers to hoard wheat in order to sell it at higher prices to the exempted firms. Commodities whose prices were controlled disappeared from the bazaars, and black marketing flourished. Nearly all the districts reported a shortage of wheat, and many reported that sugar, small change, fuel and matches could not be bought for love or money. (See Punjab Chief Secretary's Report, first half of January 1943, L/P&J/5/246, I.O.L.) The rise in the cost of living hit fixed-income groups in the towns. Some Muslim members of the provincial civil service now openly supported the League. It has been argued that Muslim officials gave the League such strength as it came to possess in the province. (See Humayun Kabir, 'Muslim politics, 1942–7', in Philips and Wainwright (eds.), *The Partition of India: Policies and Perspectives 1935–1947*, p. 390.)

20 Shaukat Hayat was conspiring with Mamdot to oust Khizar. His ministerial colleagues in their turn wanted Shaukat out. His 'unpardonably indiscreet references' to 'Pakistan' gave pro-League factions and their newspapers their opening to claim that the Unionist ministry was at an end, and it sparked off a 'mischievous and unedifying controversy' over the question whether the party in power was a League coalition, or a coalition, not pure but perhaps simple, a combination, or an union. (See Glancy to Linlithgow, 6 August 1943, L/P&J/5/246, p. 57, I.O.L.) In their turn, the pro-Khizar Unionists were trying to do down Mamdot, and hoped to get rid of him at the next Provincial League elections. This was why Mamdot in his turn curried favour with Jinnah by pressing Khizar to issue a statement acknowledging the League's control over his ministry.

21 Khizar, the Governor thought, was 'determined to take his stand on the Sikander–Jinnah Pact and to insist on retaining the term "Unionist Coalition" (both of which expressions figure in the Pact) as the correct designation of his party'. But if Jinnah pressed Khizar, Glancy was afraid that the premier might resign and thought it 'disquieting . . . that a pre-eminently Muslim Government, which, whatever its defects, has carried on for so many years with reasonable efficiency, should now collapse through the machinations of the Quaid-i-Azam and be replaced by a system of administration set

whether openly to challenge Khizar or to keep things as they were. Although Shaukat and some provincial Leaguers tried to pull members of the assembly out of the Khizar camp under the convenient pretext of backing 'Pakistan', Khizar survived. He survived because he was shrewder than Shaukat and Mamdot (which was not too difficult) and because he still had the votes of most Muslim politicians in the assembly, the support of some Hindus and Sikhs, and official backing (which was a more precarious advantage).²² But of course hanging on to the ministry was to cost the Khizar coalition dear; the demands for men and food which the war imposed upon the Punjab, the rationing and price controls they entailed, meant that the coalition ministry was inevitably tarred with the brush of unpopular governmental intervention.²³

When Jinnah met Khizar in September 1943, he had to settle for the old terms, and all he could do was to instruct the anti-Khizar groups that Muslims in the assembly should patch up their differences.²⁴ For his part, Khizar had to pay a more vocal lip-service to Jinnah. This involved going through the motions of establishing a specifically Muslim League assembly party which would be subject to League party discipline and organisation according to the best paper principles of the Quaid-i-Azam. In November 1943, Khizar deemed his Muslim parliamentary sup-

up under section 93 of the Act'. (Glancy to Linlithgow, 6 August 1943, L/P&J/5/246, p. 57, I.O.L.)

²² Glancy did not want a League ministry since it was bound to aggravate communal tensions and undermine the war effort. By the middle of 1943, recruitment in the Punjab had fallen sharply, because men were needed in the fields and the high price of food and the high wages for growing it made the army a less attractive career. (See Punjab Chief Secretary's Report, first half of June 1943, ibid). The Unionists, with their influence in the rural areas, were more likely to bring the recruits in than the League's city-slickers.

²³ The Bengal famine made the Punjab more crucial than ever for feeding India. To prevent the Punjab profiting from Bengal's distress, the Viceroy was ready to impose Section 93. (Linlithgow to Glancy, *T.P.*, IV, 179–80.) Jinnah could see some advantages in this threat of Section 93. It would warn Khizar and his ministry to toe Delhi's line, and force him to accept the price controls. In their turn, these measures would hit the Unionists' staunchest supporters in the countryside who wanted to do well out of the troubles of other Indians. Memories of the frustrating autumn of 1943 had something to do with the voters' choice in Punjab's rural localities in the crucial elections of 1945–6. (Glancy to Wavell, 30 October 1943, L/P&J/5/246, pp. 32–3.)

²⁴ Jinnah told Mamdot that Khizar had agreed to meet with the leaders of the Provincial League, and wanted them to 'put your heads together among yourselves in the first instance and try to come to a[n] unanimous decision, or at any rate backed up by a solid majority'. But the League assembly party 'must be established on a sound and proper footing as it has been agreed upon [with Khizar] and I hope that you will see to it and it must have its constitution, rules, its office-bearers, executive, etc., . . . '. (Jinnah to Mamdot, 11 September 1943, Jafri (ed.), *Correspondence with Punjab Muslim Leaders*, p. 224.)

porters to be a League assembly party. At least on paper, Jinnah's demands had been met: the assembly party was brought under the control and discipline of the Central and Provincial League Parliamentary Boards and, in matters specifically relating to Muslims, the members had to vote in accordance with the party line.[25] But these paper arrangements did not alter the fact that the League assembly party was effectively under Unionist management. Khizar's victory over Mamdot's group was subtle but sure; the Sikander–Jinnah pact had been unanimously ratified by the meeting and, by a majority vote, it was decided to incorporate it into the assembly party's constitution. Jinnah's self-appointed lieutenants now lamented that the Unionists had been able to remain independent because of the terms of the pact. So in practice things remained as they had always been.

When the A.I.M.L. resolved to strengthen its central authority at its Karachi session in December 1943, this simply underlined the gap between profession and practice, between large claims and puny realities in the control which the League had still conspicuously failed to exercise over its provincial arms. Jinnah called for a Committee of Action and a Central Parliamentary Board, whose members he would nominate. This was the 'next step' in the League's programme of creating an 'organizational machinery' in every province linked to the High Command. Its main utility would be to save Jinnah from having to make awkward decisions in provincial matters, especially when it involved supporting one Muslim faction against another. As the ultimate authority in all disputes, he would only need to intervene if he wanted to overrule the decisions taken by these two Committees. On 27 December, Jinnah appointed six members to the Committee of Action, and charged them with the task of 'organizing, co-ordinating and unifying the Provincial League[s] and the entire Muslim League organization in consonance with the Constitution, Rules and Programme of the All-India Muslim League'; its sub-committee would 'control, direct and regulate' all activities of the Provincial Leagues; it could take 'disciplinary action' against any Leaguer or office-bearer who failed to promote the aims and objects of the League, defied the decisions of the Working Committee or obstructed the League's progress in any way; and it could suspend or disaffiliate any Provincial League for failing in its duties or ignoring 'the decisions or directions of the higher bodies'. The Central Parliamentary Board was another effort at centralisation; it would serve as the authority to resolve disputes over party tickets, and all Provincial Parliamentary Boards would be subordinate to it.[26] Big words, easier to spell out than to

[25] *Eastern Times*, Lahore, 10 November 1943.
[26] Pirzada (ed.), *Foundations of Pakistan*, vol. II, pp. 449–52 and 487–8.

stick to, but it is interesting that Jinnah chose to follow the Congress's model in his efforts to centralise the League.

By 1944, when Wavell, the new Viceroy, reminded India that the Cripps offer was still open, Jinnah was still trying to bring the ministries and assemblies in the majority provinces into line.[27] Two newly-created Committees were sent to Lahore to spy out the land and see if a ministry more overtly in the League camp could be formed.[28] But the situation remained much the same. Those who wanted to do down Khizar were still mainly interested in their own 'personal advancement and . . . [could not] claim any wide Muslim support', and there was 'no reason to believe that this position has changed'.[29] The League's visiting firemen (the Election Enquiry Committee and the more ambitious Committee of Action, the paper-products of the December 1943 resolutions) met with a damp reception.[30] Jinnah's lieutenants merely 'served to accentuate the differences between the contending parties and to weaken the already unstable Punjab Muslim League organisation'.[31] Indeed if Jinnah had had a choice, he would have preferred to keep well clear of the Punjab's in-fighting; his only interest was to hang on to the ministry's allegiance at the centre. From his point of view, there was little to choose between the different Punjabi factions, but now he could no longer avoid taking sides.

So reluctantly, in March 1944, the man who had sworn after his 1936 visit never to return to the Punjab, was forced yet again to come back. His mission was simply to paper over the cracks in a province critical to his strategy but really outside his sphere of political influence. He had been outmanoeuvred by his provincial supporters into threatening Khizar with the big stick, and had been compelled to puff up a League which had yet to prove that it had the necessary bottom. He did so by adopting a belligerent stance. He criticised the Unionist party's constitution; then publicly he repudiated the Sikander–Jinnah pact. This stung Chhotu Ram, the Hindu Jat leader and the most important non-Muslim member of the ministry, into voicing Hindu and Sikh outrage at this importunate intervention. In his turn, Jinnah retorted by denouncing

---

[27] On 20 October 1943, Wavell became the Viceroy of India. On 17 February 1944, he told a joint session of the central legislature that the Cripps offer was still open.

[28] The first, the Election Enquiry Committee, was sent to investigate a petition objecting to Mamdot's re-election as president of the Punjab League and to supervise the nomination of Punjab's representatives to the A.I.M.L. Council. The second, the Committee of Action, was instructed to look into the reorganisation of the Punjab League.

[29] Punjab Chief Secretary's Report, first half of February 1944, L/P&J/5/247, I.O.L.

[30] According to the Chief Secretary, 'A cynical view is that only the hotel keepers, who benefited from the lavish entertainments given to the members of the Committee [of Action], knew of its presence in Lahore.' (Ibid.)

[31] Ibid.

Chhotu Ram's Jat Sabha as anti-Islamic.[32] He then went on to condemn the chairman of the Punjab Muslim Students Federation's reception committee for the socialistic tone of his address and advised the students not to be swept off their feet by slogans like: 'Down with the Nawabs'; instead they should turn their attention towards commerce and industry; he tried to steer them away from the politically unrewarding line of attacking rural interests, in a province where it was these interests which mattered most, by promising a League programme for the 'economic regeneration of the Muslim community'. He also rejected overtures by the Ahrars,[33] the Khaksars[34] and the Communists for a joint front.[35] In a line reminiscent of the Congress's in 1937, Jinnah called upon all non-League Muslim parties to go into voluntary liquidation and join the League's bandwagon. But when it came to stating the League's objectives in precise terms all Jinnah could do was to present platitudes about 'Pakistan' as the 'panacea for all evils', but he 'carefully avoided any reasoned explanation of where it begins and ends and what benefits it will confer'.[36] As in 1936, so eight years later Jinnah discovered that high-flying phrases did not go down well with the Punjabi notables; many Muslim members of the assembly from rural constituencies resented this outside interference in their domestic affairs. Between ten and twenty-five waverers at most – hardly the basis for a new ministry – were all

[32] Punjab Chief Secretary's Report, second half of March 1944. (Ibid.)
[33] Since 1940 the Ahrars had opposed the League's demand for 'Pakistan'. In November 1940 they had officially merged with the Congress. But the failure of the 'Quit India' movement in the Punjab had forced the Ahrars to reassess their political stance. By 1944 they were prepared to come to terms with the League if 'Pakistan' was based on Islamic principles. When Jinnah turned down their offer of help they branded him as the Kafir-i-Azam (the Great Infidel) and reaffirmed their links with the Congress. An interesting commentary on the various possible combinations of politics and Islam in the Indian setting.
[34] The Khaksars were a non-communal (but predominantly Muslim) para-military organisation under the leadership of Inayatullah Khan, better known as Allama Mashriqi. A self-avowed admirer of Hitler, whom he had met in 1926, Mashriqi saw the Khaksars as the Indian version of the German SS, and made it a point to issue impertinent 'orders' to Jinnah. In 1943 a Khaksar tried to assassinate Jinnah after which a somewhat chastened Mashriqi was reduced to embarrassing the League leader by demanding that he make terms with the Congress whenever agreement seemed least likely, for instance when Rajagopalachari produced his formula for a 'Pakistan' based on the partition of the Punjab and Bengal, or when Gandhi insisted on independence before the settlement of the communal problem in September 1944. Naturally Jinnah wanted nothing to do with the Khaksars, least of all Mashriqi.
[35] *Indian Annual Register*, 1944, vol. I, pp. 202–9.
[36] From the Punjab's standpoint, Glancy likened Jinnah to an 'ideal leader for a Demolition Squad', good for destroying but not for building something in its place. (Glancy to Wavell, 6 April 1944, *T.P.*, IV, 861.)

Jinnah could identify by way of new support. Of course the prospect of another election might, the Governor realised, change the picture, since there was no telling in what direction a 'fanatical wind . . . blowing in favour of the League candidates' might turn the weathercock of Punjabi opportunism.[37] The Unionist 'party' itself was a ramshackle coalition of opportunist politicians, without much organisation or funds, or indeed discipline, of its own. Switching from Unionist to League required no structural change in Punjab politics, let alone a change in the ideological creed of the converts. Above all it did not presuppose any radical alteration in the balance of power in the localities.

But Jinnah's snipings did have their effect upon Khizar. He now told Glancy that he had no appetite for politics and wanted to retire as soon as the war was over. But he was anxious not to leave his followers in the lurch – and the future belonged to the Congress and, willy-nilly, to the League. Khizar thought that the landlord or 'loyalist' class of the Punjab might be sacrificed sooner than they otherwise might if he decided to hold out against Jinnah. The League would deploy the mullahs to fan the fires of communalism, and would 'not hesitate to revert to other still more nefarious methods of attack'. Admitting that the Unionist party existed only in name, Khizar confessed that its disappearance would cause little regret. Of course, Khizar assured the Governor, he did not believe in 'Pakistan', yet this disheartened politician felt that the 'Pakistan slogan is bound to gain momentum and . . . it is likely to become a decisive factor in the next elections'. According to Khizar's estimates, and they were higher than those of Glancy, the number of his Muslim supporters in the assembly who would defect to Jinnah stood at thirty-two; but even after these defections the Unionists would have a comfortable majority in the house.[38] For the time being, however, Khizar's sagging morale was stiffened by some official starch. For one thing the new Viceroy did not share his predecessor's view of the relative priorities between Jinnah and the Punjab. The Punjab mattered to the army, and the army mattered to Wavell. Wavell favoured reminding 'these influential country gentlemen' on which side of their *rotis* the ghee was spread.[39] Bread and butter was something the Punjab bosses

[37] Ibid.

[38] Glancy to Wavell, 14 April 1946, ibid., p. 880–1.

[39] Wavell, influenced by military stereotypes about Indian society, thought that the time had come for the Punjab's landed aristocracy to stand up to the 'town-bred politicians'; if they did so, he thought they would discover a much greater following than they themselves were given to believe. The soldier pro-consul had a point. (Wavell to Glancy, 15 April 1944, ibid., p. 882.) Succumbing to Jinnah's pressures, Glancy warned Khizar, would lead to a 'stampede of waverers' to the League, since many of his supporters were already hedging their bets. (Glancy to Wavell, 24 April 1944, ibid., p. 924.)

understood. At the level of debate, Khizar encouraged by this benign view from the Guardians, managed to score a point over Jinnah over the fascinating question whether it was socially respectable and politically responsible for men to owe a dual allegiance to the Unionists in the province and to the League at the centre.[40] When the Governor lent a hand by turfing out Shaukat, the main trouble-maker, from the ministry, Jinnah decided that a low profile would best maintain the 'facade of Muslim unity' in a province which was the 'corner-stone of Pakistan'.[41]

So Jinnah's terms to Khizar, presented on 27 April 1944, were less an ultimatum than a plea for co-operation. All he asked for was that the ministry should call itself the Muslim League coalition and that League assembly members should belong to one, not to two parties.[42] But Khizar was not ready to accede to even these modest requests; they were 'contrary to the best interests of Muslims in this province'; they would mean repudiating a pact ratified by an overwhelming majority of the Muslim members of the Punjab assembly (fifty-seven against seven); and above all they would endanger the coalition's understandings with other communities by going back upon the 'pledged word of the Muslim community'. Moreover, these demands were an unacceptable inter-ference in provincial affairs. They would 'disturb the inner working of the Ministerial Party', and smacked of 'dictatorship and totalitarian methods'.[43] Khizar was afraid of unleashing communal passions in the Punjab. Paradoxically, he still thought that the best hope of keeping the good ship 'Punjab' on an even keel was to continue to sail under the League and its Lahore resolution, the 'sheet anchor of Muslims in the Punjab as elsewhere'. But at the same time he appealed to the 'sturdy commonsense' and provincial self-interest of the Punjabi Muslim to resist Jinnah's siren calls from the far beyond.[44]

For the time being the ministry survived, and all that Jinnah left behind in the Punjab were yet more instructions on paper on how the League was to organise itself. By two shrewd appointments, Khizar

---

[40] Encouraged by the Viceroy and the Governor, Khizar made a decent showing against Jinnah's dialectics. When Jinnah argued that no man could constitutionally belong to two parties, since it was like keeping a mistress and a wife, Khizar retorted that every Muslim knew that he was entitled to possess at least two wives (Glancy to Wavell, 21 April 1944, ibid., p. 907) – a harsh reminder to this lonely man who had lost the one woman who had broken through, albeit temporarily, his reserve in human relationships.

[41] Punjab Chief Secretary's Report, second half of April 1944, L/P&J/5/247, p. 88, I.O.L.

[42] Ibid.   [43] *Indian Annual Register*, 1944, vol. I, pp. 219–20.

[44] In a parody, deliberate or unconscious, of the Quaid-i-Azam, Khizar added: 'This is no time for petty squabbles and rivalries but for making a sincere and united effort to do our duty to our country at this critical stage of the war and to consolidate the Muslims for the constitutional struggle ahead for which we are all united.' (Ibid.)

scotched the nascent revolt in the assembly, took the wind out of the opposition's sails, and reduced the potential desertions from the Unionist benches from thirty-two to eighteen.[45] The factional struggles of the Punjab had forced a reluctant Jinnah to back a loser. Now he had no alternative but to expel Khizar from the League,[46] ending a League–Unionist alliance which had survived for seven years, and losing not only Khizar but three other Muslim ministers who resigned from the League in protest against the High Command's high-handed interference in Punjab's internal affairs.[47] This marked the beginning of a more deadly factional struggle among Muslims in the Punjab, just at a time when Jinnah at the centre most needed the appearance of solidarity. According to Makhdum Murid Hussain Quereshi, a member of an important Multan family, Mamdot and his colleagues, 'who only want to achieve their own end' had failed to give Jinnah the true picture. The League needed organisation in the towns and villages, whereas Mamdot's lot were 'satisfied in saying that the [M]uslims of the big cities bear sympathies with their organisation, but the main masses of the nation, the residents of the rural areas, are nowhere in the League and I still doubt even their familiarity with the main organisation of the nation'. Jinnah's intervention in the Punjab had 'split the whole nation' and it was 'useless to wait [and see] which party beats the other, as the efforts and activities of both parties will make the situation, bad to worse'.[48] So by mid-1944, Jinnah's mandate from the Punjab at the centre had been seriously questioned and this development had not been counterbalanced by any increase in his real power inside the Punjab. Everyone could see that his 'shares in the political market' had fallen.[49] When Jinnah met Gandhi in September 1944, he was in the familiar position of negotiating from weakness, not from strength. Not surprisingly, Jinnah stuck to his old and wholly negative stance and the talks came to nothing.

---

[45] Wavell to Amery, 16 May 1944, *T.P.*, IV, 969. The two new ministers were both influential in their respective districts: Jamal Khan Leghari was a Baluch Tumundar from the Dera Ghazi Khan district and the leader of the influential Leghari tribe; Nawab Ashiq Hussain was a member of the important Quereshi family in Multan district.

[46] In May 1944, the Committee of Action expelled Khizar from the League. Ironically the charge against him was that he had allowed Glancy to get rid of Shaukat. Jinnah called upon Khizar to ask Glancy for a satisfactory explanation of the charges against Shaukat and to resign if he did not get it. (See Punjab Chief Secretary's Report, second half of April 1944, L/P&J/5/247, p. 88, I.O.L.)

[47] The three Muslim ministers were Abdul Haye, Mohammad Jamal Khan Leghari and Ashiq Hussain.

[48] See Makhdum Murid Hussain Quereshi to Jinnah, 16 June 1944, QAP/File No. 1092, p. 251.

[49] Glancy to Wavell, 23 August 1944, *T.P.*, IV, 1223–4.

After its break with Khizar in May 1944, the League made plans to organise a drive into the Punjab localities. Having lost its Unionist allies, the League had either to construct a rural base of its own or win over some local notables from the Unionist camp. Sporadic rural rides by city-bred students, invective against Unionists and vague but strident appeals to universal Islam were hardly a recipe for success among the hard-headed lords and their local pietism. Boldly calling for a radical pro-gramme designed to appeal to the masses,[50] Mumtaz Daultana argued that it was the people not 'the landlords or the zaildar–lamburdar [sic] clans' who would make or break the League.[51] But this was a dangerous course entailing an assault upon the bastions of Punjab's rural conserva-tism, and this was not something the High Command and the Provincial League were ready to undertake. The safe way was to dangle induce-ments before the rural notables,[52] and hope by exploiting their rivalries to make terms with the winning side.

Some Punjabi Leaguers who wanted to do down both Mamdot and Daultana now calculated that their provincial prospects would improve if the League's programme had a more religious tone. In October 1944, Abdus Sattar Niazi called a meeting in Lahore to discuss making Pakistan an Islamic state.[53] The *Civil and Military Gazette* saw this as an open rebellion against Jinnah and the League. It had a point. In April 1943 at the League's Delhi session, Jinnah had carefully skated around the issue, arguing that: 'The Constitution and the Government [of

[50] So far, Daultana argued with some justification, the League had produced nothing concrete for the Punjab; it had remained 'too vaguely conditional' or else 'too legal and technical' about the Sikander–Jinnah pact. (Report of the Punjab Provincial Muslim League for June–July 1944, AIML/SHC/3/File 30, Punjab, vol. I.)

[51] Ibid. Daultana himself was a landlord. But just as the resources of conservatism inside the Congress had been strong enough in the nineteen-thirties to disarm the well-meaning radicalism of young men such as Jawaharlal Nehru and Subhas Bose, so too were Muslim India's men of substance able to keep their firebrands in check a decade later. Daultana's appeals for a more specific and 'immediate propaganda which is suited to the local needs of the Province and is democratic and anti-bureaucratic', cut no ice with the pragmatists. His proposals for a 'legislative manifesto from the Punjab League Party . . . which would distinguish the League from Khizar's Party of the "Friends of the Government" ' as a "People's party" ' fared no better – as late as December 1944, the Provincial League remained without a manifesto.

[52] One consequence of the League's unimpressive excursions into rural Punjab had been to stir its rival, the Unionist party, to revive its organisation outside the assembly, the Zamindara League. The League reacted by denouncing the Zamindara League as a mere instrument of the National War Front, which was, by 'violent coercion', milching the local landlords. Certainly landlords of Jhang district refused to pay up and opted for the League. Yet many other Unionist supporters still thought their interests would be better served by continuing to support Khizar's ministry. (Ibid.)

[53] See *Nawa-i-Waqt*, Lahore, 12 October 1944.

Pakistan] will be what the people will decide.'[54] A resolution which would have committed the League to basing the future constitution of Pakistan on Islamic principles was quietly withdrawn at Jinnah's insistence.[55] So Niazi was forced to argue that the meeting of would-be religious divines (dominated significantly by men from the U.P.) was loyal to the Lahore resolution, which in any case had nothing to say about the future government of Pakistan. By inference, every Muslim had the right to try his hand at shaping the future by convincing his co-religionists. Jinnah preferred to leave the convincing to men who mattered in the Punjab, like Daultana, who needed to keep the way open to an alliance with non-Muslims in the assembly. Not only did Daultana want to throw out a line to Hindus and Sikhs, he also was glad to see Communists joining the League. They joined on the declared basis of backing the submerged nationalities – Sindhis, Baluchis, Pathans and Bengalis just as much as the Punjabis – and not on the basis of Muslims constituting a separate nation.

With these new recruits Daultana made yet another effort to woo rural Punjab. Despite a flurry of district conferences which aimed to win round the assembly members, few of them actually changed sides. The irony of the Muslim League making a big play of its attempts to forge a united front with Hindus and Sikhs against the ministry may have been lost on the Punjab but should be spotted by its historian. Some in the League became the champions of Congress *détenus* in the hope that the assembly members who came out of jail would gratefully vote with them to bring down the ministry; the League's assembly party's manifesto declared that all minorities would be protected in Pakistan.[56] Daultana was delighted in Montgomery District to find Hindus and Sikhs ready to join the League in toppling Khizar.[57] In Okara, many 'non-Muslim friends (mainly communists and congressmen)' were present, and 'not even in the hey-day of the Congress movement in the Punjab, did that organization succeed in mass contacting the rural areas to the extent to which the Muslim League Speakers' Party has been able to do within a short space of 4 days spent in Montgomery District.' All this was seen as proof positive of the 'genuine desire of the League Executive to make it a

[54] Jinnah's address to the A.I.M.L., Delhi, April 1943, in Pirzada (ed,), *Foundations of Pakistan*, vol. II, p. 425.

[55] The resolution was drafted by Dr Abdul Hameed Kazi (Bombay). It called for Pakistan's constitution to be based on the Quran and the Hakoomat-i-Illahiya (government based on the principles of the first four Caliphs of Islam). Jinnah thought this amounted to a 'vote of censure' on every Leaguer, and his intervention ensured that the draft resolution was swept under the red carpet. (See ibid., p. 440, f.2, and p. 425.)

[56] See *Nawa-i-Waqt*, 9 November 1944.

[57] Ibid., 8 January 1945.

people's party in the real sense of the word'. But their conception of a 'people's party' verged on the absurd. At Shergarh, the four main features of the League meeting were: first, that it was a 'purely zamindars gathering – the land lords and the tillers of the soil all coming from backward areas but all eager to know'; secondly, that the 'nobles . . . the Pirs of Shergarh, Hussaingarh, Mustafa-abad and Dipalpur etc. were present in large numbers – several of them being zaildars and lambardars – the class that is generally under the Unionist thumb'; thirdly, that there were plenty of informers and police in uniform; and finally, that sterling work had been done by the Pir of Shergarh's son, the Divisional organiser of the League. The League's travelling circus had moved around in a lorry fitted with loudspeakers, flags, mottoes and slogans. No doubt the Punjabi villagers' fascination with these urban curiosities was genuine, and Jinnah's proud correspondent told the statesman that everywhere it was the lorry which 'evoked considerable interest'.[58]

The League out-groups who wanted to displace the Khizar 'ins' had no choice except to seek cross-communal alliances if they were to achieve their simple purposes, a ministry through which they could enter office.[59] This made perfect sense in the Punjab; but it emphatically underlined once more the discord between Punjabi interests and the A.I.M.L.'s stance at the centre. As Jinnah was told by a local informant, these factional struggles among Punjabi Muslims were 'bound to injure Muslim interests in the Punjab and especially our great cause of Pakistan'; that goal would 'recede further as Muslim members of [the] government Party in their own interest will claim they are non-communal and eventually will become anti-Pakistanis'.[60] The fact of the matter was that 'No Muslim League Government can ever be formed in the Punjab unless we have some Hindus and Sikhs with us.' Indeed some Muslims might cross over to the Congress, even though Congress, under a better discipline from its High Command, was unlikely to make a deal in the Punjab on Jinnah's terms.[61]

So most Muslim assembly members saw good reason to keep their options open. Even those who had crossed over now clambered back upon the fence,[62] and the organisation of the Punjab League remained

---

[58] Nazir Ahmad Khan to Jinnah, 10 January 1945, SHC/Punjab vol. 1, p. 30.
[59] A section of the Akali Sikhs had promised to support the League assembly party once seventy Muslim assembly members had joined its ranks. But by the time the Punjab assembly met in December 1944, the League had the support of only thirty members. (See *Nawa-i-Waqt*, 2 October 1944 and 21 December 1944.) So the Sikhs were kept out of a side which for the moment was reduced to sitting on the opposition benches.
[60] Sheikh Sadiq Hasan to Jinnah, 28 February 1945, SHC/Punjab vol. 1, p. 51.
[61] Ibid.
[62] Three recent converts to the League drifted back into the Unionist fold.

high-sounding in prospectus and low in performance. Many of the League's urban supporters in the Punjab felt that the League was not being properly organised and had failed to achieve a mass character. Indeed, they thought there was no real conflict between town and countryside, merely the old problem of landlord factions warring for advantage in the province.[63] In March 1945, by which time the A.I.M.L. had hoped to have triumphed in Lahore, the Unionist ministry may have been bent but it was still unbroken. The League's session for 1945 scheduled to be held in Lahore had to be postponed since holding it there would simply have advertised Jinnah's weakness in the province that mattered most to him – if the League had failed to win Punjabis at the top, there was little evidence as yet that it had succeeded in mobilising the base. As the Chief Secretary of the Punjab commented, 'During the last year the Islamic appeal behind the League has failed to galvanise the rural Muslim population'. Admittedly, the League had made an impact 'in the urban areas'; but countryfolk, in a province where villagers, not townsmen, were the men who mattered, had not been persuaded by the League's propaganda.[64]

(b) Bengal

When Cripps came to India Jinnah had at least a semblance of a title to speak for the Punjab which his pact with Sikander had given him. But in 1942 the Bengal ministry was led by a man who had broken with Jinnah the previous year, and had kept the Bengal League at bay. In Bengal all Jinnah could do to prepare for Cripps was to urge Muslims to 'follow League policy fanatically', warning them that they could not 'stand on their own legs without whole-heartedly joining the rest of India'.[65] A measure of his impotence was that he had to call upon the Governor to intervene on the League's behalf.[66]

---

[63] See *Nawa-i-Waqt*, editorial, 5 October 1944. This view was partially endorsed by the A.I.M.L.'s Committee of Action. It reported meagre progress in organising the Punjab League; a draft constitution was still being prepared and the rules for primary and district League elections had not as yet been formulated. Admittedly, some receipt books to register two-anna members for the primary Leagues had been issued, but they had not been written up. So it was a little difficult to work out what the League's membership actually was. Those districts that made a show of filling up their books claimed 36,000 primary members, enrolled in the year 1943–4. But these baptisms had touched something under one in a hundred of Punjab's Muslims. (See Committee of Action Report, no. 10, AIML/File No. 201, 26 February 1945.)

[64] Punjab Chief Secretary's Report, first half of March 1945, L/P&J/5/248, I.O.L.

[65] From the Governor-General to the Secretary of State, telegram, 16 February 1942, cited in Sen, *Muslim Politics in Bengal*, p. 169, fn. 104.

[66] Jinnah at the Sirajganj Conference had to ask the Governor to stop Huq's ministry making trouble for the League in Bengal, declaring: 'We are not going to be suppressed

Of course, the maelstrom of Bengal politics did offer some chances for those brave enough to fish in it: there were all manner of political groupings and interests, some more organised than others, some mere alliances of convenience at the top, others possessing stronger links with the base. Many of these shifting factions saw political advantage in capturing the League. But the Bengal Provincial Muslim League (dominated by this or that group) had relatively little concern for Jinnah's strategy at the centre, and conversely Jinnah was mainly a bystander in these complex Bengali affairs. But what Jinnah urgently needed was to topple Huq and have a ministry in Bengal which at least bore the League's name and accepted Jinnah as its spokesman in Delhi. Here he had to depend mainly on two sources of potential support, the Nazimuddin–Nawab of Dacca axis and Suhrawardy's agitational base in Calcutta, and hope that the unpopularity of Huq's ministry, the defection of the Mahasabha leader, Shyma Prasad Mookerji, and above all the precarious nature of the alliance between Huq's Muslims and the Forward Bloc would bring the ministry down.[67] In opposition at least, the Leaguers in the assembly might be persuaded to vote together,[68] whereas Huq's men had begun nimbly to cross the floor – the going price of a vote among the waverers was 'Rs.1000 a piece'.[69] Although Mammon had more to do with it than God, Ispahani praised Allah and reported to Jinnah that 'We are daily gaining strength in the Legislature' and that Huq's Muslims were 'cracking up'.[70] During March 1942, Huq's support dribbled away – 116 on 24 March, they were 109 three days later, when the vote was taken on two successive no-confidence motions.[71]

The Governor in Bengal, Sir John Herbert, did not like Huq and thought better of Nazimuddin. But Huq still had an inconvenient, if uncertain, majority in the house. The League, willing to wound but

---

or tyrannised by this wretched ministry that does not represent Muslims.' (*Morning News*, 16 February 1942, cited in ibid., pp. 169–70.)

[67] On 20 November 1942, Shyma Prasad Mookerji resigned as minister of finance. His overt reason was that British interference, and the influence of a 'coterie of reactionary I.C.S. officers' upon the Governor, had made a mockery of self-government. (See Broomfield, *Elite Conflict in a Plural Society*, p. 282 and Sen, *Muslim Politics in Bengal*, pp. 141–2.) In reality, he was hedging his bets. Huq survived Mookerji's resignation, but now faced one no-confidence motion after another, all engineered by the Leaguers.

[68] In the Bengal council elections, Ispahani reported with pride, tinged with some surprise, that all Leaguers 'voted strictly in accordance with the whip that was issued' while Huq's Progressive Coalition of Muslims and some members of the Forward Bloc 'who total seventy could only register twenty-nine votes for their first nominee'. (Ispahani to Jinnah, 13 March 1943, Zaidi (ed.), *Correspondence*, pp. 325–6.)

[69] Ibid.   [70] Ibid.   [71] Khaliquzzaman, *Pathway to Pakistan*, pp. 296–7.

unable to kill, was able to orchestrate no-confidence motions. But it was not strong or devious enough to fell Huq and replace him with a ministry of its own. In any event, Delhi had a different view. In Bengal the 'last thing we want', the Viceroy could see, 'is an active increase in communal tension'; a League ministry, with Scheduled Caste and European backing would inevitably 'be a serious provocation to caste Hindu feeling'.[72] In the end the Governor did force Huq to resign,[73] but there was no League ministry that he could easily slot into its place. All Jinnah could do was to stand on the sidelines. Actually he shared Delhi's attitude about the danger of virulent communalism in Bengal, and, for the time being at least, he was ready to see Section 93 rule.[74]

Since the League assembly party had at most fifty-five certain votes out of 250, Nazimuddin could only form a ministry if it was a coalition. Predictably, Huq's resignation brought new recruits into the League's camp, a baker's dozen, since the heady scent of loaves and fishes spiced with gubernatorial favour was wafting over the familiar stench of factionalism; another fifteen of the 'cursed Muslim rascals' stood by as potential recruits to those ready to vote with the League party in the assembly.[75] Ispahani had no illusions; at the best of times illusions were hard to sustain in Calcutta. As far as the politicians went, 'We Muslims are an undisciplined and unprincipled lot.' But at least the 'heart of the Muslim masses is sound' and in due course (perhaps with an optimism triumphing over experience) Ispahani expected that 'the feet of the masses will crush the very bones of these cursed politicians who put self above nation'.[76] Eventually Nazimuddin managed to cobble together a majority, and he had to do so by the usual device – patronage.[77] He had to find places in the cabinet for no less than six Hindus and Scheduled Caste

---

[72] Linlithgow to Amery, 11 April, 1943, *T.P.*, III, 881.

[73] Since the no-confidence motions had not actually been passed, Herbert could not demand Huq's resignation and impose Section 93. The Governor was thought to be acting at the behest of the European members of the assembly.

[74] As Jinnah optimistically told Ispahani, 'you will come to your own not by the back door but with honour and fully vindicating the prestige of the League'. (Jinnah to Ispahani, 29 March 1943, Zaidi (ed.), *Correspondence*, pp. 336–7.) He had sensed Delhi's dislike of Herbert's tactics and agreed that the best course was to: 'Let Section 93 continue . . . Sir Nazimuddin and Muslim League Party should not accept any other position or fall into . . . [a] trap but insist on the first condition that Sir Nazimuddin, as the leader of the Muslim League Party should be called to form the Ministry and not accept what I have read in the newspapers that the Governor has requested Sir Nazimuddin to explore the situation as a reporter.' (Jinnah to Ispahani, 3 April 1943, ibid., p. 340.)

[75] Ispahani to Jinnah, 2 April 1943, ibid., pp. 338–9.   [76] Ibid.

[77] With support from the Europeans and the Scheduled Caste members (who had been united into a new 'party' under J. N. Mandal) Nazimuddin possessed credentials for office. He bought them by increasing his cabinet from eleven to thirteen and by an

members as well as rely on the more dependable support of Europeans in the house. The old guard under the Nawab of Dacca remained the mainstay of the ministry.[78] But Suhrawardy had his own plans; and it looked as if the dissensions of the ministry, a house divided, would break into the open. Those who resented the old guard's dominance called yet again upon the High Command to intervene; and once more Jinnah had no choice but to ignore their appeal.[79] Jinnah, so his confidant in Calcutta told him, had urgently to arrange for the transfusion of new blood into the Bengal League, since otherwise the Suhrawardy–Shahabuddin gang would 'damage . . . the prestige of the organisation', bring down the ministry 'like a house of cards', and inflict 'irreparable damage' on the 'League organisation'.[80]

Bengal now had a ministry, League in name but coalition in fact, and the League outside the ministry was split down the middle, with Jinnah's closest associates excluded from the confusions of its control room. But from Jinnah's point of view this was a small price to pay for doing down Huq; he piously expressed the hope that a chastened Huq would now take 'rest for life' and 'be no more'. From the centre Jinnah might think the League in Bengal was out of the 'crucible of fire';[81] but he drew a veil

---

impressive job creation scheme which overnight brought into being sixteen more posts of parliamentary secretary. Of those who had promised to vote for the ministry as many as thirty had been lured by jobs. The composition of the assembly, in the cold statistics which mask the shifts and changes of these factions, was:

Government supporters		*Opposition*	
Muslim League	79	Congress (Official)	25
Scheduled Castes	20	Congress (Bose group–Forward Bloc)	19
Bengal Swarajists	5	Progressives	24
Independents	4	Krishak Prajas	17
Labour	2	Nationalists	13
European group	25	Scheduled Castes	8
Anglo-Indians	4	Independent	1
Indian Christians	1	Indian Christians	1
TOTAL	140	TOTAL	108

(Sen, *Muslim Politics in Bengal*, pp. 172–3.)

[78] Of the seven Muslim ministers, two, Nazimuddin and his younger brother Shahabuddin belonged to the Nawab of Dacca's family; Nawab Nasrullah, rewarded with the job as parliamentary secretary, was also a member of the same family. Though Suhrawardy was given a cabinet post, the old firm dominated the new ministry.

[79] Jinnah was urged by Ispahani to come to Bengal to prevent 'clique rule', prophesying that 'if the Cabinet does not contain younger, healthier and cleaner blood . . . it would fall within six months'. It would be 'fatal to allow it to exist'. (Ispahani to Jinnah, 15 April 1943, Zaidi (ed.), *Correspondence*, pp. 354–5.) [80] Ibid.

[81] See Jinnah's address to the A.I.M.L. session at Delhi, 24 April 1943, in Pirzada (ed.), *Foundations of Pakistan*, vol. II, pp. 405–6. But of course it was out of the fire and into the proverbial frying pan.

over the awkward truth that he had done nothing to bring about this happy result. In Bengal, just as in the Punjab, he had paid little heed to those Bengali Leaguers who wanted the High Command to take a positive line in their provincial affairs. A League ministry in Bengal was all very well; but Jinnah's nervousness about the direction it could so easily take can be seen in the way he carefully hedged his bets. He had to be ready at a moment's notice to disassociate himself from a ministry which might collapse, stripping away the façade of League support in a province which no centre had ever succeeded in controlling. His dilemma was evident at the League's annual session at Delhi in 1943 when he came close to branding the new ministry, which otherwise he might have been expected to laud as his own, as a British creation. According to Jinnah, the reason why the League was being favoured with these 'small mercies' was to expose its true character to the people 'to whom we have been making extravagant promises'. The British had deployed this tactic successfully against the Congress ministries, and the 'same trick is being played with the Muslims'. The League ministries had been called in 'so that our promises to our people are put to the test'.[82] Here was a political leader, anxious to present an united front against the Raj at the centre, well aware that the rulers were ready and able to use the levers which dissensions in the provinces between those in office and those outside it gave them against those who challenged their power at the centre. In much the same way as the Congress High Command with its provincial ministries, Jinnah had to face the danger that League ministries in office would lose the allegiance of their supporters outside, and that the gulf between 'ins' and 'outs', between ministries and party organisations, would grow uncomfortably wide.[83]

These were the normal alarms and excursions of Bengali politics. But times were not normal in Bengal. The province was India's frontier in the war against Japan. By May 1943, the spectre of famine was stalking the land, caused as much by a failure to organise adequate imports and proper distribution – mainly the government's responsibility and hence something that could be blamed upon Nazimuddin's ministry – as by an actual shortage of food. As minister for civil supplies Suhrawardy had charge of distributing food, and he was better at distributing patronage

[82] See note on the proceedings of the A.I.M.L. session at Delhi, 24 to 26 April 1943, *T.P.*, III, 920.

[83] When he exhorted the Provincial Leagues to 'exploit these Ministries' in order to 'popularise the League among the masses from whom we are mainly to draw when we are on the war path' (ibid., 921), Jinnah was trying to make the best of both worlds – the world he had arguably already lost and the world he was about to lose.

to the greedy than food to the hungry.[84] Of course the responsibility for three million deaths by starvation and disease cannot simply be laid at the ministerial door.[85] But equally it was tempting for all opposition groups to blame Nazimuddin's government. Although the ministry was mainly Muslim and League to boot, the fierce attacks upon it brushed a communal veneer over the battles in Bengal between those in office and those purporting to speak for the starving millions. But the hard, irreducible facts of economic life were reinforcing lines of division which frequently cut across the communities, and thus across a political strategy which had ostensibly to emphasise community rather than other factors more important in the competitions and collaborations of Bengal.

This was exactly the turn of events Jinnah had feared most in Bengal. Here was an unavoidably unpopular ministry which was likely to become more unpopular day by day. Somehow he had to wash the League's hands of it without too openly repudiating a ministry which after all was League in name. So he ruled that the League's party officials were not to hold posts in government.[86] This ruling had the result of forcing Suhrawardy to resign his office as secretary of the Bengal League. For years, Suhrawardy and Nazimuddin had been wrestling for supremacy inside the Bengal League. Nazimuddin was stronger in the assembly.[87] Suhrawardy in the League outside it. At the Provincial League's annual meeting in November 1943, the battle continued. With Suhrawardy no longer secretary, the Nazimuddin-backed faction took the opportunity to challenge his grip over the organisation, and Suhrawardy had to defend his exposed flanks. The elections proved that Suhrawardy had considerable influence in the League. None of the pro-Nazimuddin business magnates of Calcutta, such as Haji Adamji Daud or Ispahani, who had earlier been vice-presidents, kept their posts. Every new assistant secretary belonged to the Suhrawardy faction, and every single one of the one hundred Bengal representatives in the A.I.M.L.'s Council

---

[84] Suhrawardy peremptorily ordered stocks to be forcibly seized, purchases to be surrendered (in some cases at a much lower selling price than those at which they had been bought). Stockists were ordered to shut down their warehouses; traders were told not to sell; stationmasters were instructed to hold back wagons; carters and carriers were not allowed to shift grain as they wished and exports were banned. (See Sir Azizul Huque's speech to the central legislative assembly, 9 August 1943, Cmd. 6479, ix, 788–9.)

[85] See A. K. Sen, *Poverty and Famines: An Essay on Entitlement and Deprivation* (Oxford, 1982), and Sugata Bose, 'Agrarian Society and Politics in Bengal: 1919–1947' (Cambridge, Ph.D. dissertation, 1982), chapter 3.

[86] Sen, *Muslim Politics in Bengal*, p. 175.

[87] In 1941, Suhrawardy had tried to be leader of the League in the assembly, but had failed; in 1943, he again tried unsuccessfully to be the assembly boss. Failing inside the assembly, he decided to build up his power base outside.

owed an allegiance of sorts to Suhrawardy who had more influence over the League 'organisation' than over the ministry which had taken office in its name.[88] The main beneficiary of these struggles was Abul Hashim, standing outside the two factions but soon to become a power in his own right, and a threat to them both.[89] But by now the split in the League's leadership was reflected in the assembly and in the League outside, with Nazimuddin still holding his own in the assembly and Suhrawardy still strong outside, even though he was no longer the League's secretary. One side effect was to give Jinnah's Calcutta clique, which had no real base despite its pelf and purse, even less of a say than it had previously possessed either in the League outside or in the ministry itself. Granted, the all-India leader still had some contacts inside the ministry; but he had no line to the voters outside, which ironically, even his followers believed to be the only way to discipline the unruly factions and labyrinthine intrigues of notoriously unreliable Muslim politicians. Bengal could hardly be held up as an example to Muslim India in the support, ministerial or popular, which it gave the Quaid.

These trends predictably got worse, as the seedy politics of the assembly and the struggles in the League outside clashed in louder discord than before. Hashim, the man in the middle, decided to make his own way by a push into the districts. He was not cut of the same cloth, by conviction or by style, as the oligarchs in the ministry. Most of the time Hashim did not even bother to pretend loyalty to the ministry. His concern was to inject vitality and force into a League which had known neither. When he reviewed the state of the province in July 1944, Hashim saw that the League had no 'consolidated network of organisation spreading from one corner of the province to the other'.[90] In Bengal's twenty-seven districts, only eighteen district Leagues pretended to exist; of these, only three actually had offices – and some of these, with the ink hardly dry on their paper constitutions, had been created by a stroke of a pen, not with bricks and mortar, or money and men. Such a League was unlikely to make any impact on the local base of Bengali politics. A 'weak skeleton' was no frame for a strong body; a more 'close, well-knit and politically mature organisation' was urgently needed, not only for political ends but also for the larger social purposes that Hashim had in mind. So now he urged the district Leagues to snap

[88] Sen, *Muslim Politics in Bengal*, p. 182.
[89] Despite the 'leftist' leanings of the new secretary, Nazimuddin expected Hashim to retain his own independence of manoeuvre rather than make common ideological cause with Suhrawardy.
[90] Abul Hashim's review of the Bengal Muslim League to the secretary of the A.I.M.L., 30 July 1944, AIML/SHC/3/File No. 23, Bengal vol. 1.

into action, have proper offices, full-time workers (almost a contradiction in terms in the enervating climes of Bengal), and reading rooms with books and papers of an improving kind. Above all the Leagues must be prepared to work with anyone who wanted to tackle concrete problems which mattered to the people such as the shortage of food.[91] But the road to success in Bengal's districts could not be paved with good intentions alone. Hashim ran into a wall of 'complete apathy in the matter of building the League'. Touring some districts between April and June was an eye-opener for this enthusiast. It brought home to Hashim the 'complete amateurishness' of the League's arrangements in the districts: 'District Leaguers' showed 'a definite resistance . . . against building the League'; they were worried that raising the masses might contrive their fall;[92] they desperately wanted to hang on to their 'age-long vested interests'. This, from Hashim's point of view, just would not do. The League, he declared, could not simply get away with 'mere electioneering campaigns and tub-thumping propaganda', particularly since others, not in the League's camp, had begun to see the possibilities of exploiting the horrific grievances of a tortured countryside.[93]

As the first step, Hashim prepared a draft manifesto setting out the new objectives of the Bengal League, the very first attempt by any provincial League to define its aims, however imprecisely, to the people it purported to represent. The draft manifesto is a fascinating document. It was marked more by its wide-ranging social and economic perspectives than by its specifically political objectives. Somewhat equivocally it equated 'Pakistan' with an Islamic state, but after what was a cursory nod in the direction of the Muslim community, whether as a political or religious entity, the draft manifesto went on to speak of equality, fraternity, the rights of the poor, and the wickedness of vested interests[94]

---

91 Hashim particularly wanted to win over district and sub-divisional Krishak Prajas to the League. He had some success: from late-1943 onwards, many prominent Krishak Praja leaders joined the League. One of them, Abul Mansur Ahmad, looking back at the chances of yesteryear, argues that if the Krishak Praja members had joined the League as a group rather than as individuals, they would have had a greater say in the League Council. (See Abul Mansur Ahmad, *Amar Dekha Rajnitir Panchas Bachhar* (Fifty Years of Politics As I saw It) (2nd edn. Dacca, 1970) pp. 194–8.)

92 There was a 'lurking fear in their mind that if these organisations were democratised and strengthened, their leadership in the process of democratisation might be eliminated'. (Hashim's report, July 1944, AIML/SHC/3/File No. 23, Bengal vol. I.)

93 The old district leaders, Hashim claimed, were 'fast becoming a dead-weight retarding the growth of the League'. If the 'League refuses to discard the shackles and play the great role destined for it, it is the League that would suffer'; given the widespread distress which the famine had caused, the League could not simply 'remain idle' since 'other parties are trying to play their part'. (Ibid.)

94 The manifesto, with its progressive bent, did mention Islamic ideals and the Sharia, but

– not quite the main preoccupations of Jinnah and the Muslim League. By giving the districts more of a say in the League's Council at the top, Hashim hoped to break the dominance of the Calcutta old guard and their Dacca allies.[95] Here were shades of the Atma Sakti and Karmi Sangha groups who had challenged Calcutta's dominance in the late twenties.[96] But taking on the Nawab of Dacca, the Ahsan Manzil leaders, as well as the Calcutta business oligarchs, demanded 'a party within the party', attractive for students and would-be populists but bound to drive the ministry in office and the party outside further apart – just what Jinnah most dreaded. The Nazimuddin ministry's main problem was now the pressure building up against it inside the League.[97] Clarion calls for the ministry to respond to the discipline of a more popularly directed League had nothing to do with Jinnah's High Command but were the product of a quite different vision: a League resting on a broad popular base, divorced from the A.I.M.L. and with a radically different perspective from it.

its preamble hardly equated 'Pakistan' with an Islamic state. Among its objectives were: (1) equality before the law; (2) equal opportunities for Bengali citizens irrespective of creed, caste and class; (3) the right to education; (4) nationalisation of the jute industry and the elimination of vested interests; and (5) a declaration of rights for workers and peasants. (Draft Manifesto of the Bengal Provincial League by Abul Hashim, cited in Sen, *Muslim Politics in Bengal*, pp. 184–5.)

[95] In an effort to break Calcutta's traditional dominance, the districts were to be given more say in the League Council. Previously, representation on the League Council had depended on the size of the district's Muslim population, and Calcutta had the largest number of representatives. Hashim's scheme cut them down. The number of members of the Working Committee the president was empowered to nominate was reduced from ten to four. Out of the Working Committee's twenty-four members (excluding three *ex-officio* members) twenty were now to be elected. The posts of vice-president and assistant secretary, another feature of an organisation concerned with show not effect, were abolished.

[96] See Gallagher, 'Congress in Decline: Bengal 1930 to 1939', in Gallagher, Johnson and Seal (eds.), *Locality, Province and Nation*, pp. 275–6.

[97] According to Hashim, the ministry, with its 'own entourage of agents and henchmen', was a 'parallel show' which usually ignored the organisation. The ministers got money for themselves in the League's name and they dispensed patronage without let or hindrance. The 'refusal of the Ministerialist group to come under the discipline of the League is not only hitting the League but the Ministry as well. The recent Ministerialist crisis as a result of the defection of . . . members of the League is explained away by the Ministry as due to offer of bribes by the opposition. But this facile explanation is defective . . . The fact is that there is a fall in the Ministerialist credit due to disintegration within our own ranks. The unbridled favouritism and nepotism in which the Ministry has been indulging for some time past particularly in the matter of patronage, appointments and contracts have had serious repercussions inside our own ranks.' (Abul Hashim to the secretary of the A.I.M.L., 30 July 1944, AIML/SHC/3/File No. 23, Bengal vol. I.)

So historians who write in stirring terms about the 'Pakistan movement' in Bengal gaining ground here, doing less well there, are discussing a phenomenon which at best had the most tenuous contact, and sometimes no contact at all, with the purposes, programmes and priorities of that movement as it was conceived by Jinnah at the centre. By November 1944, Hashim claimed that the League had managed to penetrate the rural areas, particularly the eastern districts. That the League had overnight become 'revolutionary and a really mass movement', and had 'taken the masses by storm', was of course the hyperbole of a would-be demagogue. But the palpable growth in membership in districts such as Barisal, Dacca and Tippera,[98] suggests that Hashim's campaign was beginning to bite. It was put in terms which made sense to the rural voters: abolition of zamindari and the Permanent Settlement, equality and socialism – all sweet millennial tunes to an oppressed peasantry, but hardly the sort of music to reassure the League oligarchs or to enthuse Muslim grandees in other parts of India.[99]

These incursions into the base spurred Hashim and Suhrawardy in their bid to capture the Bengal League at the top. They argued that the old leaders were aged, infirm, obsolete and oligarchical, and it cannot be denied that they had a point. They wanted to turf the Dacca lot out and they called on Jinnah to back those who deserved to lead Bengal's people and to stop propping up archaic leaders such as the League's president, Maulana Akram Khan, who was a 'permanent invalid and physically unfit for work'; for the past two years the Bengal League had 'a sleeping President' who had 'sold his mind, conscience and Paper [the *Azad*] to the Khwajahs', namely the Nawab of Dacca clan.[100] The trial of strength came in November 1944. Never before in the history of the League's Council in Bengal had so many members attended a meeting; of its 500 members, 460 were there. When the old guard counted heads and hurriedly concluded that they were doomed, they tried sensibly if unconstitutionally to cancel the meeting. This almost led to revolt, but

---

[98] In Barisal, which was Fazlul Huq's home district, 160,000 members were said to have enrolled. In Dacca, 105,500 members were claimed and in Tippera, 52,000. (Raghib Ahsan to Jinnah, 15 November 1944, AIML/SHC/3 Bengal vol. IV.)

[99] One enthusiastic Bengali Muslim Leaguer wrote to Jinnah that:
'In an agricultural long-suffering, landlord–Mahajan-ridden Proja country like Bengal any mass movement is bound to become egalitarian or socialistic in outlook and character. And naturally the Bengal League is more and more becoming imbued with socialistic and anti-capitalist outlook. Particularly because abolition of Zamindari Landlordism and Permanent Settlement has become the economic creed of the Bengal League and of every Bengali Muslim, be he a Zamindar or Proja';
Jinnah could have done without this information. (Raghib Ahsan to Jinnah, 15 November 1944, ibid.)   [100] Ibid.

by now Suhrawardy, still ensconced in the ministry, was having second thoughts about giving Hashim his head with a populism which could easily backfire against the Calcutta gang. But the most he could now do was to patch up yet another compromise by which Hashim was re-elected as secretary and the old guard in the assembly lost yet more of their *ex-officio* rights in running the League.[101] This gave Hashim another chance, after November 1944, to consolidate his hold over the League. Paying the price for Suhrawardy's deal with Hashim, Nazimuddin had to promise not to align himself with the 'toadies and reactionary job-hunters', and to work his ministry in the interests of the 'masses'; but he was now fast losing control over his own supporters in the assembly. Suhrawardy had thought it politic to make terms with Hashim, since Nazimuddin was on the run. Nazimuddin's Hindu supporters took the hint and decided that the premier was not a good political future; and in this changing field of force many waverers among the Muslim members of the assembly turned towards Suhrawardy. By now, Jinnah's main lieutenants in Bengal had lost all credibility, and he had no ties with the new crop of leaders in the Bengal League. In 1941 and again in 1943, Jinnah had repudiated Suhrawardy, but now it was Suhrawardy who was clearly winning back the ground he had never willingly conceded. In the assembly, Nazimuddin's stock had fallen, Suhrawardy's was rising, and Jinnah's, as usual, was unquoted.

On 28 March 1945, twenty-one members of Nazimuddin's tottering coalition crossed the floor, and the ministerial budget was defeated by 106 votes to 97. This was the end of Nazimuddin; and in these critical last few months of the war against Japan, the Governor decided that Section 93 was the answer.[102] On 31 March 1945, hardly three months before the Simla Conference, Jinnah lost the League ministry in the province which contained about half the Muslims in India.

[101] This meant that the parliamentary group would no longer have a majority on the Working Committee, and no member of the assembly would have *ex-officio* rights to League membership unless he was returned by a district League. All Hashim had to do in return for these large concessions was to accept the old invalid Maulana Akram Khan as the League's figurehead president. Amidst hysterical scenes bordering on the absurd, the election of office-bearers was completed. According to one witness: 'Abul Hashim then embraced Akram Khan, Shaheed Suhrawardy and Nazim[uddin]. Shaheed Suhrawardy being overwhelmed with feelings of joy started weeping and fell down. Sir Nazim was all the time weeping. This was a unique scene.' (Raghib Ahsan to Jinnah, 19 November 1944, ibid.) If tears alone could have washed its politics clean, Bengal's Muslims would have achieved their land of the pure.

[102] Seeing that no stable ministry could be formed out of the existing house, Casey found he had no heart for 'the drag which an inevitably corrupt and inefficient ministry would place on Bengal administration'. (See Casey to Sir J. Colville (acting Viceroy in Wavell's absence), 30 March 1945, *T.P.*, v, 885–6.)

(c) Sind

The Punjab and Bengal were the provinces that mattered most to the A.I.M.L. Both had bare Muslim majorities, whose need to come to terms with other peoples cut against the grain of following a hard communal line. They were the two provinces where local option threatened to undermine Jinnah's uncertain mandate at the centre. But if these were the unmanageable sharks in Jinnah's waters, he also had to find ways of pulling in the lesser fish when he trawled for support: the newly-created province of Sind and the N.W.F.P., the north-western outriders of the Punjab. In Sind and the N.W.F.P. the League had failed to make even a pretence of a respectable showing in the 1937 elections. In fact the Frontier, with its overwhelmingly Muslim population, affiliated itself to the Congress while the Allah Baksh ministry in Sind, which shunted in and out of office, throughout depended on a measure of support from the Congress. In October 1942, the Governor of Sind, Sir Hugh Dow, dismissed Allah Baksh and called upon Ghulam Hussain to form a ministry. Although Ghulam Hussain had been an outspoken enemy of the Lahore resolution,[103] the Sind Muslim League now welcomed him with open arms, since he had more votes than K. B. Khuhro who wanted the job of premier. Ghulam's success in the assembly owed nothing to Jinnah and little to the Sind League. But getting Ghulam to acknowledge the League on his own terms was the only way Jinnah could 'pretend in the future that his Pakistan policy has even the most tenuous hold over the Muslims of Sind'.[104] As for the Sind Provincial League, it was a rag-tag bunch of squabbling factions and rival personalities, each anxious for the spoils of office. Adjectives failed the Governor in describing its leading lights – Khuhro, the 'dishonest rascal and careerist', Mir Bandeh Ali Khan, who 'has so far let down every one of his political associates . . . and the only thing for which he can now be trusted is to do it again', G. M. Syed, the dangerous demagogue.[105] As far as dedication to fighting for freedom was concerned there was little to choose between Ghulam Hussain and the Leaguers. In so far as they

---

[103] Ghulam Hussain was known to be 'all against Pakistan' and believed that even Jinnah himself did not have his 'heart in the proposal at all'. (Graham to Linlithgow, 1 July 1940, L/P&J/5/255, I.O.L.)

[104] Ghulam Hussain's decision to join the League gave Jinnah a line of 'honourable retreat' since even without his blessing the new ministry would have accepted office. (Dow to Linlithgow, 5 November 1942, L/P&J/5/258, I.O.L.)

[105] The two other notable Leaguers were: Abdul Majid, a convert to Islam, who thought he might do better by joining with Allah Baksh, and Gazdar, an inveterate intriguer, who could be kept in line only by paying his price. (See Dow to Linlithgow, 23 July 1941, L/P&J/5/257, I.O.L.)

could lift their eyes above their petty intrigues, the Leaguers wanted 'independent national states' for the Muslim majorities; they did not want a centre dominated by Hindus, but above all they did not want any centre which had the power to curb their avid particularism.[106] Their equivocal resolution in favour of 'independent national states' in Muslim provinces, hailed as Jinnah's triumph in Sind, was passed by the grand total of twenty-four votes against three in the absence not only of Allah Baksh's supporters but also of the Congress members in an assembly which contained sixty persons when they were all there to illuminate its proceedings.[107]

None of this mattered much.[108] What did matter in Sind was the struggle for office and here the Leaguers – Syed, Abdul Majid and Khuhro, by now president of the League – manoeuvred to oust Ghulam. They all hoped to use Jinnah's backing to push Ghulam out of office. But Jinnah had no intention of rocking the ministerial boat, even if he had been in a position to do so, which he was not. The reward for this magisterial inactivity was that the four Muslims in the Sind ministry took the train to Delhi where they solemnly endorsed Jinnah's ruling that the High Command should have draconian powers over provincial ministries, and they even made modest contributions to the Jinnah Fund.[109] This did not worry the Governor of Sind: he knew that if Jinnah pressed the Sind ministry in a direction that did not suit it, then support for the League in the province would fade away as easily as it had been conjured up.[110] The Sind ministry could afford to pretend to toe Jinnah's

[106] In its first session after the new ministry was formed, the Sind assembly passed a resolution calling for 'independent national states' since 'no constitution shall be acceptable . . . that will place Muslims under a Central Government dominated by another nation'. (*Proceedings of the Sind Legislative Assembly*, Official Report, vol. XVII, no. 6, 3 March 1943, pp. 17–43, cited in *T.P.*, III, 792, fn. 2.)   [107] Ibid.

[108] The resolution did stimulate the League into an unwonted bout of activity: some propaganda, branches opened with pomp but no circumstance and members enrolled (30,000, it was said, in the Thar Parkar district), mainly in the imagination of the enrollers. A Pakistan Conference was held in the Upper Sind Frontier district, but it was left to the *pirs* and mullahs to present the League's creed – in a predictably garbled form – to rural Muslims. (Sind Chief Secretary's Report, 5 April 1943, L/P&J/5/259, I.O.L.)

[109] Their acts of Muslim patriotism were motivated at least in part by local interests. The quarrel between the *jagirdars* (big landlords) and the tenants in Sind was given an airing at the A.I.M.L.'s session at Delhi. The *Mirs*, representing the *jagirdars*, had Ghulam's support; Syed claimed to speak for the tenants. Both sides competed for Jinnah's support. So Mir Ghulam Ali, Mir Bandeh Ali Khan Talpur, Ghulam Hussain and Khuhro gave Rs.10,000, Rs.5,000, Rs.1,000, and Rs.5,000 respectively to the Jinnah Fund. Syed who had less money but a better base succeeded in getting the League to send its men to Sind to look into the matter. (See *T.P.*, III, 922.)

[110] The Governor predicted that the entire ministry would resign from the League rather than give up office. (Dow to Linlithgow, 5 May 1943, *T.P.*, III, 946.)

line because it cost them nothing but empty words and a few rupees. Of course there were the usual excitements: it would not have been Sind if there were none. In May 1943 Allah Baksh was murdered (and to this day it remains a mystery which of his many opponents engineered the incident). But it left a gap in the patchwork quilt of Sindhi politics, and Jinnah feared that Khuhro might squeeze through it into power. With Ghulam ousted, the League's façade in Sind would collapse. By giving Khuhro and Syed a place on the A.I.M.L.'s Working Committee – the only patronage he had – Jinnah hoped to bring these trouble-makers to a centre where at least he would have them under his eye.[111]

But Jinnah was unable to curb these wayward Sindhis, as the battles over the by-election to fill Allah Baksh's seat revealed. The League chose to portray this by-election as a test of its strength; but it merely brought the ministry into further disrepute, if that was possible, and made Khuhro less loved than he already was, confirming the Governor in an opinion, already jaundiced, of the politics and politicians of the province which he had been given to run. Despite Dow's suggestion that the League should allow Allah Baksh's brother, Moula Baksh, to fight the Shikarpur by-election as a gesture of goodwill towards the family and a way of bringing Moula Baksh into the League, the ministers were overborne by Khuhro. Any election in Allah Baksh's home constituency was bound to be a fiercely contested fight, since the Khaksars, the Ahrars, the Socialist Muslims and the Jamiat-ul-Ulema all opposed the League. With the League ministers openly canvassing for their candidate, the Sind League fell to pieces. Abdul Majid now defected in support of Moula Baksh. Other Leaguers also resigned; some openly worked against the League's own candidate, while a few leading zamindars were thought to be working secretly against the ministerial candidate. In the end the League won the election by 2,000 votes, but according to the Governor, the whole affair was: 'a pitiful commentary on the state of democracy in Sind . . . both sides enlisted support less by political arguments than by bands of Pirs and Maulvis who went around threatening hell-fire to all who dared to vote against their candidate'.[112]

It was not just the conqueror of Sind, but the conquered who might

---

[111] In June 1943, Jinnah actually visited Sind. He would have liked to cut Khuhro down to size, so he laid down his usual rule that no member of the ministry could hold office in the provincial organisation. As the Governor commented: 'Jinnah appears to recognise that Khuhro's restlessness and unscrupulousness is the principal danger to the solidarity of the ministry, which Jinnah certainly does not want to see go out'. (Dow to Wavell, 18 June 1943, L/P&J/5/259, I.O.L.)

[112] See Sind Chief Secretary's Report, 16 November, 1943, L/P&J/5/529, I.O.L. and Dow to Wavell, 22 November 1943, ibid.

have adopted the message '*Peccavi*' as their motto. Sind's variant of the Indian disease – the ministry falling out with the League outside – was found in the activities of G. M. Syed who became the League's president.[113] He now claimed to be the champion of the poor against Ghulam Hussain's oligarchs. Giving Syed a place on the A.I.M.L.'s Committee of Action at Delhi, Jinnah's only remedy for the disease, did not curb his machinations in Sind. By July 1944 Syed had arranged for the Sind League to demand the ministry's resignation,[114] an inconvenient piece of timing for Jinnah, who by now had lost all semblance of authority over the ministry in the Punjab and who possessed a League ministry in Bengal which survived only by the grace of the Governor's favour.

For the time being the intrigues in Sind resolved into a Syed–Gazdar axis against the ministry, and a Haroon–Khuhro conspiracy against Gazdar and Syed. Predictably Ghulam appealed to Jinnah to discipline this rabble,[115] but Jinnah knew that his intervention could only lead to tears. Urging the Sindhi Leaguers to 'put an end to these private controversies and bickerings',[116] he concluded that 'internal strife' has been the 'bane of Sind', and confessed that he could do nothing 'more than urge upon you the necessity of maintaining the status quo for the time being'.[117] Yet another inconvenient by-election, once more at Shikarpur,[118] found Jinnah caught again in the cross-fire of the Syed and Ghulam Hussain factions. Whomever he backed, Jinnah was bound to lose; and in any event he was not able to affect the issue or discipline either camp.[119] Bemoaning the 'damage . . . already done to the prestige

[113] Khuhro was arrested for a possible hand in Allah Baksh's murder. This gave Syed his chance to take over the presidency of the Sind League.

[114] See Wavell to Amery, 11 July 1944, *T.P.*, IV, 1080.

[115] Ghulam Hussain claimed that Syed as president of the Sind League would bring about a 'Syed Raj', and only Jinnah could prevent the disruption of the League. (Ghulam Hussain to Jinnah, 7 July 1944, AIML/SHC/I/File No. 6, Sind vol. I and 24 October 1944, AIML/SHC/I/File No. 7, Sind vol. II).

[116] Jinnah to Ghulam Hussain, 16 August 1944, AIML/SHC/I/File No. 6, Sind vol. I.

[117] To counter Ghulam Hussain's allegations, Gazdar argued that the real conflict in Sind was between the Provincial League and 'an autocratic Premier'. (Gazdar to Jinnah, 6 December 1944, AIML/SHC/I/File No. 7, Sind vol. II.) But Jinnah told Gazdar that he must be 'prepared to bury the past and assure Sir Ghulam Hussain of your loyalty to him as your chief'; this was essential to keep the ministry in office. (Jinnah to Gazdar, 18 December 1944, ibid.)

[118] The League candidate elected from Shikarpur after Allah Baksh's death also died.

[119] Ghulam Hussain wanted his son to get the League ticket, but the local Parliamentary Board was dominated by Syed's faction who wanted their own man. The opposition candidate was Allah Baksh's brother, Moula Baksh. Jinnah was placed upon the horns of a dilemma. If the League lost, Jinnah would be held responsible whichever way he turned. Ghulam Hussain now launched a campaign challenging the authority of the

of the League', reluctantly he chose to back the Syed faction rather than Ghulam Hussain and his supporters.[120] In the next round of fighting between the two factions, Jinnah returned to his uncomfortable seat as an observer at the ringside.[121] The Governor thought Jinnah would have done better to back Ghulam Hussain since he was still the premier and owned the allegiance of half the Muslim members of the assembly. If Ghulam Hussain were to quit the League, most of his men would follow him out of it.[122] Jinnah's indecision, Dow argued, had this result: 'the Muslim League has unnecessarily lost two elections, the hollowness of the League façade in Sind has been well advertised . . . not only against each other but against Jinnah himself'.[123]

In February 1945, there was still a 'League ministry' in Sind, but something like half the Leaguers in the assembly were in opposition,[124]

Parliamentary Board, arguing that the 'League is not for Sayeds only, but for all the Leaguers'. (Ghulam Hussain to Jinnah, 11 December 1944, AIML/SHC/I/File No. 7, Sind vol. II.) In the end Jinnah went along with Syed's candidate, the Pir of Pagaro's brother. But the League lost the by-election despite the 'wonderful collection of Pirs and Maulvis . . . imported from outside, who took round the fiery cross and threatened with hell-fire anyone who should cast a vote against the Lord's anointed [the Pir of Pagaro's brother]'. (Dow to Wavell, 6 January 1945, L/P&J/5/250, I.O.L.)

120 Syed blamed Ghulam for having sabotaged the League's election campaign. (G. M. Syed to the convener, Central Parliamentary Board, A.I.M.L., 20 December 1944, AIML/SHC/I/File No. 7, Sind vol. II.) In his turn Ghulam argued that Syed was 'not only a dictator, but is above all law, and is a law unto himself' and Jinnah had failed in his responsibility by not taking any action for this 'unconstitutional behaviour'. (See Ghulam Hussain to Jinnah, 29 December 1944, ibid.) Jinnah's pious hope was that his Sindhi friends had learnt a lesson from their disastrous experience in Shikarpur. (See Jinnah to Ghulam Hussain, 26 December 1944, ibid.)

121 This time the by-election was in the Mir stronghold, Tando Mohammad Khan. It soon became clear that any candidate put up by Syed was bound to lose. So Ghulam wanted the League ticket to go to the Mir candidate. Syed decided against putting up a League candidate, watched and waited, and hoped to rope in the winner. On the quiet Syed set the Sind League behind the anti-Mir candidate. But this was a well-advertised secret and everyone could see that the by-election was a tug-of-war between the Mirs and the Pirs who supported Syed's faction. According to the *Sind Observer*: 'The slap that the Muslim League received in the Shikarpur constituency is quite fresh and the internal dissensions in the League circles are getting more serious than one imagines . . . *It is an open secret that the influence of the League is positively on the wane and shrewdly enough Syed steered clear of the election tangle.*' (*Sind Observer*, 6 January 1945, AIML/SHC/I/File No. 9, Sind vol. IV [my italics].) As expected, the Mir candidate won and the League was credited with yet another defeat.

122 Dow to Wavell, 9 February 1945, L/P&J/5/261, I.O.L.

123 Ibid. But Dow failed to realise how little real choice or effective influence Jinnah had in Sind.

124 As one League sympathiser lamented: 'Our organisation is in the doldrums between an inefficient and corrupt Premier and a fanatical and unsteady Provincial President.' (Hatim A. Alavi to Jinnah, 6 February 1945, AIML/SHC/I/File No. 9, Sind vol. IV.)

and the ministry and the Sind League were in open conflict. But nothing of this had much to do with the A.I.M.L., strong or weak, or the Quaid-i-Azam. As Dow told the new Viceroy, 'There are really only two parties in Sind, those who are in and those who are out, and the main question is how those who are out can get in.'[125] He might have added that Jinnah had proved to be entirely irrelevant in helping Sind to answer that main question.

(d) The North West Frontier Province

In the N.W.F.P. a powerful particularism, combined with factional divisions among the Khans, in due course paid Jinnah a faint and uncovenanted dividend. When Congress pulled out its provincial ministries, the ministry in the N.W.F.P. followed suit for reasons of its own. The local Congress's activities in the 'Quit India' movement hardly set the Frontier alight, but they did encourage the Governor to look among the Government's friends for an alternative to Section 93. His policy was to rally the forces against Congress, and he made no bones about it.[126] The Khans were his obvious choice as collaborators, and the League was a convenient tag to dignify Khans. As Cunningham conceded, 'Our Muslim Leaguers are still staunch and have been very helpful to us in doing the right sort of propaganda. Apart from them, we have large numbers of people of local influence, including many of the best-known Mullahs, working for us. Even some of the Red Shirt 'Generals', who don't like the Hindus, are helping.'[127] By early 1943, the assembly in the N.W.F.P. had been reduced to a rump of thirty-six members, with seven of them in jail and with another seven seats vacant. Aurangzeb Khan, the would-be premier, found that he needed some Hindu support, particularly since, if there was a jail delivery, the seven who were let out might vote against him. This made him reluctant to tie himself to a Provincial League which spoke, however half-heartedly, for 'Pakistan'. As the Governor saw, the 'Congress stock' may have fallen, but this did 'not mean that the prestige of the Muslim League has risen'. Everyone knew that Aurangzeb and his frontiersmen were simply after 'the loaves and the fish', and rural opinion was content to be ruled under Section 93.[128] The necessary condition for Aurangzeb to be called by the

---

125 Dow to Wavell, 10 December 1943, L/P&J/5/259, I.O.L.
126 Sir George Cunningham frankly admitted that 'anti-Congress feeling here has had to be worked up by pretty intensive propaganda on our part'. (Cunningham to Linlithgow, 28 September 1942, L/P&J/5/219, I.O.L.)
127 Cunningham to Linlithgow, 23 September 1942, L/P&J/5/219, I.O.L.
128 Aurangzeb and his men were not popular. According to Cunningham, 'Opinion does not credit them with any motives of public service . . . moreover, [there] is the very strong and widespread feeling, particularly in rural areas, that, at any rate while the war

Governor to form a ministry was having twenty-two secure votes, but he could not deliver that number, so Section 93 remained in force.[129]

When Jinnah addressed the A.I.M.L.'s session at Delhi in April 1943, there was no League ministry in the Frontier and his claim that 'Muslim public opinion is entirely with the Muslim League' was mere whistling in the cold border winds.[130] But a month later Aurangzeb pulled the rabbit out of the hat. He had managed to buy enough support among those who were prepared to sell their votes to persuade the Governor to invite him to form the ministry. In politics, and in Indian politics particularly, nothing succeeds like success, so opinion now rallied in favour of the local League 'among the Khans and other people of standing'. As the Governor expected, 'waverers' now threw 'in their lot' with Aurangzeb.[131] But Aurangzeb still needed support on the margin from Hindu and Sikh members, and he realised the dangers of being 'guided entirely by Jinnah in the formulation of policy'.[132] The Governor, not Jinnah, was Aurangzeb's real master, and it was the Governor who protected the ministry from Dr Khan Sahib.[133] The price of this protection was to keep

is on, the people are happier under the present form of Government.' (Cunningham to Linlithgow, 23 January 1943, L/P&J/5/220, p. 128, I.O.L.)

[129] Aurangzeb was able to get the promise of only sixteen firm votes in the assembly; no Hindu member was as yet willing to support him. Outside the assembly, everyone was sceptical about his chances of forming a ministry, and the Governor found 'no kind of enthusiasm' for a League ministry, 'or indeed any Ministry formed out of the present House'. (Cunningham to Linlithgow, 23 April 1943, ibid., p. 87.)

[130] Jinnah's address to the A.I.M.L. session at Delhi, 24 April 1943, in Pirzada (ed.), *Foundations of Pakistan*, vol. II, p. 406.

[131] Cunningham to Linlithgow, 24 May 1943, L/P&J/5/220, p. 90, I.O.L. The lure of jobs pulled in men behind the League. Abdur Rab Nishtar, whose previous commitment to the League was hardly outstanding, also joined Aurangzeb. (See Khaliquzzaman, *Pathway to Pakistan*, p. 301, and N.W.F.P. Chief Secretary's Report, second half of May 1943, L/P&J/5/220, p. 74.

[132] Cunningham to Linlithgow, 23 June 1943, L/P&J/5/220, p. 86, I.O.L.

[133] The Congress line was that Aurangzeb's ministry was simply the Governor's creature. It had accepted like a lamb, Cunningham reported, 'the plans we had made' for the control of foodstuffs and other supplies, and were 'really keen to carry them out'. (Cunningham to Linlithgow, 23 July 1943, ibid.) The ministers were mainly concerned to win the by-elections against Congress, and to use their position to deploy government resources in their campaign. Inside the assembly, the ministry's position remained precarious: within two months it faced a no-confidence motion and the usual in-fighting over place and person. Dr Khan exploited these splits inside the assembly to woo away some of the League's new supporters. But the Governor was determined not to permit Congress to wreck the ministry: 'I would not be ready, if Aurangzeb Khan's party were to fail, to encourage the formation of a Ministry by a small Independent Group with the nebulous support of some non-co-operating Congress Members. In spite of all these petty disagreements among the Members themselves, popular opinion continues to go in favour of the Muslim League and against Congress . . . .' (Cunningham to Linlithgow, 25 July 1943, ibid., p. 72.)

Jinnah at arm's length; the Governor had 'warned Aurangzeb at the outset to keep Pakistan in the background as much as possible'.[134] Even so, only the opposition's decision to boycott the assembly saved Aurangzeb from a no-confidence motion which it is likely he would have lost. The League's victory in four by-elections had little to do with enthusiasm for 'Pakistan', although Jinnah of course claimed this as further evidence that the Frontier was swinging behind him. In fact it was the government, not the League, that had reminded the voters where patronage and local advantage lay. Cunningham's astonishing (but in part justified) assertion that he, not the League, was responsible for rallying Islam is a true measure of Jinnah's irrelevance in the politics of the N.W.F.P.[135]

Cunningham patted himself on the back when he told Delhi that 'Muslim League successes in these by-elections are generally accepted as being a victory for the British Government over the subversive elements in the country'.[136] Certainly the League had no 'organisation for the polling', indeed it had little organisation at all. All they could do was to delight Peshawar City 'by dressing up a rather aged stork in a dhoti, with big spectacles on its beak . . . leading it through the city in a procession with a ticket marked "Mahatma Gandhi" . . . it was a cruelly true caricature. The stork died the following day of exhaustion!'[137]

With only twenty-two more or less certain and three probable votes the tenure of Aurangzeb's ministry was precarious. His opponents – whether Congressmen, Sikhs, Mahasabhites, or rival factions among the Khans – now saw that one way to smash Aurangzeb's fragile coalition might be by forcing him into the open on 'Pakistan'. Some 'out'-groups in the Provincial League, particularly those from Peshawar, called for a conference to which Jinnah would be invited. This had obvious dangers for Aurangzeb. But he 'succeeded in skating round' the problem and avoided saying anything about 'Pakistan' because this would, at a stroke, have lost him such support as he had among non-Muslim members in the assembly, and certainly would have alienated the one Sikh seat which was coming up for election.[138]

So events in the N.W.F.P. followed a pattern, by now all too familiar. Aurangzeb's main competitor in the League, Khan Bahadur Sadullah

[134] Cunningham to Linlithgow, 9 August 1943, ibid., p. 59.
[135] According to Cunningham, the League's victory at the polls 'would not, I think, have been possible had not the ground been prepared by the propaganda which *we* have been doing almost since the war started, most of it on Islamic lines'. (Cunningham to Linlithgow, 24 August 1943, ibid., p. 56 (my italic).)
[136] Ibid.   [137] Ibid.
[138] Cunningham to Wavell, 9 November 1943, ibid., p. 22.

Khan, called upon Jinnah to help him oust his faint-hearted premier.[139] But Jinnah had to follow his usual and ineffective line of appealing for unity and asking the discontented groups to come to Delhi to 'put our heads together and find a solution'.[140] It was simply eyewash to speak of the 'prestige and honour of the League' in a province where it possessed neither.[141] Taj Ali, the Frontier League's president reported that the gap between an ineffective ministry and an insubstantial League outside it was by now almost unbridgeable.[142] For the Frontier, it was business as usual: Gandhi, 'pouring money into different pockets', Leaguers 'slaughter[ing] one another', families at each others' throats, and Peshawar out of bounds for the League. The League was fast losing such credibility as it had in the Frontier: 'The different elements of the ministry . . . [were] not functioning practically for the Muslim League, but for . . . mercenary ends of their own or of their relatives. All of them sometimes press the Chief Minister in one way or the other and so the Premier runs to take their pardon for the sake of this nominal ministry'.[143] Jinnah was not about to stick his head into this hornet's nest. He told the Provincial League: 'It is up to you to realise that you have to put your house in order . . . The Centre is doing its best to help and guide, but the rest is in the Province itself.'[144] Leaving the local Leaguers to fight it out among themselves, the High Command avoided nailing its colours to any particular mast in the Frontier's affairs, because if it had done so, the Frontier's nominal allegiance to the A.I.M.L. would quickly have been ripped to shreds. But the defections inside the League's assembly party and the assaults upon it from the League outside gave Dr Khan Sahib his chance of at last bringing Aurangzeb down. With Gandhi's blessing,[145] the Frontier Gandhi's brother pushed

139 Sadullah told Jinnah that he was 'fed up' with the ministry; he had tried to 'set Aurangzeb and his party right'; as a result he had been 'crushed' and it was now his 'considered opinion' that politics in the Frontier province was the 'most dishonest life' and he at least was not prepared to live it. (Sardar Bahadur Sadullah Khan to Jinnah, 23 November 1944, AIML/SHC/4/File No. 29, NWFP vol. 1.)

140 Jinnah to Sadullah Khan, 20 November 1944, ibid.

141 Jinnah told Sadullah that the reports from the Frontier, 'if true, are not only painful but are calculated to damage the prestige and honour of the League in your Province'. (Ibid.)

142 The League ministry was by now universally detested; the Pathans were 'using filthy and unbearable words against the Ministry' and the League outside could do nothing to clean up the language of the Pathans, let alone their politics. (Taj Ali to Jinnah, December 1944, ibid.)   143 Taj Ali to Jinnah, December 1944, ibid.

144 Jinnah to Taj Ali, 18 November 1944, ibid.

145 Even Gandhi had to concede more latitude to his improbable Frontier followers than elsewhere in India. But the Mahatma who had ridden a Khilafat tiger was ready to be carried by the Frontier's stork.

aside Aurangzeb and formed a ministry of his own on 12 March 1945.[146]
Not many months before Simla, Jinnah 'lost' the Frontier to the
Congress. It was not even as if the League ministry had resigned; it had
been discredited and ignominiously tossed back into the fields of oblivion
from which Congress preoccupations nearer to home and British
patronage away from the centre had temporarily rescued it.[147]

Between 1942 and 1945, Jinnah had a relatively clear run at the centre,
but if his aim was to establish loyal League ministries in the Muslim
provinces, his success was less obvious. In the main, he had little choice
but to settle for whatever support, however grudging and nominal, the
provinces were ready to offer. There was no question of a party covering
Muslim India, organised and disciplined from the centre, and even less
of riding upon a groundswell of opinion against the old provincial bosses.
Some historians of the 'Pakistan movement' have asserted the contrary;
but in their analysis the gap between assertion and fact has not been
bridged.[148] Provincial Muslim politicians tended to align themselves to

[146] On 12 March 1945, Aurangzeb's ministry was defeated and the Governor had to invite
Dr Khan Sahib to form a new ministry.

[147] When the A.I.M.L.'s Committee of Action visited the Frontier, it discovered to its
chagrin that the League was losing the little ground it had won and that the League was
merely a cover for factional in-fighting. Many Leaguers were actually threatening to join
the Congress, and Mamdot, a member of the visiting commission, had to admit that
'there is some force in your complaint that the Muslim League is not properly organised
in your province, the remedy is not that you should leave the League and join the
Congress . . . We are fully alive to the situation created in your province owing to various
reasons and various shackles which have combined together to weaken the Muslim
League . . . have patience . . .' (Mamdot to the general secretary, Mohmand Tribes,
Mardan district, 5 August 1944, AIML/SHC/4/File No. 29, NWFP vol. 1.) Even before
Aurangzeb's fall, the Committee of Action had decided to abandon him and concentrate
its scant resources on putting the League's organisation in the N.W.F.P. into order – a
tall order!

[148] Khalid bin Sayeed's analysis of the 'Pakistan movement' is a case in point. He maintains
that the 'Muslim League bridged the gulf that yawned between the illiterate Muslim
masses and the highly Westernized elite at the top', yet he finds no evidence of the
A.I.M.L. ever adopting a comprehensive propaganda programme stating its objectives
to the people. So it is a little difficult to see how the bridge was built. Sayeed concedes
that 'not being united by any concrete programme or ideology, the League leaders soon
fell prey to squabbling and petty intrigues', but asserts that Jinnah's 'towering personality' and 'exertion of authority', combined with the League's organisation and discipline
'were such that all . . . heterogeneous elements could be kept inside the League without
impairing its unity'. One might argue that since the League leaders were directing a
movement and not a party, the growing popular sentiment for 'Pakistan' even if not
matched by real political organisation was proof of Jinnah's increasing strength during
this period. But Sayeed's own conclusions make this argument difficult to sustain: 'the
realities of Muslim politics forced even a domineering personality like Jinnah to work

the League out of calculation not commitment; their commitment remained to their own interests in their own provinces, not to the community at large or even the League at the centre. The Provincial Leagues were in the main arenas where factions wrestled for local advantage, and Jinnah could do little more than raise the A.I.M.L.'s banner over whichever factional alliance was for the time being on top, irrespective of his particular preferences or his general dislike for these unseemly wranglings in distant places. Far from being the coachman whipping Muslim provinces into line, Jinnah at the centre simply had to stand still on the side-lines, claiming victories which he had not won and denying defeats which he had not suffered. Whatever powers it claimed on paper, the League's High Command was not in fact able to play the role of arbiter, and on the few occasions it reluctantly was forced to take a hand in the Muslim provinces, its interventions had the habit of backfiring.

The price that Muslim factions in the provinces demanded for accepting the League as their spokesman at the centre was licence for an almost anarchical autonomy in their local affairs. This meant that Jinnah could not afford to be precise about the 'Pakistan demand', since what suited one local faction might upset another. Above all, his own strategy at the centre was not in the obvious, or perhaps more accurately the immediately obvious, interest of Muslim provinces. By asserting in face of the facts that there was 'no difficulty in understanding Pakistan',[149] Jinnah managed to avoid the real problems, which included the question of the partition of the Punjab and Bengal. Jinnah's only safe line was to 'discourage anything that will create dissensions in the Muslim Camp'; it avoided 'discussion or determination of fundamental rights for citizens in Pakistan, or production of a cut and dried scheme for Pakistan', since these would 'create controversies and differences of opinion'.[150] Not surprisingly, the 'Pakistan demand', or more accurately its myriad versions, had little to do with Jinnah's unstated conception of what it was, and almost everything to do with what all and sundry including his various provincial allies found most expedient in mobilising support in their own particular and differing circumstances. Jinnah was never able to reconcile his real purposes and the conflicting aspirations of his divided and warring constituents.

with the existing powerful social forces'. (See Khalid bin Sayeed, *Pakistan: The Formative Phase, 1857–1948* (Karachi, 1978), pp. 176, 197, 212, 184, 181 and 210.)

149 Jinnah's address to the A.I.M.L.'s session at Delhi, 24 April 1943, in Pirzada (ed.), *Foundations of Pakistan*, vol. II, p. 423.

150 See note on the proceedings of the A.I.M.L.'s session at Delhi, 24 to 26 April 1943, in *T.P.*, III, 921–2.

One of the most awkward problems Jinnah faced was how to reconcile the interests of Muslims in majority provinces with the needs of Muslims in minority provinces. On the face of it, the 'Pakistan demand' seemed to be the triumph of the provincial thesis of majority Muslims; but Jinnah's strategy was not – indeed it could not have been – designed simply for the benefit of the Muslim provinces.[151] If the 'Pakistan demand' was to have the support of Muslims in provinces where they were in a minority, it had to be cast in uncompromisingly communal terms. This meant that those who wanted to establish 'Pakistan' on Quranic principles of government could assert: 'Quaid-i-Azam! We have understood Pakistan in this light. If your Pakistan is not such, we do not want it'. All Jinnah could do in the face of such challenges was to carefully avoid the issue.[152] Yet a patently communal line did challenge the leaders of Muslim provinces – certainly in the Punjab and Bengal – where Muslim supremacy over undivided territories depended upon keeping Muslim ties with other communities in good repair. So Jinnah's only refuge was to keep the 'Pakistan demand' as unspecific as possible, and hope against hope that the forces of communalism would not combine to destroy his purposes at the centre. It suited the British not to expose Jinnah's fundamental dilemma; and for the time being Congress had other more pressing concerns. Since there was no all-India leader to challenge his uncertain claim to speak for Muslims at the centre, these were Jinnah's halcyon days when failure could be dressed up as success, and discreetly hidden from the public eye.[153]

---

[151] Minority-province Muslims still constituted a large section of the A.I.M.L.'s Council and dominated the Working Committee, which was nominated by Jinnah himself. Jinnah's dilemma is clearly revealed in his exhortations to Muslims in the majority provinces: 'Don't forget the Minority Provinces. It is they who have spread the light when there was darkness in the majority Provinces. It is they who were the spearheads that the Congress wanted to crush with their overwhelming majority in the Muslim Minority provinces. It is they who had suffered for you in the Majority Provinces, for your sake, for your benefit and for your advantage.' (Jinnah's address to the A.I.M.L.'s session at Delhi, 24 April 1943, in Pirzada (ed.), *Foundations of Pakistan*, vol. II, p. 407). But this was mere rhetoric to obscure differences which could not easily be reconciled.

[152] See Nawab Bahadur Yar Jang's address to the A.I.M.L., Karachi, December 1943, in ibid., pp. 485–6. Jang was the president of the All-India States Muslim League and a powerful orator in Urdu. His unique and somewhat implausible blend of Communist and Islamic ideals was in sharp contrast to Jinnah's secular vision.

[153] Other Muslim groups, like the Ahrars and Mashriqi's Khaksars were either too closely identified with the Congress or too idiosyncratic in their methods to pose a serious threat to Jinnah's claim to speak for all Indian Muslims. Maulana Maudoodi's Jama 'at-i-Islami, established in August 1941, was an outspoken opponent of the 'Pakistan' demand and had little influence beyond a small, select circle of Muslims. Although the Jamiat-ul-Ulema-i-Hind had a pro-League faction under the leadership of Shabbir

It suited Jinnah to claim that 'We want Pakistan and that commodity is available not in the Congress market but in the British market';[154] it suited him because the British were smiling upon his endeavours and because the Congress was for the moment out of play. This explains why, at this stage, Jinnah was content to stand back from the Congress, and why in its turn the Congress did not press more positively towards a settlement with Jinnah which might have flushed him into the open. Rajagopalachari did produce a formula for a settlement between Hindus and Muslims, which apparently conceded the 'principle of Pakistan'. But the 'Pakistan' Rajagopalachari envisaged was to be created out of Muslim-majority districts, not out of undivided Muslim provinces. His proposals necessarily entailed the partition of the Punjab and Bengal. But there was a further catch: the decision to cut out of India, as Rajagopalachari envisaged, would be taken not just by the Muslims but by a plebiscite of the entire population even in the Muslim-majority districts, and this might well have diluted their enthusiasm about going their own separate way.[155] None of this was what Jinnah wanted: it threatened to show up all the weaknesses in his demand. So he merely shrugged off this initiative, telling his Council that it was intended to 'torpedo' the Lahore resolution; it was the 'grossest travesty', a 'ridiculous proposal', 'offering a shadow and a husk – a maimed, mutilated and moth-eaten Pakistan, and thus trying to pass off having met our Pakistan scheme and Muslim demand'.[156]

But the real snare in the Rajagopalachari proposals lay in its suggestions for the centre. The Muslim-majority districts might, if they could carry the vote, go their own way, but only up to a point: at the centre there would still have to be common arrangements between 'Pakistan'

Ahmad Uthmani, the pro-Congress faction under Husain Ahmad Madani appeared to dominate its proceedings and spoke in favour of a composite nationalism. It was not until October 1945 that Uthmani formed the Jamiat-i-Ulema-i-Islami, mainly to assist the Muslim League in its election campaign. A Muslim leader of all-India standing who might have challenged Jinnah's leadership was Abul Kalam Azad; but Azad was too deeply ensconced in the Congress and the Quaid-i-Azam's vitriolic against him – calling Azad the Congress's 'showboy' president – had not failed to have an impact. Azad and Congress were no match for the millennial expectations which 'Pakistan' aroused. As for the provincial leaders, they were either too involved with their domestic affairs or, like Sikander Hayat Khan (who had died in December 1942) and Allah Baksh (who had been murdered in 1943), were no longer in the picture.

[154] See note on proceedings of the A.I.M.L.'s session at Delhi, 24 to 26 April 1943, in *T.P.*, III, 919.

[155] C. Rajagopalachari to Jinnah, 8 April 1944, in *Indian Annual Register*, 1944, vol. I, pp. 129–30.

[156] Jinnah's address to the A.I.M.L. Council at Lahore, 30 July 1944, in Pirzada (ed.), *Foundations of Pakistan*, vol. II, pp. 493–5.

and Hindustan for defence, commerce, communications and other essential purposes.[157] Now some of this lay close to Jinnah's unspoken hopes for the future, but the difficulty was that his power to bargain effectively depended on having the backing of undivided Muslim provinces. If he was to be a spokesman who was an equal to the Congress, not its running dog, he needed an undivided Punjab and Bengal behind him. In August 1944, a month after Jinnah had rejected Rajagopalachari's formula out of hand, he was still holding out an olive branch to his opposite numbers in the Congress, urging them to unite for the nationalist cause on equal terms against their common enemy, but asking in return for a due share of power at the centre. This had been the heart and centre of his strategy; and it was still what he was after in August 1944. Jinnah's 'Pakistan' did not entail the partition of India; rather it meant its regeneration into an union where Pakistan and Hindustan would join to stand together proudly against the hostile world without. This was no clarion call of pan-Islam; this was not pitting Muslim India against Hindustan; rather it was a secular vision of a polity where there was real political choice and safeguards, the India of Jinnah's dreams,[158] a vision unfulfilled but noble nonetheless.

Keeping open the roads into an uncertain future, Jinnah rejected the Rajagopalachari formula but at the same time agreed to talk with Gandhi. These talks took place in September 1944, but once Gandhi claimed that he could not speak for Congress, Jinnah, unwilling to commit himself to anything which the Congress High Command had not endorsed and guaranteed, had to reconcile himself yet again to the probability that talking with his old adversary was unlikely to get him anywhere. Indeed, both men stuck firmly to their old lines without conceding anything. Jinnah made much of his 'two-nation' theory, and demanded sovereign Muslim states based on the existing provincial boundaries, with Muslims alone deciding the issue of separation. He called for a treaty to settle relations between Pakistan and Hindustan. Predictably, Gandhi rejected the 'two-nation' theory; he was looking for a way of conceding some limited form of self-determination to Muslims in the majority provinces inside an undivided India, without yet committing himself to a firm guarantee about the size of the League's share of power at the centre. So the talks simply got bogged down in the old issue of whether independence should be settled first or whether the communal problem should be resolved as the necessary preliminary. Gandhi wanted

---

[157] See Rajagopalachari to Jinnah, 8 April 1944, in *Indian Annual Register*, 1944, vol. I, pp. 129–39.
[158] See Jinnah's press statement, in *Nawa-i-Waqt*, 24 August 1944.

independence first; Jinnah of course wanted his 'cut and dried' demands to be accepted by Congress before the British granted independence.[159]

Once the talks between Gandhi and Jinnah came to naught, Wavell and his advisers had to look for some other way out of the deadlock. The Viceroy could see that, for one thing, the United States was likely to raise the whole question of India's future when peace came and 'The whole empire position might be prejudiced if it was still in the present deadlock.'[160] Unless a solution was found soon, the British might, after the war, be trapped unwillingly inside India and 'compelled to direct Indian affairs for a considerable time to come'.[161] But Britain did not have the resources, administrative or military, to continue to rule India indefinitely, especially in the hard times of a post-war world. The civil service was undermanned and overworked; British soldiers would want to go home; demobilised sepoys would have to come home and would be agitational fodder on their return; and the Indian army itself might prove to be a brittle rod of order, an internal garrison no longer to be relied upon.[162] So the worried Viceroy could see ahead only troubles, a period of 'great difficulty and even danger'. All this added up in his eyes to an argument for a 'genuine and determined attempt' to secure a settlement which might save London from being 'driven' after the war 'into a move' which it did not control.[163]

In Wavell's opinion, the failure of Gandhi and Jinnah to agree on 'Pakistan' had made a 'direct solution of [the] communal problem impossible'.[164] One way forward now might be the old device of an all-India conference which would 'shelve . . . [the communal] issue for [the] time being and try to progress in other directions'.[165] By bringing the Congress and the League together into an interim government at New Delhi, Wavell hoped to pave the way for co-operation and a constitutional settlement for the future.[166] But the angle of vision from the provinces was different. An all-India conference which put Jinnah's name into the lights would give the A.I.M.L. publicity and standing even greater than it had already appropriated, 'produce a devastating effect in the Punjab' and 'could not fail to give the impression that the Muslim League was the only section of Muslims to which Government

---

[159] See Wavell to Amery, 2 October 1944, *T.P.*, v, 63.
[160] Note by Sir Francis Mudie to Wavell, 9 September 1944, ibid., 19.
[161] See Memorandum by Wavell, September 1944, ibid., 38–40.
[162] See note by Jenkins, ibid., 1.
[163] Memorandum by Wavell, September 1944, ibid., 38.
[164] Wavell to Amery, 5 October 1944, ibid., 90 (document 42).
[165] Note by Wavell, 29 September 1944, ibid., 56.
[166] Wavell to Amery, 5 October 1944, ibid., 90 (document 42).

attached importance'.[167] Instead of inflating an already dangerously inflated leader, Glancy wanted Delhi to cut Jinnah down to size by exposing the 'fallacies' of the 'Pakistan demand', which in the Punjab was an 'alarming menace to peace'.[168] Casey was also for giving hard truths about Jinnah and the demand for 'Pakistan' to the Bengali public.[169] What the Bengali Muslims were really after was freedom from central control and Government House in Calcutta saw clear hints of a specifically provincial Bengali nationalism capable of being deployed against Jinnah's centralist pretensions.[170] Suggesting a treatise on the 'Economic Consequences of Mr Jinnah', the Governor of Bengal reminded the Viceroy that the 'Pakistan' issue was 'the biggest (and indeed practically the only) hurdle standing in the way of the constitutional settlement of the Indian problem'; and it would remain so 'unless the Pakistan idea is squashed'.[171]

Wavell chose to ignore the views of the Governors of the two main provinces upon which Jinnah and the League based their claim for 'Pakistan'.[172] He preferred to press for an initiative along his own line of thinking, which gave priority to his view from the centre not to the view of the provincial parts which were eventually to play back with devastating effect upon that centre. So he returned to his plan for a conference as a prelude to a representative interim government. This interim government, he sanguinely expected, would settle the composition of a constituent assembly, and that assembly would draft the future constitution, winning Indian approbation along the way. Agreement would broaden down from precedent to precedent in the best of all possible worlds. In December 1944, Jinnah gave the Viceroy some grounds for hope by telling him that the League would be ready to take part in an interim government, under the existing constitution.[173] That was the good news;

[167] Glancy to Wavell, 26 October 1944, ibid., 141.　　[168] See ibid., 141–3.

[169] See Casey to Wavell, 11 September 1944, L/P&J/5/151, pp. 119–20, I.O.L.; 30 October 1944, *T.P.*, v, 162 and 6 November 1944, R/3/1/105, I.O.L.

[170] Even the Bengali Leaguers seemed to be 'groping after a state in which Hindus and Muslims would live together in amity' and the 'general feeling in Bengal, shared by both Hindus and Muslims' was: '(1) that Bengal is and always has been a region apart; (2) that it has never had a "fair share" from India; (3) that all-India politics and administration are increasingly dominated by Bombay and Madras, and by the provinces nearer Delhi'. (Casey to Wavell, 17 December 1944, R/3/1/105, I.O.L.)　　[171] Ibid.

[172] He was perhaps more inclined to make a note of Sir Maurice Hallet's view that for most Muslims, certainly in the U.P., the demand for 'Pakistan' was a 'forceful indication of the strength of Muslim opposition to a Hindu raj', and that 'by screaming for Pakistan' Muslims wanted to get 'coalition governments in the provinces and fifty/fifty representation at the centre'. (See note by Porter, *T.P.*, v, 247.)

[173] Note by Wavell on conversation with Jinnah, 6 December 1944, *T.P.*, v, 279–81.

Jinnah had been 'friendly' and 'forthcoming'.[174] The bad news was that he was sticking firmly to his undefined 'demand for Pakistan'. Yet nothing that Wavell had heard from his provincial Governors suggested that the demand was practical or desirable from Britain's point of view. But the Viceroy saw Jinnah's willingness to take part in an interim government as a step towards the resolution of the political deadlock. His attitude was still dominated by an exaggerated sense of the importance of Jinnah's role, which he had inherited from his predecessor. So it is not surprising that the step forward which this frustrated Viceroy planned was to prove yet another reverse in the difficult campaigns this warrior fought in the minefields of Indian politics.

[174] Ibid.

4

Centre and province:
Simla and the elections of 1945–1946

Section 1

By 1945, Viceregal Lodge and the Congress were ready to have an interim government at the centre. In January, Bhulabhai Desai and Liaquat Ali Khan, leaders of their respective assembly parties in the central legislature, discussed a scheme by which the Congress and League would each have been given forty per cent of the seats in an interim government to be created under the existing constitution, but now to be Indian in composition with the exception only of the Viceroy and the Commander-in-Chief. A settlement at the centre for the long-term would be worked out after the interim government had taken office. Rule by Section 93 would come to an end and Congress would return to office in the provinces; and by agreement would include League representatives. For the time being, no elections would be called either at the centre or in the provinces.[1] Desai's proposals gave Wavell hope of a way out of the deadlock.[2] But when he saw the Viceroy, Desai was vague about Congress's readiness to give the League equal status in the interim government.[3] Neither Jinnah nor Gandhi had endorsed the scheme.[4] Both sides were keeping their options open. The Secretary of State had been right in fearing that Desai might 'well be a stalking horse'.[5]

However, Wavell needed an initiative and asked to be allowed to come to London to consult the Prime Minister and the Cabinet. Reluctantly he was given permission. But London, with more urgent matters to deal

---

[1] Wavell to Amery, 14 January 1945, *T.P.*, v, 400 and *Indian Annual Register*, 1945, vol. I, p. 125.

[2] Wavell optimistically detected signs of a 'genuine rapprochement between certain Congress and League elements'. Desai, an 'experienced politician', was probably 'sure of his ground'. (Wavell to Amery, 14 January 1945, *T.P.*, v, 401.) Desai's proposals went 'o the India Committee in London, which reacted cautiously.

[3] See Wavell to Amery, 20 January 1945, *T.P.*, v, 423–4.

[4] It transpired that Gandhi had not given Desai authority to negotiate, and Jinnah openly denied all knowledge of the Desai–Liaquat agreement, asserting that there was 'absolutely no foundation for connecting my name with the talks which may have taken place between Nawabzada Liaquat Ali Khan and Mr Bhulabhai Desai'. (Jinnah's press interview, 22 January 1945, *Indian Annual Register*, 1945, vol. I, p. 33.)

[5] Amery to Wavell, 17 January 1945, *T.P.*, v, 412.

with, did not like his plans for an interim government in which Indians would hold all the portfolios except defence or his proposals for a constitutional conference.[6] Churchill, with his 'very old-fashioned ideas about the problem', and seeing 'no ray of hope', was still sticking to his old line, and seemed 'to favour partition into Pakistan, Hindustan, Princestan etc.'.[7] The India Committee tampered with Wavell's suggestions and wanted the legislatures, provincial and central, to produce the names of the Indian members in the Executive Council, which was in effect to be the interim government; and at the same time it wanted Parliament to strengthen the Viceroy's powers. Wavell was against both these amendments to his scheme, because they entailed a general jail delivery (since many of the members of the legislatures were still serving their sentences) and complex legislation which unavoidably would delay matters.[8] And time was what the Viceroy felt the Indian problem did not permit.

When in May 1945 the war with Germany ended, Wavell was still trying to persuade London to agree to an initiative. On 23 May, Churchill's Coalition was replaced by a caretaker government, and Churchill at last agreed to make a declaration about India before Parliament was dissolved on 15 June. On 30 May, the Cabinet discussed the terms of the declaration taking a mere forty minutes to decide upon a subject which had occupied the India Committee for eight hard weeks. There were signs that the Cabinet was by now splitting along party lines over India, with Attlee in favour of an initiative and Churchill predictably still against it. His proposals, the Viceroy told the Cabinet, had their origins in the Governors' conference of August 1944, and the Government of India was solidly behind him in wanting an initiative. Delhi was urging London to do something, not London pressing a reluctant Delhi into new directions. With the general elections in the offing, Churchill had to give way, and Wavell returned to India with authority to invite more representative Indians to join a new Executive Council, in which the Viceroy and the Commander-in-Chief would be the only English-

---

[6] Attlee thought they were 'un-democratic'. (See Penderel Moon (ed.), *Wavell: The Viceroy's Journal* (London, 1973), p. 119.   [7] Ibid., p. 120.

[8] It would be more 'democratic', the India Committee thought, if the members of the Executive Council were chosen from a panel submitted by the provincial and central legislatures. If the Executive Council was dominated by the two main Indian political parties the Viceroy would find it difficult to override it, and for this reason his powers would have to be afforced. The first proposal meant the release of all Congress *détenus* since they included many assembly members. If the negotiations failed, it would be embarrassing to lock them up again. Any extension of Viceregal powers by legislation would take time and would raise counter-demands from the Congress and in turn that would alarm Muslims and other minorities. (Ibid., p. 125.)

men. This was intended as the first step in a constructive search for a new constitution. As a goodwill gesture, Wavell let all the members of the Congress Working Committee out of jail.

Both Jinnah and Gandhi now played a waiting game, the Mahatma claiming, with some truth, that he could not speak for the Congress. Dealing with these two 'very temperamental prima donnas' was, as Wavell wryly commented, much like 'trying to get mules into a railway truck'.[9] Gandhi wanted independence to be stated specifically as the goal. But his unease about Wavell's initiative was based on quite different grounds. Wavell's proposals for sharing representation in his Council were based on drawing a distinction between caste Hindus on the one hand and Muslims on the other. This was not acceptable to the Congress. It was not prepared to admit, even implicitly, that it represented caste Hindus exclusively. As Gandhi had argued, although Congress had an 'overwhelmingly Hindu membership', it always had 'striven to be purely political'.[10] Equating Congress with caste Hindus would open Pandora's box out of which innumerable non-caste (and potentially non-Congress) Hindus might jump. This would raise the question of separate representation for non-caste Hindus, as well as deny Congress the right to speak for Congress Muslims. So Gandhi preferred to talk in terms of parity between Congress and the League.[11] Paradoxically, Congress's imperatives, or rather its weaknesses, pointed to giving Jinnah and the League a far stronger hand than Wavell wanted to concede at this stage. It also meant leaving provincial Muslims, particularly Khizar and his Unionists, to seek representation through the League rather than in having a place in the Council in their own right.

The Governor of the Punjab and his chief minister, Khizar, did not like the idea of Congress–League parity because obviously they wanted seats on the reconstituted Executive Council for non-League Muslims from the Punjab. If the Punjab ministry was to survive, a seat in the Executive Council for the Unionists was essential. Khizar understandably was bitter about the way the Punjabi Muslims were being sold short.[12] In his 'heart of hearts [Khizar] would really like the British to

---

[9] See Moon (ed.), *Wavell: The Viceroy's Journal*, pp. 142–3. Jinnah asked the Viceroy to explain his proposals and then to postpone the conference for a fortnight while he consulted the League's Working Committee. Gandhi wanted Wavell to revise his broadcast, and take account of all his objections. The mules wanted to drive the truck.

[10] Gandhi to Wavell, 17 June 1945, *Indian Annual Register*, 1945, vol. I, p. 245.

[11] As Gandhi wrote to Wavell: 'You will quite unconsciously, but equally surely, defeat the purpose of the conference if parity between Caste-Hindus and Muslims is unalterable. *Parity between the Congress and the League is understandable.*' (Ibid., [my italics].)

[12] Khizar, according to Wavell, was: 'very upset and said he had the gravest misapprehensions over what I was doing. He spoke about the loyalty of the Punjab, that there had

stay on, for a long time . . . '[13] Before any conference was called, he wanted the long-term question settled, not the other way round. But that spelt deadlock and it also involved weakening the one viable instrument capable of negotiating at the centre for Muslims generally, Jinnah and the League.

Jinnah obviously was against having an Unionist Muslim in the interim government.[14] But he could not afford to be as uncompromising as he would have liked to have been on this issue. He had just lost two League ministries in Bengal and the N.W.F.P.; in Sind the League was split down the middle. But most important of all, he had no say in the Punjab ministry. So even when Wavell made it clear that the League could not be given the right to nominate all the Muslim members of the interim government, Jinnah did not walk out, slamming the door shut, but kept it half open and did not instruct the League to boycott the conference. His dilemma was plain. Negotiations where he had no say were dangerously unacceptable; but, whether he liked it or not, negotiations were on their way. So Jinnah calculated that wrecking the conference from within might be better than sniping at it from outside. Realising that he was 'probably having a difficult ride with his followers', Wavell found the Quaid-i-Azam 'rather depressed and not sure of his position'; 'he has certainly not got the grip on his followers that Congress has'.[15] With the League's dismal record in the majority provinces, Jinnah desperately needed something to show at the centre, and this he hoped to achieve at the Conference in Simla.

On 25 June the Viceroy opened the Simla Conference. Its aims, as he explained, were quite modest: it did not intend to settle matters but rather to pave the way for a settlement.[16] Its first task was to decide how

always been a Punjab Muslim in the Executive Council since 1919, and that my approach to Congress and the League was a slap in the face for all co-operators. He said I was handing over power to the enemy, that my veto was "dead as mutton", and prophesied chaos and disaster all round.' (Moon (ed.), *Wavell: The Viceroy's Journal*, p. 144.)

13 Ibid.

14 When Wavell told him that the Unionists were to be given the right to nominate a Punjabi Muslim to the interim government, Jinnah launched into a diatribe against these traitors and claimed (quite incorrectly) 'that the fact that they had been able to run a coalition Ministry in the Punjab for so long was solely due to the sufferance of Mr Jinnah'. (Ibid., p. 146.)   15 Ibid., p. 147.

16 In his opening speech Wavell explained the purpose of the Conference: 'It is not a constitutional settlement, it is not a final solution of India's complex problems that is proposed. Nor does the plan in any way prejudice or pre-judge the final issue. But if it succeeds, . . . it will pave the way towards a settlement and will bring it nearer.' (*Indian Annual Register*, 1945, I, 239.) Maulana Azad, the Congress president, noting that these were simply stop-gap proposals, stated that his organisation would not agree to any arrangement, however provisional, which might prejudice its national character and

the Executive Council was to be composed. Interestingly enough, everyone came quickly to 'general agreement' on parity for Hindus and Muslims;[17] the real issue was who these Muslims were to be, and both Congress and League asked for time to consult their Working Committees. On 27 June, Wavell showed his hand: he was now minded to give the provinces, in particular the Punjab, as well as the all-India parties, a say. This seriously upset Jinnah,[18] and was to prove the main stumbling-block to a settlement since it seriously undermined his claim to be the sole spokesman of all Muslims. Equally Congress's demand to nominate two Muslims on the Council made a nonsense of this claim. Jinnah wanted all the five Muslims in a Council of fourteen to be members of the League.[19] Only when Wavell refused flatly to accept this and bluntly asked him whether he proposed to wreck the Conference on this issue did Jinnah step back, requesting time to consider and consult, his usual tactic when the going got rough.[20]

So the Conference adjourned for a fortnight to allow the Congress and League to produce their panel of names. Instead of submitting a panel of names, Jinnah wanted Wavell to follow Linlithgow's reassuring practice and settle the Muslim names in consultation with the League.[21] This, Jinnah claimed, was what the League had required him to demand; the

'impair the growth of nationalism or reduce it directly or indirectly to a communal body'. Ibid.

[17] Moon (ed.), *Wavell: The Viceroy's Journal*, p. 148.

[18] Wavell has recorded that: 'Mr Jinnah, who seemed rather worried and ill at ease, was a great deal more prolix and less business-like than usual.' (Ibid., p. 149.)

[19] Besides the Viceroy and the Commander-in-Chief, the Council should contain five Hindus, five Muslims, one Sikh, and one member of the Scheduled Castes. Only such a Council, Jinnah argued, could prevent Muslims from being out-voted on every issue, (but interestingly enough the only example he gave of an issue on which Muslims might be out-voted was industrial development after the war). (Ibid.)

[20] Jinnah reluctantly conceded that if the Viceroy gave the League an agreed number of nominations, and appointed the other Muslims himself (thereby denying provincial Muslims in the Congress or any other camp the right if not the fact of representation), then he was prepared to put this amended proposal to the League's Working Committee. (Ibid., p. 150.)

[21] Jinnah was asked to consult his Working Committee and send a list of eight to twelve League members who might be suitable for the Council; they could also send names of any non-Muslims who might be considered for inclusion in the Council. (See Jenkins to Jinnah, 29 June 1945, *T.P.*, v, 1174.) But Jinnah could see that this would leave the final decision entirely in the Viceroy's hands. So, after stalling for a week, Jinnah sent a predictable reply. The League's Working Committee wanted confidential discussions with the Viceroy rather than having to submit a panel of names; 'one of the fundamental principles' was that all the Muslim members of the Council had to be Leaguers; and the League was especially anxious that Muslims should have 'an effective safeguard against unfair decisions of the majority'. (Jinnah to Wavell, 7 July 1945, ibid., 1206.)

crux of the matter was that every Muslim on the Executive Council had to be a Leaguer. The device of 'confidential discussions' between the Viceroy and Jinnah was merely to save face in the likely event of non-League Muslims ending up on the Council. That would enable the League at least to claim that they had been let in on its say so. It was important for Jinnah and the League to retain the appearance of control even when the reality eluded them. But from the Viceroy's point of view all this was unconvincing prevarication. Not surprisingly, Jinnah was in a 'high state of nervous tension', spoke of being at the end of his tether and begged the Viceroy 'not to wreck the League'. The question of who was to represent Muslims had, the Viceroy could see, placed Jinnah in 'great difficulties', 'largely of his own making', but he was in danger of becoming the 'scapegoat for the failure of the Conference'. Yet Jinnah had to balance these dangers against the larger risk that his claim 'to represent all Muslims' might be badly damaged.[22] Compromise on this issue was impossible for the Quaid-i-Azam. And so the Conference did collapse.[23]

Since it was likely that Wavell would now call on the Congress and other groups to form the interim government,[24] Jinnah's only refuge was in sticking to an intransigent line. By bidding up his demands, he tried to prop up his falling stock. To Wavell's amazement Jinnah now demanded parity inside the Council with *'all other parties combined'*. Surely Jinnah would have done better to challenge Congress's list, secure in the expectation that Congress was unlikely to settle for the Viceroy's 'provisional list'.[25] All in all the Viceroy thought that Jinnah had made a 'tactical blunder'. Congress had come out of it as the model of 'sweet reasonableness',[26] and Jinnah was left attempting to shift the blame upon others, whether Khizar and Glancy, who were 'bent upon creating disruption among the Mussalmans in the Punjab'; or Gandhi and the Congress, those would-be dictators; or even poor Wavell himself who

---

22 Moon (ed.), *Wavell: The Viceroy's Journal*, p. 153.

23 Jinnah's refusal to submit a panel of names forced Wavell to concede failure: 'So ends my attempt to introduce a fresh impetus and a fresh spirit into Indian politics. I am afraid that the result may be an increase in communal bitterness and agitation in India. I wonder what comes next.' (Ibid., p. 154.)

24 In the event, Wavell decided not to risk forming a Congress-dominated interim government. Such a move would have given the League an opportunity to stir Muslim opinion against a 'Hindu Raj'.

25 If this was indeed Jinnah's claim, Wavell thought it proof that 'he had never at any time an intention of accepting the offer, and it is difficult to see why he came to Simla at all'. Moon (ed.), *Wavell: The Viceroy's Journal*, p. 155. Wavell, no match for Jinnah in this game of bluff and counter-bluff, did not see that Jinnah had come to Simla precisely to ensure its failure.   26 Ibid.

was accused of laying a cunning snare for unwary Muslims.[27] Jinnah marched back to his safe house repeating the familiar line that Muslims were a nation, not a minority. He dismissed Wavell's plans for the interim government as a device to 'shelve' the Pakistan issue, 'put it in cold storage indefinitely', establish an unitary government of India which the Congress were to be allowed to dominate.[28] In a rare moment of candour, Jinnah admitted that a Punjabi Unionist Muslim and two Congress Muslims on the Council would have cut 'at the very root and the very existence of the Muslim League', and, the 'abject surrender . . . of all we stand for'; 'it would have been a death-knell to the Muslim League'.[29] Neither the soldier whom cruel fate had made Viceroy, nor the Unionist, who had worked hard to achieve office in the Punjab, had any illusions about Jinnah's dilemma – as Khizar pointed out, it flowed from his 'totalitarian claim' that the League was entitled to a monopoly of all Muslim seats.[30]

Simla's failure, and Jinnah's intransigence, had important repercussions in London. It helped to persuade influential Labour leaders that interim settlements were not the answer, and that the time had come to find final solutions. In a final settlement, no minority could be allowed a veto; but equally, there could be no question of forcing the 'Muslim-majority provinces into a new constitutional arrangement to which they took fundamental objection'.[31] It was Cripps's old line, being reaffirmed once more. When Labour came to power with a big majority in Parliament, it was more urgent than ever for Jinnah somehow or the other to bring the Muslim-majority provinces into line for the coming elections in India.

On 26 July 1945, Labour took office and the new Prime Minister and Secretary of State, Attlee and Pethick-Lawrence, immediately called for a review of the Indian situation. With the exception of Glancy in the Punjab,[32] who feared that a League victory in the Punjab would bring bad communal trouble in its wake, all the provincial Governors wanted elections to clear the air. Even Wavell saw that the Pakistan nettle could no longer be avoided and that a clear policy was now imperative. Merely reiterating the Cripps offer would not do, since Jinnah and the League would simply refuse to co-operate and might 'even raise their demands'.[33] The Governor of the Punjab feared 'the effect of the

---

[27] The Muslims, Jinnah added, were being 'pushed' into an arrangement, which amounted to signing 'our death warrant'. (*Indian Annual Register*, 1945, vol. II, p. 138.)

[28] Ibid.   [29] Ibid., p. 139.   [30] Ibid., p. 136.

[31] Cripps's statement in London, 15 July 1945, ibid., p. 144.

[32] See Moon (ed.), *Wavell: The Viceroy's Journal*, p. 160.

[33] Wavell now stressed the 'importance of a clear policy on Pakistan when a long-term

Pakistan idea in its crude form on the Punjab'.[34] The Lahore resolution and Jinnah demanded the 'whole of the Punjab' for Pakistan. But the province contained two divisions, Ambala and Jullundur, in which not a single district had a Muslim majority. In Amritsar district, the other communities combined outnumbered the Muslims. To force an undivided Punjab into Pakistan would bring Hindus and Sikhs into 'open rebellion'. Not London, not Delhi, and certainly not Lahore could persuade Punjab's other communities to knuckle under to Muslim rule. So Pakistan necessarily would involve the partition of the Punjab. This 'would be a disaster'; 'if the Punjabis were faced with the alternatives of an Indian Union which included real safeguards for Muslims, or Pakistan with the partition of the province, they would', the Governor predicted, 'choose the former'.[35]

As Wavell reminded his new overlords in King Charles Street in the plain truths of a Raj on its way out, the 'Pakistan idea is stronger in the Muslim minority provinces than in the Pakistan Provinces'. In their majority provinces Muslims were 'already well on top, and with a little forbearance' could easily placate the minorities,[36] and 'would gain little or nothing by Pakistan'. As for Assam, it was not 'really a Muslim-majority Province' and despite the League claims could not be included in Pakistan.[37] At long last Viceregal Lodge was coming to see the need to take the 'Pakistan demand' seriously. Wavell confessed that he now saw merit in 'the Governors' view that the crudity of Jinnah's ideas should be exposed'. Chanting a new creed with the enthusiasm of a convert, he reported that until this ground had been cleared 'we cannot make . . . progress'.[38] The Governor of Assam's view that the British, having to 'some extent contributed to make Pakistan a live issue',[39] had only themselves to blame was cold comfort. Jinnah had 'found it possible to gain support . . . by consistent vagueness in his definition'. The Punjab and Bengal would never vote to partition their provinces, and if they realised that a vote for Pakistan was a vote for partition, they would reject Pakistan. Jinnah's insistence that Muslims alone should decide local option in the majority provinces was a 'preposterous proposal', making nonsense of self-determination. London and Delhi had much to answer for in their failure to ground such high-flying claims and for allowing such low-lying logic to go unchallenged. But if non-Muslims as well as

solution is attempted'. (Wavell to Pethick-Lawrence, 20 August 1945, R/3/1/105, p. 43, I.O.L.)

[34] Ibid.   [35] Ibid.

[36] Wavell to Pethick-Lawrence, 21 August 1945, ibid., p. 44B.

[37] Ibid.   [38] Ibid.

[39] Note by Clow, 22 August 1945, R/3/1/105, p. 56, I.O.L.

Muslims in the Muslim provinces were to be given the right to decide between Hindustan and Pakistan, 'what', asked Clow, 'is to happen?' 'To none of these most elementary questions', he added, 'have the Muslim League leaders even suggested an answer'. These words, written some 623 days before partition, deserved to be pasted on billboards not only in Whitehall but in every public place in Bengal and the Punjab. If only this were done, 'the Muslim League . . . would be brought much closer to reality'. 'Muslims would realise fairly quickly that Pakistan was not worthwhile and would be more ready to compromise on concessions at the Centre. As it is, a good many more of them have this in view than dare to avow it openly'.[40]

The time when the nettle should have been grasped was between July 1945, when Simla failed, and the winter elections in December 1945, but London shirked the problem. Of course the Labour Cabinet had more pressing concerns at home, and if Attlee and Cripps knew their India, Pethick-Lawrence, the Secretary of State, certainly did not. So he sat on the fence, a vantage point from which the unsure and inexperienced hope to observe every side of a question.[41] This primacy of domestic interests in London's calculations and its dithering over India was matched in a distorting mirror by Congress's reluctance for rather different reasons to face up to the Pakistan issue.[42] Three years ago, Rajagopalachari had urged it to do so; in their hundreds, Congressmen had reacted by putting their heads in the sand and their hands in the air to vote down this wise old politician from Madras. Congress's indecision in part flowed from a sense of its own weaknesses: the exposed flank of its nationalist Muslims who did not like Pakistan but were too weak to proclaim this publicly; a socially conservative organisation whose claim to represent the broad range of interests, in particular the minorities and Scheduled Castes, was always vulnerable. So Congress also fudged the issue and no less than its British counterparts, hoped against hope that Jinnah, the League and the demand for Pakistan would simply go away. But Jinnah's greatest strength was his unwillingness to go away, his capacity to stick to his guns, scraping whatever damp powder he had in the bottom of his barrels with the coolness of a warrior confidently fighting a righteous war.

With staggering nerve, Jinnah now claimed that if Muslims gave the

---

[40] Ibid., pp. 58–9.
[41] Pethick-Lawrence claimed he was anxious to 'avoid anything which might be taken up by one side or the other as calculated to influence the elections . . . ' (See Pethick-Lawrence to Wavell, 12 October 1945, ibid., I.O.L.)
[42] From the C.P., Twynam found it 'odd that the Congress apparently is averse from tackling the Pakistan problem which is after all the principal stumbling block'. (Twynam to Wavell, 25 October 1945, R/3/1/105, I.O.L.)

League a mandate in the coming elections, then it would be entitled to 'ask for Pakistan to be constituted on the basis of the existing Provinces without any further investigation or plebiscite'. This claim should publicly have been rejected by London and Delhi in terms which were short, sharp and unequivocal,[43] just as V. P. Menon, the Reforms Commissioner, urged them to. But Menon was a Hindu, and so was thought to be *parti pris*. The Viceroy could see other dangers in a clear-cut reaction along these lines. It might be seen as a declaration of war against the League, or at best a breach of neutrality. In the end Wavell did come down in favour of a cautious announcement, hedged on every side with qualifications. The announcement Wavell had in mind proposed merely to state that 'we do not intend that the constitutional future of Provinces should be determined by any one of the communities'. This would prevent Jinnah alleging 'after the elections that we had let him go to the electorate on the false assumption which we had not troubled to correct, and that the Muslim League had been treated unfairly'.[44] But London vetoed even this anodyne proposal. Jinnah's success at the polls in 1946 owed a great deal to the reluctance of the British to tell the voters what Pakistan entailed; it owed almost as much to Congress, which failed to rally its potential Muslim allies in provinces outside the League's sway. Maulana Abul Kalam Azad, who was both Congress president and a key Congress Muslim, wanted to do so by suggesting that Congress should declare publicly for a federal constitution and a weaker centre which commanded only a few all-India subjects. Ready to concede parity for Muslims at the centre, Azad was unwilling to give parity to the League.[45] Another alternative would have been for Congress to endorse Rajagopalachari's proposal and plump publicly for partition and the division of the Punjab and Bengal. But Congress's commitment to an unitary centre and Gandhi's peculiar influence, made the High Command reluctant either to accept Azad's loose federation and watered-down centre, or the logic of partitioning the two main Muslim-majority provinces as the necessary price for a strong unitary centre. With the British and the Congress sitting on the fence, Muslims, whatever their persuasion, saw the best security in having a strong spokesman in the final negotiations to settle these difficult matters. That voice, however

---

[43] See Menon to Jenkins, 20 October 1945, ibid., p. 102B.

[44] Wavell to Pethick-Lawrence, 25 October 1945, ibid., p. 609. Unfortunately the soldier who lost the desert campaigns had too sensitive an intelligence to see things clearly in black and white. But shades of grey were not the colours for painting Britain out of her corner in India.

[45] For full details of Azad's scheme see Jenkins to Abell, 25 August 1945, *T.P.*, VI, 155.

cracked, could only be that of Jinnah. If he had not yet succeeded in becoming the sole spokesman, at least Jinnah had warded off any rivals for that post. His own sheer nerve and intransigence, matched by a certain amount of dithering by his adversaries – whether British, Congressmen or Muslim politicians in the majority provinces – allowed Jinnah, potentially a broken reed in late 1945, to take the League into the elections on a groundswell of opinion rising in its favour.

Section 2

The Simla Conference came to nothing. This was fortunate from Jinnah's point of view. But it was an indication of the new turn of events. London and Delhi had shown they were ready to find places for Muslims who were not members of the League on the Executive Council, in other words in the interim government. This made it imperative for Jinnah and the League to give substance to their claims to represent the Muslims, especially in the majority provinces. Only a clear mandate from the voters in the general elections of 1945–6 would allow Jinnah plausibly to stick to his line that he alone had the right to negotiate for India's Muslims. At the same time, however, the elections would put Jinnah's pretensions to their first real test since the outbreak of war. Yet, paradoxically, those who wanted to cut Jinnah down to size had done most to improve the League's chances at the polls. By making use of the League during the war and not flushing its demands into the open, the British had helped Jinnah to survive as a political force. Saved by the bell when Cripps brought his offer to India, Jinnah also came out of the ring at Simla with his reputation as an unbending and tough fighter enhanced not only among his loyal supporters[46] but also among Muslims who were still outside the League.[47]

But Jinnah's standing owed very little to the League's political machine, which did not exist as an organised force in the majority

---

[46] For instance, Khaliquzzaman was delighted that Jinnah's tactics at Simla had succeeded: 'You have once again saved the community from a serious pit-fall and steered the ship . . . to a safe anchorage. Your grim determination and overpowering sagacity alone saved the situation. When I recall our doubtful attitude and your unfaltering resolve, the contrast becomes so palpably clear that one has to admire your capacity for leadership.' (Khaliquzzaman to Jinnah, 23 July 1945, SHC/U.P. vol. IV.)

[47] Claiming that the Simla Conference had broken down 'because the Viceroy insisted on the inclusion of Malik Khizar Hayat Khan's nominee', Jinnah, with his 'stock' now 'standing very high' and 'hailed as the champion of Islam', gave notice to Unionists in the Punjab to fall into line under the League. (Jinnah to Hatim A. Alavi, 1 August 1945, AIML/SHC/1/File No. 10, Sind vol. VI, and Glancy to Wavell, 16 August 1945, R/3/1/105, I.O.L.)

provinces. At its last annual session, held more than eighteen months earlier, the League had tried to bring its machinery, such as it was, into the centre's service. In theory, a three-man Central Parliamentary Board, all U.P. men chosen by Jinnah, now had charge of League ministries and assembly parties.[48] But the provincial bosses did not like this attempt by the centre to pre-empt their authority.[49] Nervous about local option, the High Command could not countenance the undisciplined provincial autonomy of the early forties. By claiming the final say over the choice of candidates and authority over the members of the assemblies, the Central Parliamentary Board hoped to be able to impose a three-line whip when it came to a vote on India's future. Jinnah is reputed to have once said that he cared not a whit if Muslims voted for a lamp-post provided the lamp-post was painted in the League's colours. But even lamp-posts, those beacons of a bright Muslim future, needed a maintenance department, and this the provincial Leagues, no less than their High Command, failed to set up. Hardly an example of Islamic solidarity or discipline, the local Leaguers, even by the exacting standards of Indian politics, were no amateurs in the delicate arts of feud and faction; and there was little prospect of getting them organised for electioneering on solid party lines according to the new Delhi rules.

The League faced another difficulty in its electoral strategy: if it were to spell out its demands in hard, clear constitutional terms, it would lose votes, certainly split its support, and divide the leaders. So the election campaign continued to rest on the line, unsubstantiated but plausible, that the League and Pakistan alone stood between Muslims and a black future. None of this entailed an electoral campaign, closely organised and firmly directed by the High Command. Possessing nothing like the Congress's political machinery, the League, rent by personal bickerings and short of funds, would, the Viceroy thought, do badly at the polls.[50] London also thought that Muslim dissensions at a local level would

---

[48] They were Choudhry Khaliquzzaman, Liaquat Ali Khan and Nawab Ismail Khan.

[49] The Sind Muslim League, predictably, declared that the Central Parliamentary Board's powers were: 'Unfair, and detrimental to the interests of the Provincial League, that as soon as elections are over, the elected members should cease to owe any direct responsibility to it'. (Resolution of the Sind Muslim League at its annual meeting, 3–4 June 1945, AIML/SHC/1/File No. 10, Sind vol. VI.)

[50] According to Wavell: 'The League organisation is poor – the leaders are mostly men of some social standing and do not trouble themselves much with mass contacts and local committees – and the election results might be better from Jinnah's point of view if he had time to raise money and create an efficient organisation.' Jinnah had appealed for Rs.14 lakhs for election expenses, and had received a little (Rs.1 lakh) from the Bombay-based Muslim business community. (See Wavell to Pethick-Lawrence, 12 August 1945, *T.P.*, VI, 59.)

weaken their case at the all-India level.[51] Muslim factionalism, and the absence of real political organisation, were weaknesses which, Jinnah hoped, separate electorates would continue to mask.

(a) The Punjab

For Jinnah, the elections in the Punjab were the critical test. This was the province where he had been repudiated in 1936, had conspicuously failed to dislodge the Unionists and where the provincial bosses had most to gain from local option; at Simla, Khizar's demand to have his man on the Council had been the most serious threat to the League. Yet Jinnah had somehow to push forward the League's strategy without dragging its implications for the Punjab into the open – the awkward fact that self-determination for Muslims and 'Pakistan' would mean the partition of the province. The formidable slogan of a 'crude Pakistan', 'illogical, undefinable and ruinous' though it might be, was the only line he could safely take. Perhaps uninformed Muslim patrons and their client voters, who had not fully grasped the implications of 'Pakistan' for the Punjab might cast their vote for the League, the more so since the Unionists had 'no spectacular battle-cry' with which to resist the 'false and fanatical scream that Islam is in danger'.[52]

Once more it was not what the League did, but what its opponents – the Unionists and their British allies – failed to do that gave Jinnah his chance. Even at this late stage New Delhi and Lahore might have stemmed the drift towards the League if they had rammed home the fact that Pakistan would mean the partition of the Punjab. According to Glancy, an authoritative statement would 'at least provide the Unionist Party with a rallying cry against Pakistan – something on which the electors would definitely bite. No Punjabi, however uninformed, would contemplate with equanimity so shattering a dismemberment of the Province involving in effect the disappearance of the word "Punjab" which has been held in honour for the last two thousand years.'[53] The

---

[51] The Secretary of State's comments illustrate his efforts to learn his lessons about India – its arenas, levels, and communities. But he was still a beginner. He observed that: 'the Muslim League were not standing up too well to the strain of electioneering. If they fall into local dissensions I suppose it is likely that the Muslim seats may not give a clear mandate to the League as the most representative Muslim organisation. If so, that will bring with it its own difficulties for us because although the Muslims may be divided on local issues I imagine that in big all-India issues they are much more united. It will be unfortunate if the results of the elections do not reflect properly the Muslim point of view about those issues.' (Pethick-Lawrence to Wavell, 26 October 1945, ibid., p. 411.)

[52] If the Pakistan demand was not scotched 'bloodshed on a wide scale' would be the result. (Glancy to Wavell, 16 August 1945, R/3/1/105, I.O.L.)

[53] Ibid.

Punjab government, with its network of officers and local collaborators, still controlled a potentially powerful propaganda machine. In the autumn of 1945, Government House and its district officers still had the opportunity to state authoritatively that a vote for the League was a vote to amputate the province. It is significant that no one – not Government House nor Unionist – issued such a statement. So a combination of Punjab's traditional opportunism, its new grievances and even the vague Islamic millennialism which was gaining ground at the base, all helped to make 'Pakistan' an attractive slogan.

By failing publicly to spot the blot, the Guardians were the white ants weakening the structure of the Unionist alliance. The Sikhs in particular now showed signs of breaking out. In Glancy's opinion, only a clear statement that Ambala and Jullundur would not be forced into Pakistan could prevent 'the coming elections being fought blindly on a false issue', and cut down 'the chances of a civil war'. Glancy's constant warnings show just how well he could foresee the bloody happenings of 1947. An authoritative statement from H.M.G. would be an 'entirely unexceptionable corrective to the fanatical and highly dangerous doctrine of "Islam in danger" that is now being preached by advocates of the League'.[54] Yet nothing was done to damp down communal tension, and as the Sikhs and Hindus grew more restive this tension was grist to the League's mill: Muslims must unite under the League or be ground down by their enemies.

Defections from the Unionists now came thick and fast. A ministerial coalition cobbled together to win office, the Unionists were not an organised party, and their cross-communal arrangements depended critically upon local notables whose allegiance was always a matter of calculation not commitment. As the beneficiaries of office (having enjoyed a run unbroken for a quarter of a century), the Unionists were vulnerable to the characteristic charge from 'out-groups' that they were merely sitting tight in the saddle which they had come to regard as theirs by prescription and right.[55] The electoral choices of the countryside, orchestrated whether by the favoured 'ins' or by the more numerous 'outs', were bound to be critical in a province where only eleven per cent of the Muslims had the vote and most of the voters were in the seventy-five constituencies dominated by rural notables. Those who know their Punjab agree that the choices of the rural voters are influenced and

---

[54] Glancy to Wavell, 27 October 1945, R/3/1/105, pp. 13–14, I.O.L.

[55] Anything and everything which cut against the interests of the League was used to give substance to the cry that the ministry was determined at any cost to stay in office in its 'present naked and autocratic form'. (See Report of the Punjab Provincial Muslim League for June–July 1944, AIML/SHC/3, Punjab vol. I, File No. 30.)

frequently determined by networks of local bosses consisting of zamindars,[56] *biraderi* linkages,[57] and *pirs* (or *sajjada nashins*).[58]

Forming and holding the Unionist ministries together had been convenient for those in office, but in the long run it proved to be inconvenient even for them since they inevitably neglected their constituencies. Unionists and the government came increasingly to be synonymous, hardly a recipe for popularity in wartime Punjab where government was intervening more and more in a society which liked to be left alone. Roaring inflation since 1939[59] (impressive even by present-day standards) hit wage-earners and those on fixed incomes in the towns. Gradually even some zamindars began to feel the pinch, as the cost of scarce commodities such as cloth, sugar and kerosene began to pace and then to outstrip the good prices their agricultural produce commanded. In the eastern districts petty zamindars, such as the Muslim Jats and

[56] Between 1923 and 1930 most members of the Punjab council were drawn from important landed families. The Unionist 'party' was mainly an assembly coalition with no organisation of its own. Once the Act of 1935 gave more people the vote, the Unionists continued to depend on these local networks. (See Craig Baxter, 'The People's Party vs. The Punjab "Feudalists" ', in Henry Korsen (ed.), *Contemporary Problems of Pakistan* (Leiden, 1974); and I. A. Talbot, 'The 1946 Punjab elections', *Modern Asian Studies*, 14, 1 (1980), 66–9.)

[57] The *biraderi* or kinship group is an umbrella term for that system of patronage which underpins Punjab's rural society, giving its members the support of their peers and the protection of their patrons. (See Parvez A. Wakil, 'Explorations into kin-networks of the Punjabi society: a preliminary statement', *Journal of Marriage and the Family*, 32 (November 1970) 700–7, and Hamza Alavi, 'Kinship in West Punjab villages', in *Contributions to Indian Sociology*, n.s. 6 (December 1972), 1–27, which explains some of the inner workings of the *biraderi* networks.)

[58] Rural Punjab had been converted to Islam by the proselytizing activities of Sufis, and these Sufi 'saints' were the focus of Punjab's local and fragmented structure of devotional activities. *Sajjada nashins* claimed to be the descendants of the 'saints', intermediaries between the Faithful and their God, and this cut against the grain of Islamic orthodoxy. As beneficiaries, in cash and in kind, of their special religious status, these *sajjada nashins* had become men of local standing in their own right. Often they owned land, and the interests of landlords and the religious leaders were subtly intertwined in the Punjab countryside, particularly in its western tracts. (See David Gilmartin, 'Religious leadership and the Pakistan movement in the Punjab', *Modern Asian Studies*, 13, 3 (1979).) Against these solid networks, urban and orthodox Muslims might battle, but they were unlikely to succeed, as one political worker at least clearly realised a decade before, when Ahrars had tried to undermine the landlords' hold. Provided the villages stuck with the old firm of zamindar and *pir*, the Unionists had nothing to worry about: 'Villagers, you know, follow these 'Pirs' blindly . . . Take care of the 'Pirs'. Ask them only to keep silent on the matter of elections. We don't require their help but they should not oppose us.' (Mohammad Bashir to the Unionist Party Headquarters, 9 May 1936, Unionist Papers, File D-17, cited in ibid., 504.)

[59] In Lahore the retail price index rose from a base of 100 in August 1939 to 398 in March 1946. (See Talbot, *Modern Asian Studies*, 14, 1 (1980), 73, fn. 38.)

Arains, began to drift away from the Unionists towards the League.[60] Even those who were doing well by selling food found no way to enjoy the fruits of their prosperity.[61] By late 1944 the prices of agricultural produce, which until then had kept ahead of consumer goods, began to drop sharply.[62] Landlords naturally called upon the Unionist ministry to do something about this,[63] but there was little it could in fact do: the Central Food Department, not the provincial officials, called the shots on the movement of grain out of the Punjab. This prevented the Unionists from helping their old friends,[64] and old friendships, unassisted, began to decay. By the end of 1945, grain prices did recover, but by now many zamindars had decided to look after themselves rather than to depend upon the Unionists: they stopped taking their goods to open market and relied instead on smuggling and selling on the black market.[65] This was disquieting news for Unionists in office. The prospect of a poor *rabi* crop in 1946 made the Punjabi zamindars more reluctant than ever to sell their produce locally, since by hoarding now and selling later they saw chances of making a killing. On the eve of the elections in December 1945, wheat, maize and gram had practically disappeared from the bazaars of a province proud of its role as the food basket of India.[66] So the Unionist ministry had to requisition grain, a retrograde step which cost them dear when the small farmers of the east stepped into the voting-booths.

The rules and regulations of wartime Punjab gave Lahore and its underlings more power and in some cases more patronage. This in turn gave the opponents of the Unionist ministry more to complain about and powerful levers of protest. For example, the Punjab Civil Supplies Department, with its wide discretionary powers to ration, had become a power in its own right. Khizar had given this pork-barrel to Baldev Singh, and the department, run in the main by Hindus and Sikhs, was vulnerable to the charge of doing down Muslims.[67] District and primary

---

[60] This erosion of traditional Unionist support was by no means restricted to the Muslim zamindars. Hindu zamindars, increasingly disenchanted by the wartime policies of the Unionist ministry, also switched their allegiance to the Congress. (See Prem Chowdhury, 'The Congress triumph in south-east Punjab: elections of 1946', *Studies in History*, 2, 2, (1980), 98–105.)

[61] Talbot, *Modern Asian Studies*, 14, 1 (1980), 72–3.

[62] Punjab Fortnightly Report, 20 September 1944, L/P&J/5/247, I.O.L.

[63] Punjab Fortnightly Report, 25 October 1944, L/P&J/5/247, I.O.L.

[64] Since the movement of grain out of the Punjab was controlled, the zamindars could not benefit from the higher prices in the U.P.

[65] Punjab Fortnightly Report, first half of November 1945, L/P&J/5/248, I.O.L.

[66] See Talbot, *Modern Asian Studies*, 14, 1 (1980), 74.

[67] By the end of the war Punjab's Civil Supplies Department was larger than the entire Civil Secretariat. Of the twenty-one top posts in this department, Muslims held only

Leagues, where they existed, rushed forward to voice resentments in the countryside against rationing, the requisition of food grains, and an alleged communal bias in their distribution.[68] In the winter of its discontent, the Punjab had grievances in plenty, and the League was able to benefit from them. By posing as the defenders of rural Punjab, its rich and its poor, the League was simply following its usual tactic: doing little but allowing others to shake the fruit into its basket. After all, had not the Quaid-i-Azam found the panacea for all ills, 'Pakistan'?[69] The Punjab League was hardly an impressive body since it had little money, but here and there it did try its disorganised best to do something more than to wait for victory to be handed to it on a *thali* (plate). For instance, its propagandists tried to exploit the grievances of soldiers in constituencies – Rawalpindi, Jhelum and Mianwali – where the *jawans* held the balance. In this propaganda battle the Unionists still possessed the edge, albeit somewhat blunted. Government can usually make more plausible promises provided those promises are not too far-fetched.[70] Punjab's agriculture, trade and industry were not doing well, and the demobbed soldiers wanted their reward. The soldiers of the Punjab fought for the Raj because they were mercenaries, not because they were patriots for some far-away island. If before the elections they had been given land in the canal colonies, this may just have tipped the balance in the Unionists' favour in some districts. As it was, the League, hardly the tribune of the

three. Only four of the eighteen food grain clearing agents – lucrative posts – were Muslims. (*Eastern Times*, 1 May 1945.)

[68] The Civil Supplies Department, was described as a 'Hindu raj' in Kasur, Chinoit and many other places. (See *Nawa-i-Waqt*, May–August 1945, *passim*.) Shortage of kerosene, cloth and sugar hit the rural population hardest in times of scarcity; kerosene for example never found its way into the villages. (Punjab Chief Secretary's Report, 15 August 1946, L/P&J/5/249, I.O.L.) The League called meetings in the mosques demanding jobs for Muslims in the Civil Supplies Department (*Nawa-i-Waqt*, 23 March 1945) – perhaps the first step towards the sort of Islamic state the Punjab was able to understand.

[69] According to the propaganda of the Punjab Muslim Students' Federation, the Unionist ministry was the root of all evils, and the solution to every problem in the villages was 'Pakistan'. To help the peasantry swallow this, actual nostrums were provided – the doling out of medicines, cloth and matches, albeit in small measure and in a patchy way, helped to suggest that the League's 'Pakistan' was not only a religious necessity but the answer to every social need and the solution to every economic ill. (For an account of the Punjab Muslim Students' Federation see Mukhtar Zaman's *Students' Role in the Pakistan Movement*, Karachi, 1978.)

[70] In August 1945, Khizar, too late, announced the Government's plans for a huge, one hundred crore rupees programme to reward the *jawans*; the money was to be spent on canals and electricity generators, rural construction, agriculture and industry, health, etc. (See *Nawa-i-Waqt*, 21 August 1945.) But these were promises, not cash on the nail.

armed forces, was the uncovenanted political beneficiary of *jawan* discontent in a province of soldiers.[71]

But more important by far than the League's skin-deep agitation or its rural 'constructive' work were the hard political calculations which Punjab's rural notables were now beginning to make as they scuttled out of the Unionist camp. They judged that the Unionist source of patronage and profit seemed a bad bet for the future. By 1945, Khizar's hold over the ninety-six assembly members remaining in the Unionist camp had become increasingly tenuous.[72] The only reason why the ministry was still in office, so it was commonly held, was the absence in jail of twenty-one of the thirty-three Congress assembly members and the nervous and wavering support of ten Independents, a mixed bunch of Hindus and Sikhs.[73] With the ministry so precariously supported, the rural notables had reason to reassess their allegiance to the Unionists. Even these men had been reminded by Simla that they would soon need links with an all-India party at the centre. If the British in Delhi were no longer going to be there to prop up the Unionists in Lahore, then the attractions of the old firm were bound to be less inviting – as was the tradition of cross-communal alliances when uncertainties about the future and talk of 'Pakistan' encouraged people to seek protection under the newly-unfurled umbrellas of communal solidarity.

Once the bosses, with their 'remarkable capacity for political accommodation' began to abandon the Unionist coalition and its emphasis upon keeping a balance between the communities, *biraderi* links saw to it that their clans followed the local pied pipers of the Punjab.[74] As long ago as the days, good or bad, of Ranjit Singh, who knew his Punjab, the big families had survived the vicissitudes of change at the top, in court and darbar, by knowing when expediency demanded them to be turn-coats – an old Punjabi tradition, alive and well to this day. Once the Unionists were deemed no longer the best security for their local interests, the

---

[71] Shaukat Hayat, a turn-coat to the League and an ex-soldier, made much of the discontent among demobilised Punjabi Muslim soldiers. The League set up a committee to help returning soldiers, and it too promised land and benefits to those who voted for it. This was Shaukat's first step in organising the Muslim League's Nationalist Guard which played an important role in the communal carnage in 1947.

[72] Of the ninety-six pro-Government M.L.A.s, seventy-five were Unionists, seventeen United Sikhs and four National Progressives (supporters of Manohar Lal); the opposition had seventy-eight votes – thirty-three Congressmen (twenty-one were still in jail), twenty-three Leaguers, two Ahrars and twenty Independents. (S. Oren, 'The Sikhs, Congress, and the Unionists in British Punjab, 1937–1945', in *Modern Asian Studies*, 8, 3 (1974), 417, fn. 140.)

[73] Ibid., 418, fn. 141.

[74] Talbot, *Modern Asian Studies*, 14, 1 (1980), 71.

landlords and *pirs* were ready to call in new patrons. Ranjit Singh, Dalhousie, Canning, Fazl-i-Husain, and all the old Punjab hands, understood that flexibility characterised the men who mattered in the Punjab. In their different ways, the men who ruled the Punjab had all been beneficiaries of this willingness of Punjabi notables to change sides, simply coming to terms with new masters to maintain their local mastery which mattered and was, to them, a time-honoured end. The League was yet another in the long line of those uncovenanted beneficiaries of Punjabi calculations, the more so because its lack of substance at the top prevented it posing any real threat to the realities of social control at the base. The Punjab, dynamic though some points in its economy had proved to be had not fundamentally changed its social structure and the patterns of local power had remained intact. So the tactic the League now followed – keeping its doors open to all and sundry but never threatening the *status quo* – was bound to pay dividends. Vague appeals to vaguer ideals might have rallied some popular enthusiasm, but it was not a serious threat to the old order. No one can argue that in the heady winter of 1945 Punjab's rural notability decided severally and collectively to commit *hara-kiri*, and equally no one can maintain that the League had surreptitiously discovered and openly propagated a popular programme which hurled the base against the top. This is proof, if proof is required, that the League's success in the Punjab owed much, perhaps all, to the decision to switch allegiance of elites, opportunist perhaps, even short-sighted, but, above all, dedicated to the single-minded pursuit of their narrow interests.[75] By one of those telling paradoxes which illuminate Indian politics, Shaukat Hayat and Mian Mumtaz Daultana, scions of the old Unionist leaders, came over to the League. Yet they were not rebels against their fathers' cause; nor were they iconoclasts, turning their backs on family tradition. They were in fact models of filial piety, not would-be patricides – hard-headed men who calculated that the Unionists were about to lose the backing of the big battalions at New Delhi, and so the time had come to change sides.

Shaukat Hayat and Mumtaz Daultana are early examples of a general trend by which many important families switched their loyalties and so afforced the League in the Punjab.[76] Malik Firoz Khan Noon was an

---

[75] If evidence was needed that the change of tune was conducted by the men on top, not by the massed strings of popular enthusiasm, then the parable of Ferozepur estate makes the point. Here the president of the Punjab League himself, the Nawab of Mamdot, who owned the estate, was having no such nonsense as a grass-roots League on his land, even if he was ready to fly the League's flag over his machinations at Lahore. (See Khan Rab Nawaz Khan to Jinnah, 25 March 1943, QAP/File 579/46, cited in ibid., 68.)

[76] Another example was Mian Iftikharuddin, the president of the Punjab Congress

important defector. Here was a kinsman of Khizar and a member of the Noon–Tiwana faction who resigned from the Viceroy's Executive Council, and urged Khizar and the other Unionists to join the League. Under the cloak of the need for Muslim unity at the centre, Noon was making a subtle bid for power in his own province.[77] But he let the cat out of the bag when he demanded that Muslims elected on League tickets should be free to 'form a Coalition ministry as indeed they must – and as indeed they have always done' and this 'Coalition party would be called the Unionist party'.[78] While Khizar was unpersuaded by Noon's opportunism, he had to face the fact that it had opened the gates to a flood of Unionist defections to the League, including some of his own kinsmen.[79]

That these desertions from the Unionist camp had little to do with the Punjab League and its invisible organisation, and more to do with men anxious to win tickets, is clear. 'Sensational stories of conversion to the League' took the provincial League leaders by surprise since their workers had 'not yet reached the villages in adequate numbers', and they were too busy with their own 'intrigues and . . . scramble[s] for power' to have reached down to feel the pulse below.[80] So even if the League had, unbeknown to itself suddenly become a 'mass movement', there were dangers in 'many uncontrolled elements' working in its name.[81] And since no one could actually specify their reasons for supporting the League, it was right and proper that Jinnah should have been given the credit: 'This new enthusiasm for the League is undoubtedly the result of

Committee, with stylish leanings to the left and a member of an enormously wealthy landed family. After Simla he came over to the League.

[77] Noon, who may have read Machiavelli's *The Prince*, assured Khizar that he would do his best to bring about an amicable settlement between the Punjab chief minister and Jinnah: and begged him 'not to divide the Punjab Moslems – the heart of Moslem India'. (Firoz Khan Noon to Khizar Hayat Khan, 21 August 1945, SHC/Punjab vol. IV, 15.)

[78] Ibid.

[79] Khizar was left in the lurch by two of his relatives, Malik Sardar Noon and Major Mohammad Mumtaz Khan Tiwana (*Dawn*, Delhi, 4 October 1945); Syed Amjad Ali who had been Khizar's own private parliamentary secretary, also defected to the League. Other converts included Major Mubarik Ali Shah, the M.L.A. from Jhang Central and the younger brother of the Pir of Shah Jiwana's shrine; he immediately appealed to all *sajjada nashins* to urge their faithful to rally to the League. (Ibid., 26 September 1945.) The desertions from the Punjab Congress were even more dramatic; they included, amongst many others, its president and the former leader of its provincial assembly party. If Congress Muslims felt the way the harsh winds were blowing from Delhi, it is hardly surprising that the weathercocks among the Unionists knew that the time had come to turn.

[80] Mian Bashir Ahmed to Jinnah, 14 November 1945, SHC/Punjab vol. III, p. 21.

[81] Vicky Noon (Firoz Khan Noon's wife) to Jinnah, 10 October 1945, SHC/Punjab vol. IV, 19.

your superhuman efforts and your wonderful foresight'.[82] Those who see all this as the result of a co-ordinated effort by the Punjab League to organise an election campaign face a sad disappointment if they study the facts.[83]

Indeed the Provincial League had no programme for running the elections. Its cover was patchy; its coffers were empty.[84] Yet it had the smell of a party about to have victory thrust upon it. Since it was not theirs to question why, its backers rushed helter-skelter for a place on the ladder of a League about to scale the dizzy heights of office. The seamy affairs of its turbulent branch in Lahore, one example among many, is hardly the best testimonial for a party claiming to be held together by the high ideals of patriotism and Islamic rectitude.[85] But religion was the

---

[82] Mian Bashir Ahmed to Jinnah, 14 November 1945, AIML/SHC/4, Punjab vol. III, File No. 31.

[83] Just before the elections, most League branches in districts, rural and urban alike, were still on the drawing boards. One or two district 'headquarters' were haphazardly opened (and sometimes closed); batches of Aligarh students did make a run into the country – hardly evidence of a well-laid plan to organise an electoral campaign. Rawalpindi division was an exception; here the League happened to have an energetic local man, Syed Ghulam Mustafa Shah Gilani, who actually set up a dozen or so primary branches and enrolled four and a half thousand members in the Sargodha district. (Syed Ghulam Mustafa Shah Gilani (organising secretary of the Rawalpindi division), report of activities, AIML/vol. 162.) But in other districts in the division, there was no activity. In Mianwali, the district organiser reported that there were seventeen primary Leagues with nearly two thousand members by July 1944, but eighteen months later all had gone, and not a League organisation was left in the district. (Ibid., and Mumtaz Daultana to Mian Iftikharuddin, 16 January 1946, QAP/File 588/143.) In May 1945, claims that there were 150,000 members in the Punjab League were exaggerated, but even taken at face-value are hardly evidence of a mass movement. (*Eastern Times*, 23 May 1945.)

[84] As late as January 1946, Daultana was trying to pick up a few rupees for the branches in Amritsar, Mianwali and Hoshiarpur. (Mumtaz Daultana to Mian Iftikharuddin, January 1946, QAP/Files: 588/143–50.) Daultana finally appealed to Jinnah for Rs.300,000 since a 'wonderful victory' was on the cards, but the League needed money for putting up the ante. (Daultana to Jinnah, 17 January 1946, QAP/File 257, p. 7.) Appreciating that the local League was fighting the 'hardest battle against the most treacherous foes in the Punjab', Jinnah agreed to give some money from his Central Fund. If Jinnah realised that this money was not to establish League branches but simply to buy candidates, he was not going to admit it. (Jinnah to Daultana, 17 January 1946, ibid.)

[85] On 30 September 1945, the Punjab Parliamentary Board, denouncing the 'weakness and insufficiency of the Muslim League organisation' in Lahore, called upon the Provincial Working Committee to appoint an action group to 'build up on a new, democratic, and wider basis the organisation of the two Leagues'. It made this move without telling the president of the City League. In his turn, the president complained to the High Command that he was being punished for trying to keep out the Reds, especially friends of Mamdot and Daultana. (See Punjab Lahore City Muslim League Affairs, 1945–1946, AIML/File No. 183.) High-flying ideological issues were good cover for low-flying intrigues on the ground.

resort of bankrupt commentators on these affairs. No one denies that the choices of the *pirs* mattered; but this was part and parcel of local patronage systems, with *pir* and landlord working hand in glove, rather than the profane and the religious in some improbable conflict in the plains of the Punjab. In keeping with their usual tactic, the A.I.M.L. had to take a compromising attitude over the heterodoxies and local feeling of a multitude of *pirs* who had their own particularist and idiosyncratic messages, often more material than moral. The decision by some of the least orthodox Muslim leaders of the Punjab League to create a Mashaikh Committee of twelve members[86] and stand forth as the official champions of Islam lent point to G. S. Ansari's proposal in 1943 to the A.I.M.L. Council that its policy should be one of: 'Respectfully requesting the Muslim religious heads, pirs and Sufis to help the Muslim Nation of India in its present life and death struggle.'[87] Of course there was an appeal to 'religion in danger'; it was an obvious cry. The League encouraged the prelates to give *fatwas* in its favour. Some propagandists threatened the voters that if they did not back the League they would cease to be Muslims; their marriages would be invalid and, if this did not frighten them, then they were told they would face 'ex-communication including a refusal to allow their dead to be buried in Muslim graveyards', and be debarred from 'joining in mass Muslim prayers'.[88] To counter such unsophisticated and fraudulent but effective tactics, the Unionists too had to become men of the Book. Khizar peppered his speeches with catchy quotes from the Quran to prove that Allah was 'Rabb-ul-Alameen', the Lord of everything and everyone, not the exclusive commander of the Faithful; a more logical line was that the Unionist party had nothing against 'Pakistan', but knew from long experience that only a coalition of the communities could run an undivided Punjab.[89]

So Unionists and Leaguers alike fought, the one to retain and the other

---

[86] While some of the members were men of unquestionable religious authority and power in local and provincial politics, others like the Nawab of Mamdot solemnly took the honorific title of the Pir of Mamdot Sharif; Shaukat Hayat became *Sajjada Nashin* of Wah Sharif; Firoz Khan Noon became the *Sajjada Nashin* of Sargodha Sharif and by far the most ostentatious title was appropriated by that worldly figure, the controversial secretary of the Committee, Ibrahim Ali Chishti who was designated as Fazl-i-Hind Sajjada Nashin of Paisa Akbar Sharif. (*Report of the Court of Inquiry . . . to enquire into the Punjab Disturbances of 1953* (commonly known in Pakistan as the Munir Report) (Lahore, 1954), pp. 254-5.) These were the men of god in the earthy affairs of the Punjab.

[87] G. S. Ansari to Jinnah, 25 April 1943, QAP/File 1101/105.

[88] Glancy to Wavell, 16 January 1946, L/P&J/5/249, I.O.L.

[89] V. P. Menon to George Abell, 20 November 1945, R/3/105, I.O.L.

to gain the allegiance of Punjab's notables, the men who really mattered, by means fair or foul, lay or religious. In the flux created by these tacks and turns, some *pirs* stuck with their old allies, but others saw better chances in changing sides. The permutations were endless. Pir Fazl Shah, with a shrine at Jalalpur in the Jhelum district, had kept out of local factions,[90] but his nephew, Raja Ghazanfar Ali Khan had ambitions to cut a figure in provincial politics and had persuaded his uncle to support him as early as the 1937 elections.[91] By 1946, the Pir had reconciled himself to being dragged into the mire of partisan politics and not only openly campaigned for the League but influenced other *pirs* in the locality to follow suit. The Pir had considerable influence, and one disillusioned Unionist complained that '80 per cent [of the] population of this district is "Pir-ridden".'[92] The voters were told the choice was simple, between 'Pakistan' and 'Kufiristan' (the land of the infidels).[93] In the end simplicity won the day and the League won all three seats to the assembly from Jhelum district. Another example of the way *pirs* and *biraderis* worked together to the League's advantage was in Jhang district where, with Shah Jiwana Bukhari Sayed Pir's help, two candidates related to *pirs* won both seats. In the Rawalpindi division, it was the 'out and out support of the Pir of Golra',[94] Pir Fazl Shah's brother, which took the League to its commanding heights.[95] The most spectacular success, however, was in the districts of Multan, Jhelum, Jhang and Karnal, where the League did best because the leading *pir* families decided to back it.[96]

The League's Parliamentary Board had ostensible control over the selection of candidates, and this in turn had something to do with its

[90] The Pir had a reputation of being his own man, and had his own party, known as 'Hizbullah' or 'party of God'. His writ ran mainly in Jhelum and western Gujerat districts, but he had followers in other districts too. (See Gilmartin, *Modern Asian Studies*, 13, 3 (1979), 497–8.)

[91] In 1937, Raja Ghazanfar Ali Khan fought the election on a League ticket, but had no qualms about joining the Unionists after being offered a parliamentary secretaryship by Khizar. After the split between Khizar and Jinnah in 1944, Ghazanfar saw that the tide was turning in the League's favour, so he too slipped back into the League, bringing with him, for good measure, the Pir, and his local supporters.

[92] Jhelum district organisation monthly report for December 1945, 2 January 1946, Unionist Papers, File D-44 cited in Gilmartin, *Modern Asian Studies*, 13, 3 (1979), 513, fn. 90.

[93] See Appendage to the Governor of Punjab's Report No. 587, February 1946, L/P&J/5/249, p. 147, I.O.L.

[94] Talbot, *Modern Asian Studies*, 14, 1 (1980), 68–9.

[95] Report of the Rawalpindi Divisional Organiser, 19 December 1945, Unionist Papers, File F-29, cited in Gilmartin, *Modern Asian Studies*, 13, 3 (1979), 514, fn. 92.

[96] Talbot, *Modern Asian Studies*, 14, 1 (1980), 69.

success, but in a somewhat indirect way. Only those candidates were selected whose local support was known to be strong, and they were selected with no regard to their personal credentials or their record of past services or present commitment to the League. Another factor was the League's effective propaganda against the tyranny of a bureaucracy, tarred with the Unionist brush.[97] Since the League itself had never succeeded in holding office, it made a present virtue out of its past failures and promised a new land of equal opportunities where the bureaucrats would be men of the people. This was Jacksonian democracy in an improbable setting. The League may have been surprised by how well it did at the polls, and so were the old Punjab hands who were as disappointed as the Unionist bosses at the extent of the League's success. But the historian is able to understand how it all came about. On 24 February 1946, when the results became known, it became clear that the Leaguers had won a 'greater victory than most of them appeared to have expected themselves'. But it was debatable whether this had much to do with a 'true unbiased verdict' on 'Pakistan'.[98] The League had won just under one out of three seats in an assembly of 175; the Unionists had managed to attract one vote in five, not a poor showing given the circumstances and hinting that there were still some Punjabis who could see the dangers to their province of this Gadarene rush under a League banner and the Congress itself had won more than one vote in five.[99]

---

[97] A common complaint was that the officials were 'bent upon harassing the League bitterly in the Punjab so as to vanquish it at the polls'. (See Mohammad Zakaullah (president of the Simla League) to Jinnah, 29 September 1945, AIML/SHC/3/File No. 30, Punjab vol. I.) Wavell told the Secretary of State that: 'the attitude of the average Indian politician to an election is rather like that of our own people in the eighteenth century. He argues that the Government in power has a certain pull, and it would be folly not to make use of it . . .'. (Wavell to Pethick-Lawrence, 1 October 1945, *T.P.*, VI, 304.) Jinnah of course could see how he could turn these complaints to the League's advantage; they were insurance in case the League lost the elections. In a strongly worded press statement, he claimed that the League workers were being 'coerced, threatened, intimidated and persecuted', but the Governor and the Viceroy had turned a 'deaf ear' to all 'those shameful and criminal tactics on the part of the Ministry in power. . .'. (Jinnah's press statement, February 1946, AIML/SHC/3/File No. 30, Punjab vol. I.)

[98] Glancy to Wavell, 28 February 1946, L/P&J/5/249, I.O.L.

[99] At the time of the 1945–46 elections, the population of the Punjab was roughly 28,419,000; 16,217,000 were Muslims, 7,550,000 Hindus, 3,757,000 Sikhs (*Census of India 1941*, Cmd. 6479, ix, Table VI, 11.) The electorate was 3,554,722, or about 12.5 per cent of the population; the Muslim electorate was 1,705,014, eleven per cent of the Muslims and only six per cent of the Punjab's population. But Muslims had separate electorates; the League polled 680,823 of the Muslim votes; so, by this calculation, a mere 2.5 per cent of the total population of the Punjab voted for the Muslim League.

Thus the Unionist defectors had split between the two centre parties, the League and the Congress, which had done badly at the polls in 1937.[100] They did well in the 1945–46 elections because the centre was undoubtedly going to have a greater say in the Punjab's future, something which Muslims, Hindus and Sikhs could ignore only at their cost. But a vote for the League in 1945–46 was mainly a calculated exercise in expediency; the politicians of the Punjab who became Leaguers in 1946 could, Jinnah realised, as easily desert their new allegiance as they had espoused it if they detected different straws in the wind.

But although the League did well, it did not do well enough. Its seventy-five seats in an assembly of 175 meant it had to come to terms with some of the other parties if it was to form a ministry. The communal stance which had helped to pull in the League voters now discouraged those elected on other tickets, also more communal, from entering into a coalition with the League. No one wanted to ally with the League.[101] So

The following table* gives the number of votes polled by the various political 'parties' in the Punjab.

Party	No. of votes polled	% of votes polled	Total no. of seats in the assembly
Congress	477,765	23.1	51
Unionists	419,231	20.2	21
Panthic Sikhs	160,763	7.8	21
MUSLIM LEAGUE	680,823	32.8	75
Communists	39,516	1.9	—
Others	295,238	14.2	7 (Independents)
TOTAL	2,073,336	100.0	175

* *Return Showing the Results of Elections to the Central Legislative Assembly and the Provincial Legislatures in 1945–46*, New Delhi 1948, p. 73, (henceforth *1945–46 Election Returns.*)

[100] The Congress's success at the polls was an almost mirror image of the League. Although it had no real organisation in the Punjab countryside and was as riddled with faction as the League, the Congress was able to benefit from the very different circumstances of 1945–46 to trounce its Unionist rivals. (See Chowdhury, *Studies in History*, 2, 2 (1980).)

[101] According to Daultana, the League, with Jinnah's approval, had approached Akali Sikhs before the elections. The Akalis were told that Pakistan as it was going to be, was different from the 'Pakistan' Muslim voters were being promised. As Firoz Khan Noon told Sir Evan Jenkins, he himself did not want the 'Pakistan' the League was propagating; indeed, he said he wished 'Pakistan had never been invented'. Noon however was ready to get as many seats as he could for the League on the Pakistan issue, then turn around and explain to non-Muslims that of course the League did not mean what it had been saying. Jenkins's reaction was that if this was the policy of the Punjab Leaguers, then 'surely the most reasonable and honest line to take was to give out that the League would be prepared to consider other forms of Pakistan if they were found

in the end the Governor had to call back Khizar and his rump of twenty-one Unionists to form a ministry, and he managed to do so with the help of Congress and the Panthic Sikhs. Glancy's decision not to invite the Nawab of Mamdot to form a League ministry has often been paraded by the sympathisers of the League as evidence of the old Adam of Unionism in Government House refusing to lie down. But the nature of the League's campaign during the elections and the implacable Hindu and Sikh opposition to 'Pakistan', even in watered-down Punjabi form, gives the true reason why a League ministry was a contradiction in terms in an united Punjab.

(b) Bengal

In Bengal, the complex interplay of factors which determined the choices of the Muslim voters had little to do with Jinnah and the A.I.M.L. Here the pattern of provincial particularism, the strong continuities of the local political traditions – of feud and faction, struggles between ins and outs, and the quiddities of local circumstance – qualify any notion of an united all-India Muslim movement rallying single-mindedly behind a common demand at the centre. The Bengali Muslims' idea of 'Pakistan' was very different from that of Muslims in other parts of India, and certainly different from what Jinnah had in mind. It was not a question of how Muslims would get a share of power in the rest of India, but rather the ideal of an independent sovereign state consisting of the whole of Bengal and Assam (and free of the exploitative Permanent Settlement system), which was the real motivating force behind a movement which, for the lack of a better name, called itself the Bengal Muslim League. The Bengal League was the beneficiary of groundwork prepared by decades

satisfactory, and thus heal the breach in the Muslim ranks'. But Noon frankly admitted that he did not have the 'courage to adopt this line'. (See Jenkins to Wavell, 27 November 1945, R/3/1/105, p. 110 B, I.O.L.)

After the elections, the League, in its search for a viable ministry, made further overtures to the Akalis. The Akalis, according to Daultana, agreed to support the League in the assembly, provided the League first formed a ministry. They did not want to be held responsible for putting a League ministry into office, but were ready to deal with it and benefit by alliance once it had got in. Daultana, Mian Iftikharuddin, Mian Bashir and Mamdot went to Khizar and told him that they were prepared to let him form the ministry even if he insisted on keeping out of the League. Khizar was shrewd enough to accept this offer. But all this had been done without a word of reference to Jinnah. When Jinnah was contacted in Shillong by telephone, he vetoed Daultana's proposal since it made obvious nonsense of his all-India strategy. The Leaguers now pleaded with Khizar to join the League. Khizar refused, and with his refusal all hopes for a ministry capable of keeping the Punjab united were shattered. Daultana maintains that it was Khizar who decided the fate of the Punjab in March 1946. (My interview with Mian Mumtaz Daultana, 10 February 1980, Lahore.)

of Praja Samity activities in the localities. Once the Huq–League coalition ministry introduced a series of legislative measures to improve the lot of the peasantry,[102] the Krishak Praja movement lost its impetus. Plagued with factional struggles and defections, the Krishak Praja party under Huq had been reduced to a rump. So in the early forties, the Bengal League was the only active Muslim political party in the province, its doors wide open to ex-Krishak Praja members, who continued to trickle in after 1943 and until the 1945–46 elections.[103]

At the time of the elections, Bengal was under Section 93. The fall of the Nazimuddin ministry was a blessing in disguise for the electoral prospects of the Muslim League. The ministry was unpopular (most ministries were), and this would have hampered the Provincial League's electoral campaign.[104] As the League in Bengal became more popular, the quarrel between the parliamentary party and the provincial organisation became more intense. With Huq out of the League, and the League ministry in office, the ministers did not want their freedom of action compromised by the organisation outside the assembly. After November 1944, the parliamentary 'coterie' took steps to stifle such organisation as the League possessed, particularly since it was becoming more Praja-orientated and threatened their traditional dominance in Bengali Muslim politics. Indeed, Nazimuddin went so far as to maintain that there was 'no Muslim League organisation' in Bengal.[105] Once the ministry was out of office, the Leaguers could devote all their energies to fighting inside the Bengal League without the minor distraction of trying to run a

---

[102] Such as the Bengal Tenancy (Amendment) Act, 1938; the Agricultural Debtors' (Second Amendment) Act, 1940; the Bengal Money-lenders Act, 1940 and the Bengal Secondary Education Bill, 1940.

[103] By 1945, most of the important Krishak Praja leaders had joined the League, for example Abul Mansur Ahmad, Abdulla-el-Baqui, Shamsuddin Ahmad (secretary Krishak Praja party), Nurul Islam Chowdhury and Giasuddin Ahmad. (See Sen, *Muslim Politics in Bengal*, p. 195.) For a full account of the Krishak Praja defections, see Ahmad, *Amar Dekha Rajnitir Panchas Bachhar* (Fifty years of politics as I saw it), pp. 194–8.

[104] No one was particularly sorry to see the League ministry fall. In the view of some East Bengali students, the ministry was a 'rule of a coterie'; corruption was its middle name; it had no interest in the people it claimed to represent and did not 'know the real problems of Bengal'; 'money-making' was what the ministry was in business for. Nazimuddin was described as 'a bureaucratic cowardly unsympathetic and ill-tempered man', in the pocket of his younger brother, Shahabuddin, 'the arch devil in the Party' and a shrewd 'Machiavellian, heartless villain'; Suhrawardy was cunning and ambitious, and a 'hopeless braggard'. Fazlur Rahman, the chief whip was 'rude, repulsive, devilish, dishonest'; Akram Khan, the president was a 'sentimental giant' who was far too 'old and should now retire in his den' and Abul Hashim was someone who started 'his work with vigour, but finishes badly' (Shahid Ahmed to Liaquat Ali Khan, 17 May 1945, AIML/File No. 42.)   [105] Ibid.

province with formidable problems of its own.[106] In the scramble for power, the Nazimuddin and Suhrawardy factions were dominant, and anyone who tried to challenge their monopoly was branded as a dangerous communist.[107]

As for actual League organisation, out of the twenty-seven districts of Bengal, there were by 1945 District Leagues in eighteen, but these were hardly dynamos of energy.[108] During 1944–45, the organisation held no regular elections, and enlisted hardly any primary members. Abul Hashim had his own reasons for not pressing for elections to be held within the League; as the secretary of the Bengal League, he was generally popular, but he had enemies as well in his home base, the Burdwan District League, of which he was the president. Of course, he rushed hither and yon, but one man's zeal was no alternative to a more regular system of watch and ward over the League's affairs.[109] It was encouraging to learn from Hashim that 550,000 members had been put on the lists and that membership during 1945 might even reach ten per cent of the total Muslim population of Bengal. But these figures were at best approximate since the A.I.M.L.'s inspector reported that as yet no one had been able to devise a system of finding out the actual number of League members; a daunting task even for the Recording Angel.[110]

This was hardly a description of a well-organised party, whatever may have been the trends towards a more spontaneous movement among the people below. Mindful that branch elections inside the League would be the shot from the starter's pistol to set everyone racing to cut their rivals' throats, the Working Committee of the League quite sensibly decided to postpone all such local entertainments until after the general elections. Certainly those who were 'combining to give the Muslim League a fight'

---

[106] When the League's High Command sent its inspector, Liaquat Ali Khan, to assess the Bengal situation, he found little which gave it any comfort. In Ispahani's opinion, Nazimuddin's ministry had been 'caught napping' and was 'diddled very cleverly by the Opposition' (Ispahani to Jinnah, 24 April 1945, Zaidi (ed.), *Correspondence*, p. 447.)

[107] The Muslim press in Calcutta attacked the Dacca students for their communist ideas. To counter these attacks, the students took refuge in Islam, making 'prayers . . . compulsory' for the workers. (Shahid Ahmed to Liaquat Ali Khan, 17 May 1945, AIML/File No. 42.)

[108] In the Rajshahi, Malda and Jessore districts, the District Leagues had failed to hold annual elections in 1944, and though they were still affiliated to the Provincial League, this was unconstitutional. In three other districts, 24 Parganas, Birbhum and Midnapore, no Leagues had been formed although organising committees had been set up by the Provincial League. In the four remaining districts of Chittagong Hills, Jalpaiguri, Darjeeling and Bankura, there was not even the pretence of a League office. (See A.I.M.L.'s Committee of Action's Inspection report on the general administration of the Bengal Provincial Muslim League, No. 12, 29 March 1945, AIML/2, File No. 201.)

[109] Ibid.   [110] Ibid.

were likely to take advantage of the blatantly obvious rivalries and factions which such local elections would bring to the fore.[111] Hashim's enemies in the Burdwan District League are an obvious example; they passed a no-confidence motion against him and wanted to prevent him from getting a League ticket. As the M.L.A. from Burdwan, Hashim obviously hoped to get re-elected, and the Provincial League could hardly afford to stop the League's star playing at home on a League ticket and rejected the no-confidence motion.[112]

The Working Committee of the Bengal Muslim League was desperately anxious to paper over the cracks, in all conscience wide enough, which were showing in the veneer of unity it had brushed over its own house. It had somehow to set up a Parliamentary Board without a major row. By 31 August 1945, it had launched an election fund and a provincial propaganda committee, but this was light, easy work, compared to getting an agreed Parliamentary Board. Of course everyone expected that once the Parliamentary Board had been put together, this unusual display of solidarity would go to pieces. Ispahani warned his ailing leader, who was recovering from his 'superhuman efforts' in Quetta, that there were ominous signs that the unity of the Bengal League was about to go the way of Indian unity. One local Leaguer thought that Jinnah should be on the spot to call these factions to order.[113] With an election on its way, a matter of 'life and death' for Muslim India, the Bengal leaders were as usual squabbling in an ecstasy

---

[111] Informing the High Command of the decision, the office secretary of the Bengal League explained that: 'Under the present conditions, rivalries of [a] serious nature are sure to take place between different parties for capturing the League from the Union up to the Districts and there will be serious cleavages and party factions in the rank and file of the Muslims throughout the Province. As a result our immediate task of winning the General Elections to the Legislature on behalf of the Muslim League will be greatly hampered'. (Farmuzul Huq to Liaquat Ali Khan, 4 September 1945, AIML/2, File No. 42.)

[112] The assistant secretary of the Burdwan District League and some of his henchmen passed a no-confidence motion against Hashim, and called on the Provincial League's Parliamentary Board to drop him. It was only by the device of telling the Burdwan League that a joint meeting of the Working Committee and the Parliamentary Board of the Provincial League had decided that no meetings for the purpose of passing no-confidence or confidence motions against executives of district, sub-divisional or union Leagues could be held till after the general elections were over that they saved Hashim from being denied a place on the team. (Bengal Muslim League Working Committee to Moulvi Nasirul Haque, ibid.)

[113] He wrote: 'We in this part of India, fail to understand why Mr Jinnah thought it fit to go over to Quetta at a time when practically in all the Provinces we are to form the Parliamentary Boards . . .'. (Asadullah to Liaquat, 17 September 1945, AIML/File No. 42.)

of self-interest to do down their particular local rivals. Nazimuddin and Suhrawardy were at daggers drawn,[114] trying to sign up potential supporters for their claims to lead the new ministry.[115] But despite these frantic calls to him to bring light and leading to Bengal, Jinnah was no one's fool: the solid ground of Quetta was as far away in India as he could get from the turbulent charms of Bengali politics. Those closer at hand could see the advantage of claiming that health (already precarious in the Quaid-i-Azam's case) and an interest in politics did not go together, least of all in Calcutta.[116]

On 29 September the Provincial League Council met to form the Parliamentary Board, and, as Ispahani told Jinnah: 'The squabbles that were being carried on for a couple of weeks behind the purdah . . . now come before the public and the tug-of-war for power is being demonstrated in the limelight of publicity.'[117] After rowdy scenes, in which some members were actually injured, the Provincial League elected a Parliamentary Board of nine members to nominate candidates and to run the elections.[118] Despite Nazimuddin's best efforts,

---

[114] According to one League enthusiast, both Suhrawardy and Nazimuddin 'forget the supreme importance of unity and solidarity at this moment[;] they are out for their own supremacy. Party faction spirit is running high and if it is not suppressed by an iron hand, the result would be that a Parliamentary Board would be formed that would consist of persons with party affiliations and the nominations would also go to the people of the party in power. This is most undesirable and candidates nominated by such a Board would fall far below the standard defined by Mr Jinnah.' (Ibid.)

[115] Certainly, there was 'no sign of compromise and there is very little hope that better sense would prevail upon them at this crucial moment. It was only Mr. Jinnah, who could have interfered and suppressed the faction spirit of the Leaders at this most critical moment in the life of the Muslim nation.' (Ibid.)

[116] Maulana Akram Khan, the president of the Bengal League, now decided to resign: 'the League organisation in Bengal has been deteriorating at a rapid stride and diving headlong towards a crisis. For the last seven months, I have strenuously tried, from my sick bed and moving stretcher, to retard the deterioration of my cherished organisation but all my efforts have failed and this has caused a further mental breakdown of mine [sic].' (Maulana Akram Khan to Jinnah, 24 September 1945, ibid.)

[117] Ispahani to Jinnah, 1 October 1945, Zaidi (ed.), *Correspondence*, p. 456.

[118] On the day before the actual election, Nazimuddin had 'collared four seats' and felt sure of winning at least two out of the remaining five seats which would have given him a clear majority on the Board. But Suhrawardy and Abul Hashim were able to win all five of the remaining seats. (See Ispahani to Jinnah, 1 October 1945, ibid., pp. 456–9.) The Parliamentary Board consisted of Fazlur Rahman, Khan Bahadur Nurul Amin, Maulana Akram Khan and Nazimuddin – all Nazimuddin's men and elected only because they held positions inside the Provincial League or the parliamentary party. The Provincial League Council elected the remaining members of the Parliamentary Board; they were: Suhrawardy, Abul Hashim, Ahmad Hossain, Raghib Ahsan and Moazzem Hossain. (Abul Hashim to Liaquat Ali Khan, 1 October 1945, AIML/File No. 42.)

Suhrawardy was able to secure his dominance on the Board which assured him the League parliamentary party's leadership after the elections.[119] The next day, Hindu and Muslim newspapers wrote of this hooliganism parading as politics under headlines which put to shame those few Muslims in Bengal, such as Ispahani, who, at least by their own account, 'put the League above personal ambition'. Ispahani had to admit that the 'struggle, with all its attendant ugliness, is for power in Bengal', with both Nazimuddin and Suhrawardy playing the 'game of pull baker pull devil' [sic]. He complained bitterly that: 'Not a single selfless servant of the League, including myself, not one who puts the Organisation above the individual found a place on either of the two panels.'[120]

Jinnah made short shrift of all these reports; it was entirely up to the Leaguers in Bengal to 'pull together'; no matter what the provocations or what personal intrigues and self-interest, the only issue before Muslims, according to Jinnah, was

Pakistan against Akhand Hindustan . . . I don't think that anyone of those who are ambitious will survive to realize their dreams when the Assembly meets, and even if they do, the newly elected Assembly is not going to be a permanent charter. Therefore, I do hope they will give up thinking in terms of Chief Minister and Ministers, as divided, different groups will go flying, and what is more, we shall have lost the paramount issue of Pakistan in the eyes of the world.[121]

He could have been whistling in the wind for all the notice anyone in Bengal took of these fine sentiments.

Suhrawardy's success on the Parliamentary Board did not please Government House. Nazimuddin, dispirited and anxious to get out of it all, was now minded to throw in the towel.[122] He saw Abul Hashim behind the move to get radicals and Communists into Suhrawardy's

---

[119] As Ispahani told Jinnah, both Suhrawardy and Nazimuddin wanted to become the next chief minister of Bengal, and those who did not want to be drawn into this disgraceful fight 'have been left out in the cold by both'. They only put on the Board men upon whom they could count, and all Ispahani now expected was that tickets would be handed out, conditional upon votes for one or the other of these two factions. (Ispahani to Jinnah, 1 October 1945, Zaidi (ed.), *Correspondence*, p. 457.)

[120] Ibid.

[121] Jinnah to Ispahani, 9 October 1945, Ibid., p. 462.

[122] Twynam, who was acting as Governor in Casey's absence, reported that Nazimuddin was 'shaken by his defeat . . . and . . . told me that, as a result, he was going to give up politics, to which I replied, "You mustn't do that".' (Twynam to Wavell, 5 October 1945, L/P&J/5/152, I.O.L.) Ispahani also told Nazimuddin that his decision not to stand for a seat in the legislature was a 'tragedy of great magnitude' for Bengal. (Ispahani to Jinnah, 12 November 1945, Zaidi (ed.), *Correspondence*, p. 468.)

camp; and the net result of the 'dirty play and bogus votes' of Suhrawardy's faction would be Reds under the League's charpoys.[123] But Nazimuddin decided to put a patriotic face onto a bad business and not only 'bore the defeat in silence' but placed 'every ounce of his energy to make . . . the coming elections a success'.[124] Of course Nazimuddin, and his charming little brother, Khwaja Shahabuddin, could see that their days in Calcutta were numbered; neither was prepared to stand as a candidate in the provincial elections and instead looked forward to the compensations of New Delhi. Nazimuddin got Jinnah to appoint him on the A.I.M.L.'s Working Committee, an appropriate reward for past service on a battle-field from which the commander-in-chief had kept his distance.

Having established their supremacy in the Bengal Provincial League Council and the Parliamentary Board, Suhrawardy's men naturally wanted to extend their control over all aspects of the League's activities in the province. As soon as the Parliamentary Board was formed, the Provincial League Council dissolved the election fund committee and the provincial propaganda committee, on which the Nazimuddin and Ispahani supporters still had a considerable sway. The Council now decided that all propaganda work and fund raising would be the Board's responsibility, or rather in charge of Suhrawardy's men.[125] But this made it difficult for them to raise funds for the elections since the Calcutta-based Muslim businessmen were not willing to contribute to a party run by men they profoundly distrusted. So Suhrawardy had to ask Jinnah for Rs.50,000, claiming that the subventions of the province had been improperly diverted to the centre.[126] Jinnah was having none of this; his fund was not to be spent on the ambitions of an importunate politician who had kicked out his loyal henchmen in Bengal. In any case, he was 'already incurring enormous amounts of expenditure in supervising all the Provinces' and could not give a pie to Bengal.[127] Jinnah's line was that Bengal should stand on its own feet, instead of looking to the centre for handouts, especially since 'there has been no real support to the Central Fund from Bengal'.[128]

Not surprisingly, Bengal's new leader felt no great obligation to a centre which had cut him out of his share of the League's petty cash. But Suhrawardy was now the boss of the Bengal Muslim League. His

123 Ibid.   124 Ibid.
125 Meeting of the Bengal League Council, Calcutta, 29-30 September 1945, AIML/File No. 42.
126 Suhrawardy to Jinnah, 25 October 1945, Ibid.
127 Jinnah to Suhrawardy, 30 October 1945, AIML/SHC/File No. 33, Bengal vol. III.
128 Ibid.

relations with Jinnah were bad. Yet Suhrawardy could not altogether do without Jinnah at the centre, and Jinnah could hardly deny Suhrawardy in Bengal if he wanted to claim that the province was behind him. As the leader of the League, Suhrawardy could now pretend to be a paragon of moderation, not only in dealing with his defeated rivals in the Bengal League or with Jinnah at the centre, but also in encouraging independent and non-League Muslims to make their last-minute conversions to the all-India cause. Suhrawardy wanted Jinnah to issue a 'general amnesty' to all those Muslims in Bengal who so far had remained outside the League. This was mainly to enable Huq to return to the League's fold, which would have brought the rump of the Krishak Praja party into the League camp and given Suhrawardy a few more seats in the assembly.[129] Suhrawardy also wanted Nazimuddin to contest the elections in Bengal. This was because Suhrawardy and his faction believed that Nazimuddin's 'good reputation would be useful to them'.[130] But no one was persuaded that the tiger had altered his stripes – certainly not those Muslims who formed their own National Muslim Parliamentary Board under Huq, consisting of nationalist Muslims and the rump of the Krishak Praja party with backing from the Congress and the Jamiat-ul-Ulema-i-Hind. This meant that although the League could expect to win most of the Muslim seats in the elections, it would have to fight all the way to this position.

This made the question of who selected the League candidates a critical issue; and the fight for tickets in Bengal proved as violent as the electoral campaign which followed. The nomination of League candidates by the Parliamentary Board inevitably created a great deal of dissatisfaction amongst those who failed to get tickets. The Provincial League office in Calcutta was raided by students and a demonstration was held outside Suhrawardy's house protesting against his undue interference in the selection of candidates.[131] Violence, actual and physical, was now commonplace in local politics, particularly in Calcutta where 'blood and ballot' went hand in hand. The crowds were out of control, an ominous sign for the future; the police had frequently to give them a whiff of grapeshot or a thwack of iron-bound sticks; strong-arm men broke up their rivals' meetings and charge and counter-charge, both

---

[129] Suhrawardy to Jinnah, 6 November 1945, AIML/SHC/File No. 23, Bengal vol. I.

[130] Casey to Wavell, 5 November 1945, L/P&J/5/152, I.O.L. In the end none of Suhrawardy's pre-election manoeuvres succeeded; Jinnah did not issue any statement and Huq preferred to go his own way, while Nazimuddin decided to use his 'good repute' at the centre.

[131] See Secret Report on the Political Situation in Bengal, first half of February 1946, L/P&J/5/153, I.O.L.

in words and in acts, followed one rowdy meeting after another.[132] There was not much difference in the tactics and propaganda of the League and the National Muslim Parliamentary party. But while both called religion to their aid and demanded the abolition of unholy zamindari, Huq's opposition to 'Pakistan' and his links with the Congress gave the League an excuse to brand his men as 'National traitors' sabotaging the right of Bengali Muslims to have an Islamic homeland of their own.[133] In the circumstances of 1945–46, the League had a clear edge over its rivals in propaganda terms, since the trends in British policy hinted that the A.I.M.L. and the Congress would settle the constitutional issue, and since elections in Bengal were to be fought inside separate electorates, Bengali Muslims saw their interests better protected by a communal party linked to the A.I.M.L. than by an uncertain coalition under Huq whose main prop was local Congress support. According to Abul Mansur Ahmad, an ex-Krishak Praja leader, but now the League's propaganda secretary, the League had become the real 'revolutionary people's organisation' in Bengal, the 'vanguard' of the old Krishak Praja party, while the pro-Congress Krishak Praja party had been reduced to a shambles with no platform, no primary members and no union branches. It could not even dare to deliver a speech in any public place where Muslims were gathered together.[134]

Everyone was surprised that the elections for the central assembly went off as quietly as they did; but they were less surprised by the results. In this dress-rehearsal for the general election, the Muslim League won all six Muslim seats from Bengal to the central legislative assembly. The Congress won seven, the Europeans three, and the Independent pro-Congress one. The League's success in the Muslim seats was overwhelming, and its candidates won with large majorities.[135] These results

132 According to Ashrafuddin Ahmed Choudhury, a leading member of the Bose group in the Congress and running the campaign for the National Muslim Parliamentary Board, it was impossible for the non-League Muslims to hold a meeting without it being disrupted by the League's men. (See Ashrafuddin Ahmed Choudhury, *Raj Birodhi* (Opponent of the Raj) (Dacca, 1978), *passim.*)

133 Ibid., pp. 104–6.

134 Abul Mansur Ahmad, 'The Background and Nature of Bengal Muslim Politics: It is the Muslim League which is today the vanguard of the Krishak Praja Movement', in *Millat*, Calcutta, 23 November 1945.

135 In the Calcutta and Suburbs Muslim urban constituency, the League candidate, Abdur Rahman Siddiqui, received 4,580 votes as opposed to 320 for the nationalist Muslim. Suhrawardy won the Burdwan and Presidency Divisions seat and had nearly ninety-two per cent of the total votes. In the Dacca–Mymensingh constituency, the League candidate got 12,024 as against his opponent's mere 770 votes. The League's victory in the remaining three Muslim urban constituencies was overwhelming. (See *1945–46 Election Returns*, pp. 10–21.)

persuaded Casey, who was about to give up office, that his successor,
Burrows, might soon be facing in Bengal the situation he had always
feared and tried assiduously to avoid: an exclusively Muslim ministry
facing an exclusively Hindu opposition.[136] The run-up to the provincial
elections showed that the propaganda of politics if not its substance was
coming to be drawn on sharp communal lines, a development ominous
for an united Bengal. Bengal's administrative services were getting
infected by this trend, and most Indian officials were coming out openly
in support either of the League or the Congress.[137]

The provincial elections were very different from those for the central
assembly. For one thing, the electorate was vastly larger; for another,
sending delegates to the centre where the League had its all-India *raison
d'être* was a different matter from concentrating on the squabbles at home
in Bengal. Bengali Muslims, no less than their Hindu counterparts,
could see that whatever their internal divisions, the time had come to
clamber on the bandwagons at the centre. But behind this solidarity lay a
host of conflicting aims and factions. Despite the fact that much of the
Krishak Praja party's support in the 1937 elections had now shifted to the
League, and it was mainly a matter of the old system coming to terms
with a new situation, the electoral contests in the Muslim constituencies
were fierce. There were as many as 433 candidates for the 117 rural and
urban seats.[138] In the end the League won 115 of the Muslim seats, but
not always with ease, and it lost in six. By contrast, only four of the
candidates set up by the National Muslim Parliamentary Board won, and
Huq alone succeeded against a League candidate.[139] So the League's
victory was overwhelming; it received ninety-five per cent of the total

---

[136] Of the two-hundred and fifty seats in the Bengal assembly, one hundred and twenty-
three were Muslim constituencies. Before the elections, Casey thought the League
would win at least one hundred and thirteen of the Muslim seats. With support from the
Scheduled Castes, Europeans, Anglo-Indians and Christians, it would have a clear
majority in the house. He calculated that the opposition would then consist of
approximately ninety Congress members and thirteen non-Muslims. But Casey feared
that the chronic factionalism inside the League might give the opposition a chance of
detaching some of its supporters. In this case Section 93 was again on the cards. (See
Casey to Wavell, 7 January 1946, L/P&J/5/152, I.O.L.)

[137] In Casey's opinion, on the whole 'both Muslim and Hindu officers try to do their duty
fairly', but the 'sympathies of the majority of Indian Officers lie with the Muslim
League and Congress respectively' and 'their private political feelings are stronger
than makes for good administration', which was 'one way of saying that communal
feeling has driven pretty deep into nearly all ranks of the administration in Bengal'.
(Ibid.)

[138] See *1945–46 Election Returns*, p. 71.

[139] Burrows to Wavell, 11 April 1946, L/P&J/5/153, I.O.L.

Muslim urban vote and 84.6 per cent of the total Muslim rural vote.[140]

Though it had polled almost a third of a million votes less than the Congress, overall the League was the largest single party in the assembly with a voting strength twice as large as that of the Congress and likely to be afforced by the Scheduled Caste and European members.[141] At the centre, Jinnah was calling for 'Pakistan'. But the perspective from Calcutta was quite different. Suhrawardy could see that a stable, united, and well-administered Bengal could not be achieved by the League alone, despite its successful juggling with the electoral arithmetic. He

[140] The following table gives an account of the votes for the various political parties in the elections for the Bengal assembly.

Party	No. of votes polled	% of votes polled	No. of votes polled from Muslim electorate		% of votes from the Muslims	
			Urban	Rural	Urban	Rural
Congress	2,337,053	42.2	—	11,759	—	0.5
Muslim League	2,057,830	37.2	24,182	2,032,805	95.0	84.6
Krishak Praja & nationalist Muslims	172,880	3.1	713	172,167	2.7	7.1
Hindu Mahasabha	78,981	1.4	—	—	—	—
Communists	157,197	2.8	—	3,244	—	0.1
Others (Including some pro-League Independent Muslims)	736,882	13.3	556	185,166	2.2	7.7

Of the urban Muslims entitled to vote, 77,840, or 55.4 per cent, actually voted. The League secured all six of the urban seats reserved for Muslims in the assembly. Of the total rural electorate of 4,641,687 Muslims for the 111 contested seats (seven were filled without a contest), 54.9 per cent voted. The League had secured 2,056,987 votes cast in its favour compared to the total of 373,605 Muslim votes secured by the Congress, the Krishak Praja party and the nationalist and Independent Muslims combined. (See *1945–46 Election Returns*, p. 71.)

[141] The composition of the new Bengal assembly was:

Muslim League	115	Congress	62
Independent Muslim	2	Independent Hindu	1
Muslim Labour	1	Hindu Mahasabha	1
Krishak Praja party	5	Christians	2
Scheduled Castes (reserved)	24	Anglo-Indians	4
Independent Scheduled Castes	5	Communists	3
Europeans	25	TOTAL	250

(Burrows to Wavell, 11 April 1946, L/P&J/4/153, I.O.L.)

had to contrive a coalition with at least parts of the Congress in much the same way, but now from the Muslim vantage point, as C. R. Das had attempted to do in the twenties. Burrows encouraged Suhrawardy to hold talks with the Congress leaders in the province. If a League–Congress ministry in Bengal had emerged at this stage, this would have seriously jeopardised Jinnah's all-India strategy, however much it echoed his own plans and purposes in different times and different circumstances. But all he could do was to hope that the negotiations would fail. In fact, the talks between Suhrawardy and the Bengal Congress dragged on for more than a fortnight, both in Calcutta and New Delhi. But with the Cabinet Mission in India, the Congress and the League High Commands both had more important concerns than the self-absorbed manoeuvring inside this troublesome province.

So here again, Jinnah was saved by the bell, rung this time from the Congress centre. The Congress High Command was not prepared to let the Bengal Congress Committee come to terms with the League. This would give Bengal an opportunity to assert a greater measure of provincial autonomy which the Congress High Command could not afford to countenance since it had to look to the power and unity of its centre. The negotiations ostensibly broke down on the question of how the two parties would share office in the coalition ministry and how both sides could have a veto on 'communal' legislation, something obviously more important in Bengal to the minority Congressmen than to the League.[142] But in fact the negotiations collapsed because the Congress High Command put pressure on the Bengal Congress to stand back. The breakdown of the negotiations was ominous for Bengal's future. If the coalition had come about, this certainly would have affected the resolution of the larger problems at the centre. For Bengal there was not to be another opportunity, although Bengali politicians understandably did not see this in the obscure crystal glass of Calcutta. On 22 April 1946, Suhrawardy formed a League ministry in Bengal. He had rustled up at least 126 votes (excluding the Speaker) in a house of 250. Since the Europeans, with their twenty-five seats, could be expected to vote with the ministry, Suhrawardy was in the saddle; the opposition could not

[142] Another reason for the failure, according to Burrows, was 'the usual stumbling block to coalition, namely the conflicting claims of the Congress and the Muslim League over the exclusive right claimed by the latter to nominate all Muslim members', but 'it was tacitly understood between Kiran Shankar Roy and Suhrawardy that the Congress had no Muslim whom they could seriously press on him'. Congress might have settled for six seats in a cabinet of thirteen or five in a cabinet of eleven, but were not prepared to accept five in a cabinet of twelve. Various alternatives were put forward, but none in the end proved strong enough to resist the Congress High Command's pressures. (See Burrows to Wavell, 25 April 1946, Ibid.)

hope to overturn him, and the old Nazimuddin faction had effectively been pushed out of the running. This cut down the options of those in Bengal who were not ready to accept a League solution for the province. Now that the High Command was making its reluctant allies in the Bengal League toe the line, and events inside Bengal were making agreement between the ministry and the Hindus increasingly unlikely, undivided Bengal was coming to have no future, only a past, less glorious in fact than in the legends of a people who proved to be the victims of the capital concerns of a centre which they had helped to create but had never really controlled.

(c) Sind

In Sind, the province of his ancestors, Jinnah would have liked to keep as Olympian a distance as possible from the intrigues of the provincial Sindhi politicians. He knew to his cost that most Sindhi politicians had joined the League for their own reasons and there was always the danger that they might suddenly shift out of his camp if this happened to serve their local or particularist interest. The ministry under Ghulam Hussain paid lip-service to the League's High Command. But the Provincial League under G. M. Syed was in open revolt against the ministry. Already before the elections he had made overtures to the Congress, which now showed signs of reviving since its leaders were out of jail and back in politics. In their turn, Syed's enemies organised a parallel League which passed a vote of no-confidence in him, and Syed responded in kind by forming a League of his own, the 'Syed League', which from June 1945 had its own organisation, meetings and candidates for local body elections.[143] Ineluctably Jinnah was drawn to Karachi to patch up these differences among the Sindhi politicians. As the Governor commented:

Jinnah dislikes them all (he once told me that he could buy the lot of them for five lakhs of rupees, to which I replied that I could do it a lot cheaper) and has been mainly concerned that the League ticket should go to the man most likely to be returned, his previous or subsequent loyalty to the League being a minor consideration.[144]

[143] According to Yusuf Haroon, Syed had the support of some 'big people' and the official League was divided. The situation was: 'getting worse day by day . . . general elections will soon follow and if the present state of affairs continue, the Muslim League will cut a very poor figure. Drastic changes are needed. All groups and cliques within the League field must be immediately liquidated. A solid Muslim Phalanx must be nurtured to fight the Muslims as well as the Hindu opposition to the League.' (Yusuf Haroon to Jinnah, 25 June 1945, AIML/SHC/2/File No. 10, Sind vol. VI.) Thus a province with only the most nominal commitment to the A.I.M.L. had mushroomed three Leagues in its unpropitious soil.

[144] Dow to Wavell, 20 September 1945, L/P&J/5/267, I.O.L.

Since Jinnah had neither the funds nor a dedicated group of workers in Sind, all that he wanted, or at least all he could expect, from Sind was a victory in name for the League.

There was no question of the centre calling the shots in Sind or handing out tickets from the League's headquarters; the best Jinnah could do was to persuade the local men to set up their own Provincial Parliamentary Board, which quickly set to cutting each others' throats in the scrabble for tickets once he was out of Karachi.[145] When Khuhro appealed to Jinnah against his arch-enemy Ghulam Hussain, claiming he failed to 'understand how the premier and such a ministry could be regarded as a League premier or League ministry', Jinnah was reduced to his usual anodyne platitudes, the pouring of thin oil on troubled provincial waters over which he had little control and in which he perhaps had even less interest.[146] In the end it made sense for him to keep in with the ministry that had the patronage, and keep his distance from all appeals to help convert the League in Sind into a populist party.[147] Rural Sind was the domain of its notables and Jinnah left it to them and their allies, the mullahs and *pirs*, to beguile the voters with the usual mixture of carrots and sticks afforced by religious slogans.

Sind did not have many voters – just under a million, or a little over one in five of the population. Of these voters, two-thirds were Muslim, in

---

[145] Syed maintained that some members of the Board had been promising tickets to candidates without consulting the Board. He had received requisitions from twenty-five members of the Provincial League for an emergency meeting to consider a no-confidence motion against some members of the Parliamentary Board. These members were allegedly canvassing for certain candidates even before the League's tickets had actually been allotted. So the signatories of the no-confidence motion wanted the allotment of seats to start from scratch. (See G. M. Syed to Jinnah, 3 October 1945, AIML/SHC/2/File No. 10, Sind vol. VI.)

[146] Khuhro to Jinnah, 7 October 1945, ibid. Jinnah sent Khuhro a characteristic reply: 'I do hope the Central Parliamentary Board will be able to successfully handle the matter . . . the only issue before us is Pakistan versus Akhand Hindustan and if Sind falls, God help you. There will be nothing left. All the individual dreams and cliques and groups will evaporate and Sind Muslims will stand discredited and paralysed. I do hope that the seriousness of the situation will be fully realised . . . I wish people thought less of Premier and Ministers and think more of the paramount and vital issue confronting us. If you all stand solid and close your ranks, success is within your grasp.' (Jinnah to Khuhro, 13 October 1945, ibid.)

[147] Jinnah was charged with the allegation that he lived like a 'grand Moghul in Palaces where poor Muslim masses cannot reach you' and by staying with 'the class of Capitalists and officials will never make you fit to serve them'. (M.U. Abbassi to Jinnah 5 September 1945, ibid.) Jinnah responded by claiming, contrary to the facts, that the League in Sind was already a 'people's Party'. (See Jinnah to M.U. Abbassi, 5 September 1945, ibid.)

thirty-one rural and only two urban seats.[148] No one made any secret of the fact that a contested election might cost each candidate half a lakh of rupees, since the going price among the electorate was 'a note [of one rupee] for a vote'.[149] Government House thought that the elections would cost the hundred or so candidates between fifty and a hundred lakhs, which meant that if the politicians at the top could be bought for pennies, the voters at the base would *en masse* cost substantially more – at any rate Jinnah's total fund contained less than six lakhs of rupees, hardly enough, on his own calculations, to buy just the men at the top, let alone finance a campaign in all the provinces of India.

So Sindhi politicians had to be left to their own devices. By late October 1945, the Sind Parliamentary Board had collapsed. The Sind League was split down the middle and Jinnah's Central Parliamentary Board was desperately anxious to wash its hands of the whole affair. But there was danger from Syed, who, according to the *Sind Observer* wanted 'self-determination to establish a Sindhi Pakistan without interference from the League High Command', and argued that it was the 'Nawabs and Nawabzadas [who] create all-round trouble by trying to make Sind a pawn in the All-India Muslim League game'. Syed was not prepared to accept any 'outside interference' in his 'Sindhi Pakistan', and so far as the communal problem was concerned, he was certain that it could be 'settled between the Hindus and Muslims living in the Province for centuries' and who would 'know how to get together and settle their affairs easily'.[150] This was a direct threat to Jinnah's hopes of bringing in Sind behind his all-India strategy since Syed was threatening to make a deal with the Congress.[151] Jinnah's reaction was simply to send solemn injunctions to the League that it must fight the elections 'tooth and nail'; it was, he argued: 'the duty of every Musalman to support the official Muslim League candidates. Your votes . . . are not for the individuals,

---

148 Under the Government of India Act of 1935, only 999,342 (approximately twenty-two per cent) of the population in Sind were enfranchised. Of these, 676,744 were Muslims. There were only two urban Muslim seats (with an electorate of 48,376) and thirty-one rural Muslim seats (with an electorate of 623,333), and one seat for Muslim women (with an electorate of 5,015). (See *Census of India 1941*, Cmd. 6479, ix and *1945–46 Election Returns*, p. 54.)

149 Sind Chief Secretary's Report, 2 October 1945, L/P&J/5/267, I.O.L.

150 Sind Chief Secretary's Report, Appendix I, 2 November 1945, ibid.

151 Syed planned to set up his own Forward Muslim Bloc in the hope of forming a coalition with Congress. The local Congress leader, Nichaldas, openly encouraged Syed and had offered him four seats in the ministry including the chief ministership. Dow did not think that a Congress coalition ministry in Sind was entirely implausible; Congress was better organised and the League was unlikely to remain united, and at least eight Muslim members of the assembly would join whoever formed the ministry. (See Dow to Wavell, 19 October and 3 November, 1945, ibid.)

but . . . for Pakistan . . .'[152] Fine words, but hardly matching the crore [ten million] of rupees that the Congress had allotted for the Sind elections.[153] In the 'heroic fight',[154] which according to Jinnah the Muslim League was putting up in Sind, their best ally was the organised and heavily financed push by the Congress which the Sindhi notables, and their fierce local particularism, deeply resented. In the end, the A.I.M.L.'s Committee of Action had in January 1946 to expel Syed both from the Sind League and from the central organisation. But once Syed was out, Khuhro and his gang moved in, and the Talpurs happily signed League and Khaksar pledges at the same time although these were contradictory in their declared aims.[155] Until the eve of the elections, the High Command continued to receive hysterical appeals for help from Sindhi Leaguers about which it could do absolutely nothing. A typical example was the request to the ' . . . Qaid-e-Islam, to send best front rank leaders in Sind, who must run and should perform a hurricane tour in Sind as the polling day is at hand. For God's sake wise leaders [sic] to come over here as people are in [the] dark what is League and what it desires'.[156]

The elections predictably resolved into in-fighting between the Muslim League (which nominated thirty-five candidates), the Jamiat-ul-Ulema and the Muslim Board (with fifteen candidates),[157] and Syed (who set up eleven candidates). In addition, about eighteen Muslim candidates received financial backing from the Congress.[158] The Congress leader in Sind thought he might exploit these divisions to get a Congress ministry with Muslim support and thus 'bury Pakistan in Sind'.[159] In the event, the results of the provincial elections did not quite 'bury Pakistan in

[152] Jinnah to Maher Mahmodali, 14 December 1945, AIML/SHC/2/File No. 11, Sind vol. VII.

[153] The Sind nationalist Muslims were assisted by a dozen or so mullahs imported from Baluchistan as well as by Congress money. (See Abdur Rashid Arshad Makhdum to Jinnah, 26 December 1945, AIML/SHC/File No. 11, vol. VII.)

[154] Jinnah to Maher Mahmodali, 14 December 1945, ibid.

[155] Khuhro was openly working against Ghulam Hussain in the hope of becoming the next chief minister of Sind. The Talpurs of Sind had also come out into the open with the Khaksars to form a separate group in the assembly. Khaksar nominees were not above deceiving the voters by pretending to be official League candidates. (See Abdur Rashid Arshad Makhdum to Jinnah, 14 January 1946, ibid.)

[156] Ibid.

[157] This was controlled by Maulvi Mahomed Sadiq and Abdul Samad Khan of Baluchistan; all its candidates were standing as independents.

[158] Of the fifteen from the Jamiat and Muslim Board, Congress expected six or seven to work in its camp.

[159] R. K. Sidhwa to Patel, 4 January 1946, in Durga Das (ed.), *Sardar Patel's Correspondence: 1945–1950*, vol. II (Ahmedabad, 1972), p. 317

Sind', but neither did Jinnah secure its resurrection in the desert. With the uncertain affiliation of those who won seats under its tickets, the League emerged as the largest party in the Karachi assembly but it did not have a clear majority.[160] Congress emerged as the second largest party. An indication of the League's uncertain hold in Sind was that even in the safe and separate Muslim seats in the countryside it won less than sixty per cent of the rural Muslim vote. The elections provided a clear mandate for no organisation in Sind and certainly for no principle – if they had done that, then a miracle would have occurred.

Not surprisingly, the election led to the usual manoeuvring over who was to form a ministry. For a while it looked as if Azad and Patel, who had thought it worth their while to come to Sind (and indeed the Congress High Command had invested time and money in the seamy affairs of the province), had persuaded G. M. Syed and Moula Baksh to form a 'Sind Assembly Coalition Party'. But Syed resiled from his commitments with the net result that when the jockeying for position was temporarily over, the composition of the assembly, momentarily stable, showed the Muslim League with twenty-eight seats, an equal number (twenty-eight) for the Sind Assembly Coalition party, with a few neutrals (in terms of party affiliation, that is) holding the balance.[161] Thus in the single province where the League had proudly advertised its possession of a ministry before the elections, its ability to form one after them had been placed upon a knife's edge. In the end it was not Patel, Azad or even Jinnah who settled the issue, but the Governor. It was characteristic of Sind and its affairs that Sir Francis Mudie, who had just come from Delhi where he had been Home Member,[162] decided to invite Ghulam Hussain to form a ministry yet again. It would be convenient to accept Patel's allegation that Mudie was prejudiced in favour of the League. But the heart of the matter lay in the realities of Sind which had little to do with all-India politics. It was simply that the old Sind hands

160 There were 178 candidates for the sixty seats in the Sind assembly, of which only ten were filled without a contest. The total number of electors in the contested constituencies was 880,977 of whom 453,556 or fifty-two per cent actually voted. Since the electorate in Sind was 999,343, less than half the enfranchised voted. The percentage of the total votes cast polled by the various political 'parties' in Sind was: Congress 16.6; the Hindu Mahasabha 3.2; the Muslim League 46.3 and others 29.6. Congress polled over ninety-five per cent of the general urban vote and over sixty-five per cent of the general rural vote. The Muslim League's most spectacular success was in the Muslim urban constituencies where 79.3 per cent of the votes were polled in its favour. In the rural Muslim constituencies, the League received 58.9 per cent of the votes cast. (See *1945–46 Election Returns*, pp. 54 and 79.)

161 See Mudie to Wavell, 5 February 1946, L/P&J/5/262, I.O.L.

162 Sir Francis Mudie had replaced Dow as the Governor of Sind in January 1946.

told Mudie that Syed was troublesome and Ghulam Hussain had the backing of the zamindars and the Mirs.[163] Patel, Congress's machine politician, felt sure he could knock out the ministry.[164] What Jinnah found himself facing in Sind were League politicians in a 'bad government in the hell of a fright'.[165] Whatever comfort he might take from the fact that he had a League ministry in Sind, there was no denying that he had contributed precious little to this result, that the League was in a worse position after the elections than before them, and that Sind particularism had triumphed without any concern for Jinnah's all-India strategy, or even for the demand for 'Pakistan' with implications which went beyond its narrow frontiers.

(d) The North West Frontier Province

If Jinnah had several bad moments in Sind, he was to have worse anxieties in the Frontier. Here he faced a Congress ministry in power and a skeletal Provincial League storming in the doldrums. There was no love lost between Aurangzeb Khan, the ex-chief minister, and the one other prominent Leaguer, Sardar Bahadur Sadullah Khan, who had helped to bring down the Aurangzeb ministry in March 1945 by breaking away from the League assembly party. Abdur Rab Nishtar was now Jinnah's contact in the Frontier, but Jinnah knew very little about what was happening there. In early May 1945, Jinnah had written with an intentional disingenuousness to Nishtar: 'May I know what is the League doing and what you people propose to do after the defeat of the League ministry? I have not heard anything from anyone of the four Muslim Ministers'.[166] Despite this polite enquiry, mainly for form, he saw that it was best not to interfere, and he told those local Leaguers who asked him to take a hand that it was their provincial bosses whom they should approach. The Frontier was not a canvas upon which the League could paint a bold prospect of 'Pakistan'; rather it remained a jig-saw of many tiny pieces where the Khans and their factions settled old scores without let or hindrance by any concern for the larger purposes of Muslim India or even the League. Admittedly, the defection to the League of Khan

---

[163] The new League ministry was duly formed on 8 February 1946, with all its members belonging to the Muslim League.

[164] Patel alleged that Mudie was 'using his hand' to puff up the Sind League, but warned: 'the coalition that has been made by me is not going to be disturbed and the League ministry will not last long, if the Governor had kept neutral, we would have been able to form a good and stable ministry'. (Patel to P. Subbaryan, 9 February 1946, Das (ed.), *Patel's Correspondence*, vol. II, p. 201.)

[165] See Mudie to Wavell, 9 February 1946, L/P&J/5/261, I.O.L.

[166] Jinnah to Abdur Rab Nishtar, 2 May 1945, AIML/SHC/4/File No. 29, NWFP vol. I.

Abdul Qayum Khan, a notorious 'self-seeker',[167] was a boost. But if, as the Governor reported, Jinnah's stand at Simla had led 'many of our better educated Muslims [hardly a large number] to be more pronouncedly Muslim Leaguers than they were', he still found 'no enthusiasm among that class for Pakistan in its stark separatist form'.[168]

As in Sind, so in the Frontier, it was the Congress which had more organisation and more money for its electoral campaign, and here too the League faced an undignified scrum among its supporters for leadership and tickets. The Governor predicted that the Provincial League's chances in the elections would depend on what success the High Command had in building up and brushing down its organisation in the Frontier. Pathans who looked at the League found that the League looked away from them, and even local Congressmen found its inertia mildly surprising.[169] Pleas from Peshawar lawyers to Jinnah that the 'Pathan is ready to join the League . . . it only requires us to strike now, and hard, when it is hot' could have been heard only if there had been local leadership and local organisation.[170] But there was neither leadership nor organisation. Jinnah again had the narrow choice between backing the unpopular Aurangzeb[171] or the other candidates who stood forth for the job. One seemed worse than the other, according to their competitors, and Jinnah's total helplessness was hinted at in a bitter complaint to him that 'Our worthy leaders of the High Command have brought the organisation to the edge of the precipice. One step more, and there is yawning, unfathomable abyss to engulf it.'[172]

Some young League enthusiasts tried to create a semblance of an

---

167 Cunningham to Wavell, 9 September 1945, R/3/1/105, I.O.L. Of course Qayum Khan tried to impress Jinnah with the great sacrifice he had made for the League's cause; it had been the 'most momentous decision' in his life, he told Jinnah, the result of 'anxious heart-searching and hard thinking for days on end'. (See Abdul Qayum Khan to Jinnah, 16 August 1945, AIML/SHC/1/File 2, NWFP vol. II.)

168 Cunningham to Wavell, 9 September 1945, R/3/1/105, I.O.L.

169 Jinnah's stand at Simla, according to one local lawyer, 'opened the eyes of the Pathans' and had worked 'a miracle and changed the political philosophy' of the Muslims in the Frontier. But although the Pathans had miraculously 'been converted into true political Muslims', the League in the Frontier was still in the doldrums. (Mohammad Zaman to Jinnah, 15 August 1945, AIML/SHC/4/File 29, NWFP vol. I.)

170 Ibid.

171 According to Sadullah Khan, Aurangzeb had 'no scruples to make false promises of gain in the form of contracts, permits and membership of syndicates for distribution of wheat etc.,'; and his 'constant readiness to swear by the Quran and take oaths on Talaq [divorce] both publicly and in private was responsible for the appellation of "Quran-Talaq" ministry which was generally applied to his cabinet'. (Sadullah Khan to Jinnah, 1 September, 1945, ibid.)

172 Asadul Huq to Jinnah, 20 September 1945, ibid.

organisation in an *ad hoc* manner, but despite all their efforts, the nominations to the Frontier's Parliamentary Board were settled by the time-honoured methods of dinner and discussions in smoke-filled rooms, with most of the places being given to 'ministry-mongers, reactionaries, [and] titleholders'.[173] Aurangzeb himself had been kept off the Board but his cronies still dominated it. The methods employed by Jinnah's men, in so far as they were anything more than rubber stamps for the local men who mattered, were described by the enthusiasts for some real effort as a 'perfect farce'. In less than half an hour the candidates who were deemed to have the best chance of success were given the League tickets, without a word about these candidates' commitment to the League's purposes, the situation in the constituencies or even a reference to the workers who had been given the unsavoury task of studying them.[174] In fact, Jinnah had made an intervention in the Frontier, quite uncharacteristically, in deciding to keep Aurangzeb out; and this intervention, which he was to regret sooner rather than later, probably lost the League some seats, and they did not have many to lose.[175]

With Nishtar and Qayum scrapping for the place at the top, and with each telling their backers to do down the other, it is not surprising that the Congress won the elections: it won the Frontier Muslim seat to the central legislative assembly, nineteen Muslim seats in the provincial assembly and fourteen non-Muslim seats (eleven Congress, two Independent Muslims and one Panthic Sikh). The League itself won only seventeen seats out of thirty-six reserved for Muslims. It polled more votes in the urban seats, but in the far more numerous and more important rural seats the Congress had a narrow margin over it.[176] If the

---

[173] Ibid.   [174] Ibid.

[175] According to Khaliquzzaman, both Nishtar and Qayum were against giving Aurangzeb a ticket, but after spending some time with the people in the Frontier, he himself had come to the conclusion that Aurangzeb's exclusion would do no good to the League's cause. His colleague, Qazi Isa, was also persuaded by this argument. But Jinnah went against the advice of his own men and refused to allow them to give Aurangzeb the League ticket. (Khaliquzzaman, *Pathway to Pakistan*, pp. 334–7.) But he paid the price for having an opinion about Frontier matters.

[176] Of the thirty-six Muslim seats in the Frontier assembly, three were urban and thirty-three were rural. These had been contested by 113 candidates. The total electorate in the province was 574,634 in a population of 3,038,000; of these 2,789,000 (excluding the tribal areas) were Muslim, and the total Muslim electorate was 493,296, or eighteen per cent of the Muslim population. There were 50,627 voters in the urban Muslim and 442,369 in the rural Muslim constituencies. Sixty-one per cent (30,905) cast their votes in the Muslim urban and 67.8 per cent (300,196) in the rural Muslim constituencies. The League polled 45.6 per cent (23,055 votes) of the votes cast in the urban Muslim constituencies, while Congress polled 22.2 per cent (11,241 votes), the remaining 32.2

Muslim votes cast for it are added up the Muslim League could claim a narrow edge over the Congress, but that was mere number-chopping. The facts of the matter were rather different: the Congress had the ministry; but the Governor concluded that:

Although the votes seem to show that the Frontier Muslim has come down against Pakistan, I believe that this is largely due to the fact that the Pathan simply cannot conceive of a situation in which his comings and goings would really be regulated by an outside non-Muslim authority. And from what my tribal friends tell me I think it possible even now that the League ideology is more popular with the tribes than that of Congress.[177]

Local, not all-India issues had determined the way the Pathans voted. In their electoral propaganda the League had talked 'about little but Pakistan . . . not really an intelligible war cry to ninety per cent of their hearers' since for the 'average Pathan villager in these parts, the suggestion that there can be such a thing as Hindu domination is only laughable'.[178] But Cunningham added that it 'would be dangerous . . . to assume from the present set-up that the Pathan as such will be quite happy in a unified India without safeguards for himself. If the Muslim League up here had had the sense to substitute Pathanistan for Pakistan, they would certainly have done a great deal better'.[179] The Governor might have understood how the League should have gone about winning more of the Pathan vote, but he had little understanding of what Jinnah, a stranger to this north-western extremity, was after in an electoral strategy which was always buckled and sometimes broken by the hard facts of local and provincial politics which he could not organise or control.

If the results of the 1945–46 elections alone are taken as the basis, Jinnah appears to have gone some way towards vindicating his claim to be the sole spokesman of the Indian Muslims. All the Muslim seats in the elections to the central legislative assembly were won by League candidates.[180] More importantly, the League secured nearly seventy-five per

per cent were divided between the Khaksars and the Independent Muslims. In the Muslim rural constituencies Congress did better, winning 41.4 per cent (124,201 votes) against the League's 40.7 per cent (122,373 votes), with the remaining votes split amongst nationalist Muslims, Khaksars and the Independents. This meant that Congress secured the votes of thirty-nine per cent of those Muslims who voted and the League forty-one per cent. (See *1945–46 Election Returns*, pp. 66 and 77.)

177 Cunningham to Wavell, 23 March 1946, R/3/1/105, I.O.L.
178 Cunningham to Wavell, 27 February 1946, ibid.
179 Cunningham to Wavell, 23 March 1946, ibid.
180 The League received 86.7 per cent of the total Muslim vote cast in the elections to the central assembly. Congress secured a paltry 1.3 per cent, the nationalist Muslims 8.9 per cent and non-party candidates 3.1 per cent. Of course the League had the advantage

cent of the total Muslim vote cast in the elections to provincial assemblies throughout India – a remarkable improvement on the abysmal 4.4 per cent it had registered in the 1936–37 elections.[181] But the League's electoral success disguises some awkward facts. As the actual election campaigns in the Punjab, Bengal, Sind and the N.W.F.P. have shown, Jinnah's grip over the Muslim-majority provinces was at best extremely tenuous. Poorly-organised provincial Leagues had hurriedly made terms with the old factional system; they had not won a mandate from the Muslim voters by an organisation and a programme which replaced the existing systems of local influence. Local and provincial leaders had seen advantages in aligning themselves, at least nominally, with the A.I.M.L. Yet those who had so recently and sometimes so equivocally jumped onto the League's bandwagon could just as easily jump off, if circumstances altered cases. And circumstances could change drastically, certainly in the Punjab and Bengal, if the Muslim voters were given a chance to consider the implications of the 'Pakistan' slogan for their provinces.

Another factor which could undermine Jinnah's strategy at the centre was the role played by the *pirs* and mullahs in the League's election campaign. Undoubtedly, they had contributed to the League's success at the polls; but fanning communal passions at the base was quite a different matter from having an organisation to control them. The men of religion were hardly the disciplined cadres of a League command, whether at the centre or in the provinces. Since 1937, and especially after

of separate electorates; it lost the seat to the central assembly from the N.W.F.P. which was fought for under general electorates, and could claim only 27.7 per cent of the total vote cast in the elections to the central assembly against Congress's 59.8 per cent (*1945–46 Election Returns*, p. 8.)

181 The following table shows the number and percentage of Muslim votes polled by the political parties in the 1945–46 elections to the provincial assemblies.

Constituency	Total No. of votes polled	Muslim League No. of votes polled	Muslim League % of votes polled	Congress No. of votes polled	Congress % of votes polled	Nationalist Muslims No. of votes polled	Nationalist Muslims % of votes polled	Unionist No. of votes polled	Unionist % of votes polled	Communists No. of votes polled	Communists % of votes polled	Non-party No. of votes polled	Non-party % of votes polled
Muslim Total	6,099,573	4,555,181	74.7	276,175	4.6	396,013	6.4	277,737	4.6	7,111	0.1	587,356	9.6
Muslim urban	674,649	531,089	78.7	15,834	2.3	33,588	5.0	—	—	—	—	94,138	14.
Muslim rural	5,409,423	4,016,069	74.3	260,341	4.8	358,104	6.6	277,737	6.1	7,111	0.1	490,061	9
Muslim women	15,501	8,023	51.7	—	—	4,321	27.9	—	—	—	—	3,157	20

1945–46 Election Returns, p. 55. The League polled 21.3 per cent of the total Indian vote cast in the elections to the provincial assembli[es]
It won 460 of the 533 Muslim seats in the central and provincial assembly elections. (See table of election results, *Indian Annual Regist*[er]
1946, vol. I.)

the Cripps offer of 1942, Jinnah's foremost concern had been to get League ministries into office in the Muslim provinces. To do so he had at each step to sacrifice the much harder imperatives of building real League organisations which reached effectively into the Muslim provinces. He calculated that there would be time enough later to impose effective control over Muslim India once the more urgent battle with Congress and the British had been won. This proved to be a serious miscalculation which together with the millennial expectations aroused by an undefined cry for Pakistan was soon to push Jinnah into an uncomfortably tight corner. But, for the moment, he could use the League's electoral success as an excuse to concentrate upon the three-cornered game of constitutional haggling which after all was the Quaid-i-Azam's greatest talent.

5

Jinnah's 'Pakistan' and the Cabinet Mission plan

Section 1

After the 1945–46 elections the lines were clearly drawn for the claims
and counter-claims of the end game. Congress still wanted independence
to come before settling the communal problem. This meant having an
essentially unitary form of government – one constitution and one nation
– strong enough to fulfil the purposes for which independence was being
sought, while appeasing the fears of provinces and minority groups. In
contrast, Jinnah and the League reiterated their demand that the first
step must be to accept Pakistan in principle now that the Muslim
electorate had given its verdict in favour of it. Once Congress was
prepared to recognise this, 'the whole spirit would change and we should
become friends'. If the British then 'declared their decision in favour of
Pakistan there would be no trouble' since the 'Hindus would quickly
accept it'.[1]

Another British initiative was now inevitable, and Congress at any rate
wanted to speed up matters. Seeing this, Jinnah had to show a little more
of his hand: the principle of Pakistan, he now explained, meant that the
old unitary centre of British India had to be replaced by two distinct and
separate political entities or federations organised by two constituent
assemblies, one for the Muslim provinces and the other for the Hindu
provinces. These two assemblies would then send their representatives
to yet another centre, above them both, where for the time being the
British would remain as ringmaster and umpire; at this centre, League
and Congress, representing the Muslim provinces (Pakistan) and Hindu
provinces (Hindustan) respectively, had to be given equal status, safeguarded by a 'British Crown Representative' who would 'co-ordinate the
policies of the two federations in such matters as Defence and Foreign
Affairs'.[2] By allowing this centre an executive but no legislature, Jinnah

[1] Note of conversation between Jinnah and Arthur Moore, 28 January 1946, R/3/1/105,
I.O.L.

[2] Note by George Abell on conversation between Major Wyatt and Jinnah, 5 February
1946, R/3/1/105, I.O.L. A Parliamentary Delegation had visited India in January 1946,
to meet the leading political personalities. This was generally viewed as a prelude to a
fresh British initiative.

at a stroke avoided the obvious difficulty of claiming parity of status in an all-India legislature when the federation of the Muslim provinces only contained a quarter of the country's population. If the overall centre was confined to dealing only with defence and external affairs, it could plausibly be maintained that the counting of heads, so awkward to Jinnah's case, was no longer relevant. At this centre, the League or Pakistan provinces, with their own sovereign constituent assembly, would be the equals of the Congress provinces. This would give Jinnah an important say in the negotiations about the form and powers the all-India federation was to possess.

There was some merit and some logic, albeit strained, in Jinnah's line of argument. Once it had achieved equality of status at the all-India level, the League might be able to win the safeguards for which it had been fighting all along. But there were many stumbling-blocks, not least at the provincial level. Large non-Muslim minorities in the Muslim provinces bruised the logic that the demand for Pakistan was based on the principle of self-determination. The Hindus and Sikhs of Ambala division and the Hindus of Burdwan might jeopardise the shaky dominance that Jinnah's uncertain Leaguers had in their provincial assemblies. So Jinnah privately admitted to Woodrow Wyatt, who was visiting India with a Parliamentary Delegation, that he might be prepared to let Ambala and Burdwan go; Calcutta, however, he had to have, even at the price of 'serious trouble' and civil war. This threat of communal violence was the ultimate weapon in the armoury of a politician, playing from extreme weakness for the highest stakes, who had no experience of launching or controlling an agitation. According to Wyatt, Jinnah was 'prepared to concede [a] lot more than might appear at first sight'.[3] But Jinnah's grand strategy was grounded on the mistaken assumption that the end game would be played according to a leisurely timetable. He did not think that India was about to be bundled into a snap decision by a Raj suddenly anxious to quit.[4]

As late as February 1946, Jinnah continued to remind London about its promises during the war.[5] But the context had changed: a new team

---

[3] Ibid.

[4] When Jinnah told Wyatt that he himself would welcome a two-year moratorium, in which he would take perfect rest in the Aga Khan's palace this was a comment not only on his own weariness but on what he assumed were the relatively easy-going timetables of the Raj. (See Note by George Abell, ibid.)

[5] Jinnah told the Secretary of State: 'A caretaker Government already exists . . . and there is no need to tinker with it under the new phraseology of "political Executive Council". Equally, the idea of a single Constitution-making body is fundamentally opposed to the basic principles that the Muslim League has declared times out of number. It will be perfectly futile to force such a measure upon Muslim India, as it must result in disaster,

was in charge in London and its priorities were quite different from those of the wartime coalition it replaced. The communal problem had been a convenient instrument in British policy so long as there was no question of constitutional advance. Once the war was over, it posed the largest and most inconvenient obstacle to the changes which metropolitan calculations and Indian circumstances imperiously demanded. On 15 March 1946, Attlee told the House of Commons that he could not permit a 'minority to place a veto on the advance of the majority', however important the minority might be.[6] He was proposing to send a Cabinet Delegation to India. Indians would decide their own future, and the Delegation was intended to assist them in settling their differences and in setting up a constitution-making body and a representative Executive Council for the interim period. The question whether India would remain in the British Commonwealth was to be left to the Indians to decide.

On 23 March 1946, the Cabinet Mission arrived in Karachi. It consisted of the Secretary of State, Pethick-Lawrence; that veteran of inconclusive Indian negotiations, Sir Stafford Cripps, now the President of the Board of Trade; and the First Lord of the Admiralty, Mr A. V. Alexander. Alexander was the weakest brother of this three-man team. In his first public statement, the Secretary of State announced that the Mission came with no recipe for Indian independence.[7] It did not have a formula for a compromise between the Congress demand for majority rule at the centre and the more extreme forms of the League's demand for Pakistan. The League would not be allowed to veto political advance but equally Congress would not be allowed simply to dictate. As the Viceroy's Executive Council told the Mission, the main obstacle to a compromise was an issue which for long had been swept under the carpet: the need to redraw provincial boundaries if the Muslim provinces were to be given more autonomy than they had previously possessed. However intractable this issue might prove to be, the Mission must keep working for a political settlement. The Mission could not be allowed to fail; the Executive Council insisted, it 'must refuse to permit a break·

---

not to say that it will be a breach of the solemn declaration of August 1940 and the repeated assurances of H.M.G. to that effect given from time to time.' (Jinnah to Pethick-Lawrence, 9 February 1946, R/3/1/105, I.O.L.)

[6] C. R. Attlee's speech, 15 March 1946, *Parliamentary Debates*, Fifth Series, Vol. 420, Collections 1421–22.

[7] 'The precise road towards the final structure of India's independence is not yet clear', the Secretary of State admitted, 'but let the vision of it inspire us all in our renewed efforts to find a path of cooperation'. (Pethick-Lawrence's press statement, 23 March 1946, *T.P.*, VII, 1.)

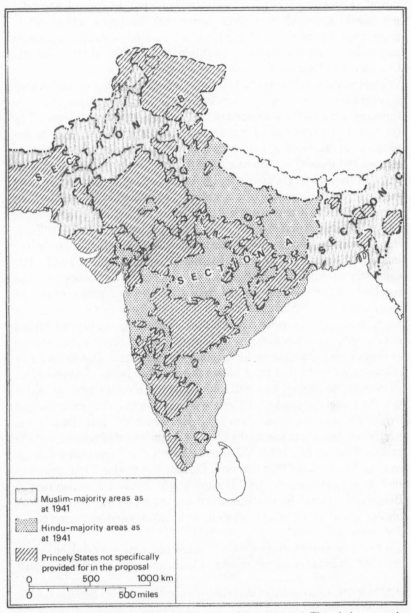

Map 4. Cabinet Mission proposal for a three-section federation, 1946. Though the proposal did not allocate Princely States to any of the three sections, it was assumed that most, if not all, would wish to enter into a federal type of union with them.

down'.[8] Delhi no longer felt it had law and order under control, and it did not think it could deal with communal outbursts which might accompany a breakdown of negotiations. This was a striking commentary on how fragile a hold the ostensible leaders of political India, British, Congress and League alike, had over the forces below.

The danger that Hindus and Muslims would set at each others' throats was a constant fear in British thinking; it was even more important in the thinking of the High Commands of the Congress and of the League. 'The big boys of Congress and League', as George Abell noted, were beginning to get 'alarmed lest their followers break loose'. If that were to happen the leaders would cease to lead, the followers would not follow and that thin crust of order which the British and their collaborators had maintained for a century and a half of rule would break down, with disorders on a scale never before seen in India, and certainly unprecedented in Britain's experience overseas. Long before the Calcutta killings, the Mission had been warned that: 'The cities of India are just in the mood for such riots, and the goonda element is out of hand. The Communists would, on present form, rejoice in the chance to make trouble . . . the effect on the Indian Army and police might be catastrophic . . .'[9] More alarming was the evidence that even if Jinnah could be squared, his provincial lieutenants might ignore his lead if it did not suit them to follow him. In the Punjab, Shaukat Hayat was calling-up ex-servicemen, apparently for a Jihad for 'Pakistan', but in fact as a manoeuvre to get rid of the Khizar ministry.[10] In Bengal Jinnah had no sway over the people, and could not bring them out in 'open revolt'.[11] But the Governor came to the wrong conclusion that this meant Bengal would be immune from disorders. He was right that Jinnah was irrelevant, but it was just in the Quaid-i-Azam's lack of control that the potential danger lay. If the Calcutta underworld and its volatile *goondas* were to break loose, then not only Jinnah, but shadier local operators such as Suhrawardy and Abul Hashim might discover that disorders in Bengal, all very well for gentlemen to float as paper tigers from their ivory towers, could spring into lethal violence in bazaars and backstreets once they were unleashed.

These ominous stirrings were still below the surface when Jinnah first met the Cabinet Mission in the calm of Viceregal Lodge. But even Jinnah

[8] Note of meeting between the Cabinet Delegation and the Viceroy's Executive Council, 26 March 1946, ibid., 7.
[9] Note by George Abell, 7 April 1946, *T.P.*, VII, 160–1; see also Thorne to Abell, 5 April 1946, ibid., 149–51.
[10] See note by Woodrow Wyatt, 28 March 1946, ibid., 22–3.
[11] Note by Burrows, undated, ibid., 67.

could no longer ignore the fact that he was unable to control powerful forces brewing at the base. He began cautiously – stating some facts and reminding the Mission of Britain's responsibilities: 'India was neither united nor divided – it was a British possession'.[12] The League was wasting its time trying to negotiate with the Congress. So H.M.G. should make an award, as it had done in 1932, this time accepting the principle of Pakistan. Once this had been done, there should be no difficulty in getting the two new states to make a mutual defence treaty, and this would assure that matters such as foreign policy, defence and communications would be dealt with by a centre.[13] By letting the Mission know that he envisaged some form of union government once power was transferred, Jinnah for the first time had come out with his real strategy. But as ever Jinnah's weak point was the question of Pakistan's boundaries. He wanted a 'viable Pakistan', not one 'carved up or mutilated'. He was prepared to give up claims to Assam and settle for the five Muslim provinces as they were; 'mutual adjustments' of boundaries could be discussed later provided this did not prejudice Pakistan's viability as a 'live State economically'. This meant Pakistan must have Calcutta; 'Pakistan without Calcutta would be like asking a man to live without his heart.'[14]

This was the view from the centre, stated by Jinnah, arrogating the role of spokesman for all of Muslim India and anxious to stifle its customary babel of tongues. But the Mission could not avoid lending an ear to mutterings from the Muslim provinces. As the Mission listened, so the worms crawled out of the intricate woodwork of Muslim India; it quickly became apparent that behind the simple cry for 'Pakistan' lay a host of complex and conflicting interests, some of which had very little to do with the shape that Pakistan was coming to assume in Jinnah's guarded exposition. Muslim provinces wanted to hang on to, perhaps even to improve, their autonomy and standing against any centre, whoever controlled it – the British, the Congress or even their very own League. These advocates of states' rights wanted their provinces to remain intact, and they wanted to keep for themselves all the patronage and profit of office in them. So provinces, the products of mere administrative convenience in times long past, were now put forward as entities whose frontiers were inviolate. According to Suhrawardy, the

---

[12] See Jinnah's meeting with the Cabinet Delegation and Wavell, 4 April 1946, ibid., 119–23.

[13] When asked to be a little more specific, Jinnah tartly responded that specificity was all very well for those with huge secretariats, like the British and the Congress; the League had a hard enough job running its one office in Delhi, let alone producing detailed schemes. (Ibid., 123–4.)   [14] Ibid., 124.

case for 'Pakistan' was Bengal's common historical traditions, its distinctive culture, and its linguistic solidarities. Religion, was conveniently forgotten in Suhrawardy's exposition.[15] So were the other provinces. Bengal was Bengali, not Muslim. That a powerful provincialism rather than commitment to 'Pakistan' lay behind the demands of most groups in Muslim provinces was proved by their fears of being dominated from the centre, even if that centre was to be the League's. It showed itself also in their readiness to sell their Muslim brothers in other provinces to buy something for themselves. The chief minister of Sind, Ghulam Hussain, thought all would be well if only all-India politics could be kept out of the provinces, and in particular out of Sind. As far as he was concerned, Hindus could have western Bengal (but not Calcutta), and the Sikhs could have their Sikhistan.[16] But Sind must be left alone by all outsiders, whatever their faith.

When his own Leaguers in the provinces demolished Jinnah's case for Pakistan with such nonchalance, it is hardly surprising that his old rivals could make an even better job of it. Khizar explained to the Mission that the Punjab's dilemma was that an united Punjab, inside Pakistan, might be good for Muslims, but Punjab's Hindus and Sikhs would never accept it. A partitioned Punjab, on the other hand would be a disaster for those Muslims left stranded in the eastern districts of the Punjab. If only Jinnah had been forced to bring these hard facts into the open by being pushed into defining clearly what Pakistan was, then at least the Punjab's unthinking enthusiasm for it might have been rather more subdued. This was the Punjab's problem, faced with the Pakistan demand. But Pakistan would also bundle Sindhis, Baluchis and Pathans into a new union with Punjabis. Although they shared a common religion, Khizar

---

[15] When gently reminded that there was a contradiction here between the Pakistan demand based on the 'two nation' theory and his own claim that Bengal and Assam should be kept together because of linguistic affinities, Suhrawardy brushed this aside as typical imperialist logic chopping. (See Suhrawardy's meeting with the Cabinet Delegation and Wavell, 8 April 1946, ibid., 163–6.)

[16] See Sir Ghulam Hussain Hidayatullah's meeting with the Cabinet Delegation and Wavell, 4 April 1946, ibid., 126. Neither Mamdot nor Suhrawardy would have been too happy at this lavish Sindhi's generosity at their expense. Mamdot, the president of the Punjab Muslim League told the Mission in unequivocal terms that Pakistan must have an undivided Punjab. This was hardly surprising. Mamdot's estate in Ferozepur was unlikely to be included in Pakistan if there were 'mutual adjustments'. Mamdot, however, disguised his personal interests by arguing that Hindus and Sikhs would be treated well in Pakistan which would be a 'democratic state'. More to the point, the Sikhs had never defined the boundaries of Sikhistan, and constituted a majority only in the Amritsar and Ferozepur districts and were in a majority in only one out of five divisions in these districts. (See the Nawab of Mamdot's meeting with the Cabinet Delegation and Wavell, 2 April 1946, ibid., 91.)

seemed to hint that the Punjabis were not minded to share much else with them. According to Khizar, the only answer was: provincial autonomy, states' rights and a weak federal centre. Khizar, the heir of that old Unionist tradition which had been eroded but not wholly broken by the League, was simply stating the time-honoured Punjab alternative which envisaged the three main Punjabi communities sharing power inside an undivided province which would have a considerable say at a weak centre. The real point of difference between Khizar and Jinnah about the powers of the centre was that Jinnah needed control over the Pakistan provinces (themselves a constituent element of a weak central federation) whereas Khizar wanted no Pakistan centre or at most a weak centre over the Muslim provinces.[17]

Muslim politicians in Sind and the N.W.F.P. who did not belong to the League told the Mission how the League had ridden roughshod over their real interests. G. M. Syed, the Sindhi leader now in exile but once a candidate for the job of chief minister in a League ministry, argued that the root of the problem was the overweening ambitions of the two High Commands, Congress and League, and their arbitrary dictates which were 'destructive not only of Provincial Autonomy but of the freedom and welfare of the Indian people'.[18] He wanted the provinces to be left alone. Before they had been bullied by all-India leaders, politicians in the provinces had known how to manage their affairs and keep everyone happy in the best of all provincial worlds. Syed wanted Azad (or free) Sind, not Pakistan. In the N.W.F.P., the Mission was bluntly told by the Congress chief minister, Dr Khan Sahib, that the League did not represent Muslims. The Pathans had no love for their Punjabi neighbours. They would never willingly join Pakistan. They wanted no centre at all but they did not fear domination by a Hindu centre. What they wanted most of all was to be entirely independent. Indeed, the Khan Sahib was not even prepared to admit that there was a meaningful *political* distinction between Hindus and Muslims. The League had won votes in the Frontier by bringing round vested interests and playing with the fires of fanaticism which would soon burn everyone's fingers. So he wanted the Frontier to be left to its own devices without interference from any centre, Hindu, Muslim or whatever.[19] An Indian version of the Balkans seemed to be the provincial Muslims' dream.

---

[17] See Khizar Hayat's meeting with the Cabinet Delegation and Wavell, 5 April 1946, ibid., 147–8.
[18] See G. M. Syed's meeting with the Cabinet Delegation and Wavell, 2 April 1946, ibid., 92–3.
[19] See Dr Khan Sahib's meeting with the Cabinet Delegation and Wavell, 1 April 1946, ibid., 74–5.

So the Muslim provinces were singing a tune different from Jinnah, particularly when non-Leaguers who had no reason to echo Jinnah's case burst into voice. No Muslim politician in the Punjab, Bengal, Sind or the Frontier had any reason within their own province to fear Congress domination; so they had a narrower, and a rather different, angle of vision about their interests from that of a grand strategist at the centre. But as ever Jinnah's line did have some support from Muslims in provinces where they were in a minority. Such Muslims, as Khaliquzzaman admitted, would gain little directly from Pakistan but indirectly they would gain something substantial. A Congress-dominated Hindustan would have to treat its Muslim minorities well, since it could not afford to fall out with Pakistan, with hostage Hindus and Sikhs in its territories.[20] Then there were the views of embryonic capitalists in western India who saw good pickings for their enterprise in a Pakistan free of Birlas, Tatas and Thakurdases. For Muslim businessmen from Bombay, who hoped to prosper in the uncompetitive markets of Pakistan, just as for the traditionally foot-loose service groups in north India who were ready to go anywhere in search of office, Pakistan promised to be a land of opportunity, not a slough of despond.[21]

Although Jinnah failed to prevent the Mission from speaking to some wayward Muslims, he did manage to get the A.I.M.L. to hold a Legislators' Convention to endorse his case emphatically. Its purpose was not to discuss the practicalities of Pakistan; it was simply to demonstrate that Muslim opinion was solidly behind its spokesman. The resolution the Convention passed was the Jinnah line of the moment: instead of two 'Independent States', the resolution now demanded for Pakistan a single 'sovereign Independent State' and two separate constituent assemblies for the Muslim and Hindu provinces, with safeguards for the minorities in Pakistan and Hindustan.[22] The call for one instead of two 'Independent States' was Jinnah's way of hauling

---

[20] See note on meeting of the Cabinet Delegation with Mohammad Ismail, I. I. Chundrigar, Choudhry Khaliquzzaman and Maulana Syed Abdur Rauf, 8 April 1946, ibid., 166–9.

[21] Khaliquzzaman frankly equated the interests of the entire Muslim community of the U.P. when he spoke of the Congress threat to Muslim landed classes. He informed the Mission that a number of Muslims, especially the educated classes, intended to migrate to Pakistan, and Muslim industrialists from Bombay might also wish to transfer their business to the Punjab. (Ibid.)

[22] The resolution 'emphatically' declared that any attempt to force an interim arrangement at the centre would 'leave the Muslims no alternative but to resist such imposition by all possible means for their survival and national existence'. (See resolution of the A.I.M.L.'s Legislators' Convention, 9 April 1946, in Pirzada (ed.), *Foundations of Pakistan*, vol. II, pp. 512–13.)

Suhrawardy and his Muslims back into line, and of stamping out ominous signs of a Bengali breakaway which threatened the tripartite negotiations at the top.[23] The resolution was hardly the product of a well-conceived effort by representative Muslims to hammer out the problems, practicalities and purposes of Pakistan. It made, for example, no mention of how Pakistan would organise its defence, although Jinnah in private admitted that 'Defence is the key pin of the problem', and was visibly shaken when he was told that if he insisted on a separate army for Pakistan, the British officers would simply quit and 'wish both Pakistan and Hindustan the very best of luck in running their own armies'.[24]

Jinnah was right in anticipating that defence would be a key issue in a transfer of power. Britain's strategic interests in the region called for a common defence structure for all of India. This, Jinnah hoped, would be the best insurance for his strategy. That strategy, if it was to do something for all Muslims including those in Hindu provinces and not merely for those in the majority provinces, required some form of common arrangements at the centre between Hindustan and Pakistan. The demand for a separate foreign policy and army for Pakistan, as Jinnah knew very well, flew in the face of British interests which depended on India remaining the keystone of Commonwealth defence. But this line had the merit of giving the League some leverage and something substantial to concede when it came to bargaining about arrangements at the centre between Pakistan and Hindustan, especially over a common defence policy.

Not surprisingly, the two options which emerged from the Mission's first round of talks with the Indian leaders both envisaged a common defence structure for India. The option which the Mission preferred was to keep an unitary India with a loose federation and a centre restricted to defence and foreign affairs. The second was to concede a sovereign but truncated Pakistan consisting of Muslim majority-districts in the north-west (that is, western Punjab, Sind, N.W.F.P. and Baluchistan) and the north-east (eastern Bengal without Calcutta, but with the Sylhet district of Assam). This sovereign Pakistan would, moreover, be expected to make a treaty of alliance, for both offensive and defensive purposes, with Hindustan. The latter option did not answer the all-important strategic

---

23 Suhrawardy had been trying to negotiate for a League–Congress coalition ministry in Bengal. (See Burrows to Wavell, 25 April 1946, *T.P.*, VII, 339–41.) By making Bengal an integral part of Pakistan (however much this flew in the face of geography), Jinnah hoped to prevent such a development, at least until he had achieved his larger purposes at the all-India level.

24 Note by Lieutenant-General A. Smith on his interview with Jinnah, 28 March 1946, ibid., 20–1.

question to the satisfaction of the military men since a sovereign Pakistan, they feared, would be the exposed flank of subcontinental defence and there was no certainty that the two sovereign states would agree to have common policies about war and peace.[25]

Both were options of difficulties rather than ideal solutions in that imperfect world in which the Mission's harassed arbitrators found themselves. Congress would be against the weak centre of the first alternative (Scheme A) and as things stood, was unlikely to accept the second, a truncated Pakistan (Scheme B); while Jinnah would bitterly complain that in the truncated Pakistan that was on offer he was being denied the large sovereign Pakistan which was his only way of ensuring that the Congress would negotiate a common centre. But whatever the reaction of the two all-India parties, the first step was to get H.M.G.'s permission for the Cabinet Mission to negotiate on the basis of the proposal for a small truncated sovereign Pakistan. The Cabinet was told that the Mission itself favoured 'something on the lines of Scheme A' but it was quite possible that it might not succeed in securing agreement for it. Unless an agreement was found between the Congress and the League, 'we risk chaos in India and no scheme of Defence will then be of any value'. Therefore it was essential to consider Scheme B, the truncated sovereign Pakistan, since this might well be 'the only chance of agreed settlement'.[26]

On 11 April 1946 the momentous question whether London was ready to divide and quit had formally been raised in the Cabinet. The Cabinet was asked to decide whether it would be prepared to deny the central article of the British Indian creed, vital to its traditional conception of metropolitan interests in South Asia. Partition had been named as the price which might have to be paid if power was to be transferred without a holocaust. The decision to be ready to tear the seamless web of Indian unity, which the British had taken more than a century and a half to weave, was taken at one short meeting of the Cabinet. However much they preferred Scheme A, the Cabinet agreed that if Scheme B was the

---

[25] The two states inevitably would become members of the United Nations in their own right, able if they were so minded to go their separate ways. Hindustan might lean towards Russia or China and go its own way heedless of British interests in Malaya, Ceylon and East and South Africa, while Pakistan might lean towards the Muslim states of the Middle East.

[26] The Mission's warning to the Cabinet was clear enough: 'We are convinced that the overriding necessity is some agreement if it can be attained and that this is the first requirement towards any effective Defence. We hope, therefore, that you will agree to our working for an agreement on the basis of Scheme B if this seems to us to be the only chance of agreed settlement.' (Cabinet Delegation and Wavell to Attlee, 11 April 1946, ibid., 221.)

only hope of an agreed settlement, then Scheme B it would have to be.[27] As the Chiefs of Staff made abundantly clear, the requirements of Britain's future strategic interests in the region, in the end, were more imperious than sticking to the old ideals of Indian unity; Scheme B was bad from the point of view of defence, but it was better than being left with an intractable set of successors; and certainly it was better than having no successors at all, the strategists' nightmare of the chaos which threatened an India left to her own devices.

Yet the detailed comments of the Chiefs of Staff which accompanied Attlee's swift reply to the Mission stressed all the difficulties and dangers of dividing India. Pakistan would consist of territory which lay across the tracks of the traditional routes into India. It would contain the bases from which the air force would have to raise an umbrella over the north-west. Pakistan would rip the old British Indian army into two. The unity of the army, even more than the political unity at New Delhi, had been regarded as essential to India's security from external attack since the very beginnings of British rule. The unity of the army had also been the rod of internal order. The Indian army, that shield of defence, had been a force capable of preventing fires at home, as well as acting as an imperial fire-brigade overseas. All this would be put at risk by Scheme B.[28] But already some of the Generals, adept at spotting silver linings in the clouds, saw merits in concentrating British interest in the areas beloved of their martial tradition, especially the Punjab. If Scheme B was the only alternative, something might be rescued from the point of view of British strategic interests: 'every effort should be made to obtain agreement for some form of central defence council to be set up which will include not only Pakistan, Hindustan and the Indian States, but also Burma and Ceylon'.[29] With the Central Defence Council providing an illusion of rescuing something of Britain's strategic requirements, London ratified its Mission's proposal to resolve Solomon's dilemma in India by giving both the claimants some part of what they wanted, at best an 'emasculated version of one or the other rival theses'; a Pakistan trimmed

---

[27] Attlee to the Cabinet Delegation and Wavell, 13 April 1946, Ibid., 260–1.

[28] To fight a war Pakistan would have to rely on Hindustan for much of its supplies; West Pakistan was likely to identify itself with other Muslim countries, which might lead it into wars of no concern to Hindustan. But the greatest danger was that the government of West Pakistan might through 'fear engendered by her own weakness uncover the vitals of India by not resisting on the natural battle ground of the hills of the Indian frontier'. Nevertheless, the Chiefs of Staff conceded that 'Scheme B will have to be accepted if the only alternative is complete failure to reach agreement and consequent chaos.' (From the War Staff Files, L/WS/I/1029: ff. 82–6, minute of Chiefs of Staff meeting, 12 April 1946, attached to Attlee's reply to the Cabinet Delegation and Wavell, 13 April 1946, *T.P.*, VII, 261.)   [29] Ibid.

to the bone, or a central government stripped of most of its real powers, and not 'worth much'. Yet both London and Delhi were at one that 'agreement is the paramount necessity'. Because the 'risk of disagreement' was 'greater', they would have to 'tolerate one or other of these alternatives'.[30]

Once the Cabinet had given the go-ahead, the way was clear to offer Jinnah the alternatives of a small Pakistan with sovereign rights and treaty relations with Hindustan, or a larger Pakistan (with some minor boundary adjustments and only excluding Assam) inside a federation with Hindustan. The great merit was that in such a federation 'Pakistan' would have equal status with Hindustan in those two matters over which a rather emasculated all-India centre was to be given authority. There was to be no union legislature and any question at the centre on which the two federal units failed to agree would be referred back to their respective group legislatures. Agreement would not be imposed by central dictate, but by agreement between the two federated governments. To make this all-India federation even more attractive for Jinnah, it was clearly stated that the Muslim-majority areas would have complete control over all their affairs except those specifically given to the centre; and at the centre 'they would meet the Hindus on a level where it was States which counted and not the number of individuals in them'. This principle of equality, which was exactly what Jinnah had been fighting for all along, was, he was now told, 'the essence of the proposal'.[31]

In the confusing story of demand and counter-demand, of tactical side steps, and strategic retreats, of propaganda aimed at turbulent followers, and proposals aimed at more hard-headed opponents, it is easy to lose track of what Jinnah was really after. Since 1940, Jinnah had maintained an immaculate silence on the inner meaning of the Pakistan demand. But once the Cabinet Mission began its enquiries and made its proposals, he allowed its members, and hence the historian, to get a tantalising hint of his real aims and a glimpse of the goal towards which he had been tacking and turning. Upon this flash of candour, so fleetingly revealed in the intentional obfuscations of Jinnah's tactics, the historian of Pakistan must pounce. Jinnah's aims had been hinted at in his talks with Wyatt (see pp. 174–5). Now the Mission had offered him the substance of what he was really after. It was not the impractical 'Pakistan' of fantasy for which the man in the street or the mullah in the mosque was wont to cry,

---

[30] At any rate, if H.M.G. had no choice but to make an award of some sort, then it was considered essential that it 'should remain free to propound more satisfactory versions of one or other of the alternatives . . . a better Pakistan, or a better All-India system'. (Croft to Monteath, 15 April 1946, ibid., 274.)

[31] See Cabinet Delegation and Wavell's meeting with Jinnah, 16 April 1946, ibid., 281–2.

nor was it the 'mutilated and moth-eaten' Pakistan which was outlined in Scheme B and which finally emerged in 1947. His Pakistan did not intend to throw the advantages of an undivided Punjab and Bengal to the winds; nor did it plan to leave the Muslims in Hindustan unprotected. Undivided provinces and protection for minority Muslims could only be achieved inside the framework of an union with an effective centre where the League had an equal say. So we must carefully assess why Jinnah did not jump more openly and more enthusiastically at what the Mission now had offered in its Scheme A. The answer is simple, but not so simple that historians have given it proper weight. In the first place, as the Secretary of State realised, there was no certainty that Congress would accept the principle of equality or parity at the centre. If Jinnah came forward with too evident an enthusiasm to embrace an offer which the Congress later might reject, he would stand exposed before his followers and would have lost the bargaining counter which his demand for the full sovereign Pakistan gave him. So he had to make a fine calculation of how to proceed. It was only by pressing for even more than he had been offered that Jinnah hoped to persuade Congress to accept the Mission's proposed all-India federal scheme as a lesser evil. Then there were his own followers to consider. Few among them would understand that the Mission had dealt them a royal flush or that equality at an all-India federal centre outweighed the advantages which a sovereign but truncated Pakistan would bring.

So the game was played in Jinnah's usual manner. He argued that equality at the centre was all very well on Cabinet paper, but would never work in *Khadi* practice. Equality could hardly be assured inside a system of government where one party had the big battalions, and the other the small. What Jinnah needed was to get all the parties to agree to dissolve the existing centre, in principle if not in fact, and then immediately to recreate it on the basis of a sovereign Pakistan. In his opinion this alone would ensure the Muslims equal treatment at the centre, since it would be an equality underwritten by the law of nations: a treaty between sovereign states. In return he was prepared to give up parts of the six Muslim provinces (though Assam could hardly be considered a Muslim province) to which he had laid claim. But unless and until Congress came forward with a clear 'yes', he would not say 'what he was willing to give up' (see p. 168). He wanted to make terms with the Congress, but only if it gave him a 'viable' state, not if it 'struck at the heart of Pakistan'. If Congress refused to budge, then Jinnah wanted the Mission to impose a settlement, and thought they were in a 'position to do it' (see pp. 174–5). In fact he would have preferred the British to give him what they had offered and what he was ready to accept by an award, since the Congress was unlikely in the end to concede such a degree of sovereignty to Pakistan which his scheme demanded. So the British should impose their solution and stay on for a few years to make it stick. Union here and now between League and Congress provinces was all very well only provided the British remained to supervise fair play to the weaker partner represented by the League.[32]

Jinnah's reasoning depended on two assumptions. The first was that if the League and Congress could not agree, the British were ready to make an award, and then stay on to enforce it. The second was that the Congress would never willingly accept the outright partition of India which the full-blown claims for a sovereign and separate Pakistan entailed. So it was safe to demand division and Pakistan since there was no risk of Congress allowing either to be conceded at the end of the day. Both these assumptions proved to be seriously misguided. The British were not ready to impose a settlement and stay on to work it, and rather than accept a weak centre for an undivided India which made nonsense of their own requirements of a strong central authority, Congress was ready reluctantly to allow contiguous Muslim regions, pared down to the bone, to go their own way. It could then impose upon its India a centre with real authority. For Congress, this was a lesser evil than accepting Jinnah's claims and settling for a weak centre shared with the League and Pakistan. Congress might have been ready to move towards a weaker centre to keep India undivided; but its own purposes required that such a centre evolve out of the existing one, perhaps giving away some of its powers, but not recasting it anew on the basis of a treaty between sovereign states. And this applied to the Indian army also, which Jinnah wanted to divide first and then to bring together again for the purposes of a common defence arrangement.

On 15 April 1946 Congress put forward its own suggestions through its Muslim president, Maulana Azad. It wanted complete independence for an undivided India. There would be one federation of fully autonomous units with residuary powers, and a centre above them with authority over certain subjects, some compulsory, others optional. The compulsory subjects would be defence and foreign affairs, while the optional list included all the remaining central subjects under the existing constitution. This, Azad felt, met all the legitimate Muslim fears.[33] But the proposal ran into all manner of difficulties. For one thing, it was probable that the Hindu provinces might be persuaded to allow the centre to retain some of the optional subjects, while the Muslim provinces were unlikely

[32] See Cabinet Delegation and Wavell's meeting with Jinnah, 16 April 1946, ibid., 285.
[33] See *T.P.*, VII, 285, fn. 3.

to be so persuaded. A federation of provinces, some with greater and others with lesser powers, was not constitutionally or practically very tidy. There would have to be some sort of executive and legislative authority to sort out the problem of compulsory and optional subjects, and this in its turn would raise the thorny question of how the provinces were to be represented in the central organs. This was the dilemma the Cabinet Mission hoped to resolve by their three-tier proposal. It was put forward by Cripps, who had borrowed it from a Punjabi Leaguer, Nawab M. A. Gurmani.[34] At the top there would be the union of all-India, in the middle the sub-federations of Pakistan and Hindustan with their separate legislatures, and below them the provinces and States or groups of States which agreed to join one or other of the two sub-federations.[35]

The Mission persuaded itself that this three-tier wedding cake was the best way to celebrate the sanctified union of Muslim and Hindu India. Even Wavell saw merits in this complex scheme, though he was not sure whether Congress would agree to the proposed sub-federations and the concentration of power which group legislatures on the second tier would entail.[36] The real point was that a group legislature on the second tier was a major concession to the League, a way of roping Jinnah into accepting the scheme. The League with its weak structure of authority over the legislatures of the Muslim-majority provinces needed a central Muslim legislature in order to keep these provinces under some control. While the Congress with its 'strong party control' might be able to work a system which only had provincial legislatures, the League would find it impossible to crack the whip on its notoriously unruly followers.[37]

On 25 April 1946, Jinnah was shown the two revised plans: in the new numbering Plan A was now the three-tier federal union and Plan B was a minimum sovereign Pakistan. In the first open indication that he might settle for something less than a sovereign Pakistan, Jinnah rejected a

---

[34] Ibid., 317, fn. 1.
[35] According to Cripps, the three-tier system would start 'at the bottom with the Provinces and such larger states or groups of states as agree to join one or other of the two groups. These units should be grouped according to the desire expressed by their popular assemblies into two groups, one of which we refer to as Pakistan and the other as Hindustan. Finally, there should be a Union of All India embracing both Pakistan and Hindustan and if it were so agreed, some or all of the states or groups of states.' (Memorandum by Sir Stafford Cripps, 18 April 1946, ibid., 306; also see Cabinet Delegation to Wavell, 22 April 1946, ibid., 315–17, documents 130 and 131.)
[36] But Alexander argued that this condition was the logical development of something to which the Congress had already agreed, and felt it 'satisfied our conscience sufficiently on the minority issue'. (See notes of meetings between the Cabinet Delegation and Wavell, 24 and 25 April 1946, ibid., 325 and 332.)
[37] Note of meeting between the Cabinet Delegation and Wavell, 25 April 1946, ibid., 334.

truncated Pakistan (Plan B) as 'definitely unacceptable' but said he was prepared to consider the three-tier federal union (Plan A) if Congress would do the same.[38] But the omens that Congress would accept the three-tier proposal were not good. Neither Gandhi nor Nehru liked the scheme; and the Working Committee was reluctant even to consider it. The Mission faced the risk of formally putting the proposal to the Congress and then having it rejected out of hand. Then the only way forward would be an award, with one option foreclosed since the main party had already declared its unwillingness to accept it. So Cripps suggested that they should 'now press the Congress hard', pointing out that since Congress had already accepted the principle of provincial autonomy, the Mission's proposal was simply a way of giving Muslims reasonable protection and taking the sting out of the Pakistan demand.[39]

But if the Mission now had a formula for a solution to the long-term constitutional problem, they had still to tackle the short-term difficulties. To get the constitution-making machinery moving, an interim government supported by both parties was essential. Congress wanted plenary powers as a condition for coming into an interim government, arguing that its followers would not be satisfied if all that happened was a change in the personnel of the existing Viceroy's Executive Council. But Wavell and the Mission argued for an interim government under the existing constitution on the grounds that Parliamentary legislation would delay getting Indians into office.[40] Wavell's new Executive Council was to be wholly Indian, except for the Viceroy himself. He would retain the right to distribute portfolios, but he would first consult Indian leaders. The Viceroy would also keep his special powers during the interim period, although, with goodwill and trust, he hoped it would not be necessary to exercise them. Wavell wanted a Council of twelve: five Congressmen including a representative of the Scheduled Castes; five Muslim Leaguers; one Sikh, and one other (Anglo-Indian, Christian or non-League Muslim). Since such a Council was bound to arouse controversy, Wavell was prepared to add a thirteenth member for good luck and maintain the communal balance. If the composition of the Council could be settled, Wavell would suggest the names of the members, but was willing to listen to objections; alternatively, he was prepared to choose names from lists sent by the parties.[41]

The long-term solution, however, overshadowed the question of the

[38] Meeting of the Cabinet Delegation and Wavell, 26 April 1946, ibid., 342.
[39] Ibid.
[40] See meeting of the Cabinet Delegation and Wavell with Maulana Azad, 17 April 1946, ibid., 294–7.
[41] See Wavell's undated note, ibid., 359–61.

interim government. Jinnah wanted the long-term issue settled first on a basis he deemed to be satisfactory. The Mission had somehow to bring the two parties to the negotiating table. If the talks produced no agreement (and no one really believed that an agreement was likely), then at least the Mission would be justified in coming out publicly with its own proposals. On 26 April, Azad thought somewhat optimistically that the Congress Working Committee might negotiate on the basis of a single federation, broken into two, and legislating separately for optional subjects.[42] The Mission saw this as a step forward. The invitation to the presidents of the two parties, couched in identical terms, stated that the Mission had in mind an union government dealing with foreign affairs, defence and communications, and two groups of provinces – Muslim and Hindu – dealing with the remaining subjects.[43] Both the parties agreed to send their representatives to confer with the Mission and the Viceroy at Simla. But agreeing to meet did not mean that they were prepared to negotiate in earnest. Azad's reply to Pethick-Lawrence now suggested that Congress was in no mood to give much away. It objected to the 'residuary sovereign rights' which the Mission planned to give to provincial governments; it maintained that 'Congress has never accepted the division of India into predominantly Hindu and predominantly Muslim Provinces', but did admit that there might have to be an optional and a compulsory list of subjects at the federal centre.[44] With such a reaction from even Azad, it is a wonder that the Mission still bothered to make the trek up to Simla.

Section 2

On 5 May 1946, the tripartite Conference opened at Simla. Congress and League each sent four representatives: Maulana Azad, Jawaharlal Nehru, Sardar Vallabhbhai Patel and Khan Abdul Ghaffar Khan from the Congress and Jinnah, Liaquat Ali Khan, Sardar Abdur Rab Nishtar and Nawab Ismail Khan from the League.[45] But no one had agreed to anything before Simla, and no one was minded to give away much at it. Jinnah wanted power to lie at the intermediate level; Congress wanted it

[42] See Cabinet Delegation to Attlee, 27 April 1946, ibid., 351.
[43] See Pethick-Lawrence to Azad, 27 April 1946, ibid., 352. (A similar letter was sent to Jinnah.)
[44] Azad to Pethick-Lawrence, 27 April 1946, ibid., 353 and 28 April 1946, ibid, 357–8.
[45] It is ironic that there were two Muslims from the Congress and three minority-province Muslims from the League who met to decide the future of India and of the Muslims in the majority provinces. But they might as well have been Catholics and Protestants in Belfast for all the love that was lost between them. Jinnah set the tone of the Conference by refusing to shake hands with Azad.

at the top. The Mission's hope was 'somehow . . . to arrive at a position which Jinnah can regard as conceding Pakistan and Congress can regard as not conceding it'.[46] Here indeed was a task for a magician, and Simla was short of wizards in the early summer of 1946.

Both parties had diametrically different conceptions of what power the union centre should possess. Finance was the nub of the matter, since power comes out of the drawers of the till. Congress wanted a self-supporting centre, with control over subjects to do with revenue. Jinnah claimed he wanted a centre with no real financial powers, a mere agent for the federations, dependent on doles from the provinces. He did not want the centre to have authority to levy taxes upon the groups. The union would have to be given a budget for defence, but that budget was to be kept to the minimum in line with previous expenditure by the two federations who would have to agree on what to give. If the union needed more money, Jinnah wanted its budget to go to the group legislatures for their approval.[47] Not surprisingly, Nehru retorted that Congress could never accept such a 'vague and airy Centre'.[48]

By his implacable opposition to an union legislature, Jinnah showed what he was really after. He would have preferred even foreign affairs and defence, the union centre's two responsibilities, to be discussed and settled in the group legislatures, and he conceded with reluctance that this was neither logical nor practical.[49] But if there was to be an union legislature, parity for the League was of the essence: different legislatures would be entitled to elect an equal number of representatives to the union legislature, and the balance between the League and the Congress had to be made immune to any changes, even if the princes were to come in later.[50]

At the end of the first long day of shadow boxing, nothing had been agreed. Congress had come out clearly against the grouping of provinces and the creation of executive and legislative machinery on the second

---

[46] Croft to Monteath, 3 May 1946, *T.P.*, VII, 410.

[47] First meeting of the Second Simla Conference, 5 May 1946, ibid., 426.

[48] Ibid., 427. Vague and airy though Nehru's critics sometimes found him, he knew better that someone had to provide the money for those with their heads in the clouds.

[49] The Secretary of State asked the Leaguers whether they envisaged India's foreign minister trotting off like some peripatetic envoy to two or three legislatures, attempting to justify his policy to three different sets of interests; and whether India's guns would have three barrels swivelling round to three points of the compass according to the conflicting demands of three houses. Jinnah thought he had made his point when he drew an analogy between the foreign policy of the British Commonwealth of Nations and the new India he wanted; but someone reminded him that the Commonwealth did not have a common foreign policy. (Ibid, 428.)

[50] Second meeting of the Second Simla Conference, 5 May 1946, ibid., 430.

tier. Such an arrangement would be 'cumbrous, static and disjointed, leading to continuous friction'.[51] The grouping scheme, with its three layers, was, Wavell confessed, far from 'ideal from the administrative point of view', but had been devised to deal with a 'psychological difficulty' and with the problems to which the Congress's own proposals for two lists of central subjects had given rise.[52] The optional subjects, the Mission decided, could best be discussed by the group legislatures. For his part, Nehru let the cat out of the bag when he hinted that Congress's proposals were not seen by it as a final solution, and the constitution it had in mind was to be something different, since provincial autonomy presented the real threat to an united India. What Nehru and Congress wanted was a 'strong and organic' centre for the union, even if its powers were to be limited to a narrower range of subjects than they preferred.[53]

Congress did not like grouping because it made the provinces the arbiters of India's future constitution and gave the League too much say at the centre. But this was precisely why Jinnah wanted a group legislature for the Muslim provinces. Both Congress and League wanted their centres to control their provinces, but the Congress wanted to control the provinces from an union legislature which it knew it could dominate while Jinnah wanted his central authority to flow from a group legislature – this was to be his centre, and from it he hoped to build up a real authority over his less amenable Muslim provinces. This was just what Congress wanted to prevent by insisting that the issue of grouping had to be decided by the all-India constituent assembly. That assembly would settle the shape of the union and *a fortiori* the provincial constitutions. Confident of victory in the constituent assembly, Congress did not believe that grouping would survive at the end of the day. It had the measure of Jinnah's weaknesses. Once Muslims entered the constituent assembly, with freedom around the corner, and Congress clearly in the saddle, Muslims, indeed even Leaguers, would in all probability exhibit that renowned Indian talent for crossing the floor. This would prove the Congress's point that Muslims were Indians just like everyone else, that Congress was a secular party open to all-comers.

Jinnah could not accept this line. Grouping alone had brought him to Simla. He had been denied a sovereign Pakistan and offered grouping instead. Now Congress wanted to take away grouping, or at best keep it at a tantalising distance which could only be reached by an united and

---

[51] See Azad to Pethick-Lawrence, 6 May 1946, ibid., 434.
[52] Third meeting of the Second Simla Conference, 6 May 1946, ibid., 436.
[53] See the third and fourth meetings of the Second Simla Conference, 6 May 1946, ibid., 437 and 441.

solid League when in fact he knew that the League was neither united nor solid. Unless he was given grouping Jinnah would not stay to talk at Simla. The uncertain hold he had over his followers was cutting down his options at the negotiating table. It was not that Jinnah was simply cussedly inflexible as the Guardians sometimes portrayed him; he was unbending because, knowing his power was so brittle, he realised that by bending a fragile League might break beyond repair. The *via tuta* for Jinnah was Pakistan or grouping for Muslim provinces, with an equal say in the constitution-making body. More than 'mere psychology or a vague feeling of sentiment' was at stake, Jinnah argued, and he was right. Grouping was the only 'way to prevent complete partition', and the groups should be allowed to set up the machinery for making the constitution, not the machinery the groups. The assembly making the constitution was not to be sovereign; sovereignty would flow only once a constitution had been agreed upon.[54] With authority to settle everything, including provincial constitutions, the constituent assemblies of the groups would only leave the three agreed subjects to the union. These group assemblies would be elected by the provincial legislatures and the Princely States would have a constituent assembly of their own. Once all these assemblies had been set up, they would send their representatives to an union assembly, tied and strictly bound to its three common subjects. Since even this emasculated centre might threaten the Muslim provinces, Jinnah wanted the groups to have the right to secede within five years – a stern reminder to the Congress to behave even-handedly towards the infant Muslim groups during the early years of the union, and also to his own followers that they would have to follow their leader.[55] This was hard play, and it depended on the other players not overthrowing the table.

Six more days of proposals and counter-proposals did not disguise the fact that the Conference had broken down over the issue of grouping, 'the whole guts' of the problem, as Jinnah pithily told the disappointed Viceroy.[56] Details are mere glosses in the margin since there was so little common ground between the Congress and the League. Jinnah laid

---

[54] See record of fourth meeting of the Second Simla Conference, 6 May 1946, ibid., 441.

[55] Patel said that this was partition, which was the reality of the grouping scheme. Jinnah assured him that he was not trying to break the union but there had to be constitutional means (just as there have to be divorce laws) to end it if it proved impossible in the 'light of experience'. (Ibid., 442.)

According to Gandhi, the grouping scheme was 'really worse than Pakistan' and there could be no question of equality between Hindu provinces and their vastly larger populations and the much smaller Muslim provinces. (Gandhi to Cripps, 8 May 1946, ibid., 466.)

[56] See note by Wavell, 13 May 1946, ibid., 540.

down the League's conditions: grouping must come before union; there had to be at least two assemblies to settle the constitution; all the Muslim provinces, both in the west and the east, had to be in one group, as the price for conceding Assam; provinces had to be denied the right to opt out until the constitution for the Muslim group had been settled.[57] In its turn, the Congress called for a sovereign constituent assembly; there was to be no parity for the Muslim group (or groups) whether in the executive or legislature at the centre, and currency and customs had to remain in the hands of the centre in addition to 'other subjects as on closer scrutiny may be found to be intimately allied to them', such as central planning.[58]

On 12 May 1946, the Simla negotiations openly collapsed. Both parties rushed to register their claims before the Mission announced its proposals in lieu of an agreed settlement.[59] The Mission was not in a position to make an award. Awards can only be made, and made to stick, if the makers are ready to impose their decisions, by force or by political persuasion. The Mission had come to India to find a way by which the British could get out of India, keeping their interests intact, but giving their responsibilities away. Its proposals of mid-May were intended to concentrate the minds of their would-be successors, not to lay down the definitive law. On 16 May 1946, the Mission proposed the three-tier system, a compromise between Jinnah's full sovereign Pakistan and Congress's 'strong and organic' centre. The union would control the three common subjects and it would have the power to raise its own revenues. It would have an executive and legislature with representatives from British India and the Indian States. There would be no parity between Congress and Muslim provinces.[60]

The 16 May statement was potentially a disaster for Jinnah. He wanted parity; he was against allowing the union centre to raise its own revenues; he did not want an union legislature at all, and had insisted that even minor decisions, whether legislative or executive, on any 'controversial' matter at the centre must have a three-fourths not a bare majority.[61] But there was worse to come. The League had demanded that the provinces and the Princely States should be sovereign in all matters except those specifically conceded to the centre. The Mission, however, spoke about

[57] See note by Wyatt on his conversation with Jinnah, 9 May 1946, ibid., 475.
[58] See Azad to Pethick-Lawrence, 9 May 1946, ibid., 476–7.
[59] See Jinnah to Pethick-Lawrence, 12 May 1946, ibid., 516–17 and Azad to Pethick-Lawrence, 12 May 1946, ibid., 518–21.
[60] See Cabinet Mission's statement, 16 May 1946, ibid., 582–91.
[61] See Jinnah to Pethick-Lawrence, 12 May 1946, ibid., 517, paragraph 8. The Mission's proposals merely suggested that any communal issue in the legislature would be decided by a majority voíe of the affected community as well as a majority of all those present and voting irrespective of community.

residuary powers for the provinces, not the 'sovereign' rights which its letters of invitation to Azad and Jinnah before Simla had mentioned.[62] Instead of one Muslim group, which Jinnah wanted, there were to be two, one consisting of the Punjab, Sind, the N.W.F.P. and Baluchistan (Group B), and the other of Bengal and Assam (Group C). The Mission's plan did entitle provinces to form groups, equip themselves with executives and legislatures, and ask for their constitution to be changed after a ten-year interval. But there was no mention of the right of secession from the union. All in all, the 16 May statement contained evidence of a greater deference to the Congress standpoint, hinting to Jinnah that perhaps he had missed the bus.

The details of the Mission's plan showed how far the League's case had fallen. The League had asked for Hindus and Muslims to have seats in the union assembly in proportion to their population; Congress preferred single transferable votes since Hindu and Sikh minorities in the Muslim provinces had been given weightage – this was standing separate representation on its head. The Mission ruled along Congress lines.[63] Muslims from all three groups could now expect a mere seventy-nine seats in a central legislature which contained 292.[64] So in the Mission's

[62] See Pethick-Lawrence to Azad, 27 April 1946, ibid., 352.

[63] According to the Mission's proposal the provincial legislatures would elect their representatives through proportional representation by a single transferable vote. (See Cabinet Delegation's statement, 16 May 1946, ibid., 582–91.)

[64] Of the 187 seats given to the Hindu provinces, twenty were for their Muslim minorities. The north-western group had thirty-five seats at the centre, of which twenty-two were for Muslims. Bengal and Assam had seventy seats, of which a bare majority of thirty-six were for Muslims. The following table gives the composition of the proposed union legislature:

Province	General	Muslim	Sikh
Group A			
Madras	45	4	—
Bombay	19	2	—
U.P.	47	8	—
Bihar	31	5	—
C.P.	16	1	—
Orissa	9	—	—
TOTAL	167	20	—
Group B*			
Punjab (28)†	8	16	4
N.W.F.P. (3)	—	3	—
Sind (4)	1	3	—
TOTAL	9	22	4

proposals the Muslim provinces of the north-west ended up with only two seats more than Muslims in the minority provinces. Punjab, which did not have a League ministry, was left in clear control of its group. Indian States, with ninety-three representatives, gave Congress a potentially overwhelming majority. Of course the Mission's proposals reflected the political arithmetic of India far more accurately than Jinnah's calculations. But that is precisely why he did not like them, was opposed to a single constitution-making body and needed a settlement by treaty between sovereign states, not by a share-out between the big and the small. For Jinnah the worst cut of all was that grouping was not made binding upon the provinces even though they would initially have to meet in groups. According to the Mission, the union assembly would begin by setting up an electoral commission.[65] Then the provincial representatives would divide according to their groups;[66] these groups would settle their provincial constitutions and decide whether they wanted group constitutions or not. In Group B, for example, Punjab was dominant but the other provinces in its group could cut loose from its sway once the constitution had been framed.[67]

Admittedly few of Jinnah's followers could understand the full implications of the Mission's proposals, but its preamble, harshly worded and openly rejecting a sovereign Pakistan, put the Quaid-i-Azam in an

Province	General	Muslim	Sikh —
Group C			
Bengal (60)	27	33	—
Assam (10)	7	3	—
TOTAL	34	36	—

*There was to be an additional representative from Baluchistan.
†These indicate the number of seats allotted to the province in the union legislature. Ibid.

65 The union constituent assembly would meet in Delhi, initially only to elect a chairman and other officers and an Advisory Committee on the rights of citizens, minorities and tribal and excluded areas. But it was obvious that if the League made the election of the chairman a communal issue the constitution-making process would be nipped in the bud.

66 In the preliminary stage the Indian States would be represented by a negotiating committee since the plan did not suggest a method of selection for State representatives. (See paragraph 19 (ii) of the statement, *T.P.*, VII, 589.)

67 There was no provincial legislature in Baluchistan which could decide to opt out of Group B. The representatives of Baluchistan were to be selected by a Shahi Jirga (or grand meeting of all the tribal *sardars*). Only after the new constitutional arrangements had been settled could a province decide to opt out of a group by the decision of its newly elected legislature. In other words, they had to parley before quitting.

impossible quandary. Until now his own followers had not questioned his tactics, however little he was wont to explain what they were. But now Jinnah was bombarded with telegrams from his followers openly questioning his line. They were bemused by his letter to Pethick-Lawrence of 12 May which seemed to give Pakistan away by conceding the principle of an union government.[68] Since the Mission's preamble so clearly rejected 'Pakistan', how could Jinnah reconcile its proposals with their demands? Jinnah took refuge behind the closed doors of his Working Committee, and called a meeting of the A.I.M.L. Council (which for the past twenty-two months he had not needed to do). Jinnah had to placate his followers, and needed time to do so. But time was running out, since the Mission and the Congress were both in a hurry. Jinnah argued for a steady unhurried pace, and asked for a month before giving his reaction to the Mission's plan.[69] Jinnah, far less sanguine of his control over events, and uncertain of winning a dangerous game, was now being questioned even by the Leaguers who previously had followed his lead blindly.[70]

But there were attractions for the Muslim provinces in the Mission's plan, so it was by no means out of the question that Jinnah could reconcile them to it. The average Punjabi, according to the Governor, would be pleased with the proposals. In Khizar's opinion, religious enthusiasm was a 'passing phase', and most Muslims in the Punjab would be 'content to settle down' and take a moderate line.[71] Equally,

---

[68] See AIML/File. No. 142 (Working Committee's Meetings 1943–1947) and AIML/SHC/ 1, Files 1 and 2 (Punjab vol. II, General Correspondence 1944–1947 and NWFP vol. II, 1944–47).

[69] See note on Jinnah's telephone conversation with George Abell, 18 May 1946, *T.P.*, VII, 619. Liaquat told Wavell that according to the League's constitution it was impossible to summon the Council at less than a fortnight's notice. But he later informed them that Jinnah had called a meeting of the League's Working Committee for 3 June instead of 10 June, and the A.I.M.L.'s Council's meeting for the 5th instead of the 15th June. (Liaquat Ali Khan's meeting with the Cabinet Delegation and Wavell, 19 May 1946, ibid., 623.)

[70] Liaquat, taking Jinnah's line, argued that calm was needed to formulate the response to the Mission's statement. No sensible decision could be arrived at in the existing 'atmosphere of emotionalism'. (See Liaquat's meeting with the Cabinet Delegation and Wavell, 19 May 1946, ibid., 628–9.)

[71] But Khizar was less optimistic about grouping; there was already friction between the Punjab and the Frontier Province over the question of a joint police force. The Pathans, understandably enough, did not want to come under the Punjab's sway. As the Governor of the Punjab commented, 'it would be certainly unwise for them to do so'. Khizar was also against having anything to do with Sind. (See Jenkins to Wavell, 17 May 1946, ibid., 604–5.) But the Syed group in Sind had already condemned the notion of grouping, arguing that their province should have nothing to do with the Punjab; they

many Bengali Muslims were relieved that the Mission had left their province undivided and essentially a 'self-governing entity', and were keen that Jinnah should accept the proposals.[72] As far as the Punjab and Bengal were concerned, Muslims had reason to be pleased with the Mission's plan. It was simply that the wording of the preamble which rejected 'Pakistan' debarred them from expressing their delight openly until Jinnah had given his clearance. By making much of 'Pakistan' in an unspecified way when he had little else in his armoury, Jinnah could not now easily reveal its inwardness or deny what had become a catch-all for a host of unattainable dreams.

On 22 May 1946 Jinnah, realising that he could no longer delay, gave his first reaction to the Mission's statement. Some of it was predictable: he regretted that the Mission had trotted out 'commonplace and exploded arguments against Pakistan and resorted to special pleadings couched in deplorable language which is calculated to hurt the feelings of Muslim India'. This was a curt nod meant for those in the gods; he went on to keep his options open. He carefully avoided rejecting the Mission's statement out of hand, arguing that it was not for him but for the A.I.M.L. Council to decide the matter.[73] By this device, more transparent to the historian than to his contemporaries, Jinnah hoped to salvage from the 16 May statement something of the Mission's pre-Simla scheme. But Congress was not ready to stand by while Jinnah tried to bring round his Council. Congress openly admitted that its policy was to go further still in the opposite direction, to 'improve' on the statement and get the sovereign constituent assembly which it wanted.[74] The Congress could scent victory. Its press was against any appeasement of the League, and the Viceroy feared that some members of the Congress High Command, led by Vallabhbhai Patel, were preparing to bid for the whole cake – 'This section has no interest in the framing of the final

wanted Sind to simply opt out of everything and become sovereign in its own right. Yet other Sindhi Muslims were seemingly happy with the proposals since they learnt from the Hindu press that they had been offered more than what Pakistan would have given them. (See Mudie to Wavell, 24 May 1946, ibid., 678.)

[72] Burrows feared that if Jinnah rejected the statement this might signal a general Jihad and the Bengal League ministry might reluctantly be forced by the High Command to resign. (Burrows's meeting with the Cabinet Delegation and Wavell, 24 May 1946, ibid., 675–7.)

[73] Jinnah's statement on the Cabinet Mission plan, 22 May 1946, in Sherwani (ed.), *Pakistan Resolution to Pakistan*, p. 118.

[74] The League had been reassured and the Congress told that the constituent assembly would become sovereign only after the constitution had been framed. (See record of meeting between Pethick-Lawrence and Cripps with Liaquat Ali Khan, Nawab Ismail Khan and Sardar Nishtar, 16 May 1946, *T.P.*, VII, 580.)

Constitution; all it wants is power, complete power, and power at once'.[75]

Jinnah was on the defensive, reluctant to face his own Working Committee and the League Council, 'nervous' and understandably alarmed at the way the Congress point of view and the line the Mission had decided to take were coming together. Everyone (except the League), the Viceroy, the Mission and the Congress were anxious to get on with making the constitution for independent India. This called for an interim government as soon as possible. But not sure that the constitution would go his way, Jinnah was anxious to delay. As he told Wyatt, what was needed was a 'surgical operation'. By this he did not mean partition, but rather a notional division of India into two groups before they joined again in a new partnership of equality. For this 'surgery' to be successful, Jinnah needed the British to remain in charge of defence and foreign affairs to hold the reconstructed centre together. In the nursery of independence, the British would have to remain in charge, disciplining the greedy and succouring the weak. Faced by such unacceptable counsels, Wyatt suggested a way out to that proud man who in the past had always relied solely on his own good judgement. Wyatt proposed that the League should pass a resolution condemning the Mission's 'outrageous' rejection of Pakistan, then state that of course Muslims never expected the British or anyone else to hand them Pakistan on a plate and were ready to win it 'by their own strong right arm'. To prove its goodwill, the League *would accept the Statement as the first step on the road to Pakistan*.[76] Jinnah was apparently 'delighted' by this advice,[77] a measure of his mounting despair.

Parity with the Congress, the League's aim, was still eluding Jinnah. He now looked to the interim government to see if he could achieve parity there. With the 'British Crown Representative', the broker between the parties, the League might still get parity in an interim

---

[75] Wavell to Henderson, 21 May 1946, ibid., 654. The leader of this section was Vallabhbhai Patel, India's Bismarck, that man of iron from Gujerat. Nehru was ready to give the Mission's plan a chance; Gandhi as ever sat on the fence, but there was no comfort for Jinnah in seeing him there. As Wavell remarked, Gandhi's stance was a trifle confusing and no one could tell where the Mahatma, 'a king chameleon', really sat (ibid.). To make matters worse for Jinnah, on 24 May the Congress Working Committee passed a resolution objecting to compulsory grouping of provinces on the grounds that this infringed on provincial autonomy, and maintaining that the constituent assembly was a sovereign body with final authority to draw up the constitution. Only after the constitution had been drawn could the provinces decide to form groups. (See enclosure no. 370, Azad to Pethick-Lawrence, 24 May 1946, ibid., 679–82.)

[76] See note by Wyatt, 25 May 1946, Ibid., 684–7 (my italics).

[77] Jinnah exclaimed: 'That's it, you've got it.' (Ibid., 687.)

government and keep it as long as that government survived. If a new constitution failed to emerge during the interim period, all the better. In Jinnah's less than perfect world he was ready to settle for a semi-permanent interim government, with the Viceroy still in charge. At least this would give him time to persuade the Congress and his own Muslims to see good sense in his solution. And good sense it was, in terms of an ideal of Indian unity; unfortunately it was no longer practical politics. Wavell could not promise Jinnah parity in an interim government; the Mission's proposals did not permit him that degree of latitude. He tried to persuade the League to keep an open mind about the Mission's plan, which it was easier to do once the Mission and the Congress fell out over their interpretation on grouping and on the status of the constituent assembly.[78] He was able to offer the League a share, less than a lion's but a lot more than a jackal's, in the interim government. Wavell gave Jinnah his 'personal assurance', on behalf of the Mission, 'that we do not propose to make any discrimination in the treatment of either party; and that we shall go ahead with the plan laid down in the statement as far as circumstances permit if either party accepts; but we hope that both will accept'.[79] With this assurance Jinnah was ready on 4 June 1946 to face his League.

Now he could tell his Working Committee that an 'assurance' from the British meant more than agreement with the Congress – the devil they knew was better than the devil they were coming to know. So he advised the Council to accept the Mission's plan on behalf of the League, condemn its preamble, but not fret too much since preamble and substance were clearly not at one. The Mission's plan in fact was a way forward for Pakistan, at least the Pakistan Jinnah was after. The proposed three-tier system gave the essence of a large Pakistan. Muslims would have their majority in two groups, and the centre, even if Congress and Hindus dominated it, had a very restricted domain. At this hedged and limited centre, parity still eluded the Muslims, but parity was more of a bargaining counter than an unnegotiable demand. Defence remained a strong card for Muslims: they would control India's frontiers and this would make them the real custodians of the centre.[80] Moreover, any constitution drawn up would be open to that decennial revision hallowed

---

[78] On 25 May, the Mission rejected the Congress's interpretation of the grouping scheme and the status of the constituent assembly; grouping was an 'essential feature' of the 16 May statement and the constituent assembly would be sovereign after, not before the making of the constitution. (See Mission's statement, 25 May 1946, paragraph 8, *T.P.*, VII, 688–9.)

[79] See Wavell to Jinnah, 4 June 1946, ibid., 799.

[80] This line was reminiscent of Iqbal's address to the All-India Muslim League at Allahabad in December 1930.

by tradition. If the worse came to the worst, the Muslim units could pack their bags and leave the union,[81] and Groups B and C would be insurance for minority Muslims, a point not lost on the four U.P. Muslims on the Working Committee.[82] If the League rejected the proposals, Jinnah warned, the British would still go ahead and the Congress would be the beneficiary. Times had changed and so had the old balance: the League no longer had a veto on constitutional advance. These harsh facts had to be faced and the League had to enter the interim government if it was to rescue some part of its aims. Even now achieving parity was not out of the question; but unless the League was in the interim government and made its voice heard, it would lose all chance of winning parity. Jinnah's reasons were a combination of special pleading and pragmatism. In the unhappy position of having to cajole and persuade men who previously had not questioned why, Jinnah was able to win the day only by promising that he would not join any interim government without parity for the League.[83] On 6 June 1946, the A.I.M.L. passed its momentous resolution accepting the Mission's statement, which, it must be stressed, had rejected Pakistan. All except thirteen Leaguers voted for it.[84] Face was saved by reiterating Pakistan as the goal,[85] and by reserving the

---

[81] Interviews with two of the most important leaders from the Punjab in the A.I.M.L. Council provide interesting insight into Jinnah's strategy. According to Mian Mumtaz Daultana, Jinnah never wanted a Pakistan which involved the partition of India and was all in favour of accepting the Cabinet Mission's proposals. The ten-year trial period was the bait Jinnah offered to the separatists in the League Council. Daultana said that this was enough time to ensure a Hindu–Muslim accommodation, and as far as this Punjabi Leaguer was concerned these 'ten years would be forever'. (My interview with Mian Mumtaz Daultana, 10 February 1980.) Shaukat Hayat claimed responsibility for bringing Jinnah round to accept the Mission's 16 May statement. According to Shaukat it was he who told the Great Leader: 'let us wait for ten years'. (Interview with Shaukat Hayat, 5 February 1980, Islamabad.)

[82] Of the twenty-one members on the League's Working Committee, eleven were from the minority provinces, including the president (Jinnah) and the general secretary (Liaquat); ten were from the Muslim-majority provinces. (See *T.P.*, VII, xxx, where the names are given.)

[83] As Jinnah later confessed, it was the Viceroy's 'assurance' which had been 'one of the most important considerations'; that assurance and the Mission's statement 'formed one whole' and without it 'we would not have got the approval of the Council to the scheme'. (Jinnah to Wavell, 8 June 1946, ibid., 841.)

[84] Those who were opposed included spokesmen of extreme religious groups like Hasrat Mohani and Abdus Sattar Niazi. The gulf between the politicians of Pakistan and its religious leaders was increasingly to come into the open. (Interview with Mian Mumtaz Daultana, 10 February 1980.)

[85] The League was 'willing to co-operate with the constitution-making machinery proposed in the scheme outlined by the Mission, in the hope that it would ultimately result in the establishment of a completely sovereign Pakistan'. (See the A.I.M.L.'s resolution of 6 June 1946, in Sherwani (ed.), *Pakistan Resolution to Pakistan*, p. 127.)

League's right to modify its stand at any time. But Jinnah got his mandate to enter the interim government and to 'take such decisions and actions as he deems fit and proper'.[86]

But for the first time Jinnah's mandate had been qualified and defined by the League's Council. Jinnah had reason to be worried. The Congress was publicly agitating against Wavell's formula of a five:five:two ratio in the interim government. That ratio, Jinnah told Wavell, had been the 'turning point in our having secured the decision of the Council'.[87] If that ratio giving Congress and the League an equal share went, then so did Jinnah's mandate. So Jinnah had to continue to demand parity for the League and the Congress in the interim government, and for good measure he demanded the most important portfolios of defence, foreign affairs, planning, development and commerce for the League. In fact Jinnah wanted the defence portfolio for himself, since he could see that this was the key post, a strong card if it could be held in Muslim hands.[88] Jinnah also had to demand the right to nominate all Muslims in the interim government.[89] As he admitted for the first time, he was 'not his own master'.[90]

There was nothing magical about the ratio Wavell had suggested; it was merely the 'most hopeful basis of settlement'.[91] Unless there was a coalition in the interim government, 'there would be a split up and chaos'. Some such ratio as five:five was the price Congress would have to pay to persuade the League to enter into a coalition with it. By accepting something like parity, Congress could get constitution-making under way; it did not commit it to accepting it in the future. But the difficulty was that Congress was not prepared to give up its right to nominate Muslims of its own. Moreover, as Nehru told the Viceroy, Congress believed that a coalition would not work because the Congress and the League were poles apart. Congress abhorred grouping: it wanted a strong centre, and it thought it could get it. In short, its party bosses 'did not think that Mr Jinnah had any real place in the country'.[92] So Congress would only settle for an interim government of fourteen: five for Congress, four for the League, one non-League Muslim, one Congress Scheduled Caste, one Indian Christian, one Sikh, and the one obligatory woman whom Congress would find.[93]

---

[86] Ibid., 128.   [87] Jinnah to Wavell, 8 June 1946, *T.P.*, VII, 841.

[88] Note by Wavell, 7 June 1946, ibid., 839.

[89] Jinnah to Wavell, 8 June 1946, ibid., 842.

[90] See note by Wyatt on conversation with Jinnah, 11 June 1946, ibid., 866–7.

[91] Meeting of the Cabinet Delegation and Wavell, 8 June 1946, ibid., 843.

[92] See Cabinet Delegation and Wavell's interview with Nehru and Azad, 10 June 1946, ibid., 855.

[93] Note by Wavell on interview with Nehru, 12 June 1946, ibid., 886–7.

On 16 June 1946, the Mission and the Viceroy announced their terms for the interim government.[94] Fourteen members were to be invited to join the Executive Council and the making of the constitution would move forward as set out in the 16 May statement.[95] The Viceroy would decide on who would have what portfolio in the interim government. It was explicitly stated that the interim government's composition, a mere expedient for the moment, was 'in no way to be taken as a precedent for the solution of any other communal question'. It was hoped to get the new Executive Council going in ten days' time. But the critical paragraph 8 of the 16 June statement made provision for breaking the Congress–League deadlock:

In the event of the two major parties or either of them proving unwilling to join in the setting up of a coalition Government on the above lines, it is the intention of the Viceroy to proceed with the formation of an interim government which will be as representative as possible of those willing to accept the Statement of May 16th.[96]

These bold words were intended to get both parties to see the light, and join the Executive Council. Parity as such had been set aside, but something very close to parity had in practice been offered to the League, if caste Hindus were seen as rough equivalents to Muslims. Other minorities – a Sikh, Parsi, Indian Christian and a member of the Scheduled Castes – had been given a place, but some of them belonged to the Congress. Wavell had made a concession to Congress's unwillingness to accept parity; in turn he looked to Congress to accept the May 16 statement and join the interim government.

But the Congress Working Committee was split down the middle. Patel was against accepting Wavell's terms for entering the interim government; Gandhi was not so sure, and on certain conditions – Gandhi's political grammar was always in the conditional – he was ready to be persuaded.[97] But the main difficulty was Wavell's failure to include

---

[94] They wearily confessed that 'no useful purpose can be served by further prolonging these discussions'; a strong and representative interim government was needed, and it was needed here and now. (See statement by the Cabinet Delegation and the Viceroy, 16 June 1946, ibid., 954.)

[95] Those invited were: Sardar Baldev Singh (Sikh representative), Sir N. P. Engineer, Jagjivan Ram (Congress Scheduled Caste), Nehru, Jinnah, Liaquat Ali Khan, Nishtar, Patel, Rajendra Prasad, Nazimuddin, Nawab Ismail Khan, C. Rajagopalachari, H. K. Mahtab and Dr John Matthai.

[96] See paragraph 8 of the statement by the Cabinet Delegation and the Viceroy, 16 June 1946, *T.P.*, VII, 955.

[97] Gandhi wanted to bring in Sarat Chandra Bose instead of H. K. Mahtab, the Viceroy's choice. This was because Bose controlled the left-wing of the party, represented Bengal and led the Congress in the central legislature. Congress also wanted Nishtar out since he

a Congress Muslim among the new members. In the end Wavell accepted all of the Congress's objections, except the one that really mattered to both sides, the inclusion of a Muslim who had no allegiance to the League. Even mild concessions by Wavell to the Congress meant acute troubles for Jinnah. His complaints about not being given parity were simply brushed aside. Pethick-Lawrence, his patience strained, told the Quaid-i-Azam that he was no longer bound by his promise to come into the interim government since parity, the condition for entry, had not been granted.[98] This made it more difficult, not easier, for Jinnah. By now Jinnah was feeling the familiar cold draught of political failure and had little choice but to come into the interim government on British terms. He asked all sorts of questions, wanted all manner of assurances, and hedged this way and that. Jinnah wanted assurance that Muslim interests would be safeguarded on the Executive Council and decisions on major communal issues would not be taken if the majority of Muslim members were opposed to it.[99] But the point Jinnah made most strongly was that the League could not sit on an Executive Council with a Muslim who was not of their persuasion: this was 'absolutely and entirely unacceptable' and if these 'Quisling[s]' were brought in, he would not be able 'to show his face anywhere'. These were the entreaties, not the demands of a man, increasingly tired and disheartened, who felt he had been 'let down'.[100] The real bone of contention remained the question of Congress's right to have a Muslim of its own; Gandhi wanted Azad, but Azad, the Congress president, was ready to stay out if it brought the League into the government.

Wavell and the Mission now were well and truly stuck on the horns of yet another dilemma. If Congress rejected their proposals, the League alone would have to be allowed to form the government. Congress had still not accepted the May 16 statement; Jinnah had, so by the Mission's terms he would have to be invited to form the government. Congress obviously could not take that lightly and the agitation it would spark off

---

was not the voters' choice in the Frontier. Wavell accepted Bose's inclusion and Congress agreed to let Nishtar in.

[98] See note of interview between Pethick–Lawrence, Alexander and Jinnah, 17 June 1946, *T.P.*, VII, 960.

[99] He was not sure whether he would come into the government himself. Some of his followers had begged him not to join the interim government since there would be no one outside capable of keeping the ramshackle party together – Jinnah at least gave the appearance of doing so. But Jinnah wanted the defence portfolio for the League. Wavell wanted to give defence to a Sikh. (See Jinnah to Wavell, 19 June 1946, ibid., 976–7.)

[100] See Wavell's note on interview with Jinnah, 18 June 1946, ibid., 971–2. In the circumstances it is easy to see why Jinnah did not summon the League Council, but only spoke with the smaller and more amenable Working Committee.

might break the grip of the right wing over the Congress leadership.[101] On 22 June 1946, the Congress Working Committee decided not to join the interim government. In an effort to 'salvage something out of the wreckage around them',[102] Cripps and Pethick-Lawrence used all their old contacts, and some of their new ones, with Congress, to get it to change its mind. After more inconclusive talks, the Congress Working Committee finally rejected the proposals for the interim government but significantly accepted the constitutional proposals of the May 16 statement.[103] Its motive was clear; it was more than confident that it would be able to change the shape of the eventual constitutional settlement.[104] By accepting the Mission's proposals of May 16, and then grounding its case on paragraph 8 of the June 16 announcement, Congress was in effect torpedoing Wavell's plans for the interim government.[105] As the Viceroy lamented, 'We have in fact been outmanoeuvred by the Congress; and this ability of Congress to twist words and phrases and to take advantage of any slip in wording is what Mr Jinnah has all along feared, and has been the reason for his difficult attitude'.[106]

Jinnah was now told that the interim government would have to be postponed. Of course he pretended to be outraged. But in fact he had deliberately withheld his decision until the Congress had definitively stated its position. If Congress had accepted, Jinnah was not minded to reject the interim government proposals; if Congress in fact turned them down, then Jinnah was eager to accept. Now British ineptitude had confused the situation, and Jinnah was ready to embarrass them by getting the League to accept the proposals for the interim government

---

[101] See record of meeting between the Cabinet Delegation and Wavell, 22 June 1946, ibid., pp. 1002–5.

[102] Sudhir Ghosh, *Gandhi's Emissary* (Bombay, 1967), pp. 166–71.

[103] See resolution of the Congress Working Committee, 25 June 1946, *T.P.*, VII, 1036–8.

[104] Bluntly Azad told Wavell: 'While adhering to our views, we accept your proposals and are prepared to work them with a view to achieve our objective.' The objective of course was a strong unitary centre. (Azad to Wavell, 25 June 1946, ibid., 1036.)

[105] As Wavell confessed, paragraph 8 of the 16 June statement had been 'rashly' conceived, since it now limited his freedom of action. The Congress could and would predictably claim that the original assurances to Jinnah no longer applied. (Note by Wavell, 25 June 1946, ibid., 1038.) Alexander complained that the Congress acceptance of the long-term proposals was 'not . . . genuine'; he had come to India with an open mind; whatever his exasperation with Jinnah's attitude, he now felt 'bound to say that the behaviour of the Congress in the last six weeks seemed to him the most deplorable exhibition that he had witnessed in his political career'. (See record of meeting of the Cabinet Delegation and Wavell, 24 June 1946, ibid., 1024.)

[106] Note by Wavell for the Cabinet Delegation, enclosure to no. 604, 25 June 1946, ibid., 1038–9.

which the proposers had reneged for the time being.[107] He realised that the League was unlikely to be asked on its own to form an interim government; Pethick-Lawrence did the Quaid-i-Azam less than justice in believing that he really thought the British would ask the League to come in on these terms.[108] Once again Jinnah could pose as the injured party and call upon his followers to rally behind him to fight another day. In this way Jinnah hoped to be able to keep open the semblance of choice in a situation where he was soon to have no choice.

On 26 June 1946, the Raj quartet, who by now were as used to making announcements as to going back upon them, told a less than expectant India that a caretaker government would be formed, not a representative interim one, but negotiations for the latter would continue when all the parties had found time for calm reflection. Jinnah reacted predictably, claiming that this was a 'breach of faith' by perfidious Albion, who was about to 'forfeit the confidence of Muslim India'.[109] But the Mission had failed to square the circle; the deadly geometry of India's triangle had defeated it. On 28 June, the trio flew back to England, its mission unaccomplished. But it left behind a leader who had sensed that the last chance to achieve what he had always really been after had lain at some point inside the critical month between the statements of 16 May and 16 June. The issue was now to be decided in circumstances over which Jinnah had little control.

[107] See A.I.M.L. Working Committee's resolution, 25 June 1946, in Pirzada (ed.), *Foundations of Pakistan*, vol. II, pp. 530–1.
[108] The Secretary of State thought that Jinnah's hope of forming a government without the Congress was a 'foolish attitude' and 'very dangerous'. But the Quaid-i-Azam hardly needed Pethick-Lawrence to tell him how to play his cards. (See meeting of Cabinet Delegation and Wavell, 26 June 1946, *T.P.*, VII, 1053.)
[109] See Jinnah's statement, 27 June 1946, ibid., 1069–73.

6

The interim government: Jinnah in retreat

The last thirteen months of British rule saw the tragic collapse of Jinnah's strategy – tragic, because the Quaid-i-Azam had always tried to keep himself above communalism in its cruder forms and had cherished his own vision of Indian unity. For six years he had managed to paint a thin veneer of solidarity and unanimity over interests which were neither solid nor unanimous. This he had achieved only by keeping his purposes to himself and by allowing his Muslim constituents to see whatever they chose to see in a Pakistan which he left intentionally undefined. When the Cabinet Mission came to India, Jinnah was forced to reveal something of his hand, particularly since the Mission's proposals of 16 May did offer him some part of what he was after. By grouping Muslim provinces compulsorily, the Mission gave Jinnah at least a chance of curbing the particularism of his constituents. But Congress did not want grouping and did not need it since its centre was much stronger than the League's; scenting victory, it was not ready to make concessions to the League. Whatever else the Mission may have failed to accomplish it did succeed, whether intentionally or not, in straining Jinnah's already uncertain hold over followers who for the first time were given a hint of their leader's purposes at the centre and began to sense the weaknesses in his bargaining position.

Some Muslims felt that 'the League was conceding all along the line' and the 'Congress did not budge an inch from their position and the Mission too resiled from the position they had originally indicated in their letter of invitation to you [Jinnah]'. The Muslims could 'not be bound to submit to a Union Centre which does not accord us a position of equality'. The League had been 'almost cold shouldered so far as the Union Centre is concerned' and could hardly 'go to the public to canvass support for the kind of Union Centre proposed by the Mission after having sworn on the Quran to fight and die for undiluted sovereign Pakistan'.[1] Here was uninformed Muslim political opinion taking its revenge on the League leadership. Yet there was some consolation for Jinnah. A section of Punjabi Muslims believed that the Mission's scheme

---

[1] Jamil-ud-Din Ahmed to Jinnah, 29 May 1946, QAP/10/File No. 1092, p. 429.

was consistent with the 'Pakistan' they wanted. According to the editor of the *Nawa-i-Waqt*, the League Council had proved its political acumen by voting to accept the Mission's proposals by a majority of ninety-five per cent. The League had not abandoned its struggle for Pakistan, it had simply entered into a new phase to achieve its ultimate goal. The ten-year period before the establishment of an independent and sovereign Pakistan was the best defence of the scheme. During these ten years the League would be able to consolidate its position in the Muslim-majority provinces and ensure a viable Pakistan, if and when it became necessary to secede from the Union.[2] But these calculations were grounded on the mistaken assumption that there was time in hand and that Congress would rather make concessions than allow the Muslim-majority provinces to go their own way.

The sands were running out for the leaders of Congress and League alike. But whereas Jinnah needed delay, speed was of the essence for Congress. Labour unrest and pressure from its left were among the reasons why the Congress right wanted power quickly. To quell Indian unrest and control internal party factions, Congress was now ready to go on the offensive against the League, portrayed as the enemy without. So it made sense for Congress to carp and criticise the Mission's plans, its cunctations and compromises. As the newly-elected president of the Congress, Nehru was not his own man, but he made up for it in the fire and fury of his rhetoric against the plan. On 10 July, Nehru's first public statement as the new Congress president did not startle those who were privy to the inner thinking of the Congress High Command. But his open repudiation of the plan gave a severe shock to those Muslims who had been lulled into complacency by their own leader's rather more curt public statements. Congress, Nehru announced, felt 'free to change or modify the Cabinet Mission Plan as it thought best'; it was 'fantastic' for the Mission to think they could tell Indians what to do ten years from now. Congress, the champion all of a sudden for provincial rights, would oppose grouping tooth and nail, since the Sindhis and Pathans were 'unanimously against grouping' and were 'afraid of being swamped by the Punjab'. There was certainly no question of Congress allowing Assam to be bundled into a group dominated by Bengal. As for the Union centre, it would be exactly what Congress always intended it to be. The three common subjects would be broadly interpreted. Foreign trade policy, currency, credit, loans and taxation would be in the hands of the centre, which would also settle all inter-provincial disputes and take measures in the event of emergencies such as administrative and econ-

---

[2] *Nawa-i-Waqt*, 8 June 1946.

omic breakdowns.³ So however limited the scope of the centre might be on paper, in practice it would inevitably have to be enlarged.

The fear of a powerful centre dominated by the Congress had been the main reason why the Muslim-majority province politicians had rallied behind Jinnah and the League. Nehru's statements seemed to suggest that the Congress High Command intended to deploy central authority to restrict their freedom of action in their provincial domains. For the League's business supporters this meant the supremacy of the Tatas, the Birlas and the Dalmias in the competitive wilds of an independent India. Other League sympathisers, bewildered already by their leader's apparent readiness to settle for less than what they thought they were fighting to achieve, interpreted Nehru's remarks in more crudely communal terms. Whatever the reactions, it appeared that Congress was not ready to meet the League, or indeed the Mission half way. Just when Jinnah was beginning to turn in the direction that he both wanted and needed to go, his own followers pressed him to stick rigidly to his earlier unbending stance which he had adopted while he was preparing for the time of bargaining in earnest. Now that the time had arrived, the constraints on the Congress High Command matched by the pressures from his own followers were threatening the freedom of action Jinnah needed and seriously undermining his tactic, which was to ask for more in the expectation, at the end of the day, of settling for less.

Jinnah was being pressed on three sides: by the Congress, his own followers and the British, who now decided to go ahead with an interim government, if necessary 'without the Muslim League'. Jinnah's claim to nominate all Muslims would not be allowed to 'stand in the way' of the interim government being formed. If he refused to come in then the League's quota would have to be filled 'so far as possible with other Muslims'.⁴ The proposals for the interim government made it unlikely that Jinnah would agree to bring the League in. The interim government was to consist of fourteen members; six members (including one Scheduled Caste representative) would be nominated by Congress; five members would be nominated by the League and the three minority representatives (including one mandatory Sikh) would be nominated by the Viceroy. No party could object to the nominees of the party. This precluded Jinnah from objecting to the inclusion of a nationalist Muslim by the Congress. The distribution of portfolios would be 'equitable' but would be settled only after the parties had agreed to join the interim government. The League's insistence that major communal issues could

³ See Nehru's press statement, Bombay, 10 July 1946, *Indian Annual Register*, 1946, vol. II, p. 143.
⁴ Pethick-Lawrence to Wavell, 18 July 1946, *T.P.*, VIII, 82–3.

be settled only by agreement between the two parties was unacceptable since 'a Coalition Government could work on no other basis'.[5] When, on 22 July, Wavell sent his proposals to both sides, Congress quickly made it clear that 'independence in action' and 'a strong Government' were its priorities.[6] In private the Viceroy might complain that this was proof positive of Congress's aim to win 'absolute power'; he called on London to restate its pledges to minorities, and to deny that it would 'recognise Congress as representing all India' or that it had any 'intention of handing over power to Congress alone'.[7] But London was not ready to follow the advice of a Viceroy who still believed that 'our own interests demand that we should not surrender tamely' and who in any case was on his way out.[8] 'Convinced that they [Congress] have got us on the run', the Raj, according to its penultimate Viceroy, was now bound 'perpetually [to be] subject to these squeezes'.[9] Only slowly was it brought home to Wavell that London had not the will, the power, or the incentive to stop this happening.

So Jinnah would look to the British in vain to come to his rescue. Yet Jinnah needed to be rescued since the League's uncertain acceptance of the Mission's plan assumed that it would be given parity in the interim government. The pressure on Jinnah to settle for nothing less than parity was overwhelming. He was curtly reminded that it was 'mandatory' for him 'to ask for Congress–League parity in the interim government', and, 'if for any reason it becomes necessary to reconsider Congress–League parity, the matter will have to be referred back to our Council and its further decision obtained'.[10] Before entering the interim government, which London and New Delhi were determined to form, Jinnah had somehow to persuade a restive League Council to let him come into office on lesser terms than parity. At the A.I.M.L. Council's meeting at Bombay, attended by 450 delegates, Jinnah accused the British of having 'played into the hands of the Congress' which was 'full of spite towards the Muslims'. Nehru's 'childish statements' had exposed Congress's designs and Muslims had no choice but to return to their original demand for Pakistan which was 'the only solution of India's problem'.[11] Unable still to define the demand for Pakistan precisely, no longer confident of his power to persuade, to command or to see the way ahead clearly,

[5] See Wavell to Nehru and Jinnah, 22 July 1946, ibid., 98–9.
[6] Nehru to Wavell, 23 July 1946, ibid., 112–13.
[7] Wavell to Pethick-Lawrence, 24 July 1946, ibid., 114–15.   [8] Ibid., 115.
[9] Wavell to Pethick-Lawrence, 28 July 1946, ibid., 127.
[10] Hatim A. Alavi to Jinnah, 12 June 1946, AIML/SHC/File No. 11, Sind vol. III.
[11] See Jinnah's address to the A.I.M.L. Council, Bombay, 28 July 1946, in Pirzada (ed.), *Foundations of Pakistan*, vol. II, p. 553.

Jinnah simply told his Council that he washed his hands of 'any decision as to the future, unless you force it down my throat'[12] – hardly the words of a Quaid, more the despairing utterances of someone at bay. But inside Jinnah's cold exterior lay an indomitable spirit, not easily broken by the slings and arrows of an unsmiling fortune. When he announced the League's decision to withdraw its acceptance of the 16 May statement, and to bid 'goodbye to constitutions and constitutional methods', Jinnah was merely reporting his Council's mood, not the inwardness of his own plans. At most this was '*au revoir*' not 'adieu' to the well-tried methods of the negotiating table, the only methods he really understood. To press for an Indian union and to accept the Mission's plan was far from folly; in fact it was 'statesmanship' of the highest order, Jinnah told his Council. This showed where his priorities really lay: 'We voluntarily delegated three subjects to the Union to work for 10 years. It is not a mistake. It is the highest statesmanship the Muslim League has achieved . . . We had the courage – it was not a mistake – to sacrifice three subjects to the Centre'.[13] None of this tallies with the notion that Jinnah had turned his back upon compromise, or that he was committed to the dangerous path of 'direct action' which his Council demanded. The League's resolution merely rejected the proposals for the interim government; it did not categorically refuse to come in. Keeping the way open to getting into the interim government, Jinnah saw to it that the 'direct action' resolution was so hedged with qualifications that once again he would be left to decide whether to launch it or not. The Working Committee was given charge of organising 'the Muslims for the coming struggle to be launched *as and when necessary*'.[14] Jinnah was to be the judge of what was necessary. So the Quaid-i-Azam, that warrior of the council chamber, that master of dialectics and dialogues, did not overnight turn into a rabble-rouser. He knew better than anyone else just how ramshackle was

---

[12] Ibid.   [13] Ibid., p. 561.

[14] See A.I.M.L.'s resolution, no. II, Bombay, July 1946, in ibid., p. 558 (my italics). No one had a clear idea of the shape 'direct action' would take. Always one to hide his own clarity behind smoke-screens of obfuscations which his bemused following could not penetrate, Jinnah characteristically kept silent about what he understood direct action to mean, and simply repeated that the League too now had a weapon for the battles ahead. (See *Nawa-i-Waqt*, 1 August 1946.) In an interview with Colin Reid, *Daily Telegraph* correspondent, Jinnah spoke of a 'mass illegal movement' – shades of Gandhi – but quickly amended 'illegal' to 'unconstitutional': not itself conclusive but a hint that the League 'had not really worked out what they were going to do'. A sub-Committee was set up to concoct a paper programme for 'direct action'. An all-India strike by Muslims was announced, but events were to show how little the League knew whom it intended to strike, and how deeply it was going to wound. When Reid, in good journalist fashion, bluntly asked Jinnah if agreement was dead, Jinnah evaded the question. (See minutes by Scott and Wavell, 1–2 August 1946, *T.P.*, VIII, 174.)

his organisation, the victim of his deliberate neglect and 'of the inherent constraints of Muslim politics, and how little capable it was of launching and controlling agitations below, whether now, tomorrow or in the forseeable future. Direct action, the 'pistol' pointed at Congress in response to its 'threat to launch mass civil disobedience' was played as a metaphor not proposed as a fact.[15] As the chief minister of Sind realised, mild and watered down though his threat of direct action may have been, Jinnah had no choice but to make it: if he 'had not agreed to something of this sort, feeling was so strong that he would have been swept aside'.[16]

After the League Council's Bombay meeting, Jinnah told the Viceroy that there was 'no chance of my Working Committee' agreeing to come into the interim government. The proposals for it were 'most detrimental to the Muslim League' and were 'obviously intended to appease the Congress'.[17] Although he was not the most acute political analyst, even Wavell was beginning to understand his Jinnah. Coming back to the old 'demand for Pakistan was in the nature of a weapon to secure better terms'.[18] The 'direct action' resolution was bound to have a bad effect on communal relations, but Wavell saw no reason to ask Jinnah for an explanation. It was clear that Jinnah had raised the threat merely to induce H.M.G. to give a definite assurance on the grouping scheme, an assurance which might enable him to bring the League into the constituent assembly and certainly into the interim government. All that H.M.G. could do was to hope for goodwill on the part of the majority party. Wavell thought he saw a 'somewhat chastened' Nehru, and wistfully hoped that Congress would now adopt a 'generous attitude as the stronger party, and offer the League the assurances which it wants'. But by now the Viceroy had come to believe that there was a 'complete lack of greatness or generosity about Indian political leaders'.[19] Much as Wavell had feared, neither Congress nor London helped him to find the 'better terms' which might have preserved the union. Wavell had either to abandon his interim government or to make terms reluctantly with a Congress of whose purposes he hardly approved. The growing unrest in some parts of India was one reason why Wavell was anxious to install a popular government at the centre. Calcutta had bad troubles already, there was trouble brewing in the U.P. as well, especially in Allahabad,

---

[15] See Jinnah's address to the A.I.M.L. Council, 29 July 1946, in Pirzada (ed.), *Foundations of Pakistan*, vol. II, p. 560.

[16] Note by Sir F. Mudie, undated, *T.P.*, VIII, 213.

[17] See Jinnah to Wavell, 31 July 1946, ibid., 156–7.

[18] See note on proceedings of the special meeting of the Executive Council, 4 August 1946, ibid., 183–6; and Wavell to Pethick-Lawrence, 31 July 1946, ibid., 154.

[19] Wavell to Pethick-Lawrence, 31 July 1946, ibid., 158.

and the communists, so it was believed, were infiltrating the ranks of the police itself. As the Governor of the U.P. commented, 'There is enough material in the present situation for not one but several revolutions. And yet nothing desperate may happen at all!'[20] The only way to prevent the Congress High Command from succumbing to pressures from its more militant groups was to burden it with responsibility. Wavell believed that the sooner this was done the better. Once inside the interim government, Congress would 'realise that firm control of unruly elements is necessary and they may put down the Communists and try to curb their own left wing'. If only the Congress leaders could be kept 'busy with administration' they might have 'much less time for politics'.[21] Certainly Patel, mindful of his rivals inside his own camp, as well as the threats posed by the League, was troubled that these difficulties might rebound against the Congress High Command. Getting into office would enable Patel and the Congress right to discipline their opponents. Anxious to get into office, Patel and the right wing, still sceptical of Nehru as their front man, threatened to resign from the Working Committee if Nehru did not fall sharply into line.[22]

On 6 August when Wavell invited Nehru to form an interim government, the Congress Working Committee accepted with alacrity; but only after Wavell had met most of Patel's points about the interim government. The Congress right was not prepared to leave seats vacant for the League, and Wavell had to agree to leave it to the Congress president to decide whether or not to ask Jinnah to bring in the League.[23] The Viceroy simply told Jinnah that he was 'sorry that things had gone the way they have', and hoped that the League would join if the Congress made a reasonable offer for a coalition.[24] As a gesture to the League the Congress Working Committee announced that it was prepared to go along with the 16 May plan, although Congress still did not 'approve of all the proposals contained in this statement'. In other words, the Congress had not in fact accepted grouping even though it was prepared to refer the matter to the Federal Court for interpretation. It also played down its view that the constituent assembly was to be sovereign; it was enough for the moment to prevent 'interference of an external power or authority'. 'Naturally', the assembly would 'function within the internal limitations which are inherent in its task and will further seek the largest measure of co-operation in drawing up the constitution of a free India

[20] Wylie to Wavell, 27 July 1946, ibid., 162.
[21] Wavell to Pethick-Lawrence, 31 July 1946, ibid., 154.
[22] See Wavell to Pethick-Lawrence, 5 August 1946, ibid., 190–1.
[23] Wavell to Pethick-Lawrence, 4 August 1946, ibid., 188.
[24] Wavell to Jinnah, 8 August 1946, ibid., 203.

allowing the greatest measure of freedom and protection for all just claims and interests'.[25] But this was just the velvet glove over the iron fist and a way of bolting the door from inside now that the Congress had decided to enter office.

All that the League could do to put a spanner into these works was to refuse flatly to enter the constituent assembly where Congress hoped to settle India's future. Jinnah had already taken the precaution of getting Leaguers to contest the elections to the union constituent assembly, in the event that he decided to bring them in. The decision to contest the elections to the constituent assembly, he explained, had been taken 'to prevent undesirable people getting in as Muslim representatives'.[26] Congress wanted the union constituent assembly to meet by mid-September. The League's line was that an assembly in which ninety-five per cent of the Muslim members were not represented could not be considered a national body. It wanted separate constituent assemblies for the Muslim and Hindu provinces which would then meet jointly to decide on common arrangements for the whole of India – the original Pakistan demand. There was little hope of agreement between the two sides on this basis. On 15 August, Nehru met Jinnah to see whether or not the League would come into the interim government. Nehru assured Jinnah that no major communal issue would be settled in the constituent assembly without the agreement of both parties; all disputes would be referred to the Federal Court, and though Congress did not like grouping and preferred to have autonomous provinces under the centre, it would 'not oppose grouping by provinces if the provinces wished it'. There would be five seats for the League in the interim government, but it could not claim a monopoly in the selection of Muslim members. Jinnah rejected the proposals, leaving Nehru with the impression that 'Jinnah had gone further than he had intended and was at a loss how to get out'. Significantly the only proposal which Jinnah put forward during the course of the talks was that all action should be held up for six months.[27] So Jinnah was back in the role of stone-waller, hoping that something somehow would turn up from somewhere.

What turned up, leaping out of the Pandora's box he himself unwittingly had helped to open, was in fact the very last thing Jinnah needed – the Calcutta killings of 16–20 August. They unleashed pent-up forces of disorder of such magnitude that they brought parts of India close to anarchy; they gave this violent chaos, the product of very different rivalries some of which had little to do with religion, a communal

[25] See Congress Working Committee's resolution, 10 August 1946, ibid., 217–18.
[26] Memo by Jinnah, undated, QAP/File No. 918.
[27] Wavell to Pethick-Lawrence, 18 August 1946, *T.P.*, VIII, 248.

colouring, and above all they destroyed the India of Jinnah's dreams. 16 August was the day the League had nominated for 'direct action'. Forty-eight hours before, Jinnah had urged Muslims to remain calm; 'direct action' day should be a day of peaceful reflection, not a day 'for the purpose of resorting to direct action in any form or shape'.[28] But by now Jinnah had much in common with King Canute: the spirits of Calcutta's underworld were minded to pay as much heed to his ineffectual commands as the tides of the North Sea. One year before partition, in an ominous dress rehearsal for performances in other parts of India, the City of Dreadful Night witnessed a mass hysteria, sparked off in the main by determined little bands of trouble-makers. In five days of rioting some 4,000 persons were killed and 15,000 were maimed and injured in Calcutta. Everyone who describes these killings runs for the shelter of communalism to explain the inexplicable, or more accurately the unacceptable, face of violence. But the killings still await their historian. All that is certain is that Jinnah had no idea of what was coming. It is not just that the politics of violence, if corporate brutalising of this sort can be so described, were anathema to him, alien to his political style and never to become a part of it, but the more powerful argument is that Jinnah did not expect, and certainly did not want, anything like this to happen. Rather he was looking for some pretext which would allow him to take his League into an interim government. It was his expectation, just as much as the expectation of the Congress High Command, that government from above would reimpose order upon a political society that was showing signs of cracking up as a result of assaults from below. A constitutional politician, a believer in rules enforced by rulers, Jinnah wanted to save not only the political unity of India, but also the reality of order upon which constitutional arrangements everywhere necessarily depend. Desperately searching for a face-saving device to excuse his backsliding on compulsory grouping, Jinnah had his own priorities savaged tooth and claw by an unthinking mob, fired by blood lust, fear and greed. Ironically, and unfairly, the horrors which lie so close to the surface of India have been laid at the door of this man of orderly constitutional advance, blamed upon his 'Pakistan' and upon the irreconcilable differences between Muslims and Hindus which his own career had consistently tried to bridge.

The Calcutta killings brought Jinnah's dilemma into the open. A constitutionalist whom fate had swung into the rough and tumble of mass politics, Jinnah's predicament was particularly cruel. He had neither party organisation nor resources to direct a movement which the more

---

[28] Cited in Chaudhri Muhammad Ali, *The Emergence of Pakistan* (Lahore, 1973), p. 75.

formidable it looked the less he controlled. To make something of 'direct action' day the ramshackle provincial Leagues had to call in the mullahs and the *pirs*. The meetings under the League's banner had nearly all taken place in and around mosques after the customary Friday prayers. There was talk of Jihad. But no official *fatwa* was issued, since a holy war could only be declared under certain conditions which were not present in the Indian situation. Nevertheless, the mullahs and *pirs* were well versed in the art of stirring religious passions. The inevitable increase in communal tensions made it all the more difficult for the League and the Congress to come to terms at the all-India level. After the troubles in Calcutta, Congress wanted nothing to do with Jinnah. Yet Jinnah desperately needed a face-saving device. As Nazimuddin confessed, an unequivocal statement by the Congress that the provinces could not opt out of the groups except as laid down in the 16 May statement might induce Jinnah to reconsider the League's Bombay resolution and enable him to abandon the dangerous course which 'direct action' had already taken.[29] Other sources close to the League believed that if the Viceroy took a firm stand on the grouping issue Jinnah would come into the interim government, even if it meant eating his own words about the nationalist Muslim issue.[30]

Convinced that a coalition government was the only way of preventing civil war in India, Wavell made a last-ditch attempt to get assurances from the Congress on the grouping scheme. But his talks with Gandhi and Nehru failed to produce the desired result. Gandhi took strong exception to Wavell's threat to postpone the constituent assembly until the grouping scheme had been settled. Wavell in his turn thought this provided 'convincing evidence that Congress always meant to use their position in the Interim Government to break up the Muslim League and in the Constituent Assembly to destroy the Grouping scheme which was the one effective safeguard for the Muslims'.[31] London strongly disagreed with the Viceroy. Attlee and Pethick-Lawrence were not ready to back Wavell's line that the constituent assembly would meet only after the grouping issue had been settled. It would have been sufficient to say that the constituent assembly would be postponed.[32] Pethick-Lawrence had complete faith in Congress's bona fides and told the Viceroy 'to avoid pressing the grouping question to a final issue before the Interim Government takes over and has had a period of office'.[33] Serious

[29] Wavell to Pethick-Lawrence, 27 August 1946, *T.P.*, VIII, 311.
[30] Wylie to Wavell, 28 August 1946, ibid., 324.
[31] Wavell to Pethick-Lawrence, 28 August 1946, ibid., 323.
[32] Pethick-Lawrence to Wavell, 28 August 1946, ibid., 332.
[33] Ibid., 332.

disagreements between Wavell and the Congress leaders on the grouping issue did not augur well for a smooth working relationship in the interim government. Congress was known to be in direct touch with the British Cabinet, leaving the Viceroy to complain that he could not 'continue to be responsible for affairs in India if some members of your Government are keeping touch with the Congress through an independent agent behind my back, as they appear to be'.[34]

With the Viceroy facing a dismissal and Jinnah's world collapsing, Congress began to build its new order. On 2 September 1946 Congress took office in the interim government and promptly filled all the seats (except two) left vacant by the League's refusal to come in with Muslims of its own persuasion. This was rubbing salt into Jinnah's wounds, but it also showed where power was coming to lie. In Congress's eyes, Jinnah, their great rival, tarred by the brush of violence, could now be treated with the same dismissive rigour of 1937. Congress was ready now for the next step: getting the constituent assembly under way, and shaping India's future constitution according to its unfettered will. This was no time for concessions, whether on grouping or on anything else. The Congress was already in office in the Punjab and the N.W.F.P. Once in the saddle, they could ride the range over Jinnah's straying flock, rope some of them in and lock them into a Congress corral. Keeping the League out of the constituent assembly was the only way Jinnah could put obstacles in the way of this plan. But somehow he also had to stiffen the League ministries in Sind and Bengal, because if they were to fall, nothing would prevent the Congress making a free run through his Muslim provinces.

In Sind, the League ministry under Ghulam Hussain had been tottering since the 1946 elections. It survived only by the grace and favour of the Governor, Sir Francis Mudie. In the assembly the pro-government and opposition groups had an equal number of seats. So there was a chance that G. M. Syed's faction might form a ministry with the help of Congress M.L.A.s and the independents. The formation of a pro-Congress ministry would have destroyed any hope of grouping the Muslim-majority provinces in the north-west. Syed and his clique were vehemently opposed to forming a group with the Punjab. One of them,

---

[34] Wavell to Attlee, 28 August 1946, ibid., 328. The Congress was getting a hearing in London through an 'independent agent', Sudhir Ghosh. Ghosh's views, which he claimed were shared by most of the Congress leaders, prove Wavell's fears. The Viceroy, according to Ghosh, 'was not the right man in the right place', and the 'relationship between Nehru and the Viceroy could only work if the personalities were sympathetic'. So the 'most important step was to replace Lord Wavell'. (See Burke to Attlee, 6 September 1946, ibid., 437).

Pir Ali Mohammad Rashidi, had openly declared that the Sindhis would never buckle down under Punjabi dominance.[35] The Congress High Command was taking full advantage of the situation in Sind. Congress propaganda had been intensified in the rural areas and there was money with which to tempt some of the Leaguers. At least one League minister, Khuhro, a long-standing aspirant for the office of chief minister, was accused of 'directly hob-nobbing with the Coalition Party'.[36] In an atmosphere thick with the usual intrigues and counter-intrigues it was the Governor who took the decisive step. Convinced that a Congress coalition would be disastrous in a province where the police force was predominantly Muslim and extremely vulnerable to communal propaganda, Mudie recommended dissolving the assembly and calling elections.[37] With the Viceroy's approval the Governor dissolved the assembly and re-appointed a League 'care-taker government' until the elections had been held.[38] This was a way of safeguarding, as far as was possible in Sindhi politics, the League's return to office. A stronger League ministry in Sind, now a possibility, would place an obstacle in Congress's triumphant progress through India, but it could be achieved only at the price of bolstering the very particularism which Jinnah found most uncompromisingly rebarbative.[39]

In Bengal (once the 'Paradise of the Indies', now more like a subcontinental version of Hell), everyone could see that one way of dampening communal fires would be to return to government by a coalition of parties and communities. Even Suhrawardy, that trimmer and tacker, could see that steering a middle, non-communal, Bengali course was the best bet for everyone, whatever their community, faction, cause or commitment. But a cross-communal arrangement in Bengal, necessary for the orderly governance of that province, made Jinnah at the centre, already shaky, shakier still. One main objective of Jinnah's strategy was to form

---

[35] *Nawa-i-Waqt*, 7 June 1946.

[36] Pir Illahi Baksh to Jinnah, 14 August 1946, SHC/File No. 11, Sind vol. VII.

[37] Mudie to Wavell, 21 August 1946, L/P&J/5/262, I.O.L. Officials in the India Office agreed that: 'In the present all-India situation a Congress coalition in Sind would be a pretty provocative step. It might well make Jinnah's return to cooperation even more difficult.' (See minutes by Turnbull and Monteath, 7 September 1946, *T.P.*, VIII, 446.) But Attlee thought it was 'madness to have an election in Sind of all places at the present moment'. (Attlee to Pethick-Lawrence, 8 September 1946, ibid., 454.)

[38] Mudie to Wavell, 21 August 1946, L/P&J/5/262, I.O.L.

[39] But as Khaliquzzaman has admitted, the Muslim League 'owed a debt of gratitude' to Mudie 'for having refused, when Governor of Sind, to hand the Province including Karachi to the mercy of Congress'. (Khaliquzzaman, *Pathway to Pakistan*, p. 393.) The League was able to secure a majority in the elections and until August 1947 Sind was the only province in the north-west with a League ministry.

coalitions with the Congress in all the provinces as well as at the centre. Having failed to secure even the bare minimum of his demands at the centre, Jinnah could not afford to let his lieutenants in the Muslim-majority provinces form coalitions with the Congress. When on 6 September Suhrawardy asked Jinnah to allow him to reopen negotiations with the Bengal Congress with a view to forming a coalition, Jinnah rejected this point blank, arguing that there was no question of any provincial coalitions with the Congress without a coalition at the centre. So Suhrawardy found himself warning the Viceroy that unless Jinnah's demands at the centre were met there was no hope of averting a catastrophic outbreak of communal violence in Bengal.[40] If anything proved that Jinnah needed a strong whip over the Muslim provinces by way of compulsory grouping, these developments at the opposite ends of India, in Sind and Bengal, made the point.[41]

Still in search of a way to get the League into the interim government, Wavell once again tried to get London to take a definite stand on the grouping issue. The time had come to 'grasp this nettle now' since everyone 'sensible really wants a settlement and few have been unscarred by recent events'. The Viceroy's unequivocal view was that the 'statement of May 16th is worthless if we have not the honesty and courage to stick to it, and I would rather lose the cooperation of the Congress at the Centre and in the Provinces than go ahead with constitution making on a one-party basis and in a way which the Mission never intended'.[42] The Secretary of State thought a settlement could be achieved even sooner if Jinnah could be forced into a compromise. The obvious thing to do was to encourage coalition ministries in Sind and Bengal.[43] Here were already signs of London's willingness to resort to ruthless squeeze play if this could break Jinnah's intransigence. One clue to Jinnah's remarkable

[40] Note by Wavell, 8 September 1946, *T.P.*, VIII, 453.
[41] As Liaquat Ali Khan confessed, assurances on the grouping scheme were a matter of life and death for the League. A mere face-saving device would not do. What was needed was a clear assurance that: (a) sections would frame group and provincial constitutions; (b) that there would be no opting out by the provinces from the groups; and (c) that the union constituent assembly would have no power to alter group or provincial constitutions except to prevent an overlapping with the union constitution whose scope could be defined by the Federal Court. On the interim government issue, Liaquat wanted assurances that there would be no nationalist Muslim in the government; that major communal issues would be decided by the representatives of the community concerned; that the selection of the minority representatives in the Viceroy's Executive Council would be made only after consultations with the two major parties; and finally that there would be equal, not equitable, distribution of portfolios (Wavell to Pethick-Lawrence, 9 September 1946, ibid., 471.)
[42] Wavell to Pethick-Lawrence, 9 September 1946, ibid., 471.
[43] Pethick-Lawrence to Wavell, 9 September 1946, ibid., 474.

resilience in the face of grave political setbacks, overwhelming odds, and unremitting squeeze play, was his extraordinary capacity to fight when all would have appeared lost to lesser men. So now he declared that the 'slate must be wiped clean and we must begin from the beginning'. He was ready to go to London to negotiate 'on an equal footing with other negotiators'.[44] For the first time, Jinnah publicly announced his readiness to break a deadlock which was becoming deadlier. If only Congress would give a little, Jinnah showed that he was willing to give more, and bend over backwards to 'take less than his present demands', 'especially as the Congress seem to aim at consolidating their power and disregarding the League altogether'.[45] But Congress was not to be moved; as Wavell feared, 'having tasted power', the High Command 'do not want to share it'.[46] By contrast Jinnah, that monster in the demonology of not very perceptive Indian and British chroniclers, that triumphant hero in Pakistani hagiography, was found by Wavell (who here, as in so many other respects, had qualities of insight which his successor, preoccupied with his own self-image,[47] did not possess) to be 'very quiet and reasonable, and . . . anxious for a settlement if it can be done without loss of prestige'.[48] Jinnah's 'main line' on the interim government, according to Wavell, 'was that he must have something with which to convince his Working Committee that he had not been defeated on every issue and was coming into the Government as a subordinate to the Congress'.[49]

By the autumn of 1946, Jinnah had been pushed into a corner from which there seemed no escape. London was clearly determined to get out of India, and to get out soon. Attlee's government did not question the need to transfer power, and its willingness to do so is a fact of history. It was simply a question of how, and how soon, the transfer could be achieved, and whether the unity of India, the nub of British interests, strategic and economic, might be rescued along the line. London still saw its way forward in cleaving faithfully to the Mission's proposals, forming an interim government, summoning the constituent assembly, encouraging the Congress and the League to come to terms inside an interim government and a constituent assembly, and hoping for the best once the main parties in India had their minds concentrated by an imminent

[44] Jinnah's statement, 9 September 1946, *The Daily Mail* cited in ibid., 478.
[45] Wavell to Pethick-Lawrence, 10 September 1946, ibid., 477.
[46] Wavell to Pethick-Lawrence, 14 September 1946, ibid., 522.
[47] In his interview with Dominique Lapierre and Larry Collins (authors of *Freedom at Midnight*), Mountbatten described Jinnah as 'a clot', 'a bastard', an 'evil genius' and the 'key to the whole thing' [partition]. (See Larry Collins and Dominique Lapierre, *Mountbatten and the Partition of India*, New Delhi, 1982, vol. I, pp. 44–7.)
[48] Wavell to Pethick-Lawrence, 26 September 1946, *T.P.*, VIII, 588.
[49] Wavell's note, 2 October 1946, ibid., 644.

transfer of power. For its part, Congress was ready to play this game. It knew that it could dominate the interim government, whatever the formal ratio of Congress and League members; it could see that the Raj's will to stay on and its resources to rule were rapidly being eroded; it predicted that it could call the shots in the constituent assembly, whether the League's representatives were there or not. It had the measure of the fragility of Jinnah's hold over the Muslim provinces.

Whatever Congress's difficulties with its own followers, however nervous the High Command may have been about its hold over its provinces, it was better placed than the League now that power at the centre was at last within reach. But Congress's big battalions still had to fight their way through obstinate pockets of resistance. There was the Viceroy, continuing to fight wars on the old basis although his leaders had declared peace on new terms, and there were the services, now a rump but by no means wholly converted to the changed purposes of their metropolis, or ready yet to welcome yesterday's enemies as today's friends, and tomorrow's unavoidable successors. There were still awkward pledges and promises – the product of circumstances which had now changed – to minorities, provinces and princes. And there was Jinnah and the League, the only spokesman of Muslim opinion at the centre and, of course, there was the provincial dilemma of the Punjab and Bengal. By taking refuge in the Cripps offer and threatening to break out of the Indian union, both these Muslim provinces hoped to get a larger measure of autonomy than they already possessed. The large concessions which the Cabinet Mission had made to the provincial demands of the Punjab and Bengal threatened the strong centre Congress wanted. But they also threatened Jinnah's position, since to keep the Punjab and Bengal undivided he would have to follow a supra-communal line which in turn would destroy the justification for the League's role at the centre. So Congress urgently needed to do its own book-keeping about the profit and loss in keeping the Punjab and Bengal undivided, and with them Jinnah and the League, inside the Indian union. It could not ignore that it had a very uncertain grip over both these provinces, not only over their politics at the top but also over their unsteady structures below. If the Punjab and Bengal were the thorns Jinnah had been carefully picking out of his side for the past six years, there were prickly bushes lying outside the Congress patch. By cutting them out of its all-India calculations, the Congress High Command could achieve its strong centre and at the same time rid itself of Jinnah and the League.

There was very little in these prospects to cheer the Quaid-i-Azam, or to suggest that the odds were not daily getting longer against his strategy. At this point his only course was somehow to claw back the substance of the Mission's proposals, in particular its commitment to compulsory grouping. To do so he had to enter the interim government, because it was only from inside the interim government that the League could prevent Congress from consolidating its authority, eroding any substance of provincial autonomy and doing away with compulsory grouping by riveting its control over the constituent assembly. Staying out of the interim government, and refusing to enter the constituent assembly, was a tactic that could only begin to work if the British stayed on as ringmasters. Direct action was a paper threat, directed at the Congress and the Raj, but quickly proving to be a snare and a delusion. Jinnah, 'no longer a young man', 'temperamentally prefer[ring] constitutional methods',[50] did not have the organisation or the resources to direct agitation once it had been invoked. The Calcutta killings underlined the point in red. Soon the gang warfare and semi-organised hooliganism of Muslim *goondas* in the localities of Noakhali showed that countryside as well as town could become the scrapyards for the predators of the underworld, snatching for instant spoils within the decaying fabric of India's social order. These disorders were just one symptom of a more generalised and diverse unrest, that endemic rivalry in a society of scarce resources, unevenly distributed, of 'have-nots' against 'haves', debtors against creditors, landless against the possessors, workers against jobbers and employers, and above all the hired hands of factions and clientage networks who unilaterally declared their independence from their patrons' control and forced their way through the fragile crust of order. To dub all these violent stirrings from below as evidence that India's myriad splits and fissures had now somehow resolved into a simple line of division between Muslims and Hindus, where community ruled and all else was secondary, is an unacceptable simplification. It has been lent a semblance of credibility by the claims and counter-claims of League and Congress, and by the categories which the Raj itself had for so long deployed in describing and regulating this complex political society and finally in justifying the way it divided and quit and the awesome turbulence it left in its wake. At best Jinnah could point to the disorders as evidence of a minefield which only agreement at the top could clear. Direct action was no answer to Jinnah's dilemma. It made the bad worse.

This left Jinnah with only the outworn devices and fading hopes of a tired and disillusioned negotiator for whom intransigence was a mask, not just an inveterate habit – the hope that the British would impose a settlement, make the last of their awards, and stay on to enforce it; the

---

[50] Wavell to Pethick-Lawrence, 21 August 1946, ibid., 275.

hope, equally forlorn, that Congress would at last see the congruence of their interests with his lifelong purpose; that at least they would give him the means to keep his own followers at bay, building him a bridge by which he could cross into the interim government. The best hope of this dying man was Wavell, a Viceroy on the way out, who had spotted the inwardness of Congress's game,[51] did not like it, but was powerless to put a stop to its progress. Everything turned on the question of who would represent Muslims inside the interim government, a small matter, it might seem, but the essence of the League's case, 'an extraordinarily intractable' issue.[52] But the Viceroy was unable to force the Congress to concede this, or indeed any other substantial point; they had no reason to do so. Wavell was left complaining that 'The Congress have not lifted a finger in helping me in getting Jinnah into the Interim Government and though I think they are right in theory on the nationalist Muslim issue they are dangerously complacent about the probable results of leaving the League out'.[53] The League, Wavell predicted, would have jumped at any excuse to come in provided 'their *amour-propre* can in some way be satisfied'.[54] It was the Congress's reluctance to expose the inherent contradictions in Jinnah's strategy which had allowed his followers to make what they wished of the Pakistan demand. Now that Jinnah's options were being narrowed under intense pressure from his following, Congress was not ready to offer him terms which might have prevented a brutal amputation of the subcontinent. Congress, just as Jinnah himself, had become the victims of the propaganda for 'Pakistan'. Talks between Jinnah and Gandhi might perhaps have produced a result, since there was common ground between these old rivals, but when the Mahatma was forced to take Patel and Nehru into account, the talks failed.[55] Here

---

[51] After an inconclusive round of talks with the Mahatma towards the end of September, Wavell concluded that: 'Gandhi's objective and the objective of the majority of the Congress . . . [is] to establish themselves at the Centre and to suppress, cajole or buy over the Muslims, and then impose a Constitution at their leisure'. (Wavell to Pethick-Lawrence, 26 September 1946, ibid., 595.)

[52] Wavell to Pethick-Lawrence, 1 October 1946, ibid., 636.

[53] Wavell had 'come to regard Gandhi's non-violence as almost pure hypocrisy', and felt that the Mahatma was 'pursuing a course deliberately which he knows and admits will lead to bloodshed' – a measure of Wavell's mounting disillusionment with the Congress leaders. (Wavell to Pethick-Lawrence, ibid.)

[54] Jinnah's main point was that the League could not accept Nehru as the vice-president of the interim government since this could not fail to give the impression that Congress was in a position of superiority. (See Wavell's note, 2 October 1946, ibid., 644.)

[55] According to Gandhi's formula the Congress would accept the League as representing an overwhelming majority of Muslims, but by the same token Congress would nominate whomever it liked as its representative in the interim government. Jinnah accepted the formula. But Nehru and Patel rejected it. So Gandhi added a new clause to get the two

again shadows of the past confused Jinnah's assessment of the present: Gandhi himself was no longer the dominant figure in Congress in office. Implacably opposed though the Mahatma was to partition, he was no longer the best guarantee that Congress would eventually negotiate, not cut, since Gandhi had already been shouldered aside by the machine politicians. Nehru, the Congress president, had 'done nothing to smooth the path for them [the League]', and Wavell predicted that the 'Coalition Government', if formed, would 'not be all pulling in the same direction'.[56]

Just how desperate Jinnah's case was is revealed by the terms on which the League eventually took its place in the interim government on 26 October 1946. 'For various reasons' – unspecified, so obvious that they 'need not be mentioned' – on 13 October Jinnah announced on behalf of the Working Committee that the League would come into the government, recognising that it would 'be fatal to leave the entire field of administration of the Central Government in the hands of the Congress'.[57] Jinnah came in without getting anything that he had demanded: he did not get parity; he did not get a monopoly of Muslim representation; he did not get the right to veto on issues concerning Muslims; he did not get the portfolios he wanted,[58] and all he was able to do to demonstrate his independence of action was to nominate a member of the Scheduled Castes as one of his Leaguers.[59] This was Jinnah trying to rub the salt back into Congress's sores. But it also was the first hint of Jinnah's ultimate intentions of extending the League's umbrella of protection to the Scheduled Castes, certainly in Bengal, and other non-Congress elements.

The League took its place in the interim government against a background of communal violence in the Noakhali and Tippera districts

Congress leaders to accept his formula, namely that the two parties would agree to work as a team and would under no circumstances invoke or allow the intervention of the Viceroy or any other authority. Jinnah could hardly afford to give up the League's only real safeguard in the interim government, and so the talks failed.

56 Note by Wavell, 12 October 1946, ibid., 703–5.
57 Jinnah to Wavell, 13 October 1946, ibid., 709.
58 Jinnah had wanted defence, commerce, transport, posts and air, and law for the League. The Congress refused to give defence and foreign affairs and offered finance instead. So Jinnah, who had wanted the defence portfolio for himself, decided to stay out on the ostensible excuse that his party organisation would suffer. Wavell's final offer was far from 'equitable'; yet Jinnah had to accept. The five portfolios he took were: Finance: Liaquat Ali Khan; Commerce: I. I. Chundrigar; Posts and Air: Abdur Rab Nishtar; Health: Ghazanfar Ali Khan; Legislative matters: Jogendra Nath Mandal (the Scheduled Caste member).
59 Jogendra Nath Mandal, a member of the Scheduled Castes, had been a member of the League's ministry in Bengal.

of east Bengal. Since the Calcutta killings, stabbings, murders and looting had become facts of life in Dacca. By the second week of October these troubles had spread into a number of towns and villages of Noakhali district. Ramganj *thana* (police station) in the north-west corner of Noakhali was the scene of organised hooliganism, loot, arson, murder and forcible conversions of Hindus to Islam. The communal situation in Noakhali had been tense long before the actual outbreak of the disturbances. Muslims were urged to enrol in a national guard and observe an economic boycott of Hindu shopkeepers or face severe penalties which did not exclude violence. Preventive and precautionary measures by the government proved to be misdirected. On 9 October a company was moved into the sub-division of Feni and armed police were brought in from outside. But troubles broke out the next day in the Ramganj *thana* instead where large bands of Muslim *goondas* terrorised the Hindu population, cordoned off villages and extracted booty and money under threat. The gangs appeared to be organised but not affiliated with any political party; they had cut off roads, making it difficult for the government to dispatch relief operations. Refugees in their thousands fled from the area with horrifying stories of the atrocities perpetrated against them and their neighbours. It was only natural to blame the League ministry. Yet communal trouble was the last thing Suhrawardy needed; he knew only too well that communal harmony was the only way he could keep a League ministry in office. The man responsible for the trouble was a 'self-styled leader', Golam Sarwar, a former member of the Bengal assembly, who ironically enough had been defeated in the 1946 elections by a League candidate. But he was a Muslim and that was all the vast majority of Hindu public opinion needed to know.[60] Even the Governor could see that 'Trouble in South-East Bengal is not a general rising of Moslems against Hindus but activity (apparently organised) of a body of hooligans who have exploited existing communal feeling and who, as they range the countryside, are temporarily joined in each locality by belligerent Muslim roughs.'[61]

So the coalition at the centre was baptised by the bloodshed in eastern Bengal. Instead of exploring the possibilities of working together, Congress decided to take the League's entry into the interim government as a declaration of war. Its leaders lambasted the League for the poor quality of its men, 'the standard of the Cabinet will be much lowered by their association', and made much of this as evidence of the League's

---

[60] Burrows to Pethick-Lawrence, 17 October 1946, ibid., 745. For a background to the troubles in the Noakhali and Tippera districts see Bose, 'Agrarian society politics in Bengal 1919–1947', (Cambridge, Ph.D. dissertation, 1982).

[61] Burrows to Pethick-Lawrence, 20 October 1946, *T.P.*, VIII, 753.

'desire to have conflict rather than to work in cooperation'.[62] The claim of at least one League member that the interim government was 'one of the fronts of the direct action campaign' seemed to prove Congress's suspicions.[63] Patel asked the Viceroy with a straight face: 'Is the Interim Government to be the arena of party politics and intrigues and for driving in the very partition wedge which the long-term arrangement has withdrawn once for all and replaced it by grouping which in itself seems to be voluntary?'[64] But this was merely a debating point. The real thrust of the Congress's attack can be seen in its immediate pressure upon both the League and the Viceroy to summon the constituent assembly at once and to make the League pay the price for coming into office, namely to withdraw its resolution rejecting the long-term plan and to enter the constituent assembly. Wavell thought this was a reasonable point and reminded Jinnah that the League's acceptance of the long-term proposals was the condition for its entry into office. But Jinnah was unmoved; he stalled in the hope that London would give him a prior assurance that Congress would not have its own way in the constituent assembly. The sections, not the assembly as a whole, had to be guaranteed the right of framing provincial constitutions and deciding on grouping. Congress's suggestion that the grouping clause might be referred to the Federal Court for its interpretation was rejected by Jinnah out of hand. He wanted grouping cut and dried before he brought the League into the constituent assembly. Congress, he argued, had never accepted the Mission's proposals unequivocally, and H.M.G. had to 'make up their minds and support what they had laid down'. Wavell found it impossible to counter this line and confessed that he was 'on rather weak ground . . . since . . . [he] entirely agree[d] with Jinnah'.[65] All Wavell could do was to tell Jinnah categorically that H.M.G. was in no position to influence the proceedings of the constituent assembly or remain in India indefinitely to ensure smooth sailing for the League. The constituent assembly was now bound to begin its proceedings on 9 December and it was in the League's best interest to come in and make sure that constitution-making followed the proposals laid down by the

[62] Nehru to Wavell, 15 October 1946, ibid., 735.

[63] Speaking to the students of the Islamia College in Lahore, Raja Ghazanfar Ali Khan said: 'We are going into the Interim Government to get a foothold to fight for our cherished goal of Pakistan and I assure you that we shall achieve Pakistan.' But the inwardness of the League's plans lay in Ghazanfar Ali's claim that once inside the interim government the Leaguers would try to convince the Congress that no Indian government could function without the co-operation of the Muslim League. (Ghazanfar Ali's speech, Lahore, 19 October 1946, enclosure to document no. 483, ibid., 756.)

[64] Patel to Wavell, 20 October 1946, ibid., 755.

[65] Note by Wavell, 30 October 1946, ibid., 832–3.

Cabinet Mission. Jinnah, who knew better than anyone else what the League's interest inexorably demanded, told the Viceroy 'if H.M.G. will not take a firm line and protect us, then leave us to our fate'. Wavell thought this might simply be Jinnah taking his usual 'extreme attitude before giving way',[66] but Jinnah was now being difficult because if he gave way on entry into the constituent assembly without any safeguards on grouping he might as well have thrown in the towel, and abandoned all that he had been striving to achieve.

Of course Jinnah now had other troubles as well, not least from an increasingly bemused following, no longer sure where their leader was taking them or where he himself wanted to go. One confused sympathiser asked: 'What is behind the screen . . . the public want your exhaustive and comprehensive statement to dispel and eliminate doubts haunting their minds and stand patiently for your views on the subject.'[67] Some thought that the League had betrayed them by this abject entry into the interim government. 'What we common people of the nation understand,' Jinnah was told, 'is that we have been misused by your colleagues who are just after ministries and nothing else.'[68] But the more percipient congratulated Jinnah for his example at the centre which paved the way for similar League–Congress pacts in the provinces, particularly in the Punjab, where there was a 'crying need for a League–Congress Pact', and called, whether in all innocence or tongue in cheek, for the High Command's clearance for a League–Congress coalition in the Punjab assembly. As one Punjabi demanded, Jinnah should 'stress the necessity of such a pact for the Punjab without further delay'.[69] Time was (and time might be) when this sort of pact tallied with Jinnah's long-term strategy. But the time was not now. The principle of Pakistan had to be accepted first and the exact shape of the centre settled afterwards. To achieve this the League needed unequivocal support from its provinces, not pacts which the Congress might use to weaken the League's already weak grip over Muslim provinces.

Jinnah's troubles with his followers were matched by the stormy reactions from Congress's own following after the League's entry into the interim government. Already the happenings in east Bengal had rocked the Congress High Command. For the first time the all-India Congress leaders were under attack from their own supporters for having failed to protect Hindu lives and property in Noakhali and Tippera:

[66] Ibid., 834.
[67] Mohammad Rashid Ahmad Dar (Rang Mahal, Lahore) to Jinnah, 26 October 1946, SHC/Punjab vol. II, p. 104.   [68] Nazir Sufi to Jinnah, 25 October 1946, ibid., 100.
[69] Muhammad Nawaz Khan (Nawab of Kot-Fateh Khan, Attock District) to Jinnah, 27 October 1946, ibid., 106.

How can leaders like Nehru and Patel watch the happenings in Bengal as helpless onlookers? The people of Bengal look up to them for help and protection. But they have no means of doing anything about it . . . If Nehru and Patel cannot keep the country in order during the interim period how are they going to make a constitution for 400 millions people [sic] and attend to the one hundred-and-one other big problems that await their attention.[70]

The League's presence in the interim government was seen as a return to Viceregal and bureaucratic rule, reducing the powers of the Congress leaders to enforce law and order and destroying the spirit of mutual co-operation which was needed at this critical juncture in Indian history. As if to add more fuel to the burning fires, the leader of the Congress Socialist Party, J. P. Narain, went on a propaganda rampage in Bihar, urging the police to disobey orders and prepare for the struggles ahead. The Congress ministry turned a blind eye to these seditious speeches, in the vain hope that action against the Congress left-wing elements combing the province might not be necessary after all. The Governor warned Wavell that Bihar was like a powder-keg and the ministry's proposal to abolish zamindari in many areas of the province was an even greater source of trouble than the communal problem itself. Fanning disputes between zamindars and *kisans* in a province where the press and the Hindu Mahasabha were churning out communal propaganda, the services were virtually paralysed, the ministry was ineffective, and the communities were arming themselves against one another, was an open invitation to disaster. When disturbances broke out towards the end of October no one was particularly surprised; it was the magnitude of the rioting which shocked and horrified everyone. This time the victims were mainly Muslims and it was time for the Muslim press to tell tales of unprecedented brutality.[71] Far from making life easier for the Congress leaders in office, the troubles in Bihar narrowed their options further still.

The experience which the Congress and the League had of failing to work together inside the interim government was short, but with communal troubles of alarming proportions in eastern Bengal and Bihar it could hardly be sweet. It all rapidly degenerated into trivial squabbling to cover the far from trivial question of how power was to be shared, not the best augury for an union government in the future. Liaquat Ali did not want to go to Nehru's tea parties, and would not recognise Jawaharlal as the government's leader, or even that the Council was a cabinet.[72] Congress in its turn, asserted that 'on no account are we prepared to

70 Sudhir Ghosh to Cripps, 31 October 1946, *T.P.*, IX, 28.
71 Dow to Wavell, 26 October 1946, *T.P.*, VIII, 812–14.
72 Nehru to Wavell, 30 October 1946, ibid., 836.

function . . . as a group facing a rival group', and after a mere ninety-six hours of joint office warned that 'we may find it not possible to continue in the Government'.[73] Bengal was in uproar, and Patel called for the dismissal of the League ministry there, and for the centre to take charge. This of course would have meant bringing Bengal under a Congress-dominated centre, and was mere provocation by Patel, not practical politics.[74] But it was ominous for Jinnah nonetheless.

If Congress in office was determined to keep up the pressure upon the League, Jinnah's expectations that Wavell was both ready and able to discipline the Congress and give the League breathing space were soon to be disappointed. By now Wavell was no longer his masters' voice. More and more, London saw the urgent sense in coming to terms with Congress, its obvious successor, if not obviously its sole successor. As Wavell and Congress grew further apart, London grew firmer in its determination to rid itself of a proconsul whose judgement it regarded as flawed, and whose preoccupations tended to be more militaristic than political. As Pethick-Lawrence and Cripps agreed a month before the League entered the interim government, it was much more important to keep the lines open to Congress than to persuade the League into office.[75] Wavell's view that London was paying too much attention to the interests of one party might have fitted in with the construct of interest of a Raj minded to stay on, but made less sense to one that was minded to leave. Wavell's contention that H.M.G. was being 'both cowardly and dishonest'[76] by not coming out into the open about the grouping issue had to be set against the Congress line that the Viceroy's initiative in bringing the League into the interim government, before it had withdrawn its rejection of the long-term proposals, was a practical blunder and 'a fine opportunity of solving our problem once and for all has been destroyed'.[77] Now the League was unlikely to leave the interim government willingly; it would continue to obstruct the affairs of government and refuse to come into the constituent assembly. As even Liaquat Ali Khan had confessed: 'the passion and determination of the Muslim League would diminish if the League once accepted the proposition that they would enter the Constituent Assembly and allow the Federal Court

[73] Ibid.
[74] See Wavell to Pethick-Lawrence, 30 October 1946, ibid., 842.
[75] Cripps thought that the threat of Muslim disturbances was not serious, and the Secretary of State echoed his sentiment that any attempt to appease the League might result in a Congress refusal to participate in the constituent assembly. This would be a more serious setback than the League's failure to participate. (See note of discussion between Pethick-Lawrence and Cripps, 27 September 1946, ibid., 614.)
[76] Notes by Wavell and Abell, 4 November 1946, *T.P.*, IX, 1.
[77] Sudhir Ghosh to Cripps, 31 October 1946, ibid., 28.

to interpret even the most vital clauses'.[78] The only arena where the League could give the Congress an effective opposition was the interim government. It could not do this in the streets, in the countryside or in the constituent assembly. This was the main reason why Congress wanted to rid the interim government of the League's presence. It pressed Jinnah to either join the constituent assembly or resign from the interim government.[79] Alternatively, Nehru threatened to resign on behalf of the Congress. Jinnah retorted in kind by issuing a statement that the decision to summon the constituent assembly on 9 December under the existing communal tensions was 'one more blunder of very grave and serious character', and that no League representative would be seen anywhere near the assembly building.[80]

All that Wavell could do to avoid a complete breakdown of the 16 May plan was to arrange for the Indian leaders to make a flying visit to London for talks. The conference, which lasted for four days, was attended by Wavell, Nehru, Jinnah, Liaquat and Baldev Singh. H.M.G.'s statement of 6 December, which issued from these talks, was hortative, not definitive. Even though it reaffirmed the Mission's proposals about grouping and expressed the view that the constituent assembly would not be allowed to force a constitution upon 'any unwilling parts of the country', this was not strong or convincing enough to bring the League into the constituent assembly.[81] A month later (and after the constituent assembly had met on 9 December, without the League) Congress gave its watered-down acceptance of the statement. But fierce opposition inside the Congress from the Hindu Mahasabhites and the left-wing socialists led by J. P. Narain even to this nominal acceptance suggested that Jinnah was right in not relying upon its bona fides in the matter.[82]

So this left Jinnah in the cold, still outside the constituent assembly. Events in the Punjab, where some Leaguers were taking the 'direct action' call as a rallying cry to bring down Khizar's ministry,[83] suggested

---

[78] Abell to Scott, 16 November 1946, ibid., 84.
[79] Nehru to Wavell, 21 November 1946, ibid., 124–5.
[80] See Jinnah's statement in the *Hindustan Times*, 22 November 1946, in ibid., 135.
[81] See H.M.G.'s statement of 6 December 1946, *T.P.*, IX, 295–6.
[82] See All-India Congress Committee's resolution, 6 January 1947, ibid., 462–3. According to Wavell the resolution had been adopted after a 'stormy debate' and: 'It was no easy business for the old guard of the Congress to get their way about this, and they had in fact to make it almost a vote of confidence in themselves'. (See Wavell to Pethick-Lawrence, 8 January 1947, ibid., 486.) It was clear that the Congress centre party, represented by Patel, Nehru, Rajandra Prasad and company, was under strong criticism from the left-wing socialists and the Hindu Mahasabhites 'and it will have to show results if it is to maintain itself'. (Note by Scott and Wavell, ibid., 488.)
[83] By January 1947, the activities of the Muslim League Nationalist Guard, and the counter-activities of the Hindu Mahasabha's para-military wing, the Rashtriya Swayam

just how precarious Jinnah's position would be if the A.I.M.L. Council was now asked to withdraw its rejection of the long-term proposals. His lieutenants in the Punjab were unlikely to pay much heed to any call to renounce direct action until they had succeeded in securing office for themselves. The shaky position Jinnah would have in the constituent assembly itself and in the Punjab (a critical base if the League was successfully to oppose Congress efforts to abandon compulsory grouping) did not warrant the League going into the assembly. A specifically Muslim attack upon Khizar's ministry in the Punjab might bring it down; the only other way to do so was by a League–Congress coalition or at least by weaning the Congress out of its alliance with Khizar. But here was the rub. Jinnah was still a bystander in Punjabi politics, whereas Congress, powerful at the centre, was increasingly not simply a bystander even in that province, and its directives from above threatened to turn a League–Congress coalition in the Punjab into a powerful weapon directed against Jinnah's standing at the centre. On 31 January 1947, a mere six months before partition, the League's Working Committee formally resolved at Karachi not to enter the constituent assembly, declaring that Congress's acceptance of H.M.G.'s 6 December exhortations was 'no more than a dishonest trick and jugglery of words'. The resolution called for the dissolution of the constituent assembly, and a declaration that the Cabinet Mission's plan had definitively and finally failed.[84]

This left Jinnah with one last straw at which to clutch, the British reaction to this breakdown between Congress and League. The Viceroy in New Delhi was coming out with an increasingly desperate series of contingency plans, like some dispirited general in retreat, regrouping at more and more improbable points in a rout which he was trying to prevent degenerating into a 'scuttle'. London saw these as devices of a military mind hopelessly lost in the maze into which India's politics had

Sewak Sangh, had brought matters to a head. On 24 January, the Punjab Government banned both organisations, and gave the League leaders an excuse to court arrest. As expected the arrest of the League leaders resulted in widespread demonstrations in Lahore. The fuse had been lit and Khizar's decision to withdraw the ban only helped to persuade the Punjabi Leaguers that success was finally in sight. According to the Governor, the League leaders were simply 'bent on defiance' and had used the denial of civil liberties as a pretext for their agitation, although they frankly admitted that the ban on the League's Nationalist Guards was a minor issue. What they intended to do was to continue 'direct action . . . until restrictions on processions and meetings were lifted and [the] Ministry resigned'. (Jenkins to Wavell, 29 January 1947, ibid., 572.) The League's High Command had no choice but to bow to Punjabi requirements. If it now withdrew the 'direct action' resolution the façade of calling the shots in the Punjab would have collapsed.

[84] See the A.I.M.L.'s Working Committee's resolution at Karachi, 31 January 1947, ibid., 586–93.

led him. Forward contingency planning was all very well in good generalship, but Wavell's ideas did not share the metropolitan angle of vision. Already early in September 1946, when the League's entry into government was uncertain, Wavell had floated the first of his plans, the 'Breakdown Plan', based on the assumption that a negotiated settlement between the two parties was impossible and, granted their depleted services, the British could at most rule India for another eighteen months. After that 'persuasion and bluff' would run out. Already Governors' powers were 'rapidly becoming a dead letter'. The only answer, and a partial one at that, would be to withdraw from the south and centre, while regrouping the remaining forces in what was left of British India. All this was to be sprung on India before March 1947, giving a full year for its implementation.[85] London received this plan with grave disquiet. All the old arguments were deployed against Wavell's plan and some new ones too (which branded the forces of disorder and agitation as belonging to the left wing, or worse). Indian unity would be sacrificed; there would almost certainly be a 'scramble for power' with 'an attempt to set up Pakistan by force either at once or in the wake of our withdrawal'. In sum, chaos would ensue, Commonwealth defence would collapse and in any case the plan would not work.[86] Not a voice was raised in the Cabinet in support of this proposal. On 30 October 1946 Wavell again pressed Attlee for a clear statement of 'how and when we are to leave India ';[87] but London liked the drift of his thinking no better than before, and now saw the spectre of 'extreme left wing elements' conspiring with 'Russians' to blow up or take over India, and so tear the whole web of British interests east of Suez. Echoing the fears of the British Cabinet, the Secretary of State predicted that: 'The extremist Left Wing elements and the Goonda elements will be anxious to exploit the situation at the expense of the wealthy classes, and the announcement of a phased withdrawal spread over a period of 14 months would give both them and the Muslims time to plan and organise attempts to seize power by violence.'[88] The Viceroy's plan was seen as a product of his immediate preoccupations which took no account of long-term British interests, both strategic and economic. As Pethick-Lawrence told Cripps, if Wavell's plan was put into effect:

We should . . . find ourselves participating in a civil war. Alternatively, if we evacuated India there would be civil war and chaos, the Russians would penetrate

[85] See Wavell to Pethick-Lawrence, 8 September 1946, *T.P.*, VIII, 454–65.
[86] See Pethick-Lawrence to Attlee, 20 September 1946, ibid., 550–2 and Pethick-Lawrence to Wavell, 28 September 1946, ibid., 621.
[87] Wavell to Attlee, 30 October 1946, ibid., 840.
[88] Pethick-Lawrence to Wavell, 26 September 1946, ibid., 621.

India, there would be no effective defence of India against external dangers, and the position of the British Commonwealth would be seriously injured because India would cease to be a participant in the Commonwealth Defence system; and if she became dominated by the Russians, communications with Australia and New Zealand would be cut.[89]

While Wavell was in London in early December he again pressed his case; he was listened to politely with deaf ears, and behind his back Attlee had already begun his search for a successor. The India and Burma Committee agreed with Wavell that once it was clear that the League would not come into the constituent assembly a further declaration of policy would be necessary. But it disagreed with his plan for a phased withdrawal. Fixing the date of the withdrawal without any certainty that power could be transferred to a responsible government, or a firm guarantee of minority rights or indeed of safeguarding British interests, was nothing short of a 'scuttle'.[90] Some members seemed inclined to accept the partition of India; they suggested that H.M.G. should state that any constitution drawn up by the existing constituent assembly would be valid for the Hindu-majority provinces. The Muslim-majority provinces would be encouraged to set up a constituent assembly of their own.[91] Wavell was vehemently opposed to anything along these lines. It contradicted the Mission's 16 May plan, and at any rate Wavell considered 'Pakistan' to be a 'thoroughly unsatisfactory solution of the Indian problem'. It would involve dividing the Indian army, the cornerstone of India's future contribution to Commonwealth defence, and a possible civil war. The need to keep the Indian army united, Wavell pointed out, was the 'most important part of my Breakdown Plan'. A complete withdrawal might mean dividing the army, whereas a phased withdrawal would indicate to the Indian leaders that 'we are really on the move' and might shock them into an agreement.[92] No one was impressed by the Viceroy's line and on 18 December while he was still in London, Attlee offered the Viceroyalty to Mountbatten. When Attlee reported the discussions between the Viceroy and the India Committee to the Cabinet the general view was that a phased withdrawal would encourage frag-

[89] See note on discussion between Pethick-Lawrence and Cripps, 27 September 1946, ibid., 614.

[90] India and Burma Committee meeting, 11 December 1946, *T.P.*, IX, 334–5.

[91] Ibid., 333.

[92] Wavell's note, enclosure to document no. 193, ibid., 346–8. Just how true Wavell's assessment was can be seen by Jinnah's reaction when Woodrow Wyatt told him that if the League and the Congress did not agree it was unlikely that the British would stay, with their officials and troops, until they agreed. The Quaid-i-Azam, according to Wyatt, was 'shocked and startled'. (See note on conversation between Jinnah and Woodrow Wyatt, 9 December 1946, ibid., p. 313.)

mentation, and above all it would be the 'first step in the dissolution of the Empire',[93] a 'defeatist' proposal in Bevin's view.[94] So the Cabinet finally rejected Wavell's plan and agreed to impose a time limit instead of an exact date for the final transfer of power.[95]

On 3 February 1947, after the League had refused to enter the constituent assembly, the Viceroy's final fling was to send home his plan for a phased transfer of authority, a variant of his earlier scheme for a phased transfer of territory. The plan bore a remarkable resemblance to the one Mountbatten eventually implemented, with the difference that while recommending a date for the withdrawal of British troops it did not propose a date for a final transfer of power. The assumption was that the withdrawal of troops, which was to be completed in the last quarter of 1948, would itself amount to a transfer of power, but this would not be announced publicly. The Indian leaders would be informed about the proposed withdrawal of troops. This would throw an increasing responsibility on the Congress and the League and would avoid a general panic in the country. The underlying principle of the plan was that the final transfer of power should not be sudden but gradual. The Secretary of State's services would be wound up first and the withdrawal of British troops would not begin before a sufficient warning had been given to provincial and central governments, at least a year in advance, about the future of the Indian army. If partition became inevitable then the Indian army would have to be divided, but a one-year warning would still be required to reduce the administrative difficulties which would accompany the transfer of power to more than one authority. During the interim period India would be treated as a Dominion and there would be 'no deliberate destruction by us of the façade of the continuing Government of India' since it was possible that India might have to continue under the existing constitution and be 'persuaded to remain in the Commonwealth rather than become independent'.[96] Essentially the plan proposed a series of decisions rather than one sweeping one which, with the League still outside the constituent assembly and the Congress insistent on its leaving the interim government, could only lead to a partition of the country. However unrealistic the plan may appear to be in retrospect it at least had the merit of recognising what was already happening in the provinces, and what would certainly happen as soon as a firm time limit was set for a transfer of power. Whether Wavell's secret

---

93 Cabinet Meeting, 31 December 1946, ibid., 428. Also see Attlee to Wavell, 8 January 1947, ibid., 490–1.
94 Bevin to Attlee, 1 January 1947, ibid., 431–2.
95 See Cabinet Meeting, 8 January 1947, ibid., 483–5.
96 See Wavell to Pethick-Lawrence, 3 February 1947, ibid., 595–602.

plans would have remained secret in a subcontinent where political secrets were for sale by the dozen in every bazaar is of course quite another matter. Curiously enough, Wavell's new plan did not reach London, or so it was claimed, until 17 February, three days before Attlee's announcement that power would be transferred by a definite time limit regardless of the form or shape which the political settlement might take. It is quite plausible that London did not wish to acknowledge a plan which went against the grain of what it had already decided to do. On 31 January, Attlee had already told Wavell that their disagreements on policy had forced him to find a new Viceroy more in tune with H.M.G.'s thinking.[97] Wavell retorted that the so-called divergence of policy was between his insisting on a 'definite policy for the Interim period and H.M.G. refusing to give me one'. While he was ready to accept London's decision lying down Wavell could not resist pointing out that 'so summary a dismissal of His Majesty's representative in India is hardly in keeping with the dignity of the appointment'.[98] But these were trivial matters compared to H.M.G.'s willingness to disregard the views of the Governors of the Punjab and Bengal, the two provinces most likely to be affected by the new policy. Both Governors believed that setting a time limit would have a disastrous effect on the communal situation and make it impossible for the two centre parties to agree.[99] Although Wavell was prepared to concede that the Governors' appreciation might well be 'unduly pessimistic' he again urged H.M.G. 'to reconsider their proposed course of action'; the 'announcement to be made now should not (repeat not) include the date of withdrawal'.[100] Since Mountbatten was not prepared to accept the appointment unless it included a definite date for the final transfer of power, H.M.G. decided to ignore the opinions of the men on the spot.[101]

[97] Attlee to Wavell, 31 January 1947, ibid., 582–3.
[98] Wavell to Attlee, 5 February 1947, ibid., 624.
[99] The Governor of the Punjab thought that an announcement of a British withdrawal from India within seventeen months and a willingness to transfer power to the existing authorities at the centre and in the provinces would mean a complete stalemate between the two main all-India parties. After all, 'what incentive is there for the contending parties to get together?' As far as he could judge: 'Few Indian politicians want an amicable settlement, except on their own terms, and the tendency will unquestionably be for all parties to seize as much power as they can – if necessary by force.' (See note by Jenkins, 16 February 1947, ibid., 729.) The Governor of Bengal felt that all would have been well if only the League was co-operating inside the constituent assembly. Since it was now unlikely to come in, he was opposed to the proposed declaration. (See note by Burrows, 14 February 1947, ibid., 705.)
[100] Wavell to Pethick-Lawrence, 17 February 1947, ibid., 733.
[101] Mountbatten had argued that world opinion would be less inclined to support H.M.G.'s policy if their critics could point out that H.M.G. were 'scuttling' without

On 20 February 1947, Attlee announced that H.M.G. intended to transfer power by a date no later than June 1948, and that Mountbatten would take over from Wavell in March 1947. Above all, Attlee made it clear that if, by June 1948, constitution-making was not taking place in a 'fully representative Assembly'

His Majesty's Government will have to consider to whom the powers of the Central Government in British India should be handed over, on the due date, whether as a whole to some form of central Government for British India or in some areas to the existing Provincial Governments, or in such other way as may seem most reasonable and in the best interests of the Indian people.[102]

This was not an acceptance of the principle of 'Pakistan' as Jinnah would have liked; it was an invitation to a scramble for power in the Muslim-majority provinces. Whichever provincial group won the race to power (or was able to stay in power) by June 1948, H.M.G. would transfer power to it in the event that an all-India agreement had not been reached. This was yet another hammer blow to the League. Bold words that they would 'not yield an inch in their demand for Pakistan' hardly disguised Jinnah's clear recognition that the agreement with the Congress inside the constituent assembly which the Mission had envisaged was now more unlikely than ever.[103] In Bengal, the Hindu Mahasabha immediately called for the partition of the province. Nehru echoed this view suggesting that once the League and Congress fell out irretrievably (now an imminent prospect), Bengal and the Punjab would have to be partitioned.[104]

Indeed, the real casualty of the 20 February announcement was Khizar in the Punjab. The League's agitation against Khizar, interpreted by the non-Muslims as evidence to set up an 'undiluted Muslim rule all over the Punjab', now took on a new ferocity.[105] Khizar's own

having the guts to admit it. Moreover, Congress was waiting for a reply to its demand that the League should be asked to leave the interim government. The India Committee considered that the declaration might persuade Congress to defer its demand for some time, at least until the League's reactions to the new policy were known.

[102] See H.M.G.'s statement of 20 February 1947, paragraph 10, ibid., 774.
[103] See Abell to Harris, 25 February 1947, ibid., 813.
[104] Wavell to Pethick-Lawrence, 22 February 1947, ibid., 785–6.
[105] Jenkins to Wavell, 15 February 1947, L/P&J/5/250, I.O.L. On 26 February, the League's agitation was called off officially after a compromise with the Punjab government. Under the terms of the agreement the ban on public meetings was lifted; the government would release all political prisoners except those convicted for offences under Section 325 of the Indian Penal Code, and would introduce new legislation to replace the Punjab Safety Ordinance. The ban on processions, however, was to continue. (*Indian Annual Register*, 1947, vol. I, 223–4.) But as the Governor could see: 'The real object of the agitation was to turn the Coalition Ministry out of office, and the settlement is therefore unreal because it makes concessions with which the agitation was not really concerned.' (Jenkins to Wavell, 28 February 1947, L/P&J/5/250, I.O.L.)

reaction was that the statement was 'the work of lunatics'; he toned it
down to 'profound dismay' but, on 2 March 1947, resigned and Section
93 was imposed in India's most important Muslim province.[106] After
twenty-three years in office, the Unionists had finally been forced to
admit defeat. This opened the way to all manner of possibilities in the
Punjab, ranging from Noon's hopes of a 'return to Unionism'[107] to
Khizar's hopes that the Punjab League might now finally grasp the
implications of Pakistan and come to terms with the minorities.[108] Some
League leaders did approach the Akali Sikhs, but the Akalis rejected
these overtures for a possible coalition on the grounds that the League
had 'bluntly refused to discuss the future of the Sikhs or to give any
assurance to them'.[109] Without firm assurances to the non-Muslim
communities about what 'Pakistan' entailed, there was no possibility of
the League taking office in an undivided Punjab. In an astonishing
revelation, Nazimuddin, who had been sent out to negotiate a settlement
between the Leaguers and the Punjab government, explained the crux of
the problem: he 'did not know what Pakistan meant', in fact 'nobody in
the Muslim League knew, so that it was very difficult for the League to
carry on long-term negotiations with the minorities'.[110] Without a
settlement between the League and the Congress at the centre there was
no prospect of a communal agreement in the Punjab. But equally without
a communal agreement in the Punjab, Jinnah was unlikely to secure his
claim for the whole province to be included in Pakistan. It is an
indication of Jinnah's priorities that he did not come out into the open

---

[106] See Jenkins to Wavell, 28 February 1947, ibid., and Jenkins to Wavell, 2 March 1947,
R/3/1/176, I.O.L. Following constitutional procedure the Governor did commission
the League president, the Nawab of Mamdot, to look into the possibility of forming a
ministry. Mamdot failed to convince the Governor that he had the support of a majority
in the house. According to the Governor: 'No names were given and I was simply asked
to accept [the] assertion that [the] League would in fact command [a] majority. Private
information suggests that Mamdot commands only 3 votes outside the League [which
by now had eighty votes] including 1 Muslim and 2 Scheduled Castes.' (Jenkins to
Wavell, 3 March 1947, R/3/1/176, I.O.L. and Jenkins to Wavell, 5 March 1947, *T.P.*,
IX, 868). Under the circumstances the Governor decided to go into Section 93 since:
'Risk of installing League Ministry of this kind even with assumed Parliamentary
majority is enormous. Without such majority installation of Ministry would in my
judgement be fraud on constitution and Instrument of Instructions. I would simply be
inviting one of [the] Parties to present communal conflict to assume charge of it without
even satisfying myself of its Parliamentary competence to do so.' (Jenkins to Wavell, 5
March 1947, telegram, ibid., 868–9.)
[107] Note by Jenkins, 6 March 1947, R/3/1/176, I.O.L.
[108] See Jenkins to Wavell, 2 March 1947, R/3/1/176, I.O.L.
[109] Jenkins to Wavell, 15 February 1947, L/P&J/5/250, I.O.L.
[110] Jenkins to Wavell, 28 February 1947, L/P&J/5/220, I.O.L.

with any formula which might have kept the Punjab united. Such a formula if it was to be accepted by Punjab's non-Muslims would have had to be non-communal and, therefore, would have undermined Jinnah's case at the centre which had to rest, at least for the moment, on a specifically communal stance. So the Punjab was to be allowed to drift towards chaos. All hopes of saving the unity of the Punjab were pipe-dreams; the province was already in the grip of communal warfare. Within two days the communal situation had deteriorated at an alarming rate. The Governor reported that 'communal tension was acute in almost every district'; Lahore, Amritsar, Multan and Rawalpindi had been badly affected and disturbances were so widespread that it was impossible for the military to reinforce at all points at the same time. The Akali leader, Master Tara Singh, declared that 'civil war' had already begun in the Punjab and threatened a Sikh uprising. With communal troubles 'gradually spreading to the rural areas all over the Punjab', a coalition ministry of all communities was 'most improbable' since 'the Muslims would insist upon Pakistan, which they are still quite unable to define; and the Hindus and Sikhs would demand the Ravi as the boundary of the non-Muslim State.'[111] Within less than six days of Khizar's resignation, the Congress High Command had called for the partition of the Punjab.[112] The Punjab had taken its revenge upon Jinnah's broken strategy. Jinnah entered the last phase of the end game with his followers in the Muslim provinces in total confusion,[113] and with only a joker – the threat of direct action – which he was understandably reluctant to play left in his pack.[114]

---

[111] See Jenkins to Wavell, 10 March 1947, *T.P.*, IX, 912–13, and Jenkins to Wavell, 9 March 1947, ibid., 902–3.

[112] See Congress Working Committee's resolution of 8 March 1947, ibid., 899–900.

[113] In the N.W.F.P. the so-called 'local League' had taken up 'direct action' to bring down the Congress ministry. This was accompanied by widespread communal disturbances in the towns and villages of the province. The military had to be called in to restore a semblance of law and order. But violent attacks on non-Muslims continued to spread both east and south of Peshawar. In Hazara district there were forced conversions of non-Muslims and Hindu temples and Sikh *gurdwaras* were reduced to ashes. (See Caroe to Wavell, 13 March 1947, ibid., 930–31.) Nehru alleged that the Governor was encouraging the 'League' agitation and called for his immediate dismissal. (Nehru to Wavell, 19 March 1947, ibid., 988–9.)

[114] Some three months or so before, when the Calcutta and Noakhali troubles had spilled over the frontiers into Bihar, and Hindus had taken the opportunity to retaliate against Muslim outrages against their brothers far away, a Delhi Leaguer, Abdus Samad, had drawn up his campaign for 'planned, co-ordinated and concerted action' in locality, town and province to fight the coming 'war'. This called for funds; it called for 'organisation down to the minutest details'; it called for a mass movement; it also, he thought, required 'politics of manoeuvring', and 'leaders who are extremely intelligent,

shrewd and past-masters in the diplomatic game'. Jinnah, the 'cold-blooded logician' might just have fitted the bill in the last item on this long list of specifications. But neither Jinnah nor the League were willing or able to gather the sinews of war. Without planning 'direct action' would 'inevitably lead to communal rioting'. 'The real remedy' (though this was hardly one which Jinnah at this late stage could think of pulling out of thin air) was 'that the Muslim League should set up a really strong and efficient All-India organization to militarise Musulamans for defence purposes . . . every Muslim Mohalla should become a veritable castle. Only then we can be safe because the enemy is already well-prepared for the attack.' (See Abdus Samad to Jinnah, 10 November 1946, QAP/8/File No. 965, p. 57.) Jinnah, the negotiator, was not capable of this metamorphosis into Jinnah the embattled and organised commander of guerillas and self-defence associations in the localities of Muslim India.

7

The end game: Mountbatten and partition

Since 1940 Jinnah's strategy had been based on the premise that India's unitary centre was a British creation which would automatically cease to exist when the British left India. Any new all-India centre would have to be agreed upon by Muslim provinces as well as by the Princely States. What Jinnah was clamouring for was a way of achieving an equal say for Muslims in any all-India arrangements at the centre. By denying that Indian Muslims were a minority and asserting that they were a nation, Jinnah advanced the constitutional lawyer's argument that since India contained at least two nations, a transfer of power necessarily involved the dissolution of British India's unitary structure of central authority, and any reconstitution of the centre would have to take account of the League's demand that Muslim provinces, the territorial expression of this claim to nationhood, should be grouped to constitute a separate state. Once the British and the Congress accepted the essence of the League's demands, then it remained, for Jinnah at least, an open question whether the Muslim state would enter into a confederation with non-Muslim provinces on the basis of parity at the centre, or whether, as a sovereign state, it would make treaty arrangements with the rest of India about matters of common concern. In either case, the League's demand was that 'Pakistan' must be conceded first, and the exact shape and powers of the new centre be arranged afterwards. But Jinnah claimed to speak for all Indian Muslims, in minority and majority provinces alike, and political geography ensured that many of his constituents could never be consolidated into a specifically Muslim territory; the Muslim nation would have almost as many citizens beyond its borders as inside them. Jinnah had tried to get round this problem by asserting that the two main Muslim-majority provinces, Punjab and Bengal, would keep their existing boundaries (and hence their large non-Muslim minorities). He also assumed implicitly, if not explicitly, that a Muslim state built around these provinces would continue to be part of a larger all-India whole in which minority Muslims outside the Muslim territory would be protected by the similar position that non-Muslims had inside it. But the difficulties he had faced since 1937 in rallying support in the Muslim provinces and in challenging their particularism had forced Jinnah to cast his demands in communal terms. Yet it was now the communal slant to his unspecific programme, directed mainly at getting the appearance of support from divided Muslims, which threatened Jinnah's political purposes at the centre. These purposes depended upon keeping the Punjab and Bengal undivided. A demand couched in communal terms cut against the imperatives of Punjabi and Bengali Muslims since their supremacy over the undivided provinces had to rest on supra-communal alliances. At no point between 1940 and 1947 was Jinnah able to resolve this fundamental contradiction. By deliberately keeping the demand for 'Pakistan' vague, and its territories undefined, Jinnah had made it possible for his followers to exploit the League's communal line without having to face its implications: the partition of the Punjab and Bengal. Indeed, Jinnah's hope seems to have been that the principle of 'Pakistan' would be conceded before he had to deal with the question of non-Muslim minorities in these two provinces. It followed that he needed a settlement based on 'Pakistan' at the centre before his followers in the Muslim provinces were allowed to settle terms with the non-Muslim populations. But seven years of virulent propaganda for Pakistan, anathema to the non-Muslims, had helped to weaken the supra-communal alliances and the internal systems of control by which social order was maintained in the Muslim provinces. Until too late, Muslims in the Punjab and Bengal, who thought they could use Jinnah and the League for their own provincial purposes, failed to realise the grave risks they ran by supporting a demand cast in communal terms.

The failure of the British, of the Congress, and indeed of his own followers, to force him to face the fatal contradiction in the 'Pakistan' demand had allowed Jinnah to concentrate upon the centre and raise his political standing there. Taking refuge in the August 1940 declaration that no constitution would be imposed which was unacceptable to 'large and powerful elements in India's national life' and on the often-repeated principle that the main political parties would have to agree between themselves on any future constitution, Jinnah's tactic was to state his maximum demand – the outright acceptance of a sovereign Pakistan built upon the undivided provinces of north-western and north-eastern India – and leaving the other sides, both British and Congress, to produce an alternative formula which gave him the substance of what he was after. Such a formula would have to give Jinnah the power to stamp the League's authority on the Muslim provinces whose particularisms were as much a threat to his strategy as they were to Congress's aim to inherit the unitary structure of British India. The Cabinet Mission's May proposals had been designed to meet Jinnah's fundamental requirement.

Compulsory grouping of provinces handed the League a centre capable of disciplining the Muslim provinces and bringing them firmly into an Indian union on its terms. But although the Congress had accepted the Mission's proposals, its acceptance had been so hedged with qualifications that it was by no means certain that grouping, so essential to Jinnah's plans, would survive. Grouping alone could guarantee Jinnah an effective say at the centre. Events since May 1946, and signs that Congress meant to break grouping, convinced Jinnah that the Mission's proposals were not a secure basis for a settlement. Winning a sovereign status for the Muslim territories, the first step in an ultimate settlement, was the only way he could ensure that the final settlement would give him what he wanted. But these territories had to include undivided Bengal and Punjab, and have a large share of the centre's spoils (particularly the army) if Jinnah was to have something with which to bargain in the making of the broader all-India arrangements. Such arrangements he always assumed would have to be made. And Jinnah needed time. The nub of Jinnah's difficulty was that his strategy required a leisurely timetable and a continued British commitment to superintending the centre. With the British acting as umpire and the principle of Pakistan conceded, Jinnah hoped to be able to play a long, slow game with the Congress to secure the substance of his demands on behalf of Muslim India. When London, without first conceding the principle of 'Pakistan' and of undivided Muslim provinces, decided to quit India by June 1948, it dealt a bitter blow to Jinnah's entire strategy.

By early 1947, the Attlee government had found its options in making policy for India narrowing rapidly. Its main priority was to get out of India quickly. To do so, it had to come to terms with the Congress High Command. By February 1947 the terms of such an understanding between the British and the Congress High Command were becoming clear. Both sides wanted India to have independence soon – the British, because they could no longer afford to stay on, and the Congress High Command because the longer a transfer was delayed the less certain it was of controlling its provinces, disciplining followers and achieving a constitution which gave it the strong unitary centre it needed. Congress imperatives were coming neatly to dovetail with London's priorities since a strong unitary government was the best way of assuring British economic and strategic interests in South Asia. It remained for Attlee's government somehow to strike a balance between transferring power quickly and leaving a strong system of government in the subcontinent to maintain the continuities of their rule. Just how delicate this balance was can be seen by the effects of the 20 February announcement. For the first time the British had placed a definite term upon their rule. But absolute certainty about a timetable was not matched by any certitudes about the procedures or forms and substance of a transfer of power. The aim of course was to encourage all parties to concentrate their minds, and come to terms. The effect was dramatically different: the prospect of the Raj coming to an end within sixteen months kicked Pandora's box wide open, unleashing just those forces that threatened a strong central government. The men at the top had evidence in plenty that the structures of government, and of public order, were already strained to their limits: an interim government which was the arena for two warring parties rather than an effective coalition; a bureaucracy etiolated by war, and by a belated policy of Indianisation and uncertainty about futures; an army whose white officers and troops were anxious to return to Britain; a police force weakened at the top, uncertain about who were its masters, and what was its role; provincial politicians poised to snatch at every opportunity and to consolidate their position in the general scramble for power; and beneath them all, threatening tides of growing disorder, much of them with a communal colouring, which neither political party, League or Congress, was in a position to deny. And most dangerous of all, the banked but still burning fires of provincialism, not least in the two most important Muslim provinces, the Punjab and Bengal, the particularism of Sind, the N.W.F.P. and Baluchistan, and the fissiparous trends in Princely India which made all the parties, Congress quite as much as the less organised and less disciplined League, nervous about their control over their followers, particularly if the uncertain crust of order were to break. Once the announcement for an early transfer of power had been made, all these difficulties were compounded. London had placed a time-bomb under an already tottering administrative structure, and had now lit the fuse. Whatever the final outcome, it seemed unavoidable that India would witness troubles on a massive scale. A main preoccupation of British policy was to shift the burden of responsibility for these troubles squarely, if not fairly, onto the shoulders of Indians themselves. To do so, both Congress and League would have to be persuaded to ratify the final settlement. Such a settlement could only be negotiated at the top. Given the constraints of the timetable, it was impossible to hold referendums on the partition of the Punjab and Bengal. There was always the danger that the two High Commands, certainly the League's, would lose the 'mandate' of the voters who would now have to face the real issues rather than the tub-thumping propaganda of the 1945–46 elections. If the two main all-India parties were repudiated by the provinces the British would not be able to negotiate an all-India settlement. For once the British had an interest in accepting the claims of both High Commands at face value. This is why, despite their doubts about

Jinnah's ability to control his followers, neither the British nor indeed the Congress could, for lack of an alternative, seriously question his claim to negotiate on behalf of the Muslim provinces. Whatever the growing conformity of purpose between the British and the Congress, they could not simply shoulder Jinnah aside in finding a final solution.

However, the Congress High Command was not convinced that concessions to Jinnah would enable him to pull the Muslim provinces (over which the League had uncertain control) firmly into an unitary India. In Congress's eyes, the Mission's proposals had the double defect of giving the Muslim provinces too much autonomy and also of giving Jinnah and the League too much weight at the centre, which together would undermine its writ over the rest of India. The price of keeping the Muslim provinces inside the union had to be a weak federal centre, incapable of controlling any of its provincial arms, not merely the Muslim provinces. But most important of all, such an arrangement would have meant giving the League a share of power at an already weak centre. The experience of the interim government had shown the Congress that power shared with the League was a power flawed and uncertain. Even without parity, the mere presence of the League in the interim government had made administration a matter of party politics, without the majority party having the option of forming a government on its own. This clearly hinted at how the central authority of the Congress might be undermined in an independent India organised along the lines of the Mission's proposals. Congress's own dissidents, whether in the provinces or at the centre, would be able to exploit its weak central authority. Shades of the deep splits of the late thirties were seen again in the voting over Liaquat Ali Khan's budget, with its proposed business profits tax; the Congress left saw attractions in what the right dubbed as a 'poor man's budget' or worse still as evidence of the League's intention to sabotage the economy.[1] Just as Jinnah feared that the Congress would

---

[1] See Ali, *The Emergence of Pakistan*, pp. 104–12 and Wavell to Pethick-Lawrence, 19 March 1947, *T.P.*, IX, 991. Liaquat Ali Khan's budget, presented on 28 February 1947, was widely interpreted as evidence of his being *parti pris*. Congress's business supporters immediately claimed that the three tax proposals recommended in the budget, namely the business profits tax, the capital gains tax and the higher duty on tea, would bring production to a standstill. British plantation owners affected by the higher duty on tea had their own axes to grind. Stock exchanges throughout the country came to a halt, and the ensuing panic in the country was given the spontaneous if unverified diagnosis of communalism or worse still 'Pakistan'. Liaquat Ali confessed that his critics were: 'so much obsessed with this idea of the Muslim League having as its goal *Pakistan* that whatever any Muslim Leaguer utters they see *Pakistan* in that . . . the moment you talk about something my friends begin to feel that it is *Pakistan*. If I talk of zonal planning and economic development of the country they see *Pakistan* in that. If I present a budget

exploit the particularism of his provincial followers in the Muslim provinces unless he got grouping, the Congress High Command for its part feared that sharing power at the centre with the League would enable the League constantly to dangle a bait before its own Congress following. It was quite conceivable that Congress, a medley of political opinions, might split up along ideological lines soon after a British withdrawal. This, together with the possibility of a re-alignment of parties along political rather than specifically communal lines, suggests why the Congress High Command was so averse to sharing power at the centre with a rival High Command.

Once Jinnah had publicly reiterated his earlier rejection of the Cabinet Mission's proposals, the Congress High Command saw a way out of the impasse. If Jinnah was not ready to bring his League into the constituent assembly, then the terms of the Mission's plan disqualified the League from staying in the interim government. Taking refuge in the official line that Congress no less than the British was reluctant to force any part of India against its will into the union, the High Command proposed to permanently eject the League and its rump of supporters from the all-India arrangements which their presence so seriously prejudiced. Within a fortnight of London imposing its deadline, the Congress came out into the open with its ultimatum which had been gathering momentum in its inner councils for some time past. If Jinnah would not accept slow death inside its embrace, then divorce, not a limited separation followed by an arranged reconstitution, was to be its order of the day. As its permanent share in the division of assets, the League could have only those districts which possessed a clear Muslim majority and were contiguous to each other. Taking the logic of Jinnah's demand to its extreme, Congress now offered him a 'Pakistan' stripped of the Punjab's eastern divisions (Ambala and Jullundur), Assam (except Sylhet district) and western Bengal and Calcutta – the 'mutilated and moth-eaten' Pakistan which Jinnah had rejected out of hand in 1944 and again in May 1946. Such a permanent settlement would at a stroke eject Jinnah from the centre, clear the way for a strong unitary government wholly under Congress's sway, and give away only parts of provinces which past experience had

which according to me is the budget which consists of principles which I believe India should follow, they say now, here is *Pakistan*.' Liaquat regretted that a budget prepared by the Finance department should be seen as an attempt by him 'to ruin the economic life of the country and then go away to *Pakistan*'; it was perfectly clear that 'today the whole of India is one and if I ruin one part of India, I am definitely ruining the other part of India'. (See Liaquat Ali Khan's speech on the Indian Finance Bill, 27 March 1947, in M. Rafique Afzal (ed.), *Speeches and Statements of Quaid-i-Millat Liaquat Ali Khan (1941–51)*, Lahore, 1967, pp. 100–5.)

shown lay outside the Congress's ken. It even left open the possibility of laying claim to the N.W.F.P. which still had a Congress ministry. In the Punjab, Khizar's resignation on 2 March and the communal fury it helped to unleash undermined any prospect of a supra-communal alliance in which the Congress could expect an effective say. In Bengal, Suhrawardy's efforts to counter the Hindu Mahasabha's demand for a partition of the province and Sarat Bose's overtures to Muslims to achieve an independent republic stressed just how uncertain Congress's grip over that province would be while eastern Bengal remained the dominant part of the political equation. So on 8 March 1947, the Congress Working Committee passed the historic resolution which demanded the partition of the Punjab,[2] a principle which would if necessary be extended, as Nehru explained, to Bengal. Two days after the resolution was adopted, Nehru called for separate ministries in the Punjab, one for its western and another for its eastern districts. He argued that this alone would prevent a full-scale civil war there.[3] The obvious corollary was the call for separate ministries in western and eastern Bengal. In this way eastern Punjab and western Bengal could be brought into the Congress fold. By publicly declaring its readiness to accept partition on these terms, the Congress had tossed a two-headed coin in the political game. If Jinnah accepted division on these terms, Congress would win its strong centre, and all the regions where it could realistically hope to exercise control. If Jinnah did not accept division on these terms, then his only alternative was to be forced back into an union where Congress was the real master, capable step by step of cutting the League out of all share of power. Before the Congress Working Committee's resolution, Jinnah still had a few limited options, at least as far as official thinking in Britain went. After 8 March this was no longer so.

As London prepared to send out the last Viceroy, its thinking showed that, while it saw no clear way forward, there was still a chance that Jinnah might be able to rescue some part of his strategy. Until now London had shied away from contemplating a sovereign 'Pakistan' with an independent centre of its own. It could no longer avoid doing so. Time and again, British policy-making had used the device of provincial autonomy to ward off the nationalist challenges to its authority at the centre, and, more recently, with the Cripps offer, to question the League's claim to solid support from the Muslim provinces. Almost until the bitter end, London and Delhi continued to raise the spectre of provincialism and the threat of balkanisation. But by early March 1947

[2] See Congress Working Committee's resolution no. 3, 8 March 1947, *T.P.*, IX, 900–1.
[3] Note by Wavell on interview with Nehru, 10 March 1947, ibid., 907–8.

there was no longer any doubt where true British interests had come to
lie: they had to afforce central authority in India. A mere four days before
the Congress Working Committee's resolution, the Secretary of State
had reviewed the alternatives, and marshalled the arguments against
'fragmentation'. It was better to have a single Muslim centre rather than
hand over power to the Muslim provinces severally. It was best to
transfer power to 'the smallest possible number of separate authorities',
and to create for them a structure of government capable effectively of
administering central functions. Several successor states would encourage the strong to overwhelm the weak, whether by force or by economic
strangulation; it might lead to civil war; it would certainly lead to a
breakdown of the existing administrative structure, and this 'worst of all
solutions' would 'probably earn for us [the British] the hostility of both
sides in the Indian dispute'.[4] Considering the four main alternatives for
the Muslim areas, the Secretary of State quickly rejected the notion of a
separate transfer severally to each of the provincial governments of
Bengal, Punjab, Sind and the N.W.F.P. The second alternative was a
transfer to three authorities, 'Hindustan' (the non-Muslim provinces
including Assam), a 'Pakistan' of north-western India, and Bengal as a
separate entity. But there were strong arguments against letting Bengal
go its own way. For one thing the north-western provinces were unlikely
to be able to afford the large defence expenditure necessary both for the
maintenance of British strategic interests and for the effective exercise of
law and order inside the new state without a large subsidy from Bengal's
revenues. Already Bengal was being cast in its usual role of milch cow for
the centre, in this case a 'Pakistan' centre which the British, however
reluctantly, were now coming to consider unavoidable. So the preferred
alternative, the 'nearest equivalent to a Judgement of Solomon' was a
transfer to two authorities, 'Hindustan' and 'Pakistan' (which the
Secretary of State assumed would include north-western India and
Bengal without Assam). Interestingly enough, the fourth alternative,
which was a transfer to two authorities, 'Hindustan' and 'Pakistan' but
with a partition of the Punjab and Bengal, was less attractive from
London's point of view because without Calcutta and the western
districts of Bengal and the eastern districts of the Punjab, 'Pakistan'
would not have resources large enough to pay for external and internal
security.[5] This review of alternatives was now in deadly earnest. If the
Muslim areas, however defined, failed to join the constituent assembly
by June 1947, they would have to be pushed into an assembly of their

[4] See memorandum of the Secretary of State, 4 March 1947, ibid., 840–50.
[5] Ibid. But then the Secretary of State's memorandum had been prepared before the
Congress Working Committee's resolution of 8 March 1947.

own; Parliament would make this a precondition for the transfer of power in June 1948. The problem of the Indian army was even more intractable. An undivided army, the best security against a total break-down of order before the transfer, would have to be divided if there were to be two separate states. If the army was to be divided, then a decision to do so would have to be taken by September 1947, which for sheer logistic reasons was the last possible date if the British were to leave by June of the following year.[6]

These were some of the difficulties which plagued London. The Congress High Command's remedy for all of them was simple. A transfer of power should take place before June 1948, by the deceptively straightforward device of deeming the interim government to be a 'Dominion Government with effective control over the services and administration . . .', and of converting the Viceroy into its 'constitutional head'.[7] The centre would thus keep all its existing powers. There would be no devolution of authority to the provinces. As for the Indian States, if they failed to join the union by June 1948, the centre would automatically slap its authority over them in matters to do with foreign affairs, defence and communications. In this way the Congress proposed to preserve the unity of India and by the way its own unity and authority. If the British were prepared to accept this remedy, the Congress for its part hinted for the first time that independent India might be ready to remain within the Commonwealth, an attractive bait for London.[8]

This line of thinking was ominous for Jinnah. Congress clearly dominated the interim government. If that interim government became in effect the government to which power was transferred, Congress would rule, leaving its relationship both with the League at the centre and with the provinces a matter to be settled after independence.[9] This was particularly ominous since there was much here to commend itself to British policy and purposes. But London was not yet quite ready to follow this drastic new line, and face its consequences. It would have meant openly retracting the pledges to the Muslims and the princes. It would have entailed a full-dress debate in Parliament and a serious row

---

6 Ibid., 843–4.
7 See Congress Working Committee's resolution, 8 March 1947, ibid., 899–900.
8 See note on proposals handed to the Secretary of State by Sudhir Ghosh, annexe II to document 524, ibid., 923–4.
9 On 13 March 1947, Krishna Menon, the secretary of the London India League and a close confidant of Nehru, had sent Mountbatten a proposal calling for the acceptance of the League's claims for 'Pakistans', subject of course to the partition of the Punjab and Bengal. This, Menon thought, was the only way of resolving the 'crisis' inside the interim government. (See Krishna Menon to Mountbatten, 13 March 1947, ibid., 946–8.)

between Labour and the Conservatives. This was why Mountbatten was sent out with instructions which were both obsolescent and contradictory[10] by a Cabinet whose perspectives on the Indian question were changing radically but not openly. If Mountbatten had not been armed with the plenipotentiary powers that he demanded and was readily given, his instruments of instruction would have made a nonsense of his mission. In fact, he came to India with a freer hand to make and to implement policy than any proconsul before him in the history of British India.[11]

When Mountbatten arrived, it was not wholly inconceivable that a settlement on the Cabinet Mission's terms might still be secured. For one thing, the Congress was bound to be anxious about the partition of the army; even a truncated Pakistan meant cutting up the army, and all the delays and dangers that this would entail. The real difficulty was how Jinnah was to be persuaded to settle for the unbending terms Congress was prepared to offer. Jinnah, Mountbatten had been warned, would be his 'toughest customer'.[12] Another view was that Jinnah's 'negative nuisance value' really stemmed from the fact that 'no one in this country had so far got into Jinnah's mind'; the Viceroy might succeed in 'breaking down his façade' and discover that Jinnah was 'much more of a realist than he made out'.[13] Nehru, who had struck Mountbatten 'as most sincere', described his rival as 'one of the most extraordinary men in history', the key to whose success was his ability to 'avoid taking any positive action which might split his followers'. But Nehru believed that 'it might be possible to frighten Jinnah into co-operation on the basis of the short length of time available'.[14] This was grist to Mountbatten's mill. A list of 'Awkward Questions to Ask Jinnah' was prepared. These placed on Jinnah the entire burden of justifying the claim to the thirteen districts in the Punjab and the eight districts (including Calcutta) of

---

[10] These instructions were: to avoid partition and obtain an unitary government for British India and the Indian States and at the same time observe the pledges to the princes and the Muslims; to secure agreement to the Cabinet Mission plan without coercing any of the parties; somehow to keep the Indian army undivided, and to retain India within the Commonwealth. (Attlee to Mountbatten, 18 March 1947, ibid., 972–4.)

[11] But the Viceroy's freedom of action was more illusory than real. The astonishing speed with which Mountbatten examined various options in his frantic search for a final settlement, and moved to others once they proved unacceptable, can only be understood against a background of growing disorder. In the choice of options the decisive factor was the Congress High Command.

[12] Pethick-Lawrence to Mountbatten, 3 April 1947, *T.P.*, x, 104.

[13] This was the opinion of Dr John Matthai, the railway and transport member in the interim government. (See Mountbatten's interview with Dr John Matthai, 25 March 1947, ibid., 16–17.)

[14] Record of interview between Mountbatten and Nehru, 24 March 1947, ibid., 12.

Bengal which did not have a Muslim majority. If Jinnah insisted on a sovereign Pakistan, he would have to accept it in a truncated form. Moreover, he would have to demonstrate how its defence would be organised. The assumption was that the resources of a truncated Pakistan would be so strained that for external defence it would need to come into a defensive alliance with Hindustan.[15] And if all these considerations were not sufficient to turn the heat on Jinnah, then the inflexibility of the time-limit certainly was. In a brutal but frank message intended specifically for Jinnah, Mountbatten told Liaquat Ali Khan that the last Viceroy had 'an appalling responsibility' in deciding what to recommend to H.M.G.; he 'intended to approach the problem in an atmosphere of stark realism'; he was 'less interested that India should be handed over on lines which might ultimately prove correct than that mechanism should be set up to avoid bloodshed after the departure of the British'.[16] Limiting bloodshed called for an united Indian army under effective control. But keeping the army intact was now inextricably linked with keeping India united. This is why Mountbatten started off by being vehemently opposed to 'abolishing the centre'; 'abolishing the centre', he assumed, would mean cutting up the army, delaying the British withdrawal, and forcing him to stay in India beyond June 1948 in the thankless role of an umpire powerless to enforce the rules.[17]

This gave Jinnah the chance to make one of his last moves on the board. By demanding a division of the army, Jinnah hoped to delay the timetable of the transfer of power, keeping the British in charge until somehow he managed to scotch the threat which the partition of the Punjab and Bengal posed and forcing the Congress to make some concessions at the centre. If Jinnah realised that the game was up, he was not ready to concede it. At his first meeting with Mountbatten on 5 April, Jinnah made no secret of what he was playing for. The Cabinet Mission, he asserted, 'had been imbued with the wrong attitude – they had come out pleading for agreement instead of laying down a solution'. Muslim India, Jinnah told Mountbatten, was up in arms and no solution could be imposed on them which did not have his endorsement; he was the 'one man to deal with'; if he resigned, that would be the 'end of the Muslim League'.[18] As the sole spokesman of Muslim India, Jinnah demanded a settlement by a British award. That award would have to accept 'Pakistan' in principle and agree that Pakistan would be entitled to an

15 See addendum to item 11, document no. 64, ibid., 100–1.
16 Mountbatten's interview with Liaquat Ali Khan, 24 March 1947, ibid., 14.
17 Viceroy's staff meeting, 5 April 1947, ibid., 128.
18 Mountbatten's interview with Jinnah, 5 & 6 April 1947, ibid., 138–9.

army;[19] that alone would enable the League to enter a 'central organization on terms of parity'.[20] Mountbatten's response was predictable. Taking Jinnah too literally, he responded too quickly that even if a settlement on these lines proved to be the 'correct solution', it needed time for its implementation, much more time than there was available. Already the five years which conservative military opinion calculated were needed for an orderly hand-over of the Indian army had to be cut down to fourteen months; if on top of that the British were expected 'to perform the miracle of cutting the Army into half', it would be impossible to get out by June 1948. This is of course just what Jinnah himself had calculated. When he was categorically told that the timetable could not be delayed, Jinnah confessed that this came as a 'shock'. He 'smiled in a cryptic way' and asked how the British proposed to leave by June 1948. Was it their 'intention to turn this country over to chaos and bloodshed and civil war?'[21] Mountbatten now pressed home his advantage: the League, he told Jinnah, had either to accept the Mission's proposals or take its 'Pakistan' carved out of India by a partition of the Punjab and Bengal. Jinnah described the threat of partitioning these two provinces as a Congress 'bluff', intended to 'frighten him off Pakistan'. Partition would 'greatly weaken . . . [a viable] Pakistan'. A Pakistan containing substantial non-Muslim minorities would be in a stronger position to bargain with Hindustan. Jinnah's only hope of forcing Congress to meet him half way in the ultimate arrangements at the centre was to keep the Punjab and Bengal undivided. He begged the Viceroy 'not to destroy the unity of Bengal and the Punjab, which had national characteristics in common: common history, common ways of life; and where the Hindus have stronger feelings as Bengalis or Punjabis than they have as members of the Congress'.[22] Congress was 'deliberately drawing a red herring across the path'. As Mountbatten insisted that what was good for the Muslims was good also for other communities Jinnah became 'more and more distressed and displeased'. Since the Lahore resolution, the demand which Jinnah and the League had orchestrated was always couched in terms of the Muslim right to self-determination. But how could that right now be denied to substantial non-Muslim minorities living in contiguous districts in the Punjab and

[19] According to Liaquat Ali Khan, a Pakistan without an army would collapse like a 'house of cards'. (Liaquat Ali Khan to Mountbatten, 7 April 1947, ibid., 152.)
[20] Record of Mountbatten's interview with Jinnah, 7 April 1947, ibid., 149.
[21] Record of Mountbatten's interview with Jinnah, 7 April 1947, ibid., 150.
[22] Record of Mountbatten's interview with Jinnah, 8 April 1947, ibid., 159. Hardly the words of a man committed to partitioning India on communal lines.

Bengal?[23] Jinnah's only retort in the face of this argument was to resort to a quite different line, namely that power should be transferred to the provinces.[24] The provinces would then decide what groups to form, and by inference whether or not to join the Pakistan or Hindustan constituent assemblies. This was a desperate attempt to avoid the partition of the Punjab and Bengal. Whatever the risks of such a course to the League's prospects of controlling the Muslim provinces, a transfer of power to the provinces severally might at least prevent the Congress from taking over at the centre without let or hindrance.

But Mountbatten's game-plan required an unrelenting pressure to be kept up on Jinnah. Turning Jinnah's proposal for a province by province transfer against him, Mountbatten blandly invited Jinnah to help him to work out the mechanics of a scheme designed to cut out the Muslim-majority districts and transfer power to them. Jinnah naturally refused to assist at his own execution. It was not, he said, what he wanted. He instead asked to see Congress's proposals for partitioning the Punjab and Bengal so that he could prepare his counter proposals. This was just a way of guarding his flanks. Jinnah could not afford to be directly associated with any scheme involving the partition of the two key provinces of Pakistan. Not only did he decide not to call his Working Committee but uncharacteristically asked the Viceroy not to spell out the procedure to be adopted in determining the will of the provinces.[25] But by now Jinnah was fighting a losing battle. When Mountbatten commented that the Quaid-i-Azam was in danger of throwing away the 'substance for the shadow', getting 'an almost unworkable truncated Pakistan which would still be obliged to share a common organisation at the Centre to arrange over-all defence',[26] we have the first hint that Mountbatten consistently failed to understand the inwardness of Jinnah's true aims, mistaking Jinnah's shadow for the substance of his demand.

Mountbatten was now convinced that if Jinnah could not be forced to accept the Cabinet Mission's proposals, and Congress could not be persuaded to meet Jinnah half-way on grouping, then a partition of Bengal and Punjab would be unavoidable. To bring the difficult contenders from 'present emotionalism to stark realism', Mountbatten set

[23] Jinnah threatened to demand a partition of Assam if Congress insisted on the partition of the Punjab and Bengal. Mountbatten gave his threat short shrift, simply saying that the League's claims on Assam would be considered on the same merits as Congress's claims on parts of the Punjab and Bengal. (See record of Mountbatten's interview with Jinnah, 10 April 1947, ibid., 186–7.)

[24] This was a line which fitted in well with the interests of his constituents in the Muslim provinces, but his weakness relative to them had made him nervous of pushing it.

[25] Record of Mountbatten's interview with Jinnah, 10 April 1947, ibid., 186–7.

[26] Ibid., 188.

out the alternatives in deliberately hard terms. On the one side, 'Plan Balkan' – a transfer in which it was left to the provinces severally to decide their future, a prospect that Mountbatten hoped would be as little pleasing to Congress (with its threat of balkanisation) as to Jinnah, who would at best end up with a divided Punjab and Bengal – a truncated Pakistan. Faced by this grave threat to its all-India centre, Congress might be cajoled into agreeing to 'Plan Union', and give the League parity inside the interim government, but only if Jinnah came in himself, and assurances on grouping which might bring the League into the constituent assembly. As for Jinnah, faced with the stark alternatives of keeping the Muslim provinces undivided, achieving the substance of autonomy for the Muslim areas, and a large say at an union centre and, on the other hand, at best a truncated Pakistan with some central organisation for defence to begin with, he might agree to the former, and settle for the Mission's proposals without further cavil or delay.[27] Indeed until 14 April Mountbatten hoped he might bring the two sides to an agreement on some such basis by convening another conference of cooler heads. If agreement on the basis of the Mission's plan was impossible then the partition machinery would have to be set into action along the lines of 'Plan Balkan'.[28] Here was a plan which was to be implemented by a centre calling for its own dissolution. It beggars belief that the Viceroy could ever have been serious about its practicality. By apparently threatening to balkanise India, Mountbatten hoped to exercise the Congress's mind in a way which might induce it to produce a formula to keep India inside the Commonwealth. Such a formula would greatly ease Mountbatten's difficulties, especially with regard to providing for an over-all defence authority after a transfer of power.[29] But until Congress produced such a formula, Mountbatten was ready to go ahead with 'Plan

[27] Viceroy's fourteenth staff meeting, 12 April 1947, ibid., 207–9 and Viceroy's conference paper, V.C.P. 28, 14 April 1947, ibid., 228–31.   [28] Ibid.
[29] There were indications that Congress was 'groping for a formula' which might keep India inside the Commonwealth. (See Mountbatten's interview with Nehru, 24 March 1947, ibid., 13.) Mountbatten considered the future of the Indian army to be his 'biggest bargaining point' with the Congress since whichever authority 'controlled an unified Army, or the most efficient divided Army, controlled India'. (Minutes of the Viceroy's fourth staff meeting, 28 March 1947, ibid., 35.) In his first interview with the Viceroy, Nehru was 'frankly astounded' to learn that the British intended to withdraw all their officers in the army and the civil service regardless of how far the nationalisation process had progressed. As far as Nehru was concerned the new government of India would want to retain the services of the British officers for some time after power was transferred. (Mountbatten to Pethick-Lawrence, 25 March 1947, ibid., 19.) Patel wanted the Secretary of State's control over the Indian services to be transferred to the government of India. But Mountbatten had rejected this point blank since a formula to keep India within the Commonwealth had to be first worked out, and 'one of the main

Balkan'. It at least had the merit of showing up the full extent of Jinnah's weaknesses. If only Jinnah could be made to realise that what he was getting was a snare and a delusion, the vision of an united India might never have to be broken.

Yet there was very little Jinnah could do. The fundamental contradiction in his strategy was playing back with a vengeance on his calculations at the centre. He needed a settlement at the centre on the basis of a 'Pakistan' consisting of undivided Punjab and Bengal. Instead the Viceroy was giving the provinces the right to decide their own future, and the procedure to determine the will of the Punjab and Bengal virtually ensured their division. The 'two-nation' theory with which Jinnah had hoped to get the League a share of power at the centre was the sword which was now cutting his Pakistan down to size. A provincial agreement in the Punjab and Bengal to keep these provinces undivided was the only way Jinnah might have rescued his strategy. But seven years of strident propaganda for 'Pakistan' and real economic grievances which were increasingly defined in communal terms had made supra-communal agreements practically impossible. The prospect of H.M.G. devolving power to provincial governments had intensified struggles between the communities since their outcome would now determine not simply control over provincial ministries but security of life and property and the entire political future of the small units that made up the complex structures of these provinces. Lulled by the false security of an undefined demand for 'Pakistan', Jinnah's followers in the Punjab and Bengal simply expected to take their undivided provinces out of the Indian union. Once this had been conceded they were prepared to mend fences with the other communities. The supreme paradox of the situation was that Jinnah was in no position to advise his followers to face reality and make concessions to the other communities until his demands had been met at the centre, and yet these demands could not be conceded unless the Punjabi and Bengali Leaguers could somehow produce a formula to keep their provinces undivided. A leader whose claims were based on such shaky foundations could not be allowed to dictate the terms of a final settlement.

This at least was what Mountbatten had concluded. Instead of holding a conference of Indian political leaders he now decided to convene one with his Governors at Delhi. The main purpose of the conference was to sound off his thinking and to prepare the ground for the new line rather than to listen to the advice of the old India hands. A partition of the

bargaining points with Pandit Nehru would be that India could not do without all the British personnel'. (See minutes of the Viceroy's second staff meeting, 26 March 1947, ibid., 24.)

Punjab, according to its Governor, would mean an 'immediate blow up'. The three communities would never take partition lying down; partition would mean a huge military problem and to 'enforce [Punjab's] partition' would require at least four operational divisions and a separate army headquarters.[30] As for Bengal, its partition would reduce eastern Bengal to a 'rural slum'. But Mountbatten was delighted to learn from the Governor that Suhrawardy was against any 'link up with the North-West Muslim Provinces' and might ditch Jinnah's lead at the centre.[31] That he was so little impressed by the opinion of the Governors of the Punjab and Bengal about the horrific consequences of partitioning their provinces (which 'Plan Balkan' was likely to entail) shows that 'Plan Balkan' and the spectre of a truncated Pakistan were in any event at this stage seen by Mountbatten as a way to ram home to Jinnah and his followers the folly of their demands: 'Anything that resulted in "torpedoing" Pakistan was of advantage in that it led the way back to a more common-sense solution'.[32] Warned that the N.W.F.P. might 'drop to bits', that dire prospect was seen by Mountbatten as a splendid opportunity to persuade the League to give up this problem region. It cost the centre two and a half crores of rupees to keep the tribes at bay, and one crore to sustain the province economically (and there were already demands for more). According to the Governor, no 'real Pakistan partition scheme' could ensure the economic future of the province. What the Governor wanted was elections in the province to clear the air and bring the two parties closer to reality. Significantly, he was prepared to 'risk any disturbances the elections themselves might bring [rather] than a continuation of the large emotional processions which were taking place . . . organized by the Muslim League in an effort to overthrow the Government'. But there was no evidence of a real League organisation in the province, and whatever the sentiments in its favour there was no certainty that the League would sweep the elections. Mountbatten, however, was not ready to call elections. Congress was vehemently opposed to such a move; it might be construed as surrendering to the League's pressures; there was no question of breaking with the Congress on the Frontier; it would 'fog the main issue' and would inevitably 'incur the annoyance of Congress'.[33]

If Mountbatten's aim was to cut Jinnah down to size, things as usual seemed to be going his way. Not only would the Punjab have to be partitioned, and Bengal too, if it did not go its independent way, but the

---

[30] Jenkins's meeting with Ismay, Mieville, Weightman and Abell, 14 April 1947, ibid., 231–3.
[31] Minutes of the first day of the Governors' conference, 15 April 1947, ibid., 254.
[32] Ibid.   [33] Ibid., 252–3.

N.W.F.P. would either remain in the Congress pocket, or be a poisoned and expensive gift which even the League might be reluctant to receive.[34] The separate state of Muslim dreams would end up by consisting simply of the mutilated rump of western Punjab and Sind. The Governor of Sind thought that even if this 'Pakistan' – hanged, drawn and quartered – had to be conceded, 'nobody could really say that this Pakistan was seriously destroying the unity of India'. The combined population of the two areas would be about fifteen million, less than four per cent of the total population of India, and such a 'Pakistan' might simply be regarded as just a large Indian State opting out of the Indian constituent assembly.[35] With an engaging if somewhat jejune enthusiasm, Mountbatten thought that he had hit upon the solution to all his problems:

This opens a new vista, since now we could go ahead giving Mr Jinnah his truncated Pakistan, whilst keeping a strong Centre for the rest of India at Delhi; all this on the assumption that the N.W.F.P. retains a Congress Government and that the Muslim League will not want the expense of trying to run a Province which needs $3\frac{1}{2}$ crores spent on it over and above its income (mostly for the tribes) and that Suhrawardy will not agree to the partition of Bengal and will throw in his lot with Congress.[36]

Naturally Jinnah would have none of this – he impassively handed back the package to the Viceroy: 'This is your scheme not mine.'[37]

With the myriad problems of Indian union and of Pakistan settled (just for the time being) in this summary manner, Mountbatten was able to turn his attention to other problems. With this load off his mind, now the most 'urgent question' was 'how to grant some form of Dominion status during 1947 if the Cabinet Mission Plan was not accepted, and it was decided that there would have to be some form of Pakistan'.[38] Jinnah had already indicated that Pakistan would want to remain inside the Commonwealth. Since Congress had still not made a similar offer this was an embarrassment to Mountbatten who told Jinnah that he could not 'possibly recommend to His Majesty's Government that they should take on such a severe liability as the moth-eaten Pakistan was bound to be'.[39] Of course Mountbatten would have been delighted if both sides had come forward with the suggestion; that would have achieved a main

---

[34] But Liaquat Ali Khan indicated that the League would rather receive this gift than face Hindustan's army on two fronts. (See minutes of the Viceroy's fifth miscellaneous meeting, 21 April 1947, ibid., 356.)

[35] Mountbatten's interview with Sir Francis Mudie, 15 April 1947, ibid., 259–60.

[36] Ibid., 260.

[37] Viceroy's Report no. 3, 17 April 1947, L/PO/433, I.O.L. and *T.P.*, x, 299.

[38] Viceroy's seventeenth staff meeting, 19 April 1947, ibid., 330.

[39] Viceroy's Report no. 3, 17 April 1947, L/PO/433, I.O.L.

objective of London's instructions to him. Not only could Mountbatten see a way of bringing Hindustan and Pakistan into the Commonwealth (and being yet again the saviour of British interests east of Suez); but once they agreed to enter this club of reason and goodwill it was on the cards that both would quickly learn the error of their separatist ways, and 'given a year's education and experience' in the hard school of independence to discover what 'partition involved', they might gain 'a different outlook' and come together in the best of all possible worlds,[40] the world that Mountbatten had created. Liaquat Ali Khan had already confessed that having had a 'fore-taste of civil war' everyone wanted an acceptable solution, and that the Viceroy would be able to 'bring considerable pressure on every group' by producing 'a plan which will get them out of their present impasse'.[41] Liaquat 'jumped' at the suggestion when Mountbatten proposed to modify the Mission's plan to allow for a central defence authority which would be supported by taxing the various groups according to their populations and the size of the armies they required. The 'goal to aim at', Liaquat thought, was an overall plan allowing all the parts of India, including the Indian States, to remain within the Commonwealth for a period of five years. It is a measure of Liaquat's desperation that he was prepared to give his 'complete support', to 'put aside all other work' and to place himself entirely at the disposal of Mountbatten's staff to work out an alternative to the partition scheme.[42] Jinnah's 'most distressed state of mind' was a good augury;[43] once the 'full horrors of working out Pakistan'[44] began to

[40] Viceroy's eighteenth staff meeting, 19 April 1947, *T.P.*, x, 348–9.

[41] According to Liaquat Ali Khan the League had a 'phobia' against the word 'Cabinet Mission'; if the same plan was put forward under a different name, 'psychologically he was sure that on both sides it would stand an incomparably better chance of being accepted than anything with the name "Cabinet Mission" attached to it'. (Mountbatten's interview with Liaquat Ali Khan, 19? April 1947, ibid., 331–3.) But Liaquat was perhaps being overly optimistic. More than psychological barriers, there were some practical considerations against the Cabinet Mission's plan. The proceedings of the constituent assembly had shown the League's provincial and business supporters that the Congress could easily deploy its numerical strength to frame a constitution providing for a strong central government. Without parity for the League in the central government constitutional safeguards were simply promises on paper. There would be nothing to prevent the centre from interfering in the Muslim provinces; the Congress might use the Indian army to discipline the Muslim provinces, and, worse still, squeeze their domestic economies to raise finances to run the centre. The first report of the Union Powers Committee proved all these fears. The proposal that customs would be in the hands of the Union centre, since it involved dealings with other countries, was evidence that the Muslim provinces would have to pay a high price for a centre which they did not want.   [42] Ibid.

[43] Viceroy's eighteenth staff meeting, 21 April 1947, ibid., 348–9.

[44] Viceroy's seventeenth staff meeting, 19 April 1947, ibid., 330.

sink in, Jinnah would be 'seriously troubled by the prospect opening out before him' and 'there would be a psychological moment at which to take advantage of it'.[45] This, the Viceroy now believed, was the way to play the game – Jinnah, whom he in any case regarded as a 'psychopathic case',[46] and the League would be subjected to a ruthless 'squeeze' and more sensible men, such as Liaquat Ali Khan (the model of sweet reasonableness), would join their new Quaid enthroned in Viceregal Lodge to find 'a more reasonable solution than this mad Pakistan'.[47]

Jinnah's sanity and steadfastness of purpose were demonstrated yet again by his cool reactions to this heavy fire. Pressing almost the last lever he possessed, he now proposed that since it was impossible actually to divide the army by June 1948, the British should make it clear immediately that the army would be divided; settle the basis for that division, and perhaps leave its implementation until later. This cold douche of realism, and the unavoidable prospect of losing much of the army if they did not come to terms, might persuade the Congress leaders to shift from their uncompromising stance. His hope was that in this way 'all intercommunal feeling would subside and Hindustan and Pakistan would be able to come together and work out the details'. Jinnah deliberately left it a tantalisingly open question whether the army would actually need to be divided at the end of the day: the implication was that if the terms were right, India's army might always march shoulder to shoulder, to discipline the common enemies of the Congress and the League beyond the subcontinent's borders.[48] The Commander-in-Chief had already argued that the Indian army could not be split into two self-sustaining armed forces. Pakistan would be responsible for all the important land frontiers of the subcontinent and so would require an army and an air force which 'would be virtually the same as those now required to defend India as a whole'. But if Pakistan and Hindustan were to have separate defence forces: 'it would seem certain that the combined total of these forces must be greater than that of the Defence Forces designed to serve a United India, since the administrative overheads must be duplicated and there would be a great loss of flexibility'.[49] Learning how to exploit the axioms of the military mind, Jinnah expressed his 'opinion' that Pakistan and Hindustan would have to make a deal since 'Pakistan and Hindustan,

45 Viceroy's eighteenth staff meeting, 21 April 1947, ibid., 349.
46 Viceroy's report no. 3, 17 April 1947, L/PO/433, I.O.L. For Mountbatten's other compliments to Jinnah, including 'lunatic', 'evil genius', 'clot', 'bastard', to name but a few, see Collins and Lapierre, *Mountbatten and the Partition of India*, pp. 40–4.
47 Mountbatten's interview with Liaquat Ali Khan, 19? April 1947, *T.P.*, x, 331–3.
48 See minutes of the Viceroy's seventh miscellaneous meeting, 23 April 1947, ibid., 381.
49 See remarks by the Commander-in-Chief, paper 3 (extract) to document 215, ibid., 423.

though they might eventually come together – and he hoped and believed that they would – would not be able to stand alone against a powerful aggressor.'[50]

Here was the narrow and stony path by which Jinnah hoped to arrive at the ultimate goal of parity in all-India arrangements by achieving parity over external defence. After all, however moth-eaten and truncated the Pakistan on offer, any division of the army on communal lines would leave Hindustan with an army of its own which was equally moth-eaten and truncated, since it would be stripped of the Muslim regiments from the Punjab that had been its mainstay for the past ninety years. Mountbatten came impressively close to getting the point (although it eluded him in the end) when he reported that this search for parity had put Jinnah into the 'ridiculous situation' in which he looked as if he might end up not only with a horribly mutilated 'Pakistan' but also still have to accept common arrangements with Hindustan at the centre. If Mountbatten had stated that Jinnah's entire strategy was aimed at securing such common arrangements, and that Jinnah was prepared to go to almost any length to achieve them, he would have been nearer the mark. As the Viceroy himself explained, 'The real difference of course lies in the fact that in the former case [i.e. a truncated but sovereign Pakistan] there would be parity at the Centre and the League could not be outvoted. But it shows what value the League sets on parity, since to obtain it they are prepared to sacrifice the richest plums of Pakistan'.[51]

But the Congress, seeing the entire cake within its grasp, was not ready to rest content with the richest plums. As Patel laid down in a few choice words: Congress had 'reached the maximum limit of their concessions'. It would not give the League parity in the interim government, even if this brought Jinnah in. If the League was not ready to accept the Mission's proposals without further ado (and without safeguards) then, quite simply, the 'Congress desired partition'.[52] Nehru, echoing his master's voice, put it more elegantly: 'Our aim is to liberate as much of India as we can, and then to deal with the question of independence for the rest. India's march towards freedom would brook no more obstruction.'[53] That this was a scarcely veiled threat to separatists, whether

[50] Minutes of the Viceroy's seventh miscellaneous meeting, 23 April 1947, ibid., 381.
[51] Viceroy's Report no. 4, 24 April 1947, ibid., 407.
[52] Mountbatten's interview with Patel, eighth miscellaneous meeting, 25 April 1947, ibid., 424–6.
[53] The Congress High Command's position, as Nehru stated once again was: 'The Punjab and Bengal will be partitioned; I am making this statement with all the responsibility I possess.' (Ibid., 337, fn. 2.)

provincial, Muslims or princes,[54] was underlined by the first report of the Union Powers Committee of the constituent assembly. The report, presented to the constituent assembly on 28 April, slammed the door shut on Jinnah and the League once and for all. By widely interpreting the three common subjects, the report effectively converted the Union centre into something very different from what the Mission had intended. 'Defence' was to include nearly all the basic industries and the Union government was to have special powers to take charge of provincial affairs in matters of 'emergency', which of course was itself subject to wide interpretations. 'Foreign Affairs' included: implementing the decisions of international conferences and treaties or agreements made with other countries; naturalisation and aliens; trade and commerce with foreign countries; import and export across customs frontiers as defined by the Union government, and, most important of all, foreign loans. 'Communications' were broadly defined as involving the control and regulation of airways, certain highways and waterways, posts and telegraphs, all telephones and broadcasting, maritime shipping, major ports, Union railways and even some minor railways.[55] Contrary to the League's insistence that the Union centre should be financed by contributions from the groups, the report specified fourteen areas where the Union centre could expect to raise revenues. These included customs and excise duties, taxes on income other than agricultural income and, except in the case of agricultural land, taxes on capital and succession and estate duties; the Union also had powers over the Reserve Bank, Public Debt, currency, coinage, legal tender, the Union judiciary, and could deal with serious economic emergencies in any part of the Union. Amongst those subjects which were to be placed under the Union's jurisdiction *by agreement* were: insurance, banking, company laws, negotiable instruments, patents, trade marks and designs, copyright, planning, ancient and historical monuments, standard weights and measures.[56] In short, the Union government was to be equipped with all the powers exercised by the existing centre, far and beyond what the Mission had considered necessary to secure an agreed constitution for the whole of India. The list of fundamental rights gave every citizen the right to move freely anywhere in the Union, to settle in any part, purchase property and to engage in any occupation. Special provision was also

[54] Nehru warned that Indian States which failed to join the constituent assembly by June 1948, would be 'regarded as hostile' to the Indian union. (Nehru's address to the All-India States' People's Conference, 18 April 1947, ibid.)

[55] See first report of the Union Powers Committee, April 1947, in B. Shiva Rao (ed.), *The Framing of India's Constitution: Select Documents*, vol. II, (New Delhi, 1967), pp. 743–7.

[56] Ibid., p. 747.

made for trade and commerce between the constituent units of the All-India Union. If these provisions were adopted the Muslim areas could not impose restrictions on the activities of Hindu businessmen and moneylenders, as they were bound to want to do. Moreover, the Punjab Alienation Act, which was designed to protect agricultural land from passing into the hands of non-agriculturists and moneylenders would have to be scrapped. Clearly then, the authors of these reports had abandoned the façade of framing a constitution with the League's co-operation. Nehru had already told the Viceroy categorically that there was no question of the High Command accepting a centre where Congress would share power with the League on the basis of equality between the two. If the only all-India arrangements that the League would make were between two sovereign states, then Congress was not ready to share power at all. After the transitional period, to sort out who was to have what, the League and its independent Pakistan would have to go its own separate way; Congress would not tolerate any deal by which it joined the League and Pakistan at an all-India level.[57] In this way the Congress High Command explicitly denied Jinnah's ultimate hopes; this was the decisive reversal, not Mountbatten's froth and fury.

On May Day 1947 the Viceroy himself admitted that Jinnah had a point: 'Mr Jinnah might be right in . . . [his] belief' that Congress had no intention of working the Mission's plan 'fairly'; 'Mr Jinnah's fears had some foundation.' Given this portentous realisation, Mountbatten was ready to admit that the Mission's plan was 'dead'.[58] The Mission's proposals, at least in the form that Jinnah was prepared to accept, gave the League the prospect of a real say at the centre. But as Patel told the Viceroy in blunt terms 'if you raise this question of parity you will incur the everlasting enmity of Congress; that is the one thing we have been fighting against and will never agree to'.[59] Parroting the new tune, Mountbatten concluded that 'anything but a clean partition would produce enmity on the part of Congress'. In the end game, Congress not the Viceroy was calling the shots. As Mountbatten (in a rare moment of candour) admitted, if he 'fell foul of Congress it would be impossible to continue to run the country'.[60] It was Congress that insisted on partition. It was Jinnah who was against partition.

[57] See Viceroy's sixth miscellaneous meeting, 22 April 1947, *T.P.*, x, 364.
[58] Minutes of the Viceroy's ninth miscellaneous meeting, 1 May 1947, ibid., 507–8. A special committee chaired by Mountbatten had already been formed on 24 April to produce a partition plan. It consisted of Lord Ismay (the Viceroy's chief of staff), George Abell, (the Viceroy's private secretary) and Sir Eric Mieville (the Viceroy's principal secretary).   [59] Viceroy's Report no. 5, 1 May 1947, ibid., 540.
[60] Viceroy's ninth miscellaneous meeting, 1 May 1947, ibid., 511.

The two main casualties of this development were, first and foremost Jinnah and his hopes of bringing all Muslims inside an Indian union where they would have their place led by a man and a party capable of disciplining their particularism and curbing Congress's overweening policies, which had spurned Jinnah's offers of help in the common cause of winning freedom for India. The other casualty, at quite the other end of the spectrum, was the provincialism of the Punjab and Bengal, whose Muslim leaders had hoped by using Jinnah and the League to afforce their provincial autonomy, but an autonomy where the exclusive beneficiaries would be the Muslims. By grasping too greedily at their provincial fruits, by pursuing monopolies rather than being content with dominant shares, by demanding too high an insurance at the centre for their possessions in the provinces, the inept, the short-sighted and above all the faction-ridden and divided Muslim politicians of the Punjab and Bengal lost the chance of keeping their domains undivided. Unlike the politicians there were some Muslims in the Punjab who could see that the Cabinet Mission's scheme was the only way to prevent an amputation of the province. The 'Pakistan' demand 'had its value as a bluff' and a 'remarkably successful' one since: 'The most important part of the [Cabinet Mission] Scheme is complete provincial autonomy, and this is, for all practical purposes, real Pakistan. One wonders what more the Pakistan of our Leaders' conception can give us.' The leaders had 'shown great political sagacity' when they accepted the Mission's scheme and it remained a 'mystery why they subsequently rejected it, for they have not yet taken us common people into their confidence on that score'. To return to the demand for Pakistan was now bound to have 'serious consequences', namely the partition of the Punjab and a civil war which 'in the absence of regular trained and disciplined armies, only means the war of the assassin'. The non-Muslims were 'not likely to withdraw their demand because they do not lose by partition as much as we do', and 'every Muslim in the Punjab realises that [a] partition of the province will be a major disaster for the community'.[61] But as Sir Evan Jenkins reported from the Punjab, the fiddling of the local Leaguers made Nero's musical endeavours in Rome seem statesmanlike by comparison. At this critical moment in their history, the Punjabi Leaguers remained hell-bent on grabbing office. Following the communal carnage in various parts of the province, organised less by the Muslim League than by the para-military wing, the Muslim National Guard – a hurried conglomeration of demobbed soldiers under the leadership of Shaukat Hayat – the

---

[61] 'An appeal to sanity and reason: Submitted for the dispassionate and serious consideration of the Punjab Muslims', QAP/8/File no. 917, pp. 327–32.

leaders were more concerned with protecting their own political futures than that of the province or even the people they purported to lead. By forming a ministry the Punjab Leaguers hoped to dish out patronage to their followers and so delay, if not avoid, a split in their rank and file. Once in power the Leaguers could stop all proceedings against their followers who had been charged for their hand in the horrific bloodbaths, particularly in the Rawalpindi division. According to the Governor, Mumtaz Daultana had on 'credible evidence' told the people in Attock district that 'if they could stick it out for a fortnight or three weeks, all proceedings against them would be withdrawn, and the officials who have suppressed the disturbances would be given a hot time'.[62] It is a true measure of Jinnah's complete lack of authority over the Punjab League that he had to go along with this utterly impractical demand for a League ministry. He did not deny Mountbatten's view that it would be 'criminal folly' to ask for a League ministry at this juncture when the Punjab was about to be sliced into two, and confessed that he was under a great deal of pressure to make this demand; he told the Viceroy: 'I entirely see your point and I respect your sincerity, though I do not agree with your decision.'[63] With the great commander unable to either direct or command it is hardly surprising that the Punjabi Leaguers were amazingly 'complacent', and had made 'no real attempt to approach the Hindus or Sikhs'. Their attitude had a certain disarming simplicity, namely that Muslims were 'entitled to rule the whole of the Punjab'; in a mirror image of the Congress line at the centre, they argued that 'when this is admitted they will be good enough to treat the non-Muslims with generosity'. The Sikhs, never a community to wait upon Muslim favour with non-violent patience, reacted in the predictable way; they were preparing for an armed offensive and had 'committed themselves so deeply to the partition of the Punjab', that it was 'difficult, and perhaps impossible for them to take a different line'. There was no prospect, Jenkins ruefully commented, of an agreed partition or an agreement to avoid it by these embattled communities. Yet 'no leader . . . [had] considered the implications and difficulties of partition'.[64]

In Bengal, Suhrawardy had long seen the implications of partition. Unlike the Leaguers in the Punjab, he was ready, indeed keen, to form a coalition ministry, since he could see that the best insurance for the dominance of some Muslims over an undivided Bengal was to bring the Congress into a junior partnership in the firm that planned to rule Bengal. But the Congress High Command put paid to this plan by

---

[62] See Jenkins to Mountbatten, 30 April 1947, *T.P.*, x, 506.
[63] Mountbatten's interview with Jinnah, 26 April 1947, ibid., 452.
[64] Jenkins to Mountbatten, 30 April 1947, ibid., 506.

endorsing the Hindu Mahasabha's demand for partition.[65] This meant that Suhrawardy's only hope was to cut loose from the centre, by asking for an united and independent Bengal. Paradoxically he had a greater chance of getting Jinnah's endorsement for this scheme than of getting it ratified by the Congress High Command. An undivided Bengal was vital for Jinnah's strategy. On 26 April 1947, Jinnah told Mountbatten that he would be 'delighted' if Bengal could remain united even if this meant it would have to stay out of Pakistan. After all, 'What is the use of Bengal without Calcutta; they had better remain united and independent; I am sure that they would be on friendly terms with us.'[66] With Jinnah's blessing, Suhrawardy now thought he had a real chance to save the unity of Bengal. But he wanted 'as long as possible to convert Bengal to the idea of being united and independent'; he asked the Viceroy to postpone a decision on partition until November 1947.[67] This was clearly out of the question, so Suhrawardy had to make the best of the limited time available.[68] There were innumerable stumbling-blocks in his way. Some Bengali Leaguers planned to use 'Pakistan' to exercise unfettered Muslim dominance over the whole province, while others preferred to see the partition of the province than share power with Hindus. This

---

[65] Interestingly, the Congress High Command's stand was strongly opposed by Sarat Bose who maintained that: 'By accepting religion as the sole basis of the distribution of provinces, the Congress has cut itself away from its natural moorings and has almost undone the work it has been doing for the last 60 years. The resolution [of 8 March 1947] is the result of a defeatist mentality [and] is no solution of the communal problem.' (*The Indian Annual Register*, 1946, vol. I, 'Chronicle of events', 15 March 1947, cited in Leonard A. Gordon, 'Brothers Against the Raj', *The Oracle*, Calcutta, July 1979, p. 43.) So there were at least some Bengali Hindus who could still see attractions in keeping their province united. But unity amongst Bengal's communities was hard enough to achieve, let alone unity between Bengal's communities.

[66] See Mountbatten's interview with Jinnah, 26 April 1947, *T.P.*, x, 452.

[67] Record of interview between Mountbatten and Suhrawardy, 26 April 1947, ibid., 448–9.

[68] Only Sarat Bose and Kiran Shankar Roy (Leader of the Opposition in the Bengal assembly) actually responded to Suhrawardy's offer to negotiate. Sarat Bose believed that if the Pakistan issue could be eliminated from eastern India it might be possible to 'bring Bengal gradually into India'. (Cited in Gordon, 'Brothers against the Raj', *The Oracle*, July 1979, p. 43.) On 28 April, talks between the unificationists began in earnest. After a preliminary round of talks between Suhrawardy, Abul Hashim and Sarat Bose, the Bengal League set up a sub-committee of six to negotiate with the Hindu leaders for a framework for Bengal's future constitution. But the League's sub-committee was divided. Four out of the six members of the committee were opposed to an independent Bengal outside the pale of north-western Pakistan, although they still claimed to be implacably opposed to the partition of Bengal. Not surprisingly, few Hindu leaders in Bengal were prepared to negotiate with Suhrawardy when his own rank and file was so divided.

forced Jinnah to maintain a calculated silence on Suhrawardy's efforts. The president of the Bengal League, Maulana Akram Khan, publicly rejected any notion of a Bengali nation in which Muslims and Hindus would share power equally. Bengali Muslims, he claimed, had been fighting for the creation of a 'sovereign Muslim State in Bengal', and such a state would be an integral part of a larger 'Pakistan'.[69] Some eastern Bengali Muslims (including two of Suhrawardy's ministers) wanted a separate eastern Bengal state. They argued that the loss of Calcutta would be 'good riddance' since it was 'a white elephant which produced no food but consumed huge amounts of food grains and that East Bengal would be happy without Calcutta'. Others thought they might do better in a separate Muslim state in eastern Bengal. The speaker of the Bengal assembly, Noorul Amin, was confident that he could become the chief minister of east Bengal and so wanted partition; Hamidul Haque Choudhury, a member of the Bengal League's Working Committee, was for partition simply because Amin had promised him a place in his cabinet. Akram Khan still wanted to retain Calcutta but was prepared to abandon the Burdwan division, perhaps as a way of ridding the League of the Abul Hashim plague. Nazimuddin as ever was simply confused; he sometimes supported Suhrawardy and at others the so-called 'division-ists'. But the most striking commentary on the extent of these divisions inside the Bengal League was provided by the members of the Calcutta League who told Jinnah:

we do not so much fear the Hindus. We do not fear the British. But we most certainly fear treachery, betrayal, sabotage, defeatism and surrender to enemy's machinations in our own ranks in Bengal . . . We apprehend that a certain section of leaders of East Bengal have not only failed in mobilising forces to counter and resist the Hindu move for partition of Bengal and the Hindu occupation of Calcutta, rather they are really happy supporting the Hindu move covertly and indirectly. They are happy to see this partition.[70]

So although the chances of Bengal remaining united and independent were remote, the Governor succeeded in getting the partition plan amended to allow the provincial assembly to vote for independence before voting for partition. This was just a way of giving Suhrawardy more time. If partition was unavoidable then the Governor wanted Calcutta to be declared a 'free city' since without Calcutta eastern Bengal would be a dismal economic proposition. But there was the danger of setting a precedent for the Sikhs in the Punjab who might demand a

---

[69] Cited in Sen, *Muslim Politics in Bengal*, pp. 234 and 235, fn. 108.
[70] Memorandum of the Calcutta District Muslim League to Jinnah, 31 May 1947, QAP/F/10.

similar status for Lahore, and the Governor had to concede that Mountbatten 'could not jeopardise the safety of all India for the sake of one Province'.[71]

This was the principle Mountbatten had to follow if he was to get an agreed settlement at the all-India level. Such a settlement he hoped would give Jinnah no more than western Punjab and Sind, which still had a League ministry. But the League's refusal to give up its claims on the N.W.F.P. was a potential obstacle in the way of Mountbatten's plans. As he admitted after a two-day visit to the Frontier, this was the 'greatest danger spot in India and the bone of contention between Congress and the Muslim League'. It appeared that the Congress ministry had been discredited, and even if Jinnah did not control the situation in the province, there was more support for the League than for the Congress. Within forty-eight hours, he had received 3,129 letters, telegrams and postcards (a remarkable number, given the percentage of illiterate Pathans) expressing support for the League and no-confidence in the Congress ministry. When he asked a deputation of local League leaders whether they had 'anything to do with Jinnah', the astounded reply was: 'Of course he is our leader.'[72] Jinnah could hardly abandon such loyal followers. After his visit Mountbatten decided it would be a 'good thing' if Congress, which had obviously lost support among the Pathans, did not contest the elections. Alternatively, a referendum or a plebiscite would have to decide the issue.[73]

Mountbatten now decided to send Abell and Ismay to London with a draft plan which not only ignored Jinnah and the leaders of the provinces that were to be partitioned but also his own Governors who saw, in the last days of the Raj, that they might govern in name but that others ruled in fact. But whoever ruled the Muslim provinces, it was not Jinnah. Always a bystander in the affairs of the Muslim provinces, Jinnah was still standing in the wings while their future was being charted out in Delhi and London. The partition plan would lead, as Jinnah predicted, 'to terrible consequences – to confusion – to bloodshed'. He publicly

---

[71] The Governor of Bengal wanted Calcutta to be placed under the joint administration of five Muslims and five Hindus elected from the two parts of the province. (See minutes of the Viceroy's ninth miscellaneous meeting, 1 May 1947, *T.P.*, x, 510–11.)

[72] Viceroy's Report no. 5, 1 May 1947, ibid., 534–6.

[73] Viceroy's Report, no. 5, 1 May 1947, ibid., 535–6. Nehru had already rejected the idea of holding elections in the Frontier. This might, he claimed, be interpreted as a sign of weakness and an endorsement of the League's use of violence to achieve political ends. (See Nehru to Mountbatten, 17 April 1947, ibid., 304–7). The Congress now alleged that the Governor, Sir Olaf Caroe, was behind the movement to remove Dr Khan Sahib's ministry, and should either be dismissed or at best be forced to resign. (See Viceroy's report, no. 5, 1 May 1947, ibid., 534.)

rejected the proposed partition of the Punjab and Bengal and called for a transfer of power to the provinces as they were then constituted. It was a 'mistake', he argued, 'to compare the basic principle of the demand for Pakistan for cutting up the provinces throughout India into fragmentation', and urged the Viceroy and H.M.G. not to fall into the 'trap' set up by the Congress and 'commit a grave error'.[74] Mountbatten was not sure whether Jinnah's 'unreasonable attitude is due to fear of his own followers or merely his maddening methods of bargaining'.[75] Even Gandhi, whom Jinnah might have expected to fight to the last ditch against partition had, according to Nehru, given his approval of 'the principle of partition' provided it involved 'the partition of Bengal and Punjab'.[76] Once the Congress Working Committee had 'virtually accepted the outline of the plan',[77] the Viceroy saw that Jinnah was powerless to prevent partition.

Of course it was not all cut and dried by 2 May when Ismay and Abell went to London with the draft plan. For one thing, Mountbatten saw that their 'departure was premature' and a 'number of difficulties inherent in the draft plan . . . had arisen'.[78] Jenkins warned against announcing 'a partition of the Punjab which no community accepts'. The partition plan assumed that the all-India parties and the Sikh leaders would at least acquiesce in implementing it. Jinnah's rejection of the partition of the provinces had 'radically changed' the situation in the Punjab. Jenkins now feared that the British would 'be manoeuvred into giving an award' which they would 'be unwilling or unable to enforce'.[79] But Mountbatten thought that the acceptance which mattered was not the Punjabis' but Jinnah's, and he expected that in the end the League could not 'absolutely refuse to acquiesce in the partition of the Punjab'.[80] The partition plan, premature though it was, was intended by Mountbatten to bring the Congress leaders to earth by testing their readiness to carry out their threats. And much as he expected, Congress did amend its position. The first hint of this had already been given by V. P. Menon, Mountbatten's constitutional adviser who, according to the last Viceroy, was 'very much in Patel's pocket' and had virtually become his 'mouthpiece'.[81] Menon's proposal was attractive from Mountbatten's point of

---

[74] See Jinnah's press statement, 1 May 1947, reproduced from *Dawn*, ibid., 543–5.
[75] Viceroy's Report, no. 5, 1 May 1947, ibid., 533.
[76] Nehru to Mountbatten, 1 May 1947, ibid., 517–19.
[77] Minutes of the Viceroy's twenty-sixth staff meeting, 5 May 1947, ibid., 618.
[78] See minutes of the Viceroy's twenty-sixth staff meeting, 5 May 1947, ibid., 617.
[79] See Jenkins to Mountbatten, 3 May 1947, ibid., 593–4.
[80] Minutes of the Viceroy's twenty-sixth staff meeting, 5 May 1947, ibid., 618.
[81] Moon (ed.), *Wavell: The Viceroy's Journal*, pp. 384, 408 and 412.

view in many respects. It proposed to transfer power on the basis of Dominion Status before June 1948. If agreement on the basis of the Mission's plan was found to be impossible, then India would have to be divided. Given the limitations of the timetable the British could at best hope to set up the machinery for partition; they could not be 'responsible for the outcome'. So it was better to transfer power to the two parties as 'constituted authorities'. Since Congress had already accepted Dominion Status for the interim period, this would reduce the pressure on the High Command to demand full independence, and they might conceivably extend this arrangement indefinitely. If, however, full power was not transferred before June 1948, the Congress would have no choice but to demand full independence. Moreover, if partition was conceded, it would become impossible to resist Congress demands to administer their own provinces 'unhampered by an uneasy coalition' with the League at the centre. There were other compelling reasons for transferring power before June 1948. It would certainly be an 'invaluable factor in the long-term view of the Indo-British relationship'. If India was divided it might take as long as five years for both parts to frame their constitutions, hold fresh elections and come to terms about common matters. If power was transferred during the interim period on the basis of Dominion Status, constitution-making would no longer be urgent. Both parties could use the 'time to think things over with leisure and sobriety' and concentrate on 'the urgent problems of administration and development'. And, much as Mountbatten himself hoped, Menon thought that once the two governments started negotiating, they might 'ultimately come right round to the view that an impassable barrier cannot be created between the two Indias and that after all a unified Constitution is better for all concerned'.[82]

It is clear that the Congress leaders were more concerned with an early transfer of power than with constitution-making. In a proposal which was similar in many respects to the Mission's proposals, Nehru suggested a transfer of power by June 1947 to the existing central government, leaving the whole question of Pakistan and the partition of Bengal and Punjab until later when the provinces had decided whether or not to form groups. It would be still open to Muslim regions to leave the Indian union, but this would only be after the constitution had been settled, and only on the condition that the Punjab and Bengal recognised that if they opted out they would be partitioned. The calculation, of course, was that the disciplines of a strong centre which the Congress would create,

---

[82] See note by V. P. Menon, appendix to document no. 222, 25 April 1947, *T.P.*, x, 438–40.

together with the change of heart which a serious consideration of the consequences of partition might bring about, would concentrate the provincial Muslim mind and make them see that they had more to gain by ditching Jinnah and the demand for Pakistan and staying on inside the union. Transferring power in this way made the large assumption that the 'Union of India' already existed and areas that decided to leave would be 'contracting out'.[83] This knocked away the main prop of Jinnah's strategy. To persuade London to fall in with this line, Nehru and Patel were ready to make a large offer. They hinted that the Congress might, after a transfer, be prepared to keep the 'Union' inside the Commonwealth,[84] and even accept Dominion Status until the new constitution had been framed.

Mountbatten swallowed the bait and claimed credit for this turn of events. He cabled Ismay that he had not expected to pull off this coup, 'but the situation has been completely changed by Patel and Nehru coming forward themselves'. Here was 'the greatest opportunity ever offered to the Empire and we must not let administrative or other difficulties stand in the way'. India (or most of it) would come into the Commonwealth, and there was a 'sporting chance' that it would remain there for all time.[85] If India did enter the Commonwealth, Mountbatten could ignore Jinnah's awkward offer, which had been registered before Congress's, of bringing Pakistan into the Commonwealth. As it always tended to be when Mountbatten was in swing, 'speed' was 'the essence of the contract'; otherwise 'we will miss the opportunity'. Dominion Status here and now would achieve a 'terrific world-wide enhancement of British prestige' and it would put the coping-stone on the 'framework of world strategy from the point of view of Empire Defence', as well as conveniently bringing about 'the early termination of present responsibilities, especially in the field of law and order'.[86]

Among the 'administrative [and] other difficulties' that Mountbatten was prepared to brush aside was London's awkward reminder that 'there is at present no Union but only a Constituent Assembly representing in the main the Provinces of Section A'.[87] He also abandoned all pretence of dealing evenly between the Congress and the League. While one side, represented by Nehru, Mountbatten's favourite, was invited to join him in Simla for 'long and satisfactory discussions' about the new plan whose author was Menon, the other, Jinnah, was not even given the slightest

---

[83] See Nehru's plan, 8 May 1947, ibid., 673–4.
[84] Minutes of the Viceroy's twenty-seventh staff meeting, May 1947, ibid., 659.
[85] Mountbatten to Ismay, 8 May 1947, ibid., 699.
[86] Mountbatten to Ismay, no. 54-SC, 11 May 1947, L/PO/427, I.O.L.
[87] Ismay to Mountbatten, 9 May 1947, *T.P.*, x, 722, document 377.

hint of the new scheme since it was thought that he 'might publish a statement which would wreck negotiations'.[88] Negotiations with one only of two contending sides was the novel concept which Mountbatten now introduced into Indian political life. There were other difficulties which Mountbatten was prepared to set aside. An 'Union' as conceived by Congress was to be given Dominion Status in a matter of weeks, forcing the Muslim districts prematurely into a birth which they were unlikely to survive. In a cavalier mood Mountbatten dismissed the vast administrative problems which a transfer on these lines would create for the regions which 'opted out'; in the Viceroy's blunt metaphor, 'Administratively it is the difference between putting up a permanent building, a nissen hut or a tent. As far as Pakistan is concerned we are putting up a tent. We can do no more'.[89] The only alleviation Mountbatten was ready to offer were his services as midwife. It would take perhaps six or eight months for Pakistan, as he conceived it, actually to come into being and in the meantime he was prepared to continue as Governor-General for both the 'Union of India' and Pakistan, at least until Pakistan's constituent assembly met and its executive was in office. All manner of good might flow from his common touch – the division of the army might be prevented; close relations between the siblings would be encouraged by a benign father, who wanted to give one son the key to the house while promising the other a tattered tent in the back and beyond. Indeed partition and Pakistan itself might never see the light of day.

But Mountbatten, in hunting with the hounds, had run ahead of his own hare. The India Committee amended the Viceroy's partition plan out of recognition. Mountbatten wanted Bengal alone to have the right to go its own way. The India Committee felt that consistency demanded that this right be extended to all the provinces: 'there must be a free choice if the scheme is to be consistent and defensible in Parliament'.[90] Even the most pliant metropolis, anxious to fall in line with its proconsul, recognised some limits to the plenipotentiary power run amuck. As far as London could see, the Viceroy's plan was based on the premise that India

---

[88] Menon, Mountbatten's constitutional adviser, had specifically asked the Viceroy not to mention the scheme to Jinnah. While Mountbatten discussed the scheme with Nehru at Simla, Menon was also there. (Minutes of the Viceroy's twenty-ninth staff meeting, 9 May 1947, ibid., p. 704.) Those who have looked at these events from Pakistan's point of view comment on Menon's equivocal role. On the one hand, he was constitutional adviser to the Viceroy, and had the duty to be even-handed in his dealings; on the other, he was known to be Patel's man (as Wavell has recorded) and was invaluable to Mountbatten as a sure way of testing Congress's pulse.

[89] Alan Campbell-Johnson, *Mission with Mountbatten*, 2nd edn., (Connecticut, 1972), p. 87.

[90] Ismay to Mountbatten, 10 May 1947, *T.P.*, x, 748.

would have to be partitioned now that the parties had failed to agree on the Mission's plan for an union of India. Since the Mission's plan had been abandoned it followed that the local option clause in the Cripps offer would become operative. Founding itself on the principle in Cripps's offer, London took the logic of 'Plan Balkan' to its own awkward conclusion. All the provinces, Hindu and Muslim alike, were to have the right to choose whether to enter the existing constituent assembly, or to group up to form a new one, or to stand out on their own.[91] Moreover, London did not accept the Congress line that an 'Union of India' already existed to which power could be transferred without further ado.

It was wholly predictable (and certainly it required no 'absolute hunch'[92] to see what was coming) that the Congress High Command would reject the plan, as amended by London, out of hand. Once again Mountbatten failed to observe protocol or the pretence of impartiality. It had been agreed to show the plan simultaneously to all the main political leaders. But Mountbatten – in an 'act of friendship' – showed Nehru the plan on the condition that he would not discuss it with his Congress colleagues, and kept the plan away from Jinnah. At the same time Mountbatten sent letters to Jinnah, Liaquat, Patel, Nehru and Baldev Singh summoning them for a final round of talks on 17 May in New Delhi.[93] Of course London's version of the plan produced a 'devastating effect' on Nehru, who saw in it the seeds of 'fragmentation and conflict and disorder'. Nehru reminded the Viceroy that Congress had only agreed to allow certain Muslim areas to opt out of the Union:

The Union was still the basic factor. In the new proposals the whole approach has been changed completely and is at total variance with our own approach in the course of recent talks. The proposals start with the rejection of an Indian Union as the successor to power and invite the claims of large numbers of succession States who are permitted to unite if they so wish in two or more States.[94]

H.M.G., Nehru lamented, 'seem to function in an ivory tower of their own isolated from realities in India'; the union of India had to be the fundamental premise of any proposals.[95] Congress clearly would have nothing to do with London's version of 'Plan Balkan'. It pressed for its

[91] See revised draft plan, ibid., 723–8.
[92] Mountbatten to Ismay, 11 May 1947, ibid., 776–7.
[93] Mountbatten to Nehru, 10 May 1947, ibid., 738 (similar letters were sent to the other Indian leaders). The subsequent postponement of the meeting was the only indication Jinnah could have had that something was amiss. Certainly it made him more cautious than ever in his negotiations with the Viceroy.
[94] See note by Nehru, 11 May 1947, ibid., 766–7.
[95] Nehru to Mountbatten, 11 May 1947, ibid., 756.

idea that the 'Union of India' existed and would continue as the basis for independent India to be accepted; and it wanted partition to be post-poned until after independence. Patel was publicly calling for an immediate transfer of power to the interim government on the basis of Dominion Status. In this way 'the central Government would form a strong centre and would have the necessary powers to put down disorder'. Congress and League would settle their differences once the British were out of the way. But the 'Majority would rule.' If the British were not ready to swallow this simple remedy then, Patel declared, 'India must be divided' but this would mean 'dividing Bengal and Punjab'.[96] On the other hand, even before he got wind of London's exact proposals, Jinnah reiterated the League's position, which was dangerously close to what London had recommended to Mountbatten, namely separation first, reunion (or not) afterwards: 'If the British decide that India must be divided and it follows that the armed forces must be divided and power transferred to the divided parts, then the Central Government must be dissolved and all power should be transferred to the two Constituent Assemblies formed and representing Pakistan and Hindustan.'[97] Since he dared not fall out with the Congress, Mountbatten did not show the plan to Jinnah in case he accepted it. So having sounded Congress on the quiet, Mountbatten told London that the plan needed a 'considerable recast both in principle and detail'. This would be done in New Delhi. The Viceroy also decided that the best course was to play the innocent. He wrote disingenuously to Ismay:

I can only hope, though after today I can be sure of nothing, that Congress will accept the plan when thus redrafted. But in case they do not, I feel that I should have a further alternative to threaten them with, in the same way as I have one to threaten Jinnah with [i.e. devolving power to the existing central government and the provincial governments]. Something on the lines of demission of power including Central Subjects to Provinces is in my mind.[98]

In the meantime he proposed to postpone the crucial meeting with Indian leaders (of both sides) until 2 June, and Ismay was to remain in London to 'pilot through my [he could just as well have said Congress's] proposals on Dominion Status'.[99] Understandably, Patel was 'delighted by the turn of events'.[100]

In recasting the plan 'in principle and [in] detail', Mountbatten followed Congress principles to the smallest essential detail. But London

[96] See Patel's statement to the Associated Press of America, 9 May 1947, ibid., 716–17.
[97] Jinnah's statement in New Delhi, 11 May 1947, ibid., 778.
[98] Mountbatten to Ismay, 11 May 1947, ibid., 779–80.
[99] Mountbatten to Ismay, telegram, no. 56-SC, 12 May 1947, L/PO/427, I.O.L.
[100] V. P. Menon, *The Transfer of Power in India* (Princeton, 1957), p. 365.

prevented him from injecting Congress's spirit into the proposed settlement. Already puzzled by the Viceroy's volte-face, London received his 'radical revisions' as 'bombshells'. Patel's demand that the existing interim government should be given a free hand in the provincial field suggested that he was trying to ditch the partition issue. Nehru's reaction to the partition plan and his advocacy of a modified version of the Mission's plan seemed to indicate that Congress was under the mistaken notion that there was 'some alternative plan which would be a substitute for partition'. There could be no question of Dominion Status 'unless the basis of partition both of territory and of the central subjects had been settled'; it would be 'contrary to assurances by H.M.G. and is not I imagine what you contemplate'.[101] Yet this was what Mountbatten was contemplating. He was not prepared to reject the Congress plan for immediate Dominion Status for the 'Union of India' and the creation of Pakistan on the same basis at a later stage. The great advantage of the Congress plan which Mountbatten referred to as 'Plan They' was that it made 'Indians really and blatantly responsible for their own future.'[102] Mountbatten was prepared to take Nehru's view that Indians should take the blame for what they were about to do. Indeed, the Viceroy was even prepared to be naïve when expediency demanded and to accept Nehru's promise of 'all manner of safeguards and assurances' for the Muslim League.[103] Mountbatten was convinced that 'Nehru is most convincingly genuine about these safeguards' and 'honestly says that the Congress leaders would be ready to give far more away to the League if left to themselves than if under British pressure'. All this would of course work only if Jinnah could be made to play. So Mountbatten had still to proceed on the assumption of partition before Dominion Status, namely the revised partition plan which was essentially an alternative Congress plan, rather inappropriately referred to as 'Plan We'.[104]

Recognising that even a Cabinet bending over backwards to give him his way could not bend as far as the grant here and now of Dominion Status, Mountbatten decided to keep that issue back until his other

---

[101] Ismay to Mountbatten, telegram, no. 6142, 12 May 1947, L/PO/427, I.O.L.

[102] Mountbatten to Ismay, ?13 May 1947, *T.P.*, x, 800.

[103] These involved undertakings to help those areas which wished to opt out of the Union, not merely to leave but also to set themselves up independently. It involved splitting up the Indian army, not interfering in the seceding areas with the help of the armed forces, agreeing to a referendum in the N.W.F.P. and creating a Boundary Commission to demarcate the areas which wanted to opt out. Congress, according to Nehru at least, would also give the League an assurance that majority rule would not be the order of the day. (See minutes of the Viceroy's thirty-first staff meeting, 12 May 1947, ibid., 781–2.) Patel's public statements made it impossible for the Muslim League to take any of the assurances seriously. [104] Ibid., 782.

revisions had been accepted. These revisions included the Congress's view that an 'Union of India' already existed. Mountbatten had found it 'difficult to disagree' with Nehru's point that the 'Cabinet Mission's plan is not dead except in a way to the Muslim League.' So the 'Union of India' had to be accepted as the basic factor in any plan to transfer power.[105] The main change that obviously had to be made was to deny the provinces the right to go their independent ways. As the Viceroy explained:

I have omitted [the] choice to Provinces for standing out independently. In principle if [the] choice is given to one Province we cannot deny it to others. If it is the desire of all parties in a particular Province to stand alone we shall not be able to prevent them, but I do not like the idea of H.M.G. giving them that choice. One of Nehru's main criticisms was that we were encouraging the Balkanisation of India.[106]

So in 'deference' to Nehru, Mountbatten did not give the Hindu-majority provinces any choice at all except to stay in the existing constituent assembly.[107] The provinces had either to like it (and remain in the existing constituent assembly) or lump it and form a new one (the Pakistan constituent assembly). The provincial assemblies in Bengal and Punjab were to meet in two parts, one representing the Muslim-majority districts and the other the rest. These two parts sitting separately would vote whether or not the province should be partitioned. A simple majority vote of either part for partition would ensure that a division took place. But in an attempt to encourage the Punjab and Bengal to see unionist sense, the plan made one concession. Before taking the fateful vote on partition, the representatives of each province would meet together (hopefully not for the last time) to see which constituent assembly they would join, whether the existing one or the one which was to be set up for the areas that opted out (Pakistan), if they somehow managed to avoid voting for partition when they met in their separate halves.[108] Significantly the Hindu provinces were not given any choice at all: they had to remain in the existing constituent assembly. And the procedure for determining the N.W.F.P.'s choice was changed to make it 'more acceptable to Nehru'; the Frontier could only opt out of the existing constituent assembly after western Punjab and Sind had voted to form a 'Pakistan' constituent assembly.[109]

---

[105] Mountbatten to Ismay, 12 May 1947, ibid., 796.
[106] Mountbatten to Ismay, 13 May 1947, ibid., 807.
[107] Ibid. [108] See revised draft partition plan, ibid., 884.
[109] See Mountbatten to Ismay, 13 May 1947, ibid., 807, and the draft partition plan, 883–7. As yet no procedure was laid down for Baluchistan; Mountbatten was still trying to find a more 'democratic' method to determine the future of the Baluchi people, if that was possible.

Understandably London was amazed by the Viceroy's revisions. After all, now that the Cabinet Mission's plan was effectively dead, 'the broad principles of the Cripps offer' (in the Secretary of State's opinion) governed the rules of the game. This suggested that a third option should be offered, 'certainly to Bengal and probably also to the Punjab'; the option 'of remaining united and framing its own constitution'.[110] Attlee summoned his Viceroy back to London to make his dramatically different case. On 18 May Mountbatten flew to London with his revised draft announcement and what essentially were Menon's proposals for how power might be transferred. According to Menon's proposals, if by some miracle unity could be preserved, then power should be transferred to the existing constituent assembly and India be given Dominion Status. If there were to be two sovereign states, they would both have Dominion Status and there would be a transfer to two constituent assemblies. There would be a common Governor-General for both states and the army would be divided between them. But the real twist in the proposals was that the existing interim government would act as the 'Dominion Government' until legislation was passed to transfer power on the basis of Dominion Status to the two states. The only 'safeguard' for the 'legitimate interests of the minorities' was to be the Governor-General.[111]

At the last moment Jinnah was given sight of the drafts, when there was nothing he could do to influence their shape. As far as the draft announcement was concerned, Mountbatten's squeeze play had begun to work its magic. Jinnah of course made the expected protests. The League, he said again, could not 'agree to the partition of Bengal and the Punjab'. It would be 'sowing the seeds of future serious trouble and the results will be disastrous for the life of these two provinces and all the communities concerned'. Calcutta had to stay in eastern Bengal, or at worst, be made a free port. Giving Calcutta to western Bengal would make it inevitable that the west would 'go to Hindustan'.[112] This and other amendments suggested by Jinnah without much hope of getting them were less significant than his outright rejection of the Mission's plan. This came in an unequivocal rejection of the draft announcement's hopes for 'negotiations between communities for an united India'. Jinnah bluntly stated that 'the Muslim League has already decided that India must be divided and Pakistan should be established'. It followed,

---

[110] Secretary of State's memorandum, 17 May 1947, ibid., 876–7.
[111] See document no. 466, ibid., 861–2.
[112] The Quaid now extended the League's umbrella of protection to the Scheduled Castes of western Bengal, and called for a referendum to allow them to make a real choice. (See the Muslim League's comments on the draft announcement, 17 May 1947, ibid., 852–3.)

in Jinnah's opinion, that the existing constituent assembly 'should [not] be allowed to continue'; it was in any case '*ab initio* invalid'. So two constituent assemblies, one for Pakistan and the other for Hindustan, should be established without further delay and 'all power' including defence, foreign affairs, communications and other central subjects transferred to the governments of Pakistan and Hindustan.[113] Since Congress had now so clearly established its sway over Viceregal policy, and had shown how it intended to push the League and its demands to one side once power was transferred, Jinnah saw that a resurrection of the Mission's plan for an united India which postponed Pakistan would inevitably mean that the Congress would be allowed to crush the League and its hopes of getting anything at all. This was the main reason why Jinnah had to settle for whatever he could get while the British remained in India. On 21 May, in what was a clear effort to show that he did not consider the agreement to be final, Jinnah asked for a 'corridor' through Hindustan connecting the two halves of Pakistan. The League, he declared, would 'fight every inch' of the way to resist the partition of the Punjab and Bengal. To dispel all doubts on whether he conceived Pakistan as a theocratic state, Jinnah categorically stated that the government of Pakistan 'can only be a popular, representative and democratic form of government'. The cabinet would be responsible to the parliament and both would be 'finally responsible to the electorate, and the people in general, without any distinction of caste, creed or sect'. This was Jinnah's way of taking the sting out of the League's communal propaganda now that the principle of Pakistan had virtually been conceded. In a vain attempt to convince the minorities in the Punjab and Bengal of the League's bona fides, Jinnah assured them that they would be 'protected and safeguarded'; they would be 'citizens of Pakistan . . . without any distinction of caste, creed or sect'. Jinnah had 'no doubt' that the minorities would be 'treated justly and fairly' and that the 'collective conscience of Parliament itself will be a guarantee that the minorities need not have any apprehension of any injustice being done to them'.[114] Jinnah justified his rejection of the partition of the Punjab and Bengal on the grounds that there would be at least twenty-five million Muslims in Hindustan.[115] Thus the demand for a 'corridor'.

Clearly then, Jinnah did not accept the settlement as final, and continued to battle to register his larger claims: namely, that the Indian army must be divided. But Jinnah was still offering the olive branch to

[113] Ibid., 851.
[114] See Jinnah's remarks on Pakistan, 21 May 1947, ibid., 929–30.
[115] See the Muslim League's comments on the draft announcement, 17 May 1947, ibid., 852.

the Congress. He maintained that the division of the army did not preclude 'friendly and reciprocal' relations between Pakistan and Hindustan: 'I envisage an alliance, pact or treaty between Pakistan and Hindustan in the mutual interest of both and against any aggressive outsider.'[116] Jinnah's unwillingness to accept the partition of the Punjab and Bengal, his demand for an unlikely 'corridor' to link the two parts of Pakistan and his offer for a defence alliance with Hindustan were, however, less significant than his outright rejection of Congress's proposal for immediate Dominion Status. Menon's proposals (which went to London with Mountbatten's revisions) for handing over power to the interim government were the most serious and immediate threat and Jinnah would have no truck with them. In his anxiety to ward off this disaster he was prepared to negotiate a grudging assent to the draft declaration. The price he exacted for appearing to go along with Mountbatten's plan (and he had little choice but to do so) was to get the Viceroy to drop the idea of transferring power to the interim government as soon as partition had been accepted in principle: 'The Muslim League will never agree to any change in the position, functions, or powers of the present Interim Government either by convention or otherwise, but it must be dissolved as soon as two Constituent Assemblies are formed; and all power should be transferred to them immediately . . . '[117] Both Nehru and Patel threatened to resign if Congress was not given full control over the Hindu provinces, the 'Union of India' in their terminology, as soon as the draft announcement had been made. As Nehru's confidant, Krishna Menon, put it succinctly: 'If Mr Jinnah wants a total separation, and that straight away, and if we agree to it for the sake of peace and dismember our country, we want to be rid of him, so far as the affairs of what is left to us of our country are concerned . . . it is not a matter of detail, but is fundamental.'[118] Although Mountbatten considered Jinnah's rejection of the partition of the Punjab and Bengal as 'blackmail', he had also come around to the view that since Congress had not genuinely accepted the Mission's plan a 'transfer of power to the Interim Government would be neither advisable nor practicable'. The 'greatest danger' now was that while Jinnah would eventually acquiesce in the partition of the Punjab and Bengal, he would not 'accept any plan as a final settlement' and the League would continue to demand a full Pakistan 'as the inalienable right of Muslims'.[119] The Congress would use this as an excuse to reject the draft announcement. As far as the Congress was concerned, accepting

---

[116] See Jinnah's remarks on Pakistan, 21 May 1947, ibid., 929–30.
[117] Jinnah to Mountbatten (via Eric Mieville), 22 May 1947, ibid., 948.
[118] Krishna Menon to Mountbatten, 21 May 1947, ibid., 940.
[119] See India and Burma Committee meeting, 22 May 1947, ibid., 953–4.

the draft announcement was contingent upon Jinnah accepting it as a 'final settlement' and on the condition that the League 'would not continue to make further claims in respect of Muslim populations in other parts of India'.[120] There would be no second helpings for the starveling state which was being created.

So on 23 May when the Cabinet reviewed the situation, the stage had effectively been set by the Congress High Command. Attlee merely repeated Mountbatten's view that there was 'no longer any prospect of a Union of India either on the basis of the Cabinet Mission's plan or any other basis'; the interim government was about to fall apart, and unless the method of the transfer was settled soon, 'widespread communal disturbances would be inevitable'. Given the League's 'recalcitrant attitude . . . some form of partition was unavoidable'. But Congress demanded that, if India was to be divided, Punjab and Bengal would have to be partitioned. So the Viceroy was authorised to convene a meeting of Indian leaders 'at which he would make a final effort to secure agreement on the basis of the Cabinet Mission's plan'. If he failed to do so, the Viceroy would announce H.M.G.'s plan along the lines of his draft declaration to transfer power 'to more than one authority'. Attlee still hoped that Bengal might yet 'decide to remain united on the basis of a coalition Government elected on a joint electorate'. Despite the real dangers of 'serious disorder and bloodshed', the Cabinet resolved that 'there appeared no alternative to partition'. If the League refused to accept the plan then H.M.G. would have to impose partition by an award. If Congress refused to accept, 'a more difficult position would arise and the whole plan would then have to be reconsidered'. But the position looked hopeful because of a 'development of major importance' – the offer of Congress leaders to keep 'Hindu India' in the Commonwealth. So the plan was now to transfer power by giving Dominion Status to both states, after swiftly passing the legislation to make this possible. Mountbatten was given a 'large measure of discretion to amend the details of this plan provided he kept within the broad limits of the policy approved by the Cabinet'.[121]

The critical factor, however, was H.M.G.'s refusal to give the interim government Dominion Status. Congress's aim had been to snuff Jinnah out at the centre, either by squashing him with their greater force in the interim government, or by expelling him from it. Since London denied it the first alternative, Congress settled for an immediate partition of India. But partition would not be construed as a division of India between Pakistan and Hindustan; it would merely mean that certain areas with

[120] Record of Henderson's conversation with Krishna Menon, 23 May 1947, ibid., 962.
[121] See Cabinet meeting minutes, 23 May 1947, ibid., 963–8.

Muslim majorities were to be seen as 'splitting off' from the 'Union of India'.[122] This was a fine way of ensuring that the League's share in the division of assets would be kept to a bare minimum. The Congress, after all, was accepting the draft announcement only on the condition that it was considered by all parties as a final settlement and 'no further claims would be put forward'.[123] So absolute partition was Congress's order of the day. And it was an order which Mountbatten had to carry out to its logical conclusion.

Before Mountbatten went to London, there was still some chance that Bengal might avoid the partitioner's axe. Suhrawardy had sounded the Viceroy out about this possibility, and Mountbatten was prepared to keep an open mind, even though his draft announcement made no provision for Bengal going its own way. Nehru had already told Mountbatten that he was 'not in favour of an independent Bengal unless [it was] closely linked to Hindustan' since 'he felt that a partition now would anyhow bring East Bengal in to Hindustan in a few years'.[124] But some elements in the Bengal Congress, and certainly Jinnah, were attracted by the notion of an independent and united Bengal. On 20 May a tentative agreement was reached between Sarat Bose, Kiran Shankar Roy, Suhrawardy and a few other Leaguers. However, the absence of four members of the League's special sub-committee to negotiate the terms of an agreement with the Bengali Hindus suggested that Suhrawardy had failed to carry his rank and file. On 24 May, a mere ten days before the announcement of the partition plan, the proposals were made public. According to the proposals, independent Bengal would decide its relations with the rest of India; there would be joint electorates and adult franchise with reservation of seats based on population for Hindus and Muslims; a new intra-communal ministry in which Muslims and Hindus (including members of the Scheduled Caste) would have an equal share: an equal share of all services, including the military and police for the two main communities, and a constituent assembly of thirty (sixteen Muslims and fourteen non-Muslims) which would frame the future constitution of Bengal.[125] But from first to last the Congress High Command had opposed the scheme for an united and independent Bengal. Bose and Roy had negotiated with Suhrawardy without the official authorisation of the Bengal Congress. Patel urged Bose to 'take a united stand' with the Congress High Command on the partition issue.[126]

[122] Record of Henderson's conversation with Krishna Menon, 23 May 1947, ibid., 962.
[123] Nehru to Mieville, 26 May 1947, ibid., 990.
[124] Mountbatten to Burrows, 16 May 1947, ibid., 850.
[125] Sen, *Muslim Politics in Bengal*, pp. 238–9.
[126] Patel to Sarat Bose, 22 May 1947, Das. (ed.), *Patel's Correspondence* vol. IV, p. 44, cited in Gordon, 'Brothers against the Raj', *The Oracle*, July 1979, p. 44.

Bose stuck firmly to his line and had the courage of his convictions to challenge Patel's view that Bengali Hindus were unanimous in wanting partition:

having been in close touch with public opinion in West and East Bengal, I can say that it is not a fact that Bengali Hindus unanimously demand partition. As far as East Bengal is concerned, there is not the slightest doubt that the overwhelming majority of Hindus there are opposed to partition. As regards West Bengal, the agitation for partition had gained ground because the Congress came to the aid of the Hindu Mahasabha and also because communal passions have been roused among Hindus on account of the happenings since August last [i.e. the Calcutta Killings]. The demand for partition is more or less confined to the middle classes. When the full implications of partition are realised and when people here find that all they will get for Western Bengal province will be roughly one-third of the area of Bengal and only about half of the total Hindu population in Bengal, the agitation for partition will surely lose support. I entirely agree with you that we should take a united stand; but I shall say at the same time that the united stand should be for a united Bengal and a united India. Future generations will, I am afraid, condemn us for conceding division of India and partition of Bengal and the Punjab. [127]

Yet the fact remained that Bose and Roy had failed to prove convincingly that the movement for an united, independent Bengal had greater popular backing than that for the partition of the province. This, together with the myopic calculations of some eastern Bengal Leaguers, allowed the Congress High Command to perform a remarkable *tour de force* in a province proud of its cultural and linguistic unities. On 27 May, Nehru formally announced that the Congress would 'agree to Bengal remaining united only if it remains in the Union'. He warned the Bengali Hindus not to be misled by Suhrawardy; an independent Bengal would mean 'the dominance of the Muslim League' and 'practically the whole of Bengal going into the Pakistan area'. [128] So although Mountbatten had persuaded London to make an exception for Bengal and allow it to become an independent Dominion, he quickly dropped his plan once Nehru had rejected the proposition out of hand. In the light of Nehru's statements 'the prospects of saving the unity of Bengal and securing its establishment as a third Dominion in India had been gravely preju- diced'. [129] There could be no question of giving Dominion Status to an embarrassingly unviable and bestially poor state of eastern Bengal. So Bengal would probably have to be partitioned and its eastern wing given

---

[127] Sarat Bose to Patel, 27 May 1947, Das (ed.), *Patel's Correspondence*, vol. IV, pp. 45–6, cited in ibid., 44.

[128] Extract from *News Chronicle*, 27 May 1947, enclosure (iii) to document 560, ibid., 1040.

[129] See India and Burma Committee meeting minutes, 28 May 1947, *T.P.*, X, 1014.

the unenviable choice of either joining Hindustan or the even more distant Pakistan.[130]

There had never been much hope of preventing a partition of the Punjab. By May 1947, the province had become the arsonists' paradise and the Governor in a gross understatement of fact declared that 'communal hostility is now universal'.[131] Stabbings and fires were by now facts of Punjabi life. Muslims had the support of the Punjab police; Sikhs and Hindus were backed by Hindu big-business and the personal armed police of the Rajas of Patiala, Faridkot and Nabha to name only a few. The battle for the walled city of Lahore was ominous for the rest of the province. The Governor's request for an additional brigade for Lahore alone was turned down on the grounds that troops had to be deployed in areas where trouble was expected to follow the draft announcement. The Governor's warnings that there would be large-scale disturbances after June in Jullundur, Amritsar, Lahore, Sheikhupura, Lyallpur and Montgomery also went unheeded. The Punjab was almost certain to erupt after the announcement on 2 June. By the time Mountbatten returned to India, bands of armed Sikhs and Hindus (who had possibly purchased their weapons from enterprising Muslims) were sacking Muslim villages in the non-Muslim-majority district of Gurgaon.[132] The unity of the Punjab was already a thing of the past. The main question was whether the Boundary Commission's report could be implemented before the province drifted beyond the brink of total chaos. The situation in the N.W.F.P. was quite as alarming. The Frontier Gandhi with the Congress High Command's backing had raised the explosive issue of a 'Pathan national Province' which would be free to make 'its own alliances as may suit it'.[133] This was the first public call for 'Pakhtunistan', an idea which is alive and well to this day. But for strategic and practical reasons the British had already decided that the N.W.F.P. could not be allowed to stand alone; it would have to choose between the two constituent assemblies, and it could do so only after western Punjab and Sind had voted to form the Pakistan constituent assembly. Similarly, Baluchistan's 'will' was to be determined by a mere nod of the Shahi Jirga, although for good measure it had been decided that a Commission consisting of a Congress, a League and a British representative would consult each Jirga.[134] A Pakistan consisting of western Punjab, Sind, the N.W.F.P., Baluchistan, eastern Bengal and

---

[130] Ibid., 1015.
[131] Jenkins to Colville, 25 May 1947, ibid., 985 and 21 May 1947, ibid., 927–8.
[132] See Liaquat Ali Khan to Mountbatten, 30 May 1947, ibid., 1033–4.
[133] Caroe to Colville, 22 May 1947, ibid., 944.
[134] See annex II to document no. 516, ibid., 951.

Sylhet district was hardly the Pakistan of Jinnah's dreams. Yet this was all he could now expect to get. Congress, his own followers and above all the contradictions in his own strategy had reduced Jinnah's Pakistan to the moth-eaten version which he had rejected so vehemently on more than one occasion. But, as the British could see, Jinnah was so 'determined on the principle of Pakistan' that he was 'unlikely to throw away the chance of getting a limited Pakistan in an attempt to get the whole'.[135]

On 30 May Mountbatten returned to India. There were just two days before his meeting with all the leaders. The plan obviously could only be amended if all the parties at the centre agreed. But Mountbatten did not intend to have any real discussions, even at the centre. Certainly he was not minded to consult provincial leaders except to find an excuse for dropping Bengal's option for remaining united and independent. Bengal could only remain united and independent if both High Commands agreed. On 31 May, Suhrawardy met Mountbatten and informed him that the Congress High Command would not permit Bengal to vote for independence. The Bengal Muslim League had disowned the proposals for an united and independent Bengal even though it still rejected the partition of the province in principle. Suhrawardy believed that the only way to ease communal tensions during the partition period was to declare Calcutta a free city.[136] But when Mountbatten sent Patel a proposal to give Calcutta such a status for six months, the Congress's man of iron retorted: 'Not even for six hours.'[137] With the problem of Bengal now conveniently out of the way, Mountbatten could concentrate his mind on the all-India issues. He planned to give all sides the least amount of time possible. London had a fortnight; the Indian leaders were to have twenty-four hours to consult their Working Committees before the plan was announced on 3 June. On 2 June at 10 a.m. Mountbatten met with Congress and League leaders, and one Sikh leader,[138] handed them the plan and brusquely informed them that, in view of the 'terrific sense of urgency',[139] power would be transferred to two separate states as soon as Parliament had passed the India Bill.[140] So there was no possibility of

135 This was the opinion of Sir John Colville, who was acting as Viceroy in Mountbatten's absence. (See Mieville to Mountbatten, 26 May 1947, ibid., 991.)

136 Suhrawardy to Mieville, 31 May 1947, *T.P.*, XI, 20.

137 Viceroy's Report no. 8, 5 June 1947, L/PO/433, I.O.L.

138 These included Nehru, Patel and Kripalani (the Congress president), Jinnah, Liaquat, Nishtar and Sardar Baldev Singh.

139 See minutes of the Viceroy's meeting with the Indian leaders, 2 June 1947, *T.P.*, XI, 39.

140 The India Bill was to be finalised after consultations with the Indian leaders. There were many controversial issues which could delay the Bill. For instance, the power of the central governments over the provinces; negotiations between Britain and the two states

holding referendums in the Punjab and Bengal on the partition issue. As the Viceroy had anticipated, all the party leaders promised to co-operate. Interestingly, while the leaders (including Jinnah) were prepared to give their 'personal assurances' to co-operate, they sensibly maintained that 'they could not agree to the plan'.[141] The Congress leaders were confident that their Working Committee would accept; Jinnah did not intend to commit himself before he had consulted his Council. Jinnah asked for a week to get its opinion; Mountbatten said he could not wait for a day, let alone a week. So Jinnah had to agree to give the League Working Committee's reactions verbally and not in writing, the very same day.[142]

Mountbatten had planned the last moves to force Jinnah into submission with great care. He had his staff draw up a detailed plan for his talk with Jinnah. The Quaid was to be told that he was getting the 'partition' for which he had been fighting for 'so many years', and, attributing to the leader the words of his lieutenant, that he had once said that he would 'sooner have a few acres of the Sind desert' provided it was his 'very own, rather than have a united India with a majority rule'.[143] But the long and the short of it was that Jinnah would simply be ordered to accept the partition of the Punjab and Bengal regardless of whether or not he 'entirely agree[d] with it'. After all, Jinnah could always console himself with the thought that there was 'nothing . . . final in this world'.[144] On 2 June, one hour before the deadline at midnight, the Quaid-i-Azam returned to Viceregal Lodge hoping somehow to persuade the Viceroy not to announce the partition plan publicly. Playing for time and for another round of negotiations, Jinnah warned the Viceroy that the League's Council might not accept the plan. When the Viceroy retorted that this would mean 'chaos . . . and you [Jinnah] will lose Pakistan, probably for good', Jinnah simply shrugged his shoulders and said: 'What must be, must be.' But Mountbatten had expected prevarication along these lines and was ready to deal with it. Since he had taken the precaution of getting London's authority to make an award if necessary, he now pretended to lose his temper, secure in the knowledge that Jinnah had no square to which to escape. In a move of quite staggering audacity

over the sterling balances; the future of the Andaman and Nicobar Islands (which both parties claimed); and the date of the actual transfer of power as well as the title of the states. (See minutes of the India and Burma Committee meeting, 28 May 1947, *T.P.*, x, 1016–19.)

[141] Mountbatten to the Secretary of State, no. 1258-S, 2 June 1947, L/PO/429, I.O.L.
[142] Ibid.
[143] See Mountbatten's interview with Liaquat Ali Khan, 3 April 1947, *T.P.*, x, 102 to confirm this.
[144] See draft brief for Mountbatten's talk with Jinnah before the 3 June announcement, R/3/1/150, I.O.L. But in Jinnah's unhappy world, the settlement proved to be final.

(but one which underlined the fragility of Jinnah's position in relation to his own followers), Mountbatten threatened that he himself would appropriate the Quaid's role and speak for the League:

Mr Jinnah! I do not intend to let you wreck all the work that has gone into this settlement. *Since you will not accept for the Muslim League, I will speak for them myself.* I will take the risk of saying that I am satisfied with the assurances you have given me, and if your Council fails to ratify the agreement, you can place the blame on me.[145]

If Jinnah had been sure of his following, he could have laughed this out of court. As it was, he had to sit quietly while Mountbatten proceeded to give him instructions on how he was to behave the next day in the headmaster's study. The following morning, when the Indian leaders came together for their fateful meeting, the Quaid-i-Azam, the spokes-man of India's Muslims, the father of a nation about to be born, was meekly to accept the partition of Pakistan's two main provinces and when Mountbatten said: 'Mr Jinnah has given me assurances which I have accepted and which satisfy me', Jinnah would under 'no circum-stances contradict that', and, when the Viceroy looked in his direction, the Quaid would 'nod . . . [his] head in acquiescence'.[146] And that is how it was to be.

Of course there were last-minute bids by all sides to vary the terms of the announcement. The League continued to reject the partition of the Punjab and Bengal, while the Sikhs wanted the plan to contain specific instructions to the Boundary Commission which took account of their claims on certain districts in the Punjab. In its turn, the Congress wanted the N.W.F.P. to be given the right to opt for independence and then decide its future relations with the rest of India. To give the Frontier such an option would have been to turn the logic of the partition plan on its head. It was at Nehru's request that Mountbatten had withdrawn the right of each province to opt for independence. If this was now re-introduced, H.M.G. would insist on extending the right to all the provinces. So raising this point was out of the question. The Congress also wanted H.M.G. to give an assurance that if the rest of India decided to leave the British Commonwealth, Pakistan would be expelled. Even Mountbatten saw that this 'dangerous' demand by the Congress would have 'wrecked the whole chance of agreement'. Nehru and Patel finally agreed to withdraw a proposal which negated the very basis of Dominion

---

145 Campbell-Johnson, *Mission with Mountbatten*, p. 103 (my italics).

146 Ibid. Mountbatten may have discovered a device by which Jinnah could avoid taking the full responsibility of giving his explicit approval to the plan; but the report that Jinnah's 'delight was unconcealed' must be viewed with scepticism. (Mountbatten to the Secretary of State, no. 1277-S, 3 June 1947, L/PO/429, I.O.L.)

Status. If Jinnah had got wind of it, he would almost certainly have used it as an excuse to reject the plan on the grounds that the Congress had not accepted the basic principle, namely the sovereignty and independence of Pakistan.[147] Fortunately for Mountbatten, none of the points raised by any side was acceptable to the others. He told London that 'although they [the Indian leaders] did not agree to [the] plan as indeed I had anticipated they had virtually accepted it'.[148] On 3 June 1947, at 10 a.m. precisely, Mountbatten, with Nehru on his right and Jinnah on his left, declared that the plan to partition India remained 'as near 100% agreement as it was possible to get, and that in his judgement, what was being done was in the best interests of the people of India'.[149] Not a single leader challenged the Viceroy's assessment. Jinnah, who might have, according to Campbell-Johnson, confirmed Mountbatten's version of his position 'by the appropriate silence and nod of the head'.[150] For a strategist who had always, and with reason, been reluctant to come into the open about his real aims, it was appropriate that at the fateful moment he should have remained silent. India's political future was thus resolved in less than four days after Mountbatten's return from London. The Viceroy's relief was undisguised, and he admitted 'how miraculously lucky' this was for H.M.G.[151]

Now that the partition issue had been settled, Mountbatten hoped that a new spirit would emerge amongst the leaders. And for a fleeting moment the Indian leaders did seem willing to bury the past. Here was 'the prospect of building a fine future'. But as soon as the Viceroy had handed out a thirty-four page pamphlet on 'The Administrative Consequences of Partition' the Indian leaders were seen in their true colours.[152] When Mountbatten suggested that the problem of partition would be discussed in 'a Cabinet meeting', Jinnah quickly corrected him: 'You mean the Viceroy's Executive Council! A spade should be called a spade.'[153] It was clear that the status of the interim government, certainly its composition, would make the parting of ways less than amicable. Working within the limitations of the policy outlined by H.M.G., Mountbatten had somehow to keep the interim government intact until the partition plan had been ratified by Parliament. If either party

---

[147] Mountbatten to the Secretary of State, no. 1284-S, 3 June 1947, L/PO/429, I.O.L., and Kripalani's letter of 2 June 1947 as cited in Mountbatten to the Secretary of State, no. 1279-S, 3 June 1947, ibid.

[148] Mountbatten to the Secretary of State, telegram, no. 1282-S, 3 June 1947, ibid.

[149] Minutes of the Viceroy's meeting with the Indian leaders, 3 June 1947, *T.P.*, XI, 74.

[150] Campbell-Johnson, *Mission with Mountbatten*, p. 103.

[151] Mountbatten to the Secretary of State, no. 1284-S, 3 June 1947, L/PO/429, I.O.L.

[152] See minutes of the Viceroy's meeting with the Indian leaders, 3 June 1947, *T.P.*, XI, 74.

[153] Ibid., 76.

resigned, the interim government would have to be dissolved and this undoubtedly would compromise Mountbatten's position as an arbiter. So despite Congress's insistence that the League should be asked to leave the interim government, Mountbatten had to play for time until power had been transferred to the two governments. This meant that the dissolution of the interim government had to wait until the Muslim provinces had voted on which constituent assembly they would join. This was expected to take about six weeks. With the interim government already falling to bits, 15 August was the only plausible date for a transfer of power.[154]

On 3 June 1947, as planned, Mountbatten and Attlee simultaneously announced that India would be partitioned and power would be transferred to two separate states on the basis of Dominion Status. Nehru recommended the partition plan as a 'big advance towards complete independence', while Jinnah simply left it to the League Council to decide whether to accept the plan as 'a compromise or a settlement'.[155] Jinnah obviously wanted to keep the way open for a different result. On 9 June, the date agreed upon by Mountbatten and Jinnah, the A.I.M.L. Council formally announced that it accepted the plan, not as a settlement but 'as a compromise'.[156] Six days later the A.I.C.C. accepted the partition plan as a final settlement.[157] The vote of the Muslim provinces was now merely a formality. On 20 June at a preliminary joint meeting of representatives from western and eastern Bengal, 126 against 90 voted to keep the province united and to take it into a new constituent assembly. At a separate meeting, representatives from western Bengal voted by 58

---

[154] Now that the principles had been settled, the partition machinery had to start rolling. A Partition Committee consisting of Patel, Prasad, Liaquat and Nishtar was set up. It was to be assisted by a steering committee consisting of H. M. Patel (cabinet secretary) and Muhammad Ali (adviser in the military finance department). The main principles of partition and much of the actual separation were expected to be completed by 15 August. The Indian army was not expected to be divided until March 1948 and this was to be carried out under a separate committee, namely the Joint Defence Council. As soon as the decision of the Muslim provinces was known, a Partition Council would replace the Partition Committee. It would consist of two top-ranking leaders each from the Congress and the League with Mountbatten as chairman without arbitral functions. These functions would rest with a special Arbitral Tribunal which would be set up simultaneously and would consist of three members, all of whom would have judicial experience and would be selected by the Partition Committee. The services of the Arbitral Tribunal would be available to the partitioned provinces as well.

[155] See Nehru's broadcast on 3 June 1947, *T.P.*, XI, 94–7 and Jinnah's broadcast on 3 June 1947, ibid., 97–8.

[156] See A.I.M.L. Council's resolution, 9 June 1947, in Pirzada (ed.), *Foundations of Pakistan*, vol. II, p. 568.

[157] See A.I.C.C.'s resolution, 15 June 1947, *T.P.*, XI, 397–8.

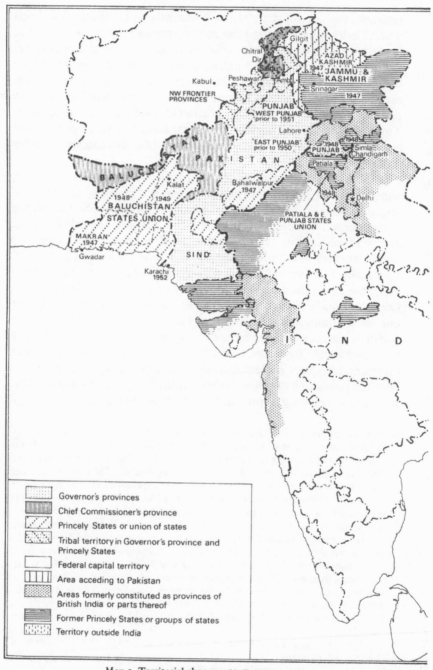

Map 5. Territorial changes, 1947–1955.

to 21 to partition the province and remain in the existing constituent assembly. The eastern Bengal representatives voted to keep the province undivided by 106 to 35 votes, and by 107 against 34 votes to join a new constituent assembly. In a separate vote, 107 representatives were in favour and 34 against amalgamating eastern Bengal with Sylhet.[158] Three days later at the joint preliminary meeting of the Punjab assembly, 91 members voted to join a new constituent assembly and to keep the province undivided while 77 voted to stay in the existing constituent assembly.[159] The eastern Punjab representatives then decided to partition the province and remain within the existing constituent assembly by 50 votes against 22. In contrast the western Punjab representatives voted to join a new constituent assembly and to keep the province undivided, by 69 votes against 27.[160] So the future of Bengal and the Punjab was decided by the western and eastern halves respectively. On 26 June, the Sind assembly decided by 33 votes to 20 to join a new constituent assembly.[161] By 17 July the N.W.F.P.,[162] Sylhet[163] and Baluchistan[164] had all opted for a new constituent assembly. Pakistan, however truncated and moth-eaten, was now a reality. But its exact geographic boundaries remained as unspecific as they had always been. A Boundary

---

[158] Mountbatten's Report no. 10, 27 June 1947, ibid., 681.

[159] According to a Reuter's report the 168 members of the Punjab assembly met in a festive mood to decide the fate of their province; they 'laughed and joked as they shook hands in the lobbies of the Assembly building'. Just contrast this with the 'fire-blacked ruins' of Lahore and scores of villages throughout the Punjab. (See report from Reuter Indian Service, 23 June 1947, ibid., 566.)

[160] Ibid.

[161] Mountbatten's Report no. 10, 27 June 1947, ibid., 681.

[162] On 17 July the future of the N.W.F.P. was finally decided in a referendum (boycotted by the Congress) in which nearly 50.49 per cent of the electorate voted for a new constituent assembly. The following are the results of the referendum:

Valid votes for Pakistan	289,244
Valid votes for Hindustan	2,874
Majority for Pakistan	286,370

The total votes cast in the referendum were 292,118, as against 375,989 cast in the 1945–46 elections, or fifteen per cent less than those cast in the last elections when there was no boycott by the Congress. (Mountbatten's Report no. 14, 25 July 1947, L/PO/433, I.O.L.)

[163] On 7 July in the Sylhet referendum a majority of 55,578 voted in favour of the district joining east Bengal, and therefore Pakistan. (Mountbatten's Report no. 13, 18 July 1947, ibid.)

[164] On the face of it Baluchistan had come out completely in favour of joining Pakistan. But although all fifty-four members present voted to join the Pakistan constituent assembly, three members of the Shahi Jirga and five out of the ten members of the Quetta municipality were conspicuously absent from the proceedings. (Mountbatten's Report no. 11, 4 July 1947, *T.P.*, x, 896.)

Commission award had to decide this issue, which for so long had been deliberately avoided by the League.[165]

Meanwhile Jinnah continued his constitutional battles in New Delhi. He was not ready to vacate Delhi before the partition process had been completed. Jinnah had no illusions about where power in the subcontinent lay. Congress's demand for a reconstitution of the interim government without the League once the Muslim areas had voted to form a new constituent assembly was seen by Jinnah as a grave threat to Pakistan's future. Mountbatten was tempted to bow down to Congress pressures but had to admit finally that Jinnah was correct by the letter of the law. The interim government could not be reconstituted until Parliament had passed the India Bill. Having postponed his departure to Karachi Jinnah now came up with the ingenious suggestion that Pakistan and Hindustan should celebrate their parting of ways by getting their constituent assemblies to meet simultaneously in New Delhi. Missing the irony in Jinnah's proposal Mountbatten thought this 'would be a good gesture for the future happy relations between the two Dominions'. But Nehru, Patel, Prasad and Gandhi, who knew Jinnah better, 'absolutely blew up', and said they could under no circumstances allow the Pakistan constituent assembly to meet anywhere near the vicinity of New Delhi.[166] So another attempt by Jinnah to bring Pakistan and Hindustan on an equal footing at Delhi met with a Congress rebuff. But it was an objective Jinnah had pursued for too long to lose sight of now that Pakistan was finally within reach. His insistence that Mountbatten should become the super Governor-General over the two Dominions, each of which would have its own separate Governor-General, was partly in pursuit of the same objective. Jinnah wanted a British Crown Representative with arbitral powers to supervise the partition process, particularly the division of the Indian army. Congress's invitation to Mountbatten to remain as a constitutional Governor-General over its areas and Mountbatten's refusal to become an arbiter convinced Jinnah of the futility of having a common Governor-General for the two Dominions. He knew only too well how difficult it would be for the government of Pakistan to discipline the particularisms of its constituent units and at the same time set up an effective administrative structure to make centralised authority

---

[165] The Boundary Commission consisted of two representatives from each party. After the usual bickerings both parties agreed to the appointment of Sir Cyril Radcliffe as the chairman of the Commission. Radcliffe also chaired the meetings of the Punjab and Bengal Boundary Commissions and had the final word; this was considered to be the only insurance of getting the boundaries settled by 15 August. (Mountbatten's Report, no. 10, 27 June 1947, ibid., 681–2.)

[166] Mountbatten's Report, no. 10, 27 June 1947, ibid., 690–1.

a reality. To share a common Governor-General with Hindustan would have given Congress an excuse to use this joint office to make terms separately with the Muslim areas in the event that the Pakistan constituent assembly fell to pieces. It was to avoid this disaster that Jinnah had to exercise the powers of a Governor-General himself and in the process consolidate the League's authority over the Muslim areas.[167]

On 2 July 1947, Jinnah formally told Mountbatten that he intended to become Pakistan's first Governor-General. Of course Mountbatten was outraged. It complicated the partition process, as planned by him, and especially the already odious business of dividing the Indian army. Both parties wanted separate Commanders-in-Chief in charge of two newly-reconstituted armies by 15 August. Since the division of the army was not expected to be completed before 31 March 1948, a British Commander-in-Chief had to remain in charge and it was preferable that he should take orders from a Governor-General common to both Dominions. Yet this was precisely why Jinnah wanted to become the Governor-General for Pakistan. He knew that as Governor-General he would have wide-ranging powers over the Muslim areas, powers which he could not possibly afford to let any other individual exercise. Moreover, as the Governor-General of Pakistan, Jinnah felt he would be better placed to ensure the division of the army, and the army was what he needed most of all to clamp central authority over Pakistan's provinces. At any rate, the Prime Minister of Pakistan would have to take orders from the Governor-General. 'In my position', Jinnah told the bemused Viceroy, 'it is I who will give the advice and others will act on it.'[168] Mountbatten concluded that Jinnah had either gone 'mad' or was suffering from an acute form of 'megalomania'. Yet there was some method in Jinnah's apparent madness. He wanted Mountbatten to remain on the Congress side as a 'steadying influence' and confessed that he was 'afraid of what the Congress Government might do to Pakistan'. Liaquat Ali Khan in his turn asked Mountbatten to stay on in India until the partition process was complete because 'otherwise there will be terrible trouble and Pakistan will suffer severely'.[169] All this suggests just how deeply nervous the League leaders were about their ability to sustain Pakistan as a separate and independent state. They distrusted Congress's intentions, and they were uncertain of their own followers once Pakistan had been achieved. But it is nevertheless significant that until the bitter end the League continued to protest against Hindustan adopting the title 'Union

[167] For an analysis of Jinnah's decision, see my article 'Inheriting The Raj: Jinnah and The Governor-Generalship Issue', forthcoming in *Modern Asian Studies*, 19(1985).
[168] Mountbatten's Report no. 11, 4 July 1947, ibid., 899.
[169] Ibid., 900.

of India'. A commentary perhaps that Jinnah never quite abandoned his strategy of bringing about an eventual union of India on the basis of Pakistan and Hindustan.

If Jinnah was still hoping that there would be a period of convalescence after the 'surgical operation', his hopes were shattered finally by the wholesale butchery which accompanied partition, particularly in the Punjab. More than any other province, it was the Punjab which had provided Mountbatten and the Congress High Command with the ammunition with which to hustle Jinnah into a snap decision. But the reaction in the Punjab to the actual partition of the province remained the most serious threat to the hurriedly-contrived all-India settlement. This is why Mountbatten deliberately avoided disclosing the details of the Boundary Commission's award to the political leaders until 18 August, three days after the grant of Dominion Status. Fierce disagreements on the award were inevitable and could well have smashed the apparent settlement. The fact that power was transferred to two governments, neither of which knew the exact geographical boundaries of their respective states, adds yet another curious twist to Mountbatten's handling of the partition of India. Certainly the Viceroy's tactic of postponing the award did nothing to prevent an eruption in the Punjab. Everything that was 'humanly possible', so we are told, was done to control the situation. The Joint Boundary Force was reinforced by two more brigades, but the situation was 'long past mere military action and require[d] political leadership of a high order'.[170] If anything it was a complete failure of responsible political leadership which had brought anarchy to the Punjab. While Punjab writhed and turned under the impact of decisions taken in distant places, Mountbatten boldly claimed credit for having accomplished, in less than two and a half months, one of the 'greatest administrative operations in history'.[171] On behalf of the Hindus, Sikhs and Muslims who were slaughtered in their hundreds of thousands, and the refugees who in their millions stumbled fearfully across the frontiers of the two states, the historian has a duty to challenge Mountbatten's contention and ask whether this 'great operation' was not in fact an ignominious scuttle enabling the British to extricate themselves from the awkward responsibility of presiding over India's communal madness.

170 Mountbatten's Report, no. 17, 16 August 1947, L/PO/433, I.O.L.

171 Mountbatten's address to the Indian Continent Assembly at New Delhi, 15 August 1947, in *Time Only to Look Forward, Speeches of Rear Admiral The Earl Mountbatten of Burma* (London, 1949), p. 64.

Glossary

Ahrar	literally 'the free'; Muslim political party founded in the Punjab in 1931 by Mazhar Ali Khan and Maulana Ataullah Shah Bukhari
Akhand	united
anna	the sixteenth part of a rupee
Arains	a cultivator caste in the Punjab
Azad	free
bandemataram	literally 'hail to the mother'; title of song in Bankim Chandra Chatterjee's novel *Anandamath* with Hindu communalist overtones
bazaar	market
biraderi	literally 'brotherhood'; patrilineal kinship group
charpoy	a bed with a wooden frame covered by netted string
crore	one hundred lakhs or ten million
darbar	the court of a ruler
fatwa	political opinion as enunciated by the leader of a Muslim religious congregation
gadi	seat or chair to designate religious or political office
ghee	clarified butter
goonda	hooligan
gurdwara	a Sikh temple
Hindu Mahasabha	an avowedly communal political organisation based on Hindu revivalism
jagirdar	big landlord
Jat	name of a Rajput tribe from the Punjab
jawan	soldier
Jihad	the religious duty of Muslims to establish, if necessary by force, the sway of Islam over the non-Islamic world, the Dar-al-harb (the abode of war) and to defend also by force the Dar-ul-Islam
khadi	hand-spun and hand-woven cloth
Khaksar	literally 'humble'; a para-military organisation led by Allama Mashriqi
Khans	title used generally by the Pathans and by the British to refer to the landlords or tribal leaders
Khudai Khidmatgars	literally the 'servants of God'; organisation led by Abdul Ghaffar Khan, the 'Frontier Gandhi'
kisan	peasant; cultivator
krishak	peasant or cultivator
lakh	one hundred thousand
lambardar	village headman

majlis	gathering or assembly
Makhdum	title for religious leader
Mashaikh	plural of Shaikh; used for persons known for their piety
maulvi	title used for Muslim religious leader
Mir	a chief or leader in Sind
mohalla	a ward or a quarter
mullah	title used for Muslim religious leader
pir	term used for spiritual guide
praja (or *proja*)	tenant
pundit	learned or wise man; usefully refers to a learned Brahmin
purdah	veil
Quaid-i-Azam	The Great Leader
Rabb-ul-Alameen	God of the whole world
rabi	the spring harvest
Raj	kingdom, rule or sovereignty
roti	bread
rupee (Indian)	Indian currency
sajjada nashin	literally one who sits on the prayer rug; custodian of a Sufi shrine
sardar	chief of tribe
satyagraha	civil disobedience campaign
sepoy	soldier or policeman
Shahi Jirga	grand meeting of all tribal *sardars*
Sharia	Islamic law
Sufi	Muslim mystic; the word 'sufi' comes from the coarse woollen garment, *suf*, worn by the early Muslim mystics
talaq	Muslim term for divorce
taluqdar	used for a landlord in the U.P. who collected revenue from his own and other estates; after the Mutiny, Oudh *taluqdars* were given proprietary rights over the land for which they collected revenue
tehsildar	officer in charge of a tehsil, a revenue subdivision of a district
thali	a plate
ulema	persons versed in Islamic religious sciences
vakil	advocate or lawyer
zaildar	officer in charge of a group of villages
zamindar	term is used loosely to refer to any landholder, large or small.

Select bibliography

Manuscript sources

India Office Library, London (I.O.L.)

Mian Fazl-i-Husain Papers Mss.Eur.E.352
Linlithgow Papers Mss.Eur.F.125
Political Department Miscellaneous (Governors' Reports for the Muslim-majority provinces and the U.P.) L/P&J/5.
Private Office Papers L/PO. Papers of the Office of the Private Secretary to the Viceroy R/3/1.
Political Department Collection L/P&J/8.

National Archives of Pakistan, Islamabad

Quaid-i-Azam Papers QAP/– microfilm copies and photostat copies of the 'Partition Papers'.
All-India Muslim League Papers AIML/– microfilm copies.
Syed Shamsul Hassan Collection SHC/– microfilm copies. (Although part of the All-India Muslim League Records this collection forms a separate archival group.)

Karachi

Syed Shamsul Hassan Collection. The complete collection of Syed Shamsul Hassan (honorary secretary of the All-India Muslim League) is in the possession of his son, Khalid Shamsul Hassan, who kindly allowed me to take photostat copies of those papers which were not available in the National Archives in Islamabad.

Published sources

This dissertation has relied heavily on N. Mansergh, E. W. R. Lumby and Penderel Moon (eds.), *Constitutional Relations Between Britain and India: The Transfer of Power 1942–7*, in eleven volumes, 1970–1982. The first four volumes have been edited by N. Mansergh and E. W. R. Lumby, and the remaining seven by N. Mansergh and Penderel Moon:

Volume I: *The Cripps Mission, January–April 1942*. London, 1970.
Volume II: *'Quit India', 30 April–21 September 1942*. London, 1971.
Volume III: *Reassertion of authority, Gandhi's fast and the succession to the Viceroyalty, 21 September 1942–12 June 1943*. London, 1971.
Volume IV: *The Bengal Famine and the New Viceroyalty, 15 June 1943–31 August 1944*. London, 1973.

Volume V: *The Simla Conference, Background and Proceedings, 1 September 1944–28 July 1945*. London, 1974.
Volume VI: *The post-war phase: new moves by the Labour Government, 1 August 1945–22 March 1946*. London, 1976.
Volume VII: *The Cabinet Mission, 23 March–29 June 1946*. London, 1977.
Volume VIII: *The Interim Government, 3 July–1 November 1946*. London, 1979.
Volume IX: *The fixing of a time limit, 4 November 1946–22 March 1947*. London, 1980.
Volume X: *The Mountbatten Viceroyalty, Formulation of a Plan, 22 March–30 May 1947*. London, 1981.
Volume XI: *The Mountbatten Viceroyalty, Announcement and Reception of the 3 June Plan, 31 May–7 July 1947*. London, 1982.

Official publications

Report of the Indian Franchise Committee, 1932. Command Paper No. 4086, V6485.
The Government of India Act, 1935. Delhi, 1936.
Returns showing the Results of Elections in India, 1937. Command Paper No. 5589.
Census of India 1941. Command Paper No. 6479.
Speeches by the Marquess of Linlithgow, vol. II. Simla, 1944.
Mitra, N. N. (ed.), *The Indian Annual Register, 1944–1947*. Calcutta.
Return Showing the Results of Elections to the Central Legislative Assembly and the Provincial Legislatures in 1945–46. New Delhi, 1948.
Report of the Court of Inquiry . . . to Enquire into the Punjab Disturbances of 1953. Lahore, 1954.
Legislative Assembly Debates. V/9/124, I.O.L.
Parliamentary Debates. Fifth series, vol. 420, collections 1421–22.

Newspapers and periodicals

Civil and Military Gazette, Lahore, 1936–47. Punjab Public Library, Lahore.
Dawn, Delhi, 1943–46. Microfilm, Seeley Library, Cambridge.
Eastern Times, Lahore, 1943–46. Punjab Public Library, Lahore.
Harijan (Ahmedabad).
Nawa-i-Waqt, Lahore, 1945–46. Office of the Nawa-i-Waqt, Lahore.
Sind Observer, Karachi, 1936–44. National Archives of Pakistan, Islamabad.
Tribune, Ambala, 1936–44. Microfilm, Centre of South Asian Studies, Cambridge.

All-India Muslim League sources

Ahmad, Jamil-ud-Din (ed.), *Historic Documents of the Muslim Freedom Movement*. Lahore, 1970.
Pirzada, Syed Sharifuddin (ed.), *Foundations of Pakistan: All-India Muslim League Documents: 1906–1947*. 2 vols. Karachi, 1969–70.
Sherwani, L. A. (ed.), *Pakistan Resolution to Pakistan, 1940–1947: A Selection of Documents Presenting the Case for Pakistan*. Karachi, 1969.

Printed secondary works cited

Afzal, M. Rafique (ed.), *Speeches and Statements of the Quaid-i-Azam Mohammad Ali Jinnah, 1911–34 and 1947–48*. Lahore, 1966.
— (ed.), *Speeches and Statements of Quaid-i-Millat Liaquat Ali Khan (1941–51)*. Lahore, 1967.
— (ed.), *Malik Barkat Ali: His Life and Writings*. Lahore, 1969.
Ahmad, Abul Mansur, *Amar Dekha Rajnitir Panchas Bachhar* (Fifty Years of Politics as I saw it). (Bengali) 2nd edn., Dacca, 1970.
Ahmad, Waheed (ed.), *Diary and Notes of Mian Fazl-i-Husain*. Lahore, 1976.
— (ed.), *Letters of Mian Fazl-i-Husain*. Lahore, 1976.
Alavi, Hamza, 'Kinship in West Punjab villages', in *Contributions to Indian Sociology*, n.s. 6 (December, 1972), 1–27.
Ali, Chaudhri Muhammad, *The Emergence of Pakistan*. Lahore, 1973.
Ali, Chaudhuri Rahmat, *Pakistan: The Fatherland of the Pak Nation*. Revised edition, Lahore, 1978.
Aziz, K. K., *The All-India Muslim Conference, 1928–35, a Documentary Record*. Karachi, 1972.
Batalvi, Ashiq Husain, *Iqbal Ke Akhari Do Saal* (Iqbal's last two years). (Urdu.) 3rd edn., Lahore, 1978.
Baxter, Craig, 'The People's Party versus the Punjab feudalists', in Henry Korsen (ed.), *Contemporary Problems of Pakistan*. Leiden, 1974.
Bose, Sugata, 'Agrarian society and politics in Bengal: 1919–1947'. Cambridge, Ph.D. dissertation, 1982.
Broomfield, J. H., *Elite Conflict in a Plural Society: Twentieth-Century Bengal*. Berkeley, 1968.
Campbell-Johnson, Alan, *Mission With Mountbatten*. 2nd edn., Connecticut, 1972.
Collins, L. and Lapierre, D., *Mountbatten and the Partition of India: March 22–August 15, 1947*, vol. I, New Delhi, 1982.
Coupland, Reginald, *Indian Politics: 1936–1942*. London, 1944.
Choudhury Ashrafuddin Ahmed, *Raj Birodhi* (Opponent of the Raj). (Bengali) Dacca, 1978.
Chowdhury, Prem, 'The Congress triumph in South-East Punjab: elections of 1946', *Studies in History*, 2, no. 2 (1980), 81–110.
Das, Durga (ed.), *Sardar Patel's Correspondence: 1945–1950*. Ten vols. Ahmedabad, 1972.
Dundas, John L., *Essayez, the Memoirs of Lawrence, Second Marquess of Zetland*. London, 1956.
Gallagher, John, 'Congress in decline: Bengal 1930 to 1939', in John Gallagher, Gordon Johnson and Anil Seal (eds.), *Locality, Province and Nation: Essays on Indian Politics, 1870–1940*. Cambridge, 1973.
Ghosh, Sudhir, *Gandhi's Emissary*. Bombay, 1967.
Gilmartin, David, 'Religious leadership and the Pakistan movement in the Punjab', *Modern Asian Studies*, 13, 3, (1979), 485–517.
Gordon, Leonard, A., 'Brothers against the Raj', *The Oracle*. Calcutta, July 1979.
Gordon, Richard, 'Non-cooperation and Council entry, 1919 to 1920', in John Gallagher, Gordon Johnson and Anil Seal (eds.), *Locality, Province and Nation: Essays on Indian Politics, 1870–1940*. Cambridge, 1973.

Hardy, Peter, *The Muslims of British India*. Cambridge, 1972.

Hasan, Mushirul, *Nationalism and Communal Politics in India, 1916–1928*. New Delhi, 1979.

Husain, Azim, *Mian Fazl-i-Husain: A Political Biography*. London, 1966.

Jafri, S. Qaim Hussain, *Quaid-i-Azam's Correspondence with Punjab Muslim Leaders*. Lahore, 1977.

Jalal, Ayesha and Seal, Anil, 'Alternative to partition: Muslim politics between the wars', *Modern Asian Studies*, 15, 3, (1981), 415–54.

Kabir, Humayun, 'Muslim politics, 1942–7', in C. H. Philips and M. Wainwright (eds.), *The Partition of India: Policies and Perspectives, 1935–1947*. London, 1970.

Khaliquzzaman, Choudhry, *Pathway to Pakistan*. Lahore, 1961.

Low, David Anthony (ed.), *Soundings in Modern South Asian History*. London, 1968.

Menon, Vapal Pangunni, *The Transfer of Power in India*. Princeton, 1957.

Minault, Gail, *The Khilafat Movement, Religious Symbolism and Political Mobilization in India*. New York, 1982.

Momen, Humaira, *Muslim Politics in Bengal: A Study of Krishak Praja Party and the Elections of 1937*. Dacca, 1972.

Moon, Penderel (ed.), *Wavell: The Viceroy's Journal*. London, 1973.

Moore, R. J., *Churchill, Cripps, and India, 1939–1945*. Oxford, 1979.

Mountbatten, Lord Louis, *Time Only to Look Forward, Speeches of Rear Admiral The Earl Mountbatten of Burma*. London, 1949.

Oren, S., 'The Sikhs, Congress and the Unionists in British Punjab, 1937–1945'. *Modern Asian Studies*, 8, 3, Cambridge (1974), 397–418.

Page, David, *Prelude to Partition: The Indian Muslims and the Imperial System of Control 1920–1932*. Oxford, 1982.

Pandey, B. N., *The Indian Nationalist Movement, 1885–1947, Select Documents*. London, 1979.

Philips, C. H. and Wainwright, M. (eds.), *The Partition of India: Policies and Perspectives, 1935–1947*. London, 1970.

'A Punjabi', *Confederacy of India*. Lahore, 1939.

Rao, B. Shiva (ed.), *The Framing of India's Constitution: Select Documents*, vols. I–III of a five-volume series. New Delhi, 1966–68.

Reeves, P. D., 'Changing patterns of political alignment in the general elections to the United Provinces Legislative Assembly, 1937 and 1946', *Modern Asian Studies*, 5, 2, (1971), 111–42.

Rizvi, Gowher, *Linlithgow and India: A Study of British Policy and the Political Impasse in India, 1936–43*. London, 1978.

Robinson, Francis, *Separatism among Indian Muslims: The Politics of the United Provinces' Muslims (1860–1923)*. Cambridge, 1974.

Saiyid, Matlubul Hasan, *Mohammad Ali Jinnah: A Political Study*. 3rd edn. Lahore, 1962.

Schwartzberg, Joseph E. (ed.), *A Historical Atlas of South Asia*. Chicago and London, 1978.

Seal, Anil, 'Imperialiam and nationalism', in John Gallagher, Gordon Johnson and Anil Seal (eds.), *Locality, Province and Nation: Essays on Indian Politics, 1870–1940*. Cambridge, 1973.

Sen, A. K., *Poverty and Famines: An Essay on Entitlement and Deprivation*. Oxford, 1982.

Sen, Shila, *Muslim Politics in Bengal: 1937-1947*. New Delhi, 1976.

Spate, O. H. K., *India and Pakistan: A General and Regional Geography*. London, 1954.

Talbot, I. A., 'The 1946 Punjab elections', *Modern Asian Studies*, 14, 1, (1980), 65–91.

Tomlinson, B. R., *The Indian National Congress and the Raj, 1929–1942, The Penultimate Phase*. London, 1976.

Wakil, Parvez A., 'Explorations into kin-networks of the Punjabi society: a preliminary statement', *Journal of Marriage and the Family*, 32 (November 1980).

Zaidi, Z. H. (ed.), *M. A. Jinnah–Ispahani Correspondence*. Karachi, 1976.

Zaman, Mukhtar, *Students' Role in the Pakistan Movement*. Karachi, 1978.

INDEX

Abell, George, 178, 267–8
Aga Khan, 52fn, 175fn
Agriculturist party (U.P.), 20, 29–32
Ahmad, Abul Mansur, 105fn, 152fn, 159
Ahrars, 21fn, 91, 111, 120fn, 140fn,
    143fn
Ahsan, Raghib, 107fn, 155fn
Akali Dal, 23fn, 66, 97fn, 150fn, 151fn,
    238–9
Alexander, A. V., 176, 189fn, 206fn
Ali, Chaudhuri Rahmat, 12fn, 53–5
Ali, Malik Barkat, 21, 63, 64fn, 85, 87fn
Ali, Mohammad, 7fn
Ali, Taj, 117
Aligarh, 3fn; constitutional scheme, 53–4
All-India Congress Committee, see Indian
    National Congress
All-India Muslim Conference, 10–13, 30
All-India Muslim League: 4–5, 123;
    acceptance of 3 June 1947 plan, 287;
    Allahabad session, 1930, 12, 52; and
    1935 Act, 4; and all-India federation,
    20, 189, 212; and Bengal, 20fn, 24–5,
    39–41, 64, 68–9, 82, 102–3, 106, 109,
    151, 153, 154fn, 157, 159–60, 162–3,
    172, 241–4, 246, 252–3, 276–7, 285;
    Bombay session, 1936, 20; Bombay
    session, 1946, 211–13; and British,
    4–5, 18, 45–51, 102, 123–4, 126,
    128–36, 174–5, 179, 210, 213, 217,
    220–2, 232, 235, 241–4, 247, 249, 279;
    and Cabinet Mission, 176, 189,
    192–209, 211–12, 220fn, 221, 227,
    230–2, 237, 242–3, 258, 260, 262, 275;
    and central defence authority, 252,
    258; and Communal Award, 20; and
    communal disorder, 178, 225–6,
    239fn, 240fn, 244; and Congress, 4–5,
    7–10, 19, 33–5, 38, 126, 128, 130–2,
    134–7, 174–6, 179, 188, 192, 194,
    200–1, 203–6, 207fn, 208–11, 213–15,
    217–32, 235, 237–8, 241, 245–7, 249,
    254, 259–63, 267, 269–70, 273–5,
    278–80, 287, 291–2; constitution of
    1938, 40–1; and constitutional

schemes, 53–8; and Cripps offer,
    78–82, 132, 247; Delhi session, 1943,
    86, 95–6, 101–2, 110fn, 115, 119,
    120fn, 121; and 'direct action',
    212–13, 216–17, 240fn; and elections,
    1936–37, 4, 18–32, 38; and elections,
    1945–46, 134–8, 171–3, 244;
    foundation of, 3fn, 7; and Indian
    army, 292; and interim government,
    1946–47, 190, 202–3, 210–18, 221–31,
    235, 246, 249, 254, 260, 269, 278,
    287, 291; and Islam, 96, 120, 137,
    147, 172, 217; and Jinnah, 4–5, 7,
    9–10, 13–14, 18–20, 124, 130–2, 136,
    173, 182, 192–4, 198–203, 210–18,
    232, 241–3, 246, 251–5, 259–60,
    262–3, 267, 273, 276–7, 284–5, 287,
    291–2; Karachi session, 1943, 89, 120;
    Lahore resolution, 1940, 57–61, 252;
    Lahore session, 1940, 57–60;
    Legislators' Convention, 1946, 182–3;
    Lucknow session, 1916, 7; Lucknow
    session, 1937, 39–41; and Muslim
    business interests, 182, 210, 258fn;
    and N.W.F.P., 20fn, 28, 33, 40–1,
    82fn, 115, 117, 118fn, 168–72, 181,
    253, 256–7, 267; organisational
    structure, 5, 19–20, 40–1, 50, 89–90,
    118–19, 136–8, 172–3, 189, 212–13,
    216–17, 240fn, 244–5; and 'Pakistan'
    demand, 4–5, 137, 174–5, 182–3,
    202–3, 208–9, 211, 213, 241–3, 245fn,
    246fn, 260, 262, 290–1; and partition,
    276–7, 285; Patna session, 1938, 45;
    and Punjab, 20–2, 39–41, 63–4, 82,
    86, 90–8, 109, 123, 136fn, 172, 232,
    241–4, 246, 252–3, 263, 276–7, 285;
    and 1919 reforms, 9–10; and separate
    representation, 4; and Simla
    Conference, 138; and Sind, 28, 33,
    40–1, 64–5, 82fn, 110–14, 137fn,
    163–7, 172, 181, 253; and U.P., 20fn,
    30–3, 40–1, 137; use of religion, 5,
    242
Ambala, 2, 133, 175, 246

301